Emerging Issues and Methods in Personality Assessment

Emerging Issues and Methods in Personality Assessment

Edited by

John A. Schinka
James A. Haley VA Medical Center
and
University of South Florida, College of Medicine

Roger L. Greene
Pacific Graduate School of Psychology

Routledge
Taylor & Francis Group

LONDON AND NEW YORK

First published 1795 by Franks Cass and Company Limited

2 Park Square, Milton Park, Abingdon, Oxon OX14 4RN
711 Third Avenue, New York, NY 10017, USA

Routledge is an imprint of the Taylor & Francis Group, an informa business

First issued in paperback 2016

New impression 1971

Transferred to Digital Printing 2006

ISBN 978-1-138-96864-6 (pbk)
ISBN 978-0-8058-2676-0 (hbk)

Contents

Preface

This book represents a collection of articles that were written for, and recently published as, special sections in three consecutive issues of the *Journal of Personality Assessment*. The origins of the collection lie in several casual conversations with other personality assessment researchers at professional meetings over the past several years. As is often the case, these informal discussions were more stimulating and freewheeling than the formal presentations and focused on a broad range of topics including the merits of new and revised personality instruments, evolving methods of personality scale development, models of personality, and the appropriate use of complex and occasionally arcane statistical procedures as applied to data in personality assessment. Many of these conversations concluded that the topic of discussion would be a great theme for a symposium at the next national professional meeting. On rare occasions, this was in fact accomplished, but more commonly no tangible outcome resulted. In retrospect, however, the increasing frequency of these conversations appears to be a testimony to a groundswell of interest and activity in the study of personality in the broad sense—models, measurement issues, developmental pathways, and even molecular genetics (Benjamin et al., 1996; Ebstein et al., 1996).

We were subsequently invited by Bill Kinder, the editor of the *Journal of Personality Assessment*, to serve as action editors for a series of special sections focusing on methodologic issues and advances in personality assessment. We responded by organizing sections for three issues, addressing respectively present and anticipated research issues with commonly used personality instruments, current issues in personality assessment, and applications of statistical methods to personality assessment. Our subsequent solicitations of articles on specific topics were quickly accepted by a list of contributing authors whose names are well-known to personality assessors. In fact, the reputations of contributing authors and the quality of their contributions suggested to the publisher of the *Journal* that the articles might be compiled into an edited text for distribution to a larger audience. Thus we were invited to organize this compilation.

The organization of this book parallels that of the *Journal* issues in which the articles originally were published in early 1997. No changes have been made in any of the substantive articles. Introductions to the special sections that appeared in each of the issues largely stand as they were originally published.

The contributing authors enjoy reputations as unquestionable experts in their given areas of research. From one standpoint, this would suggest a situation requiring minimal editorial effort. Instead, these authors demand the same rigor of editorial review that they apply in their own editorial duties. We were fortunate to have had the support of outstanding reviewers to assist in this task, all of whom are well known within the area of personality assessment. For their advice and counsel in this regard, we extend our appreciation to Robert P. Archer, James Choca, Michael Clark, Glenn Curtiss, Larry Greenbaum, Alan Harkness, Stephen Hibbard, Seth Kalichman, Mark Maruish, Kevin L. Moreland, Sarah I. Pratt, Paul Retzlaff, Jacob Sines, James Truckenmiller, Rodney Vanderploeg, Martha Wetter, Nancy H. Wrobel, and Eric Zillmer.

Decisions regarding numerous editorial and technical issues were facilitated greatly by Bill Kinder, Editor of the *Journal of Personality Assessment*. We would also like to extend our appreciation to Larry Erlbaum and Robert Kidd of Lawrence Erlbaum Associates for their support and assistance. On our behalf and that of the other contributing authors, we express our appreciation to colleagues, patients, and students who serve as inspiration, test cases, and critics of our ideas and formulations.

In this, as well as all of our other significant professional and personal endeavors, the encouragement and guidance of Gail Schinka and Mary Sharon Greene play a fundamental role in our accomplishments.

—John A. Schinka
—Roger L. Greene

REFERENCES

Benjamin, J., Li, L., Patterson, C., Greenberg, B., Murphy, D. L., & Hamer, D. H. (1996). Population and familial association between the D4 dopamine receptor gene and measures of novelty seeking. *Nature Genetics, 12*, 81–84.

Epstein, R., Novick, O., Umansky, R., Priel, B., Osher, Y., Blaine, D., Bennett, E. R., Nemanov, L., Katz, M., & Belmaker, R. H. (1996). Dopamine D4 receptor (D4DR) exon III polymorphism associated with the human personality trait of novelty seeking. *Nature Genetics, 12*, 78–80.

PART I

Personality Assessment Instruments: Current Status and Future Directions

In this first collection of chapters, Irving Weiner and Roger Greene have provided lucid commentaries on the current status of the Rorschach and MMPI-2, respectively. Because these instruments are the most commonly researched and discussed in clinical personality assessment, their comments are valuable in themselves. Their presentations also set the stage for chapters by John Exner and Alex Caldwell that address important issues that will face both researchers and clinicians in the near future with these same two instruments. The remainder of the chapters in this special section address similar issues for instruments whose importance has come to the forefront of personality evaluation in the past decade: the Minnesota Multiphasic Personality Inventory—Adolescent (MMPI-A: Butcher et al., 1992), the Interpersonal Adjective Scales (IAS-R: Wiggins, 1995) and the Inventory of Interpersonal Problems–Circumplex version (IIP-C; Alden, Wiggins, & Pincus, 1990), the revised NEO Personality Inventory (NEO-PI-R: Costa & McRae, 1992), and the third edition of the Millon Clinical Multiaxial Inventory (MCMI-III: Millon, 1994). The authors addressing these issues—Robert Archer for the MMPI-A, Jerry Wiggins and Krista Trobst for the IAS and IIP-C, Robert McCrae and Paul Costa for the NEO-PI-R, and Theodore Millon and Roger Davis for the MCMI-III—participated not only in the development of the respective instruments, but continue to lead the research effort in the application of these instruments in both clinical and research settings.

REFERENCES

Alden, L. E., Wiggins, J. S., & Pincus, A. L. (1990). Construction of circumplex scales for the Inventory of Interpersonal Problems. *Journal of Personlaity Assessment, 55*, 521–536.

Butcher, J. N., Williams, C. L., Graham, J. R., Archer, R. P., Tellegen, A., & Kaemmer, B. (1992). *Minnesota Multiphasic Personality Inventory–Adolescents.* Minneapolis: University of Minnesota Press.

Costa, P. T., Jr., & McCrae, R. R. (1992). *Professional manual for the Revised NEO Personality Inventory.* Odessa, FL: Psychological Assessment Resources.

Millon, T. (1994). *Manual for the Millon Clinical Multiaxial Inventory-III.* Minneapolis, MN: National Computer Systems.

Wiggins, J. S. (1995). *Interpersonal adjective scales: Professional manual.* Odessa, FL: Psychological Assessment Resources, Inc.

1

Current Status of the Rorschach Inkblot Method

Irving B. Weiner

Department of Psychiatry
University of South Florida

The current scientific, clinical, and professional status of the Rorschach Inkblot Method (RIM) is reviewed with respect to its psychometric properties, the applied purposes it can be expected to serve, the extent of its use, and the nature of prevailing attitudes toward it. Available evidence indicates that the RIM is a psychometrically sound measuring instrument that provides valid assessments of personality characteristics and can facilitate differential diagnosis and treatment planning and evaluation. The RIM continues as in the past to be widely used by both clinicians and researchers. However, the esteem in which it is held by practitioners, who are generally agreed that clinical psychologists should be competent in Rorschach assessment, is not universally shared by academicians, many of whom presently question the future place of Rorschach training in graduate education.

How fitting it is to contemplate the status of the Rorschach Inkblot Method (RIM) in 1996, the 75th anniversary of Hermann Rorschach's (1921/1942) publication of *Psychodiagnostics*. Surely, in today's fast-paced world such longevity speaks to the quality of a clinical method and to the genius of its creator. From shaky Swiss beginnings through times of repudiation and renaissance, its survival repeatedly threatened both by excessive enthusiasm and unwarranted disparagement, the RIM has emerged worldwide as a frequently used and highly regarded measure of personality functioning. Although there has long been and remains a formidable corps of Rorschach detractors who deplore its use and demean its value, the distinction of the inkblot method derives not from its age, but from its well-documented capacities to elucidate the human condition.

Except in passing, this article will address neither the history of Rorschach assessment nor previous debates concerning its merit; both of these topics are considered in detail elsewhere (see, e.g., Ellenberger, 1954; Exner, 1993, chap. 1; Weiner, 1977, 1996). Instead, this article focuses on the current status of the RIM,

3

with specific attention to (a) its scientific status, as inferred from its psychometric properties; (b) its clinical status, as determined by the purposes that it can be expected to serve in applied practice; and (c) its professional status, as defined by how widely it is being used and by the nature of prevailing attitudes toward it.

By way of further introduction, comment may be in order concerning the preference reflected here to refer to the Rorschach as a method and not merely as a test. Like other personality tests, the Rorschach includes scores and indices that measure aspects of personality functioning. The Rorschach is more than a test, however, because its utility is not limited to applications of the scores and indices that it yields or to interpretive strategies rooted in any one theoretical frame of reference. Rather, as I have elaborated elsewhere (Weiner, 1994b, 1995c), the Rorschach is a multifaceted method of generating structural, thematic, and behavioral data that can be applied in both quantitative and qualitative terms and can be interpreted from many different theoretical perspectives. Accordingly, to recognize that the Rorschach functions not only as a personality test but as a method of generating useful information in other ways as well, it seems appropriate to refer to it as the RIM.

SCIENTIFIC STATUS

The scientific status of a measuring instrument is a function of its psychometric properties. By prevailing standards, an instrument is considered psychometrically sound when (a) trained examiners can reach reasonable agreement in scoring its variables; (b) estimates of its reliability indicate that it provides reasonably accurate information, that is, the "obtained" scores it yields closely approximate what the "true" scores are; (c) its demonstrated corollaries identify purposes for which it is reasonably valid; and (d) normative data concerning its descriptive statistics among various populations are adequate to allow comparisons of individuals to appropriate reference groups (Anastasi, 1988, chaps. 4–8).

The RIM, when administered and coded according to the Comprehensive System (Exner, 1993), satisfies each of these four psychometric requirements. Additionally, even though no other general Rorschach system has been demonstrated to rest on a solid scientific foundation, numerous special scales and indices developed outside of the Comprehensive System have shown sufficient interrater agreement, retest reliability, and construct validity to be considered psychometrically sound.

Turning to the evidence in these respects, studies of interrater agreement indicate that all of the variables coded in the Comprehensive System can be reliably scored. The levels of agreement typically found exceed 90% for location scores, pairs, Populars, and Z scores; are somewhat lower for form quality and content categories; and fall to the middle or lower 80s for determinants and Special Scores (Exner,

1991, pp. 459–460; 1993, p. 138). McDowell and Acklin (1996) recently reported an overall mean percentage agreement of 87% in a study of Rorschach interrater reliability.

The capacity of an instrument to be reliably scored does not guarantee that interrater agreement will in fact characterize a particular research study, however. For this reason, the *Journal of Personality Assessment (JPA)* began in 1991 to require Rorschach research articles to include the level of scoring agreement achieved by the examiners in the study being reported (Weiner, 1991). A required minimum of 80% agreement has not reduced the frequency with which Rorschach research articles have been appearing in *JPA*, which would seem to indicate that adequately trained researchers are having no difficulty in coding the instrument reliably. This being the case, there is certainly reason to expect that adequately trained practitioners as well as researchers are scoring the Rorschach reliably in their work.

The reliability of Rorschach data has been documented in a series of retest studies with both children and adults over retest intervals ranging from 7 days to 3 years. Among 100 nonpatient adults who were reexamined after 3 years, 13 core variables showed stability coefficients of .80 or more (*Z frequency, Lambda, M, Active movement, FC, SumC, Affective Ratio, Sum T, Sum V, X+%, Egocentricity Ratio, Sum Critical Special Scores,* and *Experience Actual*); six other core variables had stability coefficients greater than .70 (*Response Total, Passive movement, CF + C, Popular, FM,* and *Experienced Stimulation;* Exner & Weiner, 1995, pp. 21–27).

As for the validity of Rorschach assessment, the scientific merit of the instrument was confirmed in a series of meta-analytic reviews that led Parker, Hanson, and Hunsley (1988) to conclude that the RIM has demonstrated adequate validity by usual psychometric standards and is comparable to the Minnesota Multiphasic Personality Inventory (MMPI) in this respect. Applying procedures developed by Hedges and Olkin (1985) for calculating unbiased estimates to the results of 411 studies, Parker et al. derived population estimates of convergent validity coefficients of .41 for the Rorschach and .46 for the MMPI, with there being no statistically significant difference between these values.

Subsequent to the Parker et al. (1988) study, Shontz and Green (1992) published an evaluation of trends in Rorschach research in which they identified a need for methodologically improved studies concerning practical applications of the instrument. In this same article, however, they indicated that "definitive statements can now be made about the psychometric properties of the Rorschach," because the meta-analytic reviews have "all concluded that the Rorschach is reliable and valid when it is properly used" (p. 149).

With respect to the importance of adequate normative data, the Rorschach Comprehensive System provides detailed descriptive statistics for each of its coded variables on a sample of 700 nonpatient adults stratified to represent the 1980 U.S.

census; on 1,390 children and adolescents separately for each age from 5 to 16; and on patient reference groups of 320 hospitalized schizophrenics, 315 hospitalized depressives, 440 diagnostically unspecified outpatients, and 180 outpatients with character disorders (Exner, 1993, chap. 12). The size and diversity of these normative and reference samples provide more standardization information than is available for most psychological assessment measures and establishes the RIM as adequately normed for a U.S. population.

Looking beyond the Comprehensive System, evidence of adequate interscorer agreement, retest reliability, and criterion or construct validity has emerged as well for numerous specific Rorschach scales and indices developed for special assessment purposes, many of which are based largely on codification of thematic imagery. Among examples of such psychometrically sound specific scales currently receiving attention in the literature are the Rorschach Defense Scales (Cooper, Perry, & Arnow, 1988), the Rorschach Oral Dependency Scale (Bornstein, 1996), the Ego Impairment Index (Perry, Viglione, & Braff, 1992), the Mutuality of Autonomy Scale (Urist, 1977), and several other measures of object relatedness (Stricker & Healey, 1990). The development of these scales, along with ongoing research with the Comprehensive System, provides abundant evidence that the RIM is a psychometrically sound personality assessment instrument and one that lends itself to continuing discovery of new ways to codify and apply the data it generates.

Finally, with respect to the scientific status of the RIM, considerable attention has been paid of late to the application of appropriate methodology in Rorschach research and data analysis. For current information concerning methodological issues in investigative work with the Rorschach, the reader is referred to contributions by Exner (1995) and Weiner (1995b).

CLINICAL STATUS

The clinical status of an assessment instrument is determined by the purposes it can be expected to serve in applied practice. The current clinical status of the RIM thus depends on what Rorschach assessors are able to do with the data they obtain. Present knowledge in this regard can be summarized in reference to four clinically relevant assessment tasks: personality description, differential diagnosis, treatment planning and evaluation, and behavioral prediction.

Personality Description

Because the RIM is basically a personality assessment instrument, descriptions of personality functioning hold the key to the purposes it can be expected to serve. The range of appropriate Rorschach applications and the utility of whatever conclusions and recommendations the instrument suggests will always be a function of (a) the relevance of particular personality characteristics to the assessment task at hand and (b) the accuracy with which the RIM describes these personality characteristics. With respect to describing personality functioning, it is helpful to consider separately what Rorschach data can indicate about personality structure and personality dynamics.

Personality structure.   *Personality structure* refers to the nature of people as defined by their current frame of mind (personality states) and their abiding dispositions to think, feel, and act in certain ways (personality traits). Personality states comprise a broad range of relatively transitory affects and attitudes that are elicited by situational circumstances and are coterminus with them. Of such states, the one best measured by the Rorschach is a generally elevated level of subjectively felt distress that combines elements of anxiety and depression. As documented in the Comprehensive System (Exner, 1993), acute situational distress is suggested by the general index of $D < AdjD$ and by specific elevations in m (helplessness), Y (hopelessness), T (loneliness), V (guilt/remorse), and Color-Shading Blends with Y (dysphoria).

Traits comprise a broad range of fairly stable personality characteristics and orientations of which the following, as again documented in the Comprehensive System volumes (Exner, 1991, 1993; Exner & Weiner, 1995), have valid Rorschach correlates: (a) preferred patterns of attending to experience and capabilities for doing so openly, consistently, efficiently, and realistically; (b) characteristic styles of using ideation and capacities to think coherently and logically; (c) preferred ways of experiencing and expressing emotions and abilities to modulate affect sufficiently and pleasurably; (d) customary methods of managing stress and resources for doing so adequately; (e) clarity of identity formation and nature of attitudes toward oneself; and (f) attitudes toward other people and preferred style of interpersonal relatedness.

Personality dynamics.   *Personality dynamics* refers to the nature of people as defined by the underlying needs, attitudes, conflicts, and concerns that influence how they are likely to think, feel, and act at particular points in time and in particular kinds of circumstances. Personality dynamics are revealed on the Rorschach by responses in which participants attribute characteristics to their percepts that go beyond the stimulus properties of the inkblots; thus, percepts involving movement, distortions of form, or embellishment with qualities other than shape, shading, and color are likely to reflect projection onto the blots of a participant's internal psychological processes and thereby provide clues to the nature of these processes (Exner, 1989; Schachtel, 1966, chap. 2).

Numerous variables coded in the Comprehensive System for response contents and embellishments have been demonstrated to measure dynamic aspects of personality functioning, such as *MOR* (concerns about the adequacy of one's body), *COP* (positive attitudes toward interpersonal collaboration), and *Food* (unmet dependency needs). In addition, as noted earlier, various scales based on codification of thematic imagery are proving valid for assessing personality dynamics, especially with respect to defensive style and object relatedness.

However, Rorschach assessment of personality dynamics has not yet been as thoroughly validated as assessment of personality structure. This does not signify that such validation has proved elusive or is for any reason beyond accomplishing. Rather, it is simply the case that Rorschach assessment of personality dynamics has yet to receive the extent of systematic research attention that it deserves. Given that there already exist adequately validated Rorschach variables and scales for describing many dynamic aspects of personality functioning, there is good reason to expect that future studies will continue to generate confirmatory findings of this type. While awaiting comprehensive validation of clues to personality dynamics, Rorschach clinicians can continue to draw on theoretical principles, clinical guidelines, and an extensive literature to generate valuable hypotheses concerning participants' underlying needs, attitudes, conflicts, and concerns (see, e.g., Aronow & Reznikoff, 1976; Lerner, 1991; Schachtel, 1966; Schafer, 1954).

Differential Diagnosis

The original monograph *Psychodiagnostics* is subtitled "A diagnostic test based on perception" (Rorschach, 1921/1942). As Rorschach may have anticipated, given his brilliance, subsequent advances in conceptualization indicate that his instrument goes well beyond this initial characterization in three respects: (a) the RIM functions as more than a test, as previously noted, and is better conceived as a method of generating data; (b) the inkblot method is based as much on association as on perception; and (c) Rorschach findings identify aspects of personality functioning and only secondarily bear on diagnostic status (Weiner, 1994b).

In this last regard, early efforts to construct Rorschach sign lists for diagnostic purposes foundered badly, primarily because they failed to tap the richness of the RIM for elucidating dimensions of personality (see Goldfried, Stricker, & Weiner, 1971). Reliable contributions of the RIM to differential diagnosis eventually emerged only in concert with systematic conceptualizations of psychopathology that made it possible to link certain Rorschach variables with certain disorders on the basis of personality processes common to both (Weiner, 1986).

At present, the Rorschach Comprehensive System provides indices for schizophrenia (*SCZI*) and depression (*DEPI*) that can prove helpful in identifying these two conditions, provided that they are used not in an uninformed actuarial manner but rather in light of numerous qualifications and special considerations elaborated by Exner and Weiner (1995, chaps. 5 & 6). Recent work by Gacono and Meloy (1994) suggested that a similarly sound and useful index of psychopathic personality can now be constructed. These diagnostic indices are clinically useful because the personality characteristics they are known to measure play a clearly formulated role in the conditions to be diagnosed. In addition, although further documentation is needed, accumulating data indicate that there are on the horizon adequately conceptualized and empirically valid Rorschach indices for bipolar disorder, borderline and schizotypal personality disorder, and acute and chronic stress disorder (Weiner, 1995a).

The future utility of Rorschach findings in diagnosing various other conditions will depend on how successfully these conditions can be delineated in terms of personality characteristics that are reasonably specific to them. If a condition of interest to psychologists cannot be shown to entail some unique personality features, Rorschach data are unlikely to identify the presence of this condition or to help differentiate it from other conditions. Conversely, the more that can be learned about structural and dynamic aspects of personality that contribute to or are determined by types of disorder, the more effective the RIM will become in diagnosing these disorders.

Treatment Planning and Evaluation

Currently emerging concepts and findings are demonstrating potentially important Rorschach contributions to the planning, conduct, and evaluation of psychological interventions. These contributions include identifying treatment targets and possible obstacles to progress, selecting appropriate treatment modalities, and monitoring change and improvement over time.

Regarding treatment targets, Rorschach findings provide a wealth of information concerning what needs to be accomplished in therapy to help a particular patient feel better and function more effectively. Each translation of a deviant or generally undesirable Rorschach finding into its implications for maladaptive personality characteristics identifies a potential goal of the treatment, such as a low Affective Ratio indicating a need for the person to become more comfortable with feelings, a small number of Populars indicating a need to become more cognizant of conventional reality, and an excess of passive movement responses indicating a need to become more assertive and self-reliant.

The relative degree to which particular Rorschach deviations from normative expectation are manifest or seem entrenched can also prove helpful in deciding which among several alternative treatment targets are most important to address and in what order it might be most fruitful to address them. Thus patients with an unusually large D of -3 and only a modestly elevated *MOR* of 3 probably need attention first and foremost to their high level of subjectively felt distress rather than to their predilection for pessimistic thinking, even though the latter could also become a worthwhile treatment target later on.

Obstacles to progress in treatment come in various forms. Generally speaking, however, there is good reason to expect that people who are rigid and set in their ways, who are satisfied with themselves and free from subjectively felt distress, who are disinclined to be introspective, and who are averse to close and trusting interpersonal relationships will have difficulty becoming engaged and participating effectively in most forms of psychotherapy. These obstacles to progress have been translated into Rorschach indices of personality characteristics that need to be recognized and confronted in order for treatment to be sustained and achieve its maximum possible success (Weiner, 1994a).

As for selecting an appropriate modality, data analyses are underway that should help tap the rich potential of the RIM for identifying personality characteristics associated with relative aversion or receptivity to alternative treatment approaches. In this work, Exner (personal communication, October 27, 1995) has begun to examine longitudinal data on 497 patients who took the Rorschach prior to entering various types of psychotherapy. Thus far, some interesting relationships have emerged between Rorschach patterns and treatment modality among patients differing in their early treatment course.

Among 73 of Exner's 497 participants who dropped out of treatment early (within 8 weeks), those who were in behavioral therapy were especially likely to have an introversive EB but not to show any consistent patterns of interpersonal difficulty; by contrast, early dropouts from dynamic, cognitive, and experiential forms of therapy did not display any particular EB style (introversive or extratensive) but were especially likely to demonstrate difficulty in forming interpersonal attachments ($T = 0$). EB style in Exner's sample was also differentially associated with modality among 123 patients who remained in treatment and were rated by their therapists as making very good progress after 4 months. Those who were progressing well in dynamic therapy were particularly likely to be introversive, whereas those who were progressing well in some form of brief therapy (fewer than 18 sessions) were particularly likely to be extratensive.

There was also a group of 117 patients who remained in therapy but were regarded as making slow progress after 4 months. Of these patients, those in behavioral therapy were particularly likely to show interpersonal neediness ($T > 1$), whereas those in other types of therapy were notable for being unusually insulated against subjectively felt distress (D or $AdjD > 0$). These preliminary findings offer great promise for being able to use the Rorschach to good effect in recommending specific treatment modalities for patients with particular personality characteristics.

Finally, the capacity of the RIM to identify needs for change and corresponding treatment targets makes it obvious that baseline and follow-up testing can provide valuable information concerning progress in treatment and reliable assessment of treatment outcome. Large-scale studies reported in recent years leave little doubt that adequately conceptualized Rorschach indices can monitor change effectively in numerous forms of treatment (Abraham, Lepisto, Lewis, Schultz, & Finkelberg, 1994; Blatt & Ford, 1994; Exner & Andronikof-Sanglade, 1992; Weiner & Exner, 1991).

Behavioral Prediction

Personality assessors are well-advised to remember Lewin's observation that behavior is a complex and interactive function of personality (what people are like) and the environment (the circumstances in which people find themselves). Because personality assessment methods provide information only on the personality side of Lewin's equation, they can rarely stand alone as predictors of behavior. Being a personality assessment method, the RIM by itself has demonstrated limited predictive validity during its 75-year history, and there is little reason to expect it to attain much single-handed predictive power in the future.

Once it is recognized that the RIM is not by nature a predictive instrument, its limitations in this regard can be qualified in four respects. First, because personality traits are fairly stable in adults, Rorschach trait variables are likely to provide reasonably accurate longitudinal predictions of personality style, even over many years' time. Long-term retest data confirm the validity of the RIM for this purpose (Exner, 1993, p. 46; Janson & Stattin, 1994).

Second, to the extent that a particular behavior is determined largely by personality characteristics, with a minimum of nonpersonality variance (i.e., environmental influence), Rorschach variables become increasingly likely to achieve better-than-chance prediction of who is likely to do what. In the preceding discussion of treatment planning, for example, the likely importance of personality style in determining receptivity to various forms of treatment, with nonpersonality variables playing a lesser role, no doubt accounts for such findings as the difficulty of introversive individuals becoming involved in behavioral therapy but progressing particularly well in dynamic therapy.

Third, when assessment questions are framed within the context of foreseeable environmental circumstances, Rorschach findings can help to anticipate how participants are likely to respond to them. For example, participants with a minus *D-score* (excessive subjectively felt distress) and a high *Lambda* (narrow focus of attention) are likely to function more comfortably in a well-structured, clearly defined, and uncomplicated situation in which they know what is expected of them than in an ambiguous, open-ended, and complex situation in which there are few guidelines to follow; by contrast, participants with an unbalanced *a:p* ratio (cognitive inflexibility) and a high *Xu%* (idiosyncratic perception) are likely to adapt better to an unstructured, free-wheeling situation in which they are free to do things their own way than to a highly regimented situation in which they are expected to conform to someone else's rules.

Fourth, although the current status of the RIM does not support unqualified predictions of the future, Rorschach data formulated in terms of personality characteristics can contribute to cautious estimates of behavioral potentials. Thus, it is reasonable to suggest that people whose Rorschach responses identify marked anger and resentment, limited impulse control, an expressive coping style, a self-righteous nature, an aversion to passivity and dependency, and poor judgment are at greater risk than most people for behaving aggressively toward others.

PROFESSIONAL STATUS

The professional status of a clinical method is reflected in the frequency with which it is used and the esteem in which it is held. With respect to the RIM, these aspects of its current status are measured by how widely the instrument is being utilized for clinical and research purposes and by the nature of presently prevailing attitudes toward it.

Clinical and Research Use of the RIM

It seems forever that prophets of doom have been forecasting the demise of Rorschach testing. Even assessment psychologists personally committed to the inkblot method are often heard to lament its declining use. This article cannot plumb the origins of these forecasts and laments; it can, however, report that the former are false and the latter unnecessary.

Repeated surveys of psychological test usage over the past 35 years have shown a substantial and consistently sustained frequency of Rorschach assessment in clinical settings. In 1961 Sundberg (1961) reported that more than 80% of 185 agencies he surveyed were using the Rorschach. Subsequent surveys by Lubin, Wallis, and Paine (1971) of 251 clinical settings; by Lubin, Larsen, and Matarazzo (1984) of 221 settings; and by Piotrowski and Keller (1989) of 413 outpatient mental health facilities all found similarly that more than 80% of the responding agencies used the Rorschach. With the RIM maintaining its percentage of use and the number of mental health facilities having increased considerably since 1961, it seems reasonable to conclude that more rather than fewer Rorschach examinations are being conducted now than in the past.

The 1990s have brought cause for concern that managed care environments and restricted third-party payments may discourage assessors from employing relatively comprehensive and costly measures such as the Rorschach (see Acklin, 1996). Nevertheless, in a recent survey by Watkins, Campbell, Nieberding, and Hallmark (1995) of 412 clinical psychologists engaged in providing assessment services, 82% indicated that they use the Rorschach in their assessments. The only methods mentioned by a greater percentage of these respondents were the clinical interview (95%), the Wechsler Adult Intelligence Scale–Revised (93%), the MMPI/MMPI–2 (85%), and Sentence Completion methods (84%).

Before the case is rested with respect to the clear evidence of widespread Rorschach testing, it should be noted that the surveys just mentioned pertain only to the United States. There exists beyond our shores a flourishing international Rorschach community of scholars and practitioners, and preliminary surveys abroad confirm the popularity of the RIM worldwide as well as in the United States (Piotrowski, Keller, & Ogawa, 1993). Bearing witness to the international stature of the instrument are thriving graduate programs and training institutes in Rorschach assessment in many countries of the world, both East and West; the current prospering of the International Rorschach Society and the large attendance at its triennial meetings; and the inception in 1993 of an annual journal, *Rorschachiana: Yearbook of the International Rorschach Society*, that in its first three volumes has published clinical and research articles from 17 different countries.

Turning to research applications of the RIM, two surveys can be cited to document extensive use of the instrument in investigative pursuits, both past and present. Reynolds and Sundberg (1976) reported some years ago that the two most extensively researched personality instruments were the RIM and the MMPI. As evidence in this regard, they utilized Buros' (1974) *Mental Measurements Yearbook* to identify 4,580 Rorschach references through 1971 with an average yearly rate of 92 references. For the MMPI, a younger instrument, the total number of references was 3,840 and the yearly rate 132.

As for the present, Butcher and Rouse (1966) found in a literature search that research articles published on the MMPI/MMPI–2 from 1974 to early 1994 far outnumbered those involving any other instrument. In each of these years the second most frequently researched personality assessment instrument was the Rorschach, with far more published articles than any other measure except the MMPI/MMPI–2. Minor variations in annual frequency aside, the volume of published Rorschach research was fairly stable over this 20-year period, with 99 articles in 1974, 96 articles in 1993, and an annual 20-year mean of 95.8. Butcher and Rouse (1996) drew the following conclusion from their data: "Whether viewed from the perspective of research attention or practical usage, the Rorschach Inkblot technique continues to be among the most popular personality assessment methods, and predictions about the technique's demise appear both unwarranted and unrealistic" (p. 91).

Prevailing Attitudes Toward the RIM

Not surprisingly, the attitudes that mental health professionals hold toward the RIM vary widely with their background, training, and personal preferences. Hence what one hears about Rorschach assessment will depend on whom one asks. The overall tenor of prevailing attitudes toward the RIM, beyond what can be inferred from the extensive use to which it is being put in research and practice, can best be gauged from the results of surveys of graduate programs and training sites in clinical psychology.

According to published surveys of APA-approved graduate programs, the RIM was being taught in 94% of these programs in 1974, 93% in 1984, and 85% in 1993 (Piotrowski & Zalewski, 1993; Ritzler & Alter, 1986). Although these percentages could be seen as signifying a decline in the teaching of Rorschach assessment, it is probably more reasonable to regard them as evidence of a sustained and widespread commitment among accredited doctoral programs to teach students something about the inkblot method. As further evidence in this regard, a recent survey of 235 student affiliates of the Society of Personality Assessment indicated that Rorschach instruction was included in 94% of their graduate programs and was a required course or part of a required course in 85% (Hilsenroth & Handler, 1995).

To be sure, the presence of Rorschach instruction in graduate programs does not ensure adequate instruction in the inkblot method. Negative attitudes toward the instrument and an increasingly crowded curriculum have combined over the years to reduce the instructional time typically allotted to Rorschach assessment. Indeed, in the Piotrowski and Zalewski (1993) survey, 45% of the responding clinical directors predicted that the use of projective personality assessment in academic settings would decline in the near future, and 46% felt that the extent of projective test usage in applied clinical settings is unjustified.

However, as Watkins (1994) pointed out, the opinions of these survey respondents merely echo what many academic clinical faculty have been saying for the last 25 years, without there being a shred of evidence to document either declining interest in or decreasing use of projective techniques. With specific respect to Rorschach assessment, moreover, even the Piotrowski and Zalewski respondents ranked the RIM first among projective tests with which doctoral clinical students should be familiar, and 85% of them included it in their listing of the five most important projective methods for students to learn. Watkins (1994), commenting on these data and survey information he reviewed previously (Watkins, 1991), quite correctly suggested that clinical directors have been giving projective techniques a "bum rap" by continuing to denigrate the teaching and use of these assessment methods despite clear indications that they are in fact widely used, taught, and valued.

The reservations of many academic clinicians concerning the value of Rorschach assessment are not shared by practitioners. Craig and Horowitz (1990) reported that more than 95% of diagnostic practicum sites they surveyed recommended that clinical students receive training in the Rorschach. In the previously mentioned survey by Watkins et al. (1995), 90% of the responding clinical practitioners expressed the belief that clinical students should be competent in Rorschach assessment.

CONCLUSION

What, then, can be said about the current status of the RIM as it passes age 75? Well-established as a psychometrically sound assessment instrument with numerous known corollaries in personality functioning, it is also a dynamic instrument for which new interpretive methods continue to emerge and about which there is much yet to learn. Already proved useful as an aid in differential diagnosis and treatment planning and evaluation, it has considerable potential for contributing to applied clinical practice that remains to be tapped in the future. Widely used and highly valued by clinicians and researchers in many countries of the world, it appears despite its fame not yet to have received the academic respect it deserves and, it can be hoped, will someday enjoy.

REFERENCES

Abraham, P. P., Lepisto, B. L., Lewis, M. G., Schultz, L., & Finkelberg, S. (1994). An outcome study: Changes in Rorschach variables of adolescents in residential treatment. *Journal of Personality Assessment, 62,* 505–514.

Acklin, M. W. (1996). Personality assessment and managed care. *Journal of Personality Assessment, 66,* 194–201.

Anastasi, A. (1988). *Psychological testing* (6th ed.). New York: Macmillan.

Aronow, E., & Reznikoff, M. (1976). *Rorschach content interpretation.* New York: Grune & Stratton.

Blatt, S. J., & Ford, R. Q. (1994). *Therapeutic change: An object relations perspective.* New York: Plenum.

Bornstein, R. R. (1996). Construct validity of the Rorschach Oral Dependency Scale. *Psychological Assessment, 8,* 200–205.

Buros, O. K. (Ed.). (1974). *Tests in print II.* Highland Park, NJ: Gryphon.

Butcher, J. N., & Rouse, S. V. (1996). Personality: Individual differences and clinical assessment. *Annual Review of Psychology, 47,* 87–111.

Cooper, S. H., Perry, J. C., & Arnow, D. (1988). An empirical approach to the study of defense mechanisms: I. Reliability and preliminary validity of the Rorschach Defense Scales. *Journal of Personality Assessment, 52,* 187–203.

Craig, R. J., & Horowitz, M. (1990). Current utilization of psychological tests at diagnostic practicum sites. *Clinical Psychologist, 43,* 23–36.

Ellenberger, H. F. (1954). The life and work of Hermann Rorschach (1884–1922). *Bulletin of the Menninger Clinic, 18,* 173–219.

Exner, J. E., Jr. (1989). Searching for projection in the Rorschach. *Journal of Personality Assessment, 53,* 520–536.

Exner, J. E., Jr. (1991). *The Rorschach: A comprehensive system: Vol. 2. Interpretation* (2nd ed.). New York: Wiley.

Exner, J. E., Jr. (1993). *The Rorschach: A comprehensive system: Vol. 1. Basic foundations* (3rd. ed.). New York: Wiley.

Exner, J. E., Jr. (Ed.) (1995). *Issues and methods in Rorschach research.* Mahwah, NJ: Lawrence Erlbaum Associates, Inc.

Exner, J. E., Jr., & Andronikof-Sanglade, A. (1992). Rorschach changes following brief and short-term therapy. *Journal of Personality Assessment, 58,* 59–71.

Exner, J. E., Jr., & Weiner, I. B. (1995). *The Rorschach: A comprehensive system: Vol. 3. Assessment of children and adolescents* (2nd ed.). New York: Wiley.

Gacono, C. B., & Meloy, J. R. (1994). *The Rorschach assessment of aggressive and psychopathic personalities.* Hillsdale, NJ: Lawrence Erlbaum Associates, Inc.

Goldfried, M. R., Stricker, G., & Weiner, I. B. (1971). *Rorschach handbook of research and clinical applications.* Englewood Cliffs, NJ: Prentice-Hall.

Hedges, L. V., & Olkin, I. (1985). *Statistical methods for meta-analysis.* Orlando, FL: Academic.

Hilsenroth, M. J., & Handler, L. (1995). A survey of graduate students' experiences, interests, and attitudes about learning the Rorschach. *Journal of Personality Assessment, 64,* 243–257.

Janson, H., & Stattin, H. (1994). Recurring objects in Rorschach records over a period of about 30 years: How often do people report the same thing again? *Rorschachiana, 19,* 156–170.

Lerner, P. (1991). *Psychoanalytic theory and the Rorschach.* Hillsdale, NJ: The Analytic Press.

Lubin, B., Larsen, R. M., & Matarazzo, J. D. (1984). Patterns of psychological test usage in the United States: 1935–1982. *American Psychologist, 39,* 451–454.

Lubin, B., Wallis, R. R., & Paine, C. (1971). Patterns of psychological test usage in the United States. *Professional Psychology, 2,* 70–74.

McDowell, C., & Acklin, M. W. (1996). Standardizing procedures for calculating Rorschach interrater reliability: Conceptual and empirical foundations. *Journal of Personality Assessment, 66,* 308–320.

Parker, K. C. H., Hanson, R. K., & Hunsley, J. (1988). MMPI, Rorschach and WAIS: A meta-analytic comparison of reliability, stability, and validity. *Psychological Bulletin, 103,* 367–373.

Perry, W., Viglione, D., & Braff, D. (1992). The Ego Impairment Index and schizophrenia: A validation study. *Journal of Personality Assessment, 59,* 165–175.

Piotrowski, C., & Keller, J. W. (1989). Psychological testing in outpatient mental health facilities: A national study. *Professional Psychology, 20,* 423–425.

Piotrowski, C., Keller, J. W., & Ogawa, T. (1993). Projective techniques: An international perspective. *Psychological Reports, 72,* 179–182.

Piotrowski, C., & Zalewski, C. (1993). Training in psychodiagnostic testing in APA-approved PsyD and PhD clinical psychology programs. *Journal of Personality Assessment, 61,* 394–405.

Reynolds, W. M., & Sundberg, N. D. (1976). Recent research trends in testing. *Journal of Personality Assessment, 40,* 228–233.

Ritzler, B., & Alter, B. (1986). Rorschach teaching in APA-approved clinical graduate programs: Ten years later. *Journal of Personality Assessment, 50,* 44–49.

Rorschach, H. (1942). *Psychodiagnostics: A diagnostic test based on perception.* New York: Grune & Stratton. (Original work published 1921)

Schachtel, E. G. (1966). *Experiential foundations of Rorschach's test.* New York: Basic Books.

Schafer, R. (1954). *Psychoanalytic interpretation in Rorschach testing.* New York: Grune & Stratton.

Shontz, F. C., & Green, P. (1992). Trends in research on the Rorschach: Review and recommendations. *Applied and Preventive Psychology, 1,* 149–146.

Stricker, G., & Healey, B. J. (1990). Projective assessment of object relations: A review of the empirical literature. *Psychological Assessment, 2,* 219–230.

Sundberg, N. D. (1961). The practice of psychological testing in clinical services in the United States. *American Psychologist, 16,* 79–83.

Urist, J. (1977). The Rorschach test and the assessment of object relations. *Journal of Personality Assessment, 41,* 3–9.

Watkins, C. E., Jr. (1991). What have surveys taught us about the teaching and practice of psychological assessment? *Journal of Personality Assessment, 56,* 426–437.

Watkins, C. E., Jr. (1994). Do projective techniques get a "bum rap" from clinical psychology training directors? *Journal of Personality Assessment, 63,* 387–389.

Watkins, C. E., Jr., Campbell, V. L., Nieberding, R., & Hallmark, R. (1995). Contemporary practice of psychological assessment by clinical psychologists. *Professional Psychology, 26,* 54–60.

Weiner, I. B. (1977). Approaches to Rorschach validation. In M. A. Rickers-Ovsiankina (Ed.), *Rorschach psychology* (2nd ed., pp. 575–608). Huntington, NY: Krieger.

Weiner, I. B. (1986). Conceptual and empirical perspectives on the Rorschach assessment of psychopathology. *Journal of Personality Assessment, 50,* 472–479.

Weiner, I. B. (1991). Editor's note: Interscorer agreement in Rorschach research. *Journal of Personality Assessment, 56,* 1.

Weiner, I. B. (1994a). Rorschach assessment. In M. Maruish (Ed.), *The use of psychological testing for treatment planning and outcome assessment* (pp. 249–278). Hillsdale, NJ: Lawrence Erlbaum Associates, Inc.

Weiner, I. B. (1994b). The Rorschach Inkblot Method (RIM) is not a test: Implications for theory and practice. *Journal of Personality Assessment, 62,* 498–504.

Weiner, I. B. (1995a, March). *Clinical assessment with the Rorschach Comprehensive System.* Workshop presented at the meeting of the Society for Personality Assessment, Atlanta, GA.

Weiner, I. B. (1995b). Methodological considerations in Rorschach research. *Psychological Assessment, 7,* 330–337.

Weiner, I. B. (1995c). Searching for Rorschach theory: A wild goose chase. *Proceedings of the XIV International Rorschach Congress* (pp. 23–32). Lisbon, Portugal: Gulbenkian.

Weiner, I. B. (1996). Some observations on the validity of the Rorschach Inkblot Method. *Psychological Assessment, 8,* 206–213.

Weiner, I. B., & Exner, J. E., Jr. (1991). Rorschach changes in long-term and short-term psychotherapy. *Journal of Personality Assessment, 56,* 453–465.

2

Current Status of MMPI–2 Research: A Methodologic Overview

Roger L. Greene, Roy Gwin, and Mark Staal

Pacific Graduate School of Psychology

MMPI–2 research since 1990 has been reviewed to assess whether Butcher and Tellegen's (1978) concerns and suggestions about MMPI research were being followed. Guidelines are provided for when the MMPI–2 is appropriate to administer, how to describe the sample used, assessing validity of the profile, what scores to analyze, and how to report the results. Suggestions also are presented for research within several current areas of debate in the MMPI–2: codetype comparability between the MMPI and MMPI–2, incremental validity of new or existing scales, obvious and subtle subscales, emphasis on item content, development of new scales, and correcting profiles for specific medical and physical conditions.

Research with the MMPI–2 (Butcher, Dahlstrom, Graham, Tellegen, & Kaemmer, 1989) is proceeding at a high rate in a multitude of clinical and research areas. A review of the MMPI–2 research since 1990 was undertaken to examine whether the current research is heeding the original concerns and suggestions raised by Butcher and Tellegen (1978) about MMPI research and to provide guidelines for improving the overall quality of MMPI–2 research.[1]

Potential problems in the use of the MMPI–2 will be reviewed roughly in the order that a researcher should consider them in designing and carrying out an MMPI–2 study. Then suggestions will be provided for conducting and reporting research within several areas of current debate in the MMPI–2 field. These guidelines and suggestions should be helpful to both researchers, in designing and reporting their projects, and clinicians, in knowing what types of information should be reported when they are reading a published study on the MMPI–2.

---

[1] Butcher, Graham, and Ben-Porath (1995) recently published a similar critique of research with the MMPI–2 that should be consulted.

WHETHER TO USE THE MMPI–2

Butcher and Tellegen (1978) advised researchers not to use the MMPI with groups for which some other instrument might be more appropriate. Their recommendation continues to be relevant for the MMPI–2, plus there are a number of relatively new personality inventories available for researchers to consider. Helmes and Reddon (1993) noted that psychopathology is defined more clearly today than 50 years ago, but modern developments in theories of psychopathology generally are not evident in the MMPI–2 because of the emphasis on continuity with the original MMPI.

Emphasis on Psychopathology

The MMPI–2 is a restandardization of the MMPI, and the MMPI–2 clinical scales are still measures of various forms of psychopathology (Butcher et al., 1989) and not measures of general personality even though some positive personality or emotional factors are assessed (e.g., Dominance, Social Responsibility, and Gender Role—Feminine and Masculine). Differential weighting of psychopathologic elements also occurs because the T-score distribution ranges from 30 to 120, with seven standard deviations above the mean for measuring psychopathology and only two standard deviations below the mean for measuring positive traits in clinical populations (Ward, 1994).

Appropriate Settings

The MMPI–2 is appropriate for clinical and personnel settings in which the researcher or clinician is interested in a broad-band instrument to assess or screen for Axis I psychopathology and to a lesser extent for Axis II psychopathology. If the Morey, Waugh, and Blashfield (1985) personality disorder scales become available through commercial or hand-scoring services for the MMPI–2 and further research substantiates their validity, they could facilitate its usefulness with Axis II disorders. When a specific form of psychopathology is being investigated, it is likely that an individual test that has been validated specifically for that purpose will be more appropriate than a general screening instrument like the MMPI–2. It is highly unlikely that the MMPI–2 will be appropriate for circumstances in which the researcher is interested in more general personality characteristics of putatively normal individuals.

Short Forms

The use of short forms for the MMPI or MMPI–2 is not appropriate given their low concordance rate and the lack of substantial research conducted to validate them (Butcher et al., 1995; Butcher & Hostetler, 1990; Butcher & Tellegen, 1978). In addition, any subsequent inferences drawn from the short form should not be based on the standard normative data or from assumptions of equivalence to the full administration of the MMPI–2.

DESCRIPTION OF SAMPLE

In addition to the usual information on the number of participants and their age, gender, and education, a complete description of any clinical sample is necessary. This additional information is vital because many studies are conducted on generic samples, that is, samples of "convenience," rather than a specific diagnostic group.

Generic Samples

If a generic sample of patients is being used, the setting (psychiatric, medical, rehabilitation), type of treatment (inpatient, outpatient, day treatment), typical diagnoses (at a minimum percentage of Axis I or Axis II diagnoses and whether psychotic or not), and reason for referral (voluntary, court-mandated) should be provided. MMPI–2 scale elevations and codetypes can vary drastically as a function of any of these variables, and such information is needed if any type of meaningful comparisons between and among studies is to be made.

Specific Diagnostic Groups

When specific diagnostic groups are being compared on the MMPI–2, researchers should delineate the bases for making the diagnoses as well as their reliability. Clinicians' judgments of diagnoses are unlikely to qualify as an adequate "gold-standard" criterion without substantial documentation, and a structured interview will be needed in most circumstances. The researcher should insure that the MMPI–2 is not part of the process for making the diagnosis to eliminate a potential source of confounding.

Number of Participants

An acceptable ratio of participants per variable needs to be maintained with minimal estimates running from 10 to 15 participants per variable, that is, each group will need to have a minimum of 130 participants if all 13 standard validity and clinical scales are to be analyzed. Because clinical participants frequently are limited in number, researchers may prefer to develop specific hypotheses about individual

MMPI–2 scales. For example, if two diagnostic groups are being contrasted for their level of depression, it is not necessary to test all 13 scales to evaluate this hypothesis even though the entire MMPI–2 has been administered. If the these two groups are expected to differ by 5 T points (.5 standard deviation), a sample size of 50 persons per group is needed to achieve power of .80 at the .05 level of significance (Cohen, 1988).

Ethnicity

The expansion of ethnic representation in the MMPI–2 normative group has renewed interest in researching its potential ethnic bias. Timbrook and Graham (1994) found few ethnic differences between Blacks and Whites within the MMPI–2 normative group and other investigators have started to examine this issue in Asian Americans (Stevens, Kwan, & Graybill, 1993) and Mexican Americans (Canul & Cross, 1994; Whitworth & McBlaine, 1993). There are a plethora of issues that need to be considered by anyone who is doing research in this area and a number of references to be consulted (Dahlstrom, Lachar, & Dahlstrom, 1986; Dana, 1990; Dana & Whatley, 1991; Greene, 1987; Zalewski & Greene, 1996). At a minimum, researchers should determine that the persons actually identify themselves as a member of the specific ethnic group and assess their level of acculturation (Cuellar, Harris, & Jasso, 1980; Parham & Helms, 1981; Suinn, Rikard-Figueroa, Lew, & Vigil, 1987). Surname and/or skin color are unlikely to be reliable measures of ethnicity, even though they are the two most frequently used indexes. If any differences are found on the MMPI–2 that can be attributed to ethnicity after controlling for variables such as profile validity, education, and socioeconomic status, their empirical correlates need to be determined. Given the large number of studies on this issue, the paucity of studies that have reported any empirical correlates of ethnicity is dismaying.

VALIDITY CONSIDERATIONS

Researchers need to provide explicit information on three specific aspects of validity: item omissions, consistency of item endorsement, and accuracy of item endorsement. It is also important for researchers not to confuse measures of these last two forms of validity as sometimes occurs when infrequency scales are used as measures of inconsistency of item endorsement (see Greene, 1991, in press). Researchers should report the specific number and percentage of persons that are excluded within each of these areas.

Finn (1996) advocated a new paradigm for therapeutic MMPI–2 assessment wherein the psychologist becomes a participant-observer rather than an objective observer. The psychologist collaboratively explores the client's situation and usual ways of being in a manner that minimizes power imbalances and demonstrates respect, empathy, and caring for the person. In this paradigm the MMPI–2 becomes an opportunity for dialogue with the client about characteristic ways of responding to usual problem situations and should essentially eliminate any intentional reason(s) for persons to distort their responses to the MMPI–2.

Omissions

Item omissions occur much less frequently on the MMPI–2 because of the elimination of objectionable items and rewording of obscure language. Nevertheless, researchers should screen the data carefully for item omissions. Persons who omit more than 30 items should be removed from data analysis if they cannot be encouraged to answer these items. More conservative cutting scores of 10 or more omissions probably are appropriate in most situations because of the relative infrequency (less than 1% in most psychiatric samples) with which items are omitted.

Consistency

It is extremely important that MMPI–2 data be screened for consistency of item endorsement because reliable data are necessary for any analysis. The recommended cutting scores on the *Variable Response Consistency Scale (VRIN)* have ranged from 10 (69T) to 14 (84T; Berry et al., 1991; Butcher et al., 1989; Greene, 1991), so researchers will need to report the specific cutting score used. Alternatively, they could report the number of persons that would have been excluded by using each of the cutting scores in the aforementioned range as well as the final cutting score selected.

These recommended cutting scores are based on the assumption that the person has maintained the same response style throughout the MMPI–2. If there is any reason to suspect that the person's motivation has changed at some point during the test, researchers need to report measures of consistency that are sensitive to such vicissitudes (cf. Berry et al., 1991; Greene, 1991, in press).

Accuracy

There are a multitude of scales and indexes that can be used to assess accuracy of item endorsement, that is, whether persons have distorted their responses to make themselves appear more or less psychopathologic. Researchers also need to screen their MMPI–2s to remove the more extreme cases of response distortion before undertaking any analyses. Infrequency scales (e.g., F and/or F_B) are the most common measures of the accuracy of item endorsement, closely followed by the Gough (1950) Dissimulation Index ($F - K$). Typical cutting scores on F and F_B range from raw scores of 20 to 23 and T scores of 100 to 110 (Butcher & Williams, 1992; Graham, 1993; Greene, 1991). The Psychiatric F ($F[p]$; Arbisi & Ben-Porath, 1995) scale, 27 items that are endorsed infrequently in psychiatric samples, also appears promising as a measure of the accuracy of item endorsement in clinical samples.

If researchers are going to utilize some other measure of accuracy of item endorsement, they should provide a rationale for its use being more appropriate in this specific setting or with this specific group of persons.

Once researchers have provided the basic information on the validity of the MMPI–2 profiles that are being investigated and excluded those cases that do not meet each criterion, the next issue becomes what scores to analyze.

WHAT SCORES TO USE

There are two basic issues a researcher must decide on in selecting the specific scores to be analyzed: (a) whether raw scores or T scores are to be used, and (b) whether these scores should be K-corrected. Each of these issues will be examined in turn.

Raw Scores

Butcher and Tellegen (1978) recommended using raw scores in research computations rather than T scores unless data from both genders are to be combined or codetypes are to be analyzed. This recommendation is still germane to the MMPI–2, particularly if a single scale is being examined. When multiple scales are being analyzed and it is important that the scales have essentially the same distribution, uniform T scores, which are described in the next section, will be more appropriate.

T Scores

The MMPI utilizes linear T scores in its standardization of raw scores that preserves the relative skewness of individual scales but results in scales that are not comparable in terms of percentile distribution. Although Colligan, Osborne, and Offord (1980, 1984) proposed normalized T scores as an alternative to linear T scores, the restandardization committee (Butcher et al., 1989) chose to adopt a uniform T-score format for the eight clinical scales and all content scales. The use of uniform T

scores has resulted in percentile comparability across scales while maintaining the relative skewness of the underlying distributions (Tellegen & Ben-Porath, 1992). Uniform *T* scores will facilitate comparisons between and among the clinical and content scales because of the similarity of their distribution of scores and should be used in most analyses.

K-Correction

Meehl and Hathaway (1946) developed the *K* scale to identify individuals who were defensive in endorsing the MMPI items and to adjust the low scores upwards of these patients. The resulting corrections to the raw MMPI/MMPI–2 scores are known as the *K*-correction that is applied to five of the clinical scales (*Hs, Pd, Pt, Sc,* and *Ma*). Butcher and Tellegen (1978) recommended that scores on the clinical scales be used without *K*-correction and the *K* scale be used as a separate indicator because its role as a "suppressor" variable cannot be assumed when individual scales are being analyzed. This recommendation applies to research with the MMPI–2 for the same reasons. Researchers will need to look up the non-*K*-corrected *T* scores in Table A–2 (pp. 56–57) of the *MMPI–2 Manual* (Butcher et al., 1989) because they cannot be read directly from the standard profile form.

When the researcher is interested in examining the correlates of MMPI–2 codetypes, *K*-corrected *T* scores will need to be used to compare the obtained results with the extant literature because it is based on *K*-corrected *T* scores. Even in this circumstance, researchers still should examine whether non-*K*-corrected *T* scores provide better relationships with the correlates under investigation.

It is remarkable that in over 50 years there has been virtually no research on the *K*-correction process, and that this correction procedure was not examined nor validated when it was extended to the MMPI–2. Such research clearly is needed.

REPORTING AND ANALYZING DATA

The means and standard deviations for the standard validity and clinical scales for the various groups under consideration are reported in most studies, and this practice should continue. This information is preferred to providing only profiles of the data because measures of variance are unavailable when data are presented only in profile form. Profiles of the data, when means and standard deviations for all scales are included, are desirable because clinicians are accustomed to seeing the data in profile format.

Group Means/Profiles

As Butcher and Tellegen (1978) noted, presenting only group data may be misleading because the individuals within the group may not have the pattern of scores or specific codetype illustrated in the mean profile. It is even possible for no single individual to have the codetype that is indicated by the group data! Their recommendation that researchers report the frequency with which the various codetypes occur has fallen on deaf ears, as can be seen, for example, in virtually any study that has reported the results of cluster analysis of MMPI/MMPI–2 data. Researchers should report the specific codetypes that are found within any group data and the frequency with which each codetype occurs.

Standard Error of Estimate

If profiles of the data are provided, the standard error of measurement for each scale should be indicated. In addition, researchers should consider whether their obtained results exceed the standard error of estimate, which will be approximately 3 to 6 T points for most MMPI–2 scales.

Statistical Analyses

MMPI–2 studies typically involve multiple dependent variables because the 13 standard validity and clinical scales will be analyzed. The researcher should consider whether a multivariate or univariate analysis is appropriate (Huberty & Morris, 1989), and use some method of correcting for experiment-wise error rate such as the Bonferroni correction regardless of the analysis employed. It is not appropriate to conduct separate t tests on all 13 scales in the standard profile, and it is even more problematic to conduct separate t tests on the standard scales between and among several groups of patients.

AREAS OF CURRENT DEBATE
WITHIN THE MMPI–2 FIELD

There are several areas of research within the MMPI–2 that have been the focus of debate in the past few years. Each of these areas will be summarized briefly along with suggestions for how to direct research to address these issues.

Codetype Comparability

Although very little was changed in terms of item composition between the standard validity and clinical scales of the MMPI and MMPI–2, research on codetype comparability has been very popular with over 40 published studies since 1990. At least four factors will increase the overall level of concordance that is reported in these studies: (a) using only "well-defined" codetypes (codetypes where all other clinical scale elevations are at least 5 T points below the two highest scales) rather than nonrestrictive codetypes (codetypes based simply on two highest scales regardless of other elevations), (b) eliminating "within-normal-limits" profiles before calculating concordance, (c) using clinical samples rather than college students or the MMPI–2 restandardization sample, and (d) administering only Form AX (containing all of the MMPI and MMPI–2 items in a single instrument) rather than separate administrations of the MMPI and MMPI–2. Consequently, there are a wide range of opinions on the degree of codetype comparability between the MMPI and MMPI–2 ranging from 50% to 90% using well-defined codetypes, and 40% to 70% for nonrestrictive codetypes (cf. Dahlstrom, 1992; Edwards, Morrison, & Weissman, 1993a, 1993b; Graham, Timbrook, Ben-Porath, & Butcher, 1991; Morrison, Edwards, Weissman, Allen, & DeLaCruz, 1995). Rarely do these researchers report whether the degree of concordance varies as a function of specific codetype, although it does (see Greene, 1991, pp. 247–251), and none of the studies of the comparability of the MMPI and MMPI–2 have actually examined the empirical correlates of the two instruments despite calls for such research (Dahlstrom, 1992).

Little appears to be gained by further research investigating the concordance between MMPI and MMPI–2 profiles because it begs the question of what are the correlates of MMPI–2 scales and codetypes. Instead, researchers should ascertain the specific empirical correlates of well-defined MMPI–2 codetypes and then investigate whether these relationships change when nonrestrictive codetypes are included. Researchers also should consider replotting the MMPI–2 as an MMPI using Appendix K from the *MMPI–2 Manual* (Butcher et al., 1989) to assess whether the correlates provide a better fit to the MMPI or the MMPI–2 codetype. Such a procedure also will be necessary so that the results can be compared to the existing literature on the correlates of MMPI codetypes.

Incremental Validity of Scales

Butcher and his colleagues (Ben-Porath, Butcher, & Graham, 1991; Butcher, Graham, & Ben-Porath, 1995) have advocated that any new scale or index should contribute incrementally to the prediction of relevant behaviors. This rationale can be justified to the extent that it limits the proliferation of scales, but it seems to overlook the numerous instances of the differential validity of scales across settings and situational demands, and the even more numerous occasions in which investigators have failed to report the differential validities of closely related (conceptually or correlationally) measures of the primary construct of interest. The three alcohol and drug scales on the MMPI–2 (Addiction Acknowledgment scale [AAS], Weed,

Butcher, McKenna, & Ben-Porath, 1992; Addiction Potential scale [APS], Weed et al., 1992; and MacAndrew Alcoholism Scale–Revised [MAC–R], MacAndrew, 1965) are correlated significantly, yet provide valuable information about this area from a variety of perspectives. Persons abusing alcohol or drugs who will endorse the face-valid items on the AAS will be very different to work with clinically than persons who avoid endorsing the AAS items yet who are identified by the APS or MAC–R. High scorers on the APS also tend to be different from high scorers on the MAC–R. Otto, Lang, Megargee, and Rosenblatt (1988) demonstrated a similar point for different MMPI alcohol scales as a function of instructions to alcoholics to deny their alcohol-related problems.

Studies reporting the results for the two scales developed to identify posttraumatic stress disorder (*PK*, Keane, Malloy, & Fairbank, 1984; *PS*, Schlenger & Kulka, 1987) typically have not included data from conceptually related measures such as Scales 7(*Pt*), *A* (Welsh, 1956), *Mt* (Kleinmuntz, 1960), and other markers for the first factor of the MMPI/MMPI–2 despite zero-order correlations among these five scales that often are in the .85 to .95 range. In this case, investigators who omit reporting the performance of these conceptually related scales with the results of *PK* and *PS* not only fail to document their incremental validity, they leave open the question of whether *PK* or *PS* possess any substantive validity at all.

There are a number of other sets of similar scales that warrant serious investigation along the lines suggested. Such investigations may provide valuable differential information, even when they fail to demonstrate incremental validity for one or more of the measures studied. In the interests of brevity, only some of these various sets of scales will be listed: defensiveness (Lie [*L*]; Correction [*K*]; Superlative [*S*], Butcher & Han, 1995); depression (Scale 2[*D*]; Content Depression [*DEP*]; Depression, Wiggins, 1966); hostility (Hostility [*Ho*], Cook & Medley, 1954; Content Anger [*ANG*]; Content Cynicism [*CYN*]; Content Type A [*TPA*]; Authority Conflict and Hostility, Wiggins, 1966; and Tryon, Stein, & Chu's Suspiciousness and Resentment and Aggression, Stein, 1968); and masculinity–femininity (Scale 5[*Mf*]; Gender Role–Feminine; Gender Role–Masculine). The inclusion of other pertinent scales not only addresses incremental and differential validity, but it also helps to clarify the concept themselves.

Obvious and Subtle Subscales

There has been a renewed debate in the last decade over the usefulness of obvious and subtle subscales of the MMPI–2. One issue within this debate is whether obvious or subtle subscales are better predictors of external criteria (cf. Dahlstrom, 1991; Jackson, 1971; Weed, Ben-Porath, & Butcher, 1990; Wrobel & Lachar, 1982). The other issue is the usefulness of the obvious and subtle subscales as a measure of overreporting (malingering) and underreporting (defensiveness) of psychopathology with advocates both pro (Brems & Johnson, 1991; Dannenbaum & Lanyon, 1993; Dush, Simons, Platt, Nation, & Ayres, 1994; Greene, 1988; Lees-Haley & Fox, 1990) and con (Schretlen, 1988; Timbrook, Graham, Keiller, & Watts, 1993; Weed et al., 1990).

Hollrah, Schlottmann, Scott, and Brunetti (1995) provided an overview of the methodologic issues that arise in determining the convergent and discriminative validity of the obvious and subtle subscales of the MMPI/MMPI–2. Any researcher who is contemplating work in this area should consult their article. Several conclusions of Hollrah et al. are worthy of noting here: (a) there are pervasive difficulties with the measures used to evaluate the subtle subscales, (b) there is a propensity to validate the obvious subscales with self-report measures comprised only of obvious statements, (c) many studies use nonpsychiatric samples that may restrict the range of scores on these scales, and (d) the decision to use obvious and subtle ratings for general psychopathology or specific scales needs to be predicated on the issue being investigated.

Emphasis on Item Content

Despite the empirical roots of the MMPI that eschewed looking at the content of the individual items, interest in item content began with the identification of "critical" items (Grayson, 1951; Koss & Butcher, 1973; Lachar & Wrobel, 1979) and has continued with the development of content scales for the MMPI (Wiggins, 1966) and MMPI–2 (Butcher, Graham, Williams, & Ben-Porath, 1989). More recently, Nichols and Greene (1995) developed a Structural Summary for the MMPI–2 that is based entirely on content analysis.

This growing trend to emphasize content in the interpretation of the MMPI–2 may be impeded by the inherent limitations of the item pool because the original derivation of MMPI scales did not consider the substantive meaning of the items and there was no need to be comprehensive nor exhaustive in selecting potential items (Butcher & Tellegen, 1978; Helmes & Reddon, 1993), although Hathaway and McKinley (1940) tried to be quite comprehensive at sampling the domain of self-reported symptoms and complaints of distress. Researchers, who are interested in examining forms of psychopathology that were not well delineated in the late 1930's, may find the item pools of more recently developed instruments more fruitful.

This emphasis on the item content can be problematic for scales that have a relatively limited number of items such as some of the Harris and Lingoes (1955) clinical subscales and the MMPI–2 Content Component scales (Ben-Porath & Sherwood, 1993). It is not clear whether these subscales should only be interpreted when the parent scale is elevated above a T score of 60 (Ben-Porath & Sherwood, 1993) or any elevation on a subscale of 65 or higher is reflective of a content area of particular importance for this individual. The former position is more conservative and clearly appropriate given the psychometric limitations of some of these subscales, whereas the latter position holds that this content area is important for the person regardless of its psychometric qualities. Most of these subscales have little empirical validation, which suggests that clinicians should be very judicious in their use of them and that it is an important research area in the coming years.

Development of New Scales

New scales can be developed using either an empirical or content-based method-ology. One of the inherent limitations of content-based approaches has been detailed earlier. An empirical methodology that uses a chi-square analysis for selecting items for a new scale determines only that the two groups endorse each item differently, and may identify many redundant items. Logistic regression also determines whether such items contribute unique variance to the differentiation of the two groups and provides weights for these individual items. Such weighting of items that contribute unique variance is feasible in this era of computers and deserves serious consideration rather than relying on the unitary weighting of all items identified by a chi-square analysis. Davis, Offord, Colligan, and Morse (1991) provided an example of using logistic regression to develop a new alcoholism scale for a medical setting.

Regardless of how the items for the scale are selected, item-total correlations should be examined and coefficient alpha, or some other form of reliability, should be reported. A receiver operating characteristic (ROC) curve should be constructed for the new scale (Cleary, Booker, & Kessler, 1987; Swets, 1986) that demonstrates the relationship between all levels of sensitivity and specificity. If the new scale is designed to supplant an existing scale, the two ROC curves should be plotted together so that they can be compared directly. Finally, researchers should report the positive and negative predictive power for the scale for typical bases rates encountered in the clinical setting (Baldessarini, Finkelstein, & Arana, 1983). Davis et al. (1991) and Svanum and Ehrmann (1993) provided examples of the use of ROC curves with new and existing MMPI/MMPI–2 scales.

Corrections for Specific Medical or Physical Conditions

A series of studies over the last few decades has investigated whether the MMPI/MMPI–2 scales are biased against specific medical or physical conditions: cerebrovascular accidents (Gass & Lawhorn, 1991), multiple sclerosis (Baldwin, 1952; Marsh, Hirsch, & Leung, 1982; Meyerink, Reitan, & Selz, 1988), neurologic dysfunction (Alfano, Finlayson, Stearns, & Neilson, 1990; Cripe, Maxwell, & Hill, 1995; Gass, 1991), and physical disability (Taylor, 1970). The usual paradigm in these studies is to ask a panel of experts to review the item pool to identify those items that would be answered in the deviant direction based on the presence of the specific medical or physical condition in question. The items identified by these experts are then deleted, the MMPI/MMPI–2 is rescored, and *T* scores are computed in the usual manner, that is, no attempt is made to correct for the items that have been deleted from any scale. Not surprisingly, the standard profile is lower once these items have been deleted, and those scales from which the largest number of items are deleted are affected the most. Based on these decreases in scale elevation, researchers conclude that the MMPI/MMPI–2 is biased against the medical or physical condition being investigated and their correction should be used.

There are a surprising number of assumptions that are made in these studies that need to be substantiated: (a) the patients with the medical or physical condition are a homogeneous group, (b) the only reason patients endorse the correction items is because of their medical or physical condition rather than because they reflect their concern about their physical functioning, and (c) the MMPI/MMPI–2 scale can be interpreted in the usual manner after some number of items has been removed. In addition, none of these sets of correction items has been cross-validated or supported if cross-validated (Dunn & Lees-Haley, 1995).

Research that examines whether patients with a specific medical or physical condition have different empirical correlates when any correction items are removed is needed. Clinicians should be very hesitant to use any of these sets of correction items until they have been validated empirically across several settings.

SUMMARY

There has been and will continue to be a wide variety of research with the MMPI–2. These guidelines and suggestions should facilitate an overall improvement of the quality of research with this venerable instrument and allow both researchers and clinicians to integrate the results of many disparate studies. Hopefully another decade of MMPI–2 research will not see the same methodologic errors being perpetuated.

ACKNOWLEDGMENTS

We appreciate the feedback of Alex Caldwell, David Nichols, and two anonymous reviewers.

Bill N. Kinder served as Action Editor for this chapter.

REFERENCES

Alfano, D. P., Finlayson, A. J., Stearns, G. M., & Neilson, P. M. (1990). The MMPI and neurologic dysfunction: Profile configuration and analysis. *The Clinical Neurologist, 4*, 69–79.

Arbisi, P. A., & Ben-Porath, Y. S. (1995). Interpretation of F scales for inpatients: Moving from art to science. *Psychological Assessment, 7*, 424–431.

Baldessarini, R. J., Finkelstein, S., & Arana, G. W. (1983). The predictive power of diagnostic tests and the effect of prevalence of illness. *Archives of General Psychiatry, 40,* 569–573.

Baldwin, M. V. (1952). A clinico-experimental investigation into the psychologic aspects of multiple sclerosis. *Journal of Nervous and Mental Disease, 115,* 299–342.

Ben-Porath, Y. S., Butcher, J. N., & Graham, J. R. (1991). Contribution of the MMPI–2 content scales to the differential diagnosis of schizophrenia and major depression. *Psychological Assessment, 3,* 634–640.

Ben-Porath, Y. S., & Sherwood, N. E. (1993). *The MMPI–2 content component scales: Development, psychometric characteristics, and clinical application.* Minneapolis: University of Minnesota Press.

Berry, D. T. R., Wetter, M. W., Baer, R. A., Widiger, T. A., Sumpter, J. C., Reynolds, S. K., & Hallam, R. A. (1991). Detection of random responding on the MMPI–2: Utility of F, Back F, and VRIN scales. *Psychological Assessment, 3,* 418–423.

Brems, C., & Johnson, M. E. (1991). Subtle-obvious scales of the MMPI: Indicators of profile validity in a psychiatric population. *Journal of Personality Assessment, 56,* 536–544.

Butcher, J. N., Dahlstrom, W. G., Graham, J. R., Tellegen, A., & Kaemmer, B. (1989). *Minnesota Multiphasic Personality Inventory–2 (MMPI–2): Manual for administration and scoring.* Minneapolis: University of Minnesota Press.

Butcher, J. N., Graham, J. R., & Ben-Porath, Y. S. (1995). Methodological problems and issues in MMPI, MMPI–2, and MMPI–A research. *Psychological Assessment, 7,* 320–329.

Butcher, J. N., Graham, J. R., Williams, C. L., & Ben-Porath, Y. S. (1989). *Development and use of the MMPI–2 content scales.* Minneapolis: University of Minnesota Press.

Butcher, J. N., & Han, K. (1995). Development of an MMPI–2 scale to assess the presentation of self in a superlative manner: The S scale. In J. N. Butcher & C. D. Spielberger (Eds.), *Advances in personality assessment* (Vol. 10, pp. 25–50). Hillsdale, NJ: Lawrence Erlbaum Associates, Inc.

Butcher, J. N., & Hostetler, K. (1990). Abbreviating MMPI item administration: What can be learned from the MMPI for the MMPI–2? *Psychological Assessment, 2,* 12–21.

Butcher, J. N., & Tellegen, A. (1978). Common methodological problems in MMPI research. *Journal of Consulting and Clinical Psychology, 46,* 620–628.

Butcher, J. N., & Williams, C. L. (1992). *Essentials of MMPI–2 interpretation.* Minneapolis: University of Minnesota Press.

Canul, G. D., & Cross, H. J. (1994). The influence of acculturation and racial identity attitudes on Mexican-Americans' MMPI–2 performance. *Journal of Clinical Psychology, 50,* 736–744.

Cleary, P. D., Booker, T. B., & Kessler, L. G. (1987). Evaluating the use of mental health screening scales in primary care settings using receiver operating characteristic curves. *Medical Care, 25,* 90–98.

Cohen, J. (1988). *Statistical power analysis for the behavioral sciences* (2nd ed.). Hillsdale, NJ: Lawrence Erlbaum Associates, Inc.

Colligan, R. C., Osborne, D., & Offord, K. P. (1980). Linear transformation and the interpretation of MMPI T scores. *Journal of Clinical Psychology, 36,* 162–165.

Colligan, R. C., Osborne, D., & Offord, K. P. (1984). Normalized transformations and the interpretation of MMPI T scores: A reply to Hsu. *Journal of Consulting and Clinical Psychology, 52,* 824–826.

Cook, W. W., & Medley, D. M. (1954). Proposed hostility and Pharisaic-virtue scales for the MMPI. *Journal of Applied Psychology, 38,* 414–418.

Cripe, L. I., Maxwell, J. K., & Hill, E. (1995). Multivariate discriminant function analysis of neurologic, pain, and psychiatric patients with the MMPI. *Journal of Clinical Psychology, 51,* 258–268.

Cuellar, L., Harris, L. C., & Jasso, R. (1980). An acculturation scale for Mexican-American normal and clinical populations. *Hispanic Journal of Behavioral Science, 2,* 199–217.

Dahlstrom, W. G., (1991, July). *Correlates of each of the subtle and obvious subscales of D, Hy, Pd, Pa, and Ma (Wiener & Harmon).* Paper presented at the MMPI–2 Summer Institute, Colorado Springs, CO.

Dahlstrom, W. G. (1992). Comparability of two-point high-point code patterns from original MMPI norms to MMPI–2 norms for the restandardization sample. *Journal of Personality Assessment, 59*, 153–164.

Dahlstrom, W. G., Lachar, D., & Dahlstrom, L. E. (1986). *MMPI patterns of American minorities.* Minneapolis: University of Minnesota Press.

Dana, R. H. (1990). Cross-cultural and multi-ethnic assessment. In J. N. Butcher & C. D. Spielberger (Eds.), *Advances in personality assessment* (pp. 1–26). Hillsdale, NJ: Lawrence Erlbaum Associates, Inc.

Dana, R. H., & Whatley, P. R. (1991). When does a difference make a difference? MMPI scores and African-Americans. *Journal of Clinical Psychology, 47*, 400–406.

Dannenbaum, S. E., & Lanyon, R. I. (1993). The use of subtle items in detecting deception. *Journal of Personality Assessment, 61*, 501–510.

Davis, Jr., L. J., Offord, K. P., Colligan, R. C., & Morse, R. M. (1991). The CAL: An MMPI alcoholism scale for general medical patients. *Journal of Clinical Psychology, 47*, 632–646.

Dunn, J. T., & Lees-Haley, P. R. (1995). The MMPI–2 correction factor for closed-head injury: A caveat for forensic cases. *Psychological Assessment, 2*, 47–51.

Dush, D. M., Simons, L. E., Platt, M., Nation, P. C., & Ayres, S. Y. (1994). Psychological profiles distinguishing litigating and nonlitigating pain patients: Subtle, and not so subtle. *Journal of Personality Assessment, 62*, 299–313.

Edwards, D. W., Morrison, T. L., & Weissman, H. N. (1993a). The MMPI and MMPI–2 in an outpatient sample: Comparisons of code types, validity scales and clinical scales. *Journal of Personality Assessment, 61*, 1–18.

Edwards, D. W., Morrison, T. L., & Weissman, H. N. (1993b). Uniform versus linear T scores on the MMPI–2/MMPI in an outpatient psychiatric sample: Differential contributions. *Psychological Assessment, 5*, 499–500.

Finn, S. (1996). *Using the MMPI–2 as therapeutic assessment.* Minneapolis: University of Minnesota Press.

Gass, C. S. (1991). MMPI–2 interpretation and closed head injury: A correction factor. *Psychological Assessment, 3*, 27–31.

Gass, C. S., & Lawhorn, L. (1991). Psychological adjustment following stroke: An MMPI study. *Psychological Assessment, 3*, 628–633.

Gough, H. (1950). The F – K dissimulation index for the MMPI. *Journal of Consulting Psychology, 14*, 408–413.

Graham, J. R. (1993). *MMPI–2: Assessing personality and psychopathology* (2nd ed.). New York: Oxford University Press.

Graham, J. R., Timbrook, R. E., Ben-Porath, Y. S., & Butcher, J. N. (1991). Code-type congruence between MMPI and MMPI–2: Separating fact from artifact. *Journal of Personality Assessment, 57*, 205–215.

Grayson, H. M. (1951). *A psychological admissions testing program and manual.* Los Angeles: Veterans Administration Center, Neuropsychiatric Hospital.

Greene, R. L. (1987). The MMPI and ethnicity: A review. *Journal of Consulting and Clinical Psychology, 55*, 497–512.

Greene, R. L. (1988). The relative efficacy of F – K and the obvious and subtle scales to detect overreporting of psychopathology on the MMPI. *Journal of Clinical Psychology, 88*, 152–159.

Greene, R. L. (1991). *The MMPI–2/MMPI: An interpretive manual.* Needham Heights, MA: Allyn & Bacon.

Greene, R. L. (in press). Assessment of malingering and defensiveness by multiscale personality inventories. In R. Rogers (Ed.), *Assessment of malingering and defensiveness* (2nd ed.). New York: Guilford.

Harris, R. E., & Lingoes, J. C. (1955). *Subscales for the MMPI: An aid to profile interpretation.* Unpublished manuscript, University of California.

Hathaway, S. R., & McKinley, J. C. (1940). A multiphasic personality schedule (Minnesota): I. Construction of the schedule. *Journal of Personality, 10,* 249–254.

Helmes, E., & Reddon, J. R. (1993). A perspective on developments in assessing psychopathology: A critical review of the MMPI and MMPI–2. *Psychological Bulletin, 113,* 453–471.

Hollrah, J. L., Schlottmann, R. S., Scott, A. B., & Brunetti, D. G. (1995). Validity of the MMPI subtle items. *Journal of Personality Assessment, 65,* 278–299.

Huberty, C. J., & Morris, J. D. (1989). Multivariate analysis versus multiple univariate analysis. *Psychological Bulletin, 105,* 302–308.

Jackson, D. N. (1971). The dynamics of structured personality tests: 1971. *Psychological Review, 78,* 229–248.

Keane, T. M., Malloy, P. F., & Fairbank, J. A. (1984). Empirical development of an MMPI subscale for the assessment of combat-related posttraumatic stress disorder. *Journal of Consulting and Clinical Psychology, 52,* 888–891.

Kleinmuntz, B. (1960). Identification of maladjusted college students. *Journal of Counseling Psychology, 7,* 209–211.

Koss, M. P., & Butcher, J. N. (1973). A comparison of psychiatric patients' self-report with other sources of clinical information. *Journal of Research in Personality, 7,* 225–236.

Lachar, D., & Wrobel, T. A. (1979). Validating clinicians' hunches: Construction of a new MMPI critical item set. *Journal of Consulting and Clinical Psychology, 47,* 277–284.

Lees-Haley, P. R., & Fox, D. D. (1990). MMPI subtle-obvious scales and malingering: Clinical versus simulated scores. *Psychological Reports, 66,* 907–911.

MacAndrew, C. (1965). The differentiation of male alcoholic outpatients from nonalcoholic psychiatric outpatients by means of the MMPI. *Quarterly Journal of Studies on Alcohol, 26,* 238–246.

Marsh, G. G., Hirsch, S. H., & Leung, G. (1982). Use and misuse of the MMPI in multiple sclerosis. *Psychological Reports, 51,* 1127–1134.

Meehl, P. E., & Hathaway, S. R. (1946). The K factor as a suppressor variable in the MMPI. *Journal of Applied Psychology, 30,* 525–564.

Meyerink, L. H., Reitan, R. M., & Selz, M. (1988). The validity of the MMPI with multiple sclerosis patients. *Journal of Clinical Psychology, 44,* 764–769.

Morey, L. C., Waugh, M. H., & Blashfield, R. K. (1985). MMPI scales for DSM-III personality disorders: Their derivation and correlates. *Journal of Personality Assessment, 49,* 245–251.

Morrison, T. L., Edwards, D. W., Weissman, H. N., Allen, R., & DeLaCruz, D. (1995). Comparing MMPI and MMPI–2 profiles: Replication and integration. *Assessment, 2,* 39–46.

Nichols, D. S., & Greene, R. L. (1995). *The MMPI–2 Structural Summary manual.* Lutz, FL: Psychological Assessment Resources.

Otto, R. K., Lang, A. R., Megargee, E. I., & Rosenblatt, A. I. (1988). Ability of alcoholics to escape detection by the MMPI. *Journal of Consulting and Clinical Psychology, 56,* 452–457.

Parham, T. A., & Helms, J. E. (1981). The influence of Black students' racial identity on preferences for counselor's race. *Journal of Counseling Psychology, 28,* 250–257.

Schlenger, W. E., & Kulka, R. A. (1987, August). *Performance of the Keane–Fairbank MMPI scale and other self-report measures in identifying post-traumatic stress disorder.* Paper presented at the meeting of the American Psychological Association, New York.

Schretlen, D. J. (1988). The use of psychological tests to identify malingered symptoms of mental disorders. *Clinical Psychology Review, 8,* 451–476.

Stein, K. B. (1968). The TSC scales: The outcome of a cluster analysis of the 550 MMPI items. In P. McReynolds (Ed.), *Advances in psychological assessment* (Vol. 1, pp. 80–104). Palo Alto, CA: Science & Behavior Books.

Stevens, M. J., Kwan, K., & Graybill, D. (1993). Comparison of MMPI–2 scores of foreign Chinese and Caucasian-American students. *Journal of Clinical Psychology, 49*, 23–27.

Suinn, R., Rikard-Figueroa, K., Lew, S., & Vigil, P. (1987). The Suinn-Lew Asian self-identify acculturation scale: An initial report. *Educational and Psychological Measurement, 47*, 401–407.

Svanum, S., & Ehrmann, L. C. (1993). The validity of the MMPI in identifying alcoholics in a university setting. *Journal of Studies on Alcohol, 54*, 722–729.

Swets, J. A. (1986). Form of empirical ROCs in discrimination and diagnostic tasks: Implications for theory and measurement of performance. *Psychological Bulletin, 99*, 181–198.

Taylor, G. P. (1970). Moderator-variable effect on personality-test item endorsements of physically disabled patients. *Journal of Consulting and Clinical Psychology, 35*, 183–188.

Tellegen, A., & Ben-Porath, Y. S. (1992). The new uniform T scores for the MMPI–2: Rationale, derivation, and appraisal. *Psychological Assessment, 4*, 145–155.

Timbrook, R. E., & Graham, J. R. (1994). Ethnic differences on the MMPI–2? *Psychological Assessment, 6*, 212–217.

Timbrook, R. E., Graham, J. R., Keiller, S. W., & Watts, D. (1993). Comparison of the Wiener–Harmon subtle-obvious scales and the standard validity scales in detecting valid and invalid MMPI–2 profiles. *Psychological Assessment, 5*, 53–61.

Ward, C. L. (1994). MMPI–2 assessment of positive attributes: A methodological note. *Journal of Personality Assessment, 62*, 559–561.

Weed, N. C., Ben-Porath, Y. S., & Butcher, J. N. (1990). Failure of the Wiener and Harmon MMPI subtle scales as personality descriptors and as validity indicators. *Psychological Assessment, 2*, 281–285.

Weed, N. C., Butcher, J. N., McKenna, T., & Ben-Porath, Y. S. (1992). New measures for assessing alcohol and drug abuse with the MMPI–2: The APS and AAS. *Journal of Personality Assessment, 58*, 389–404.

Welsh, G. A. (1956). Factor analysis A and R. In G. S. Welsh & W. G. Dahlstrom (Eds.), *Basic readings on the MMPI in psychology and medicine* (pp. 264–281). Minneapolis: University of Minnesota Press.

Whitworth, R. H., & McBlaine, D. D. (1993). Comparison of the MMPI and MMPI–2 administered to Anglo- and Hispanic-American university students. *Journal of Personality Assessment, 61*, 19–27.

Wiggins, J. S. (1966). Substantive dimensions of self-report in the MMPI item pool. *Psychological Monographs, 80*(22, Whole No. 630).

Wrobel, T. A., & Lachar, D. (1982). Validity of the Wiener subtle and obvious scales for the MMPI: Another example of the importance of inventory-item content. *Journal of Consulting and Clinical Psychology, 50*, 469–470.

Zalewski, C., & Greene, R. L. (1996). Multicultural usage of the MMPI–2. In L. A. Suzuki, P. J. Meller, & J. G. Ponterotto, (Eds.), *Handbook of multicultural assessment: Clinical, psychological, and educational applications* (pp. 77–114). San Francisco: Jossey-Bass.

3

The Future of Rorschach in Personality Assessment

John E. Exner, Jr.

Rorschach Workshops
Asheville, North Carolina

This article considers the Rorschach and its prospects for the next century in the context of two broad issues in psychology, as well as some test specific challenges confronting those interested in the Rorschach and its applications. The broad issues are the matters of personality as a topic of study in psychology, and the relation of findings about personality to treatment planning. The specific issues concern the definition of the Rorschach, research about the test stimuli, and the expansion of information concerning the interpretive usefulness of some structural variables that are poorly conceptualized or for which interpretation may be overly generalized. Some recommendations concerning collaborative research efforts are also offered.

Any critique of the Rorschach and its prospects for the next century probably should include some consideration of at least two broad interrelated issues as well as some test specific challenges confronting those interested in the Rorschach and its applications. The broad issues concern the matter of personality as a topic of study in psychology, and the relation of findings about personality to treatment planning. The specific issues concern the definition of the Rorschach, much needed research regarding the test stimuli, and the expansion of information concerning the interpretive usefulness of some structural variables that are poorly conceptualized or for which interpretation may be overly generalized.

PERSONALITY, INDIVIDUAL DIFFERENCES, AND TREATMENT PLANNING

Psychology, as a science, allows little leeway for individual differences among people within a group. Nearly 60 years ago, Allport (1937, pp. 6–10) bemoaned the fact that psychology was taking a pathway that disregarded Wundt's admonition that there is no psychological law to which exceptions are not more numerous than agreements. Allport expressed concern that this disregard would prompt psychology to dismiss the issue of individual differences in much research concerning people and their behaviors. Nearly 25 years later, Allport (1961, pp. 8–16) reaffirmed his concerns and warned that the study of personality and/or psychopathology was being sharply limited by an exaggerated emphasis on psychology as a nomothetic discipline. He noted that the tendency to ignore the uniqueness of each person was already causing embarrassment among those searching for ways to account for the uniformity of behaviors. He also cautioned against research orientations that might tend to dismember the total person in ways that would present only fragments of information about whole people, and then attempt to extend that information in ways that would neglect individual differences.

A review of contemporary psychology suggests that Allport's prediction that the study of individual differences might be sacrificed in favor of greater emphasis on the development of nomothetic laws seems to have been realized. A notable decline seems to have occurred regarding personality as a topic of study. It is true that object relations theory has gained considerable interest during the past two decades, but it is usually cast in a framework of pathology rather than as a broader theory of personality as such. In effect, there is far less concern in contemporary psychology with the issues of personality and individual differences than was once the case, and this reduced concern has also become pervasive in the clinical applications of psychology.

It is difficult to identify the causes that have led to a reduction of interest in the issue of personality and/or individual differences. Certainly, the difficult challenges confronting those attempting personality research has prompted some to become vested in other areas, and there is no doubt that the de-emphasis on the uniqueness of the individual was stimulated during the 1960s when radical behaviorism became prominent among some practicing in clinical psychology. It brought with it the notion of the black box, and the message that there is no such thing as personality, or even if there is, it cannot be measured through psychological testing. This movement created a new group of psychologists who not only avoid personality assessment, but who campaign actively against it, favoring instead the tactics of observation and counting critical incidents as ways of understanding people and identifying targets for intervention. It does not disregard individual differences, but attempts to study them in ways that are rather superficial.

The tendency to disregard individual differences probably has also been stimulated by the publication of the *Diagnostic and Statistical Manual of Mental Disorders* (*DSM–III;* American Psychiatric Association [APA], 1980) and subsequent *DSM* versions that contain a variety of checklists of symptoms and behaviors that are used to diagnostically classify people in distress. Those who formulated *DSM–III* disavow any direct relation between diagnostic categories and personality as such, "Another misconception is that all individuals described as having the same mental disorder are alike in all important ways" (p. 6). They also warn that a diagnosis does not lead directly to some specific form of treatment, "they may differ in other important ways that may affect clinical management and outcome" (p. 6), and "Additional information about the individual being evaluated beyond that required to make a *DSM–III* diagnosis will invariably be necessary [for treatment planning]" (APA, 1980, p. 11).

These cautions are often disregarded and many practitioners in psychiatry and psychology formulate treatment plans based on diagnosis. In fact, contemporary psychiatry and psychology is marked by a notable emphasis on specific treatments, and a remarkable accumulation of fads concerning treatment have been generated during the past two decades. New propositions about entities such as borderlines, anorexia, bulimia, obsessive compulsive disorders, panic disorders, multiple personalities, anxiety reactions, antisocial personalities, posttraumatic stress disorders, and the like, have created a cadre of specialists. These specialists often suggest that their credentials provide an implicit promise of cure, or at least a clear understanding of the problem.

Unfortunately, personality assessment has played an almost negligible role in contributing to these propositions, and research concerning these issues struggles to reach even a mediocre level. Stated simply, people who purport themselves to specialize in the treatment of these disorders have little interest in personality assessment for, by their logic, they already know what is wrong with the prospective patient and have the methodology readily available for correction. This unreasonable logic neglects the individual as a unique entity, and even more important, is based on the naive assumption that symptom presentation dictates a specific form of treatment. In effect, it is an extension of the medical model to which many psychologists seem to object so strenuously.

The question then, is whether the Rorschach will have relevance to the tasks of applied psychology and psychiatry in the future? If the issue of personality is unimportant, and if the issue of the person, as a unique entity, is unimportant, then the Rorschach is unimportant. On the other hand, if the future of treatment planning in mental health care includes concern for basic personality structure, the etiological aspects of behavior, or the issues of individual assets and liabilities represented in the personality of the participant, the future of the Rorschach will remain bright. In such a context, it is obvious that future research about the Rorschach should expand existing findings concerning the efficacy of the test in treatment planning (Exner & Sanglade, 1992; Garwood, 1977; Weiner, 1994a; Weiner & Exner, 1991). There are also numerous other issues concerning the test that should be addressed.

DEFINING AND UNDERSTANDING THE RORSCHACH

The Rorschach has existed for 75 years, having been published in September, 1921. During that period, it often has been the focus of considerable criticism, some of which was clearly justified. However, it is also clear that some criticism occurred because the format of the Rorschach deviates rather markedly from other psychological tests. The Rorschach is very complex, generating many scores that must be interpretively woven together carefully to derive the full measure of its yield. When this occurs, the product is considerable as it permits the study of personality from both nomothetic and idiographic perspectives.

The Comprehensive System for the Rorschach was designed to contend with many of the criticisms of the test that had developed through the 1960s. As noted earlier, many of these criticisms were quite valid. Some were created by the fact that there were many different approaches to the manner in which the test was administered and scored, and the way in which results were interpreted. The several approaches also permitted a considerable variability to occur in response production, and as such, validated criticisms that the test could not be standardized. Thus, it seemed logical to devise a standard methodology concerning the use of the Rorschach and its applications.

The standardization represented by the Comprehensive System seems to have generated some success with regard to its use and its empirical integrity, but criticisms do continue and, in some ways, they probably become an important source of issues that need to be addressed and research that needs to be accomplished in the future.

The Rorschach has often seemed so complex that some have preferred to define it as being "not a test." For instance, Zubin, Eron, and Schumer (1965, pp. 237–239) argued quite persuasively that it is a form of semistructured interview, and many, such as Holzman, Thorpe, Swartz, and Herron (1961, pp. 3–10) suggested that substantial differences in response productivity and the nomothetic instability that it creates for variables leads to the conclusion that the Rorschach could never be appropriately standardized as a test. Others, such as Lerner (1991, pp. vii–viii, 4–5) asserted that a theoretical basis for the Rorschach is necessary to identify its appropriate place in psychological assessment.

Weiner (1993, 1994b) attempted to deal with the issue of Rorschach theory by arguing that "there is not and will not be any overarching theory of the Rorschach as a test, because the Rorschach is not a test" (Weiner, 1993, p. 29). Unfortunately, that statement contains two serious flaws. The first is the implication that a test requires some underpinning theory. It is true that many tests are linked to a theory, but such linkage is not a test requirement. Many psychological tests are atheoretical. Any review of the MMPI, for example, will be hard pressed to find a theoretical basis for this well-developed test of personality features.

The second flaw is the statement that the Rorschach is not a test. To paraphrase a well-known quote, a test by any other name is still a test, and the Rorschach is a test by any traditional definition. For instance, Anastasi (1987) wrote, "A psychological test is essentially an objective and standardized measure of a sample of behavior" (p. 22). The Anastasi definition is similar to many others offered throughout the history of tests and measurement such as Cronbach (1960, p. 21), Freeman (1962, p. 46), and even Freeman (1926, p. 17), and all are commensurate with the *Standards for Educational and Psychological Tests* (American Psychological Association, 1974). In the *Standards* it is noted that a test "may be thought of as a set of tasks or questions intended to elicit particular types of behavior when presented under standardized conditions and to yield scores that will have desirable psychometric properties such as high reliability and high validity" (p. 2).

Viewed in this context, the Rorschach, although somewhat more complex than many psychological tests, surely meets the criteria as a test if any of the previously mentioned definitions are applied, and to offer a substitute rubric may be likened to the baby and the bathwater. Despite these criticisms of Weiner, however, it is very important that his basic message not be neglected. While discounting the need for a Rorschach theory and calling attention to the complexity of the test, he also gives considerable emphasis to the fact that the interpretative yield of the test can be cast in any of a variety of theoretical models concerning personality and/or behavior.

In other words, the presence or absence of an underpinning theory is irrelevant, as the data are the data. They have been generated through the use of the Rorschach as a standardized procedure, whether it be called a method, technique, instrument, or even a test. Moreover, the data are presented in light of information regarding the temporal reliability of its variables and a large number of studies indicating that it has validity concerning the aspects of personality structure that it has been purported to measure.

The question then is not really whether the Rorschach should be called a test. Weiner (this issue) attempted to clarify this with his statement that it "is more than a test." The main issue is whether the data of the test have value to the study of personality and, in turn, whether those data can be understood in the context of one or more theories, and finally, whether the data can be useful to the therapeutic well-being of the subject.

It is true that the Rorschach does not offer a precise measure for any single personality trait. Nor does it test directly for most of the common diagnostic categories, and there is no total score that may be used to gauge the breadth, depth, or maturity of personality. However, it does provide a source from which many personality features can be evaluated, not by single scores, but by the study of clusters of scores and the enhancement of objective findings with careful thematic analysis. In effect, the Rorschach, as a test, provides a broad array of data concerning many characteristics of the individual that, if read correctly, provide an in-depth portrait of the individual as an individual. It is also important to emphasize that the portrait can be sharpened much more by additional research concerning the test.

RORSCHACH RESEARCH AND THE
STUDY OF PERSONALITY

The accumulated Rorschach literature involves more than 200 books and between 8,000 and 9,000 articles, about two-thirds of which were published between the mid 1940s and the early 1970s. Nearly 60% of the articles are research works but, unfortunately, a substantial number of the research studies have been flawed in one way or another. Many older studies involved rather unsophisticated designs or methods of analysis that were inappropriate. Most more recent studies are not marked by those problems; however, there has been a pervasive tendency in Rorschach research to focus rather narrowly on specific hypotheses related to one or two variables in a manner that disregards the broader personality features that may exist within the population studied. Fortunately, some researchers, beginning with Rorschach himself, have concentrated more directly on some of the basic personality features that seem apparent in the routine data of the test and many important findings have evolved that should be exploited much more in future research.

Rorschach was quite intrigued by the fact that the stimulus characteristics of the blots tend to generate significantly different patterns of response. One group of participants tends to perceive moving figures in the blots quite frequently and attend only modestly to the color features of the blot stimuli. Another group tends to respond more frequently to the color features and interprets movement in the blots much less than the first group. Rorschach (1921) identified these distinctive response styles as introversive and extratensive "types" and devoted nearly one fourth of his monograph to empirical and theoretical explications concerning them (pp. 72–119). Gradually, considerable data has accumulated to suggest that they do, indeed, represent very different personalities. They differ in basic approaches to problem solving and decision making and there is some evidence to suggest that they differ rather markedly in several physiological characteristics. In fact, these two groups differ significantly ($p < .01$) in the mean values for 22 important Rorschach variables (Exner, 1993, pp. 265–276). There is also evidence to suggest that when either of these stylistic features are markedly dominant within the individual, they promote less flexibility and more inefficiency in problem solving or decision making (Exner, 1991, pp. 6–16). These response styles and their dominance is an issue of basic personality that wants sorely for much more research.

As research concerning the test has accumulated, several other revelations concerning personality response styles have unfolded. One data set appears to identify people who are stylistically prone to be more passive than expected in their decision making and in their interpersonal relations. Another cluster of variables seems to detect participants who are stylistically guarded in their approach to the world and people in it, and the presence of a single variable apparently indicates that a person may be much more self centered than should be the case. When the value for another variable exceeds a certain level, it appears to indicate that the participant tends to approach the environment in a very narrow and potentially ineffective manner, whereas another cluster of variables identifies people who are prone to an unusual level of perfectionism or even obsessiveness. Still another data set seems to identify people who are cautious, or even fearful about emotions, and tend to avoid direct emotional exchanges with the world.

These are all basic features of personality, but unfortunately, probably not enough information has been developed about any of them, and especially about their interrelationships. They represent ways in which people function psychologically and if the current body of data regarding these styles is expanded, conceptualizations regarding personality, individual differences, and symptom development may become more precise than has been the case.

Unfortunately, many researchers have neglected the issue of response styles when selecting subjects or analyzing data. A great deal of contemporary Rorschach research ignores the necessity of using data concerning response styles as a way of subclassifying subjects, or avoids the possibility that fundamental differences in personality styles impact very directly on the validity of test results, especially those derived from relatively small samples. Variables concerning these stylistic features must be regarded very carefully in research. In some instances they should be used as classification variables, but that is often difficult in a small sample study. When such classification is not practical, data concerning stylistic features should probably be used in some sort of covariation to avoid clouding results with analyses that add apples and oranges inappropriately.

It is very important to note that none of the stylistic features noted earlier equate directly with psychopathology. It is important, however, to note that if some sort of pathology or maladjustment is present, any of these stylistic features may relate to the difficulties, and any plan for intervention should be developed with concern for these features.

RORSCHACH RESEARCH AND
THE RESPONSE PROCESS

One of the key objectives for future research that probably should be afforded considerable priority concerns the stimulus characteristics of the blots. As noted earlier, Rorschach literature includes a large number of research studies, but less than 50 deal with specific stimulus features of the blots. Unfortunately, for several decades researchers proceeded on the assumption that the blots are ambiguous figures and thus, subject to an almost infinite number of interpretations. However, much data, beginning with Rorschach's own studies, have suggested strongly that each of the blots has salient stimulus characteristics that restrict or at least discourage certain interpretations or responses and encourage certain other classes of response to be given.

This is probably best illustrated by the presence of Popular responses to each of the 10 blots. These are answers that occur at least once in every three records and that tend to be uniform across cultures with only a few variations. The saliency of some blot features is also illustrated by frequency data that have been used to define form quality in the Comprehensive System. For example, ordinary or conventional form quality use has been defined by using the criterion of any response reported to a *W* or *D* area in at least 2% (190 or more) of the 9,500 records used to create the Form Quality Table. Those records contain more than 209,000 answers. When the actual number of ordinary responses is calculated, there are only 834 listed for *W* and *D* areas to the ten blots. Even when a more liberal criterion is applied to include responses to *Dd* areas, the number is increased only to 979 answers. These findings clearly support the postulate that each blot does have very salient stimulus features, but unfortunately, work concerning which features promote which kinds of answers is very sparse.

As more information unfolds regarding the salient or critical stimulus features of each blot, more research concerning the issue of thematic analysis and the accurate identification of projected material can evolve. Currently, thematic analysis of the supposedly projected material in responses involves more speculation than should be the case. The level of speculation about what is projected and what is not probably can be reduced considerably as more information about the critical stimulus features of the blots increases. Likewise, added information concerning the critical stimulus features of the blots may also play a very key role in enhancing the understanding of some of the stylistic features of personality discussed earlier. In other words, how do response styles contribute to the decisions of participants taking the test about which responses they will select and which responses they will discard, even though the stimuli may be relatively equivalent for either?

OTHER RESEARCH CONCERNS FOR THE FUTURE

The research needs that have been noted earlier are high priority issues but, by no means, represent all of the topics that are currently important. Many others warrant substantial concern. There are numerous Rorschach variables for which the validation data are "soft," that is, empirical findings concerning interpretation may be over generalized, or in some instances, empirical findings are, at best, difficult to understand in a conceptual framework. For example, there is no satisfactory conceptualization about why animal movement responses seems to relate to mental activity prompted by need states or why inanimate movement answers seem related to a similar kind of mental activity that is situationally provoked.

Similarly, there is no satisfactory conceptualization about why diffuse shading responses seem to be situationally related while a "close cousin," achromatic color answers seem to represent a more trait-like feature. Likewise, it is quite difficult to detect those instances in which elevations in vista and texture answers should be regarded as situationally related phenomena versus those in which they reflect a more enduring aspect of the psychology of the subject. New research concerning any or all of these variables may well lead to some change in the manner that the *Adj es* is calculated.

Research concerning several content scores, such as blood, fire, explosions, household, and science, is essentially nil, and the findings concerning food answers are, at best, limited. It is clear that blood, fire, and explosion answers do occur differentially when the introversive and extratensive response styles are considered, but why this occurs and how best to interpret these responses remains an unsolved puzzle.

It is also very clear that other classes of scores such as the *COP* and *AG* responses need to be studied much more precisely than has been the case. Currently, all *COP* and *AG* answers are given equal weight and nomothetically equal meaning, but it is quite obvious to the astute Rorschacher that some *COP* answers are less positive than others and some *AG* answers are less worrisome than others. The development of new, easily applied criteria for a more refined differentiation within each of these scoring categories may well lead to empirical findings that can reshape the interpretative propositions that are developed from them, and especially if new findings are studied in the context of response styles.

It should be obvious that, to this point, no mention has been made about research needs and issues of psychopathology. This is not to imply that the Rorschach cannot or should not be used to study psychopathology, but it should be interpreted as a reaffirmation that the Rorschach is not a diagnostic test that yields data from which participants are pigeon-holed easily into most of the *DSM* diagnostic categories.

It is true that the Revised Schizophrenia Index (*SCZI*) is reasonably sturdy in identifying people who are seriously disturbed but, even as revised, the value of 4 still probably yields more false positives than should be the case, especially among younger participants. A well-organized longitudinal study of young people, especially those who are troubled, could contribute enormously to a resolution of this issue and might even lead to a separate index for younger clients. In a similar vein, the relation between the Revised Depression Index (*DEPI*) and the Coping Deficit Index (*CDI*) has not been studied sufficiently and it remains unclear whether subjects who are positive on both indices are really affective disturbances, or is the positive *DEPI* finding some sort of by-product of the coping problems? As with the *SCZI,* some of the *DEPI* and *CDI* data are confusing when they appear in the records of youngsters, and again, a well-designed longitudinal study would go far to resolving some of these important issues.

Finally, two other issues are of considerable importance. The first is the relatively small sample sizes that constitute the nonpatient normative data for youngsters. They are too small, and currently can be applied only with the greatest caution. Collecting nonpatient data, especially from children, poses a considerable challenge. It does seem possible, however, that such a challenge could be addressed through a series of well-designed longitudinal studies. Any longitudinal study requires a lengthy collaborative effort, and for some the prospects might seem dim. However, there is considerable enthusiasm about the Rorschach throughout the world and the prospect of mounting collaborative research may be brighter than any time in the past. Hopefully, the new generation of Rorschach researchers will accept this difficult challenge and create more collaborative research, both within and across cultures.

Obviously, such studies could improve knowledge about the Rorschach substantially. Even more important, however, they would also represent milestones in the broader scheme of research about personality and individual differences.

REFERENCES

Allport, G. W. (1937). *Personality: A psychological interpretation*. New York: Holt.

Allport, G. W. (1961). *Patterns and growth in personality*. New York: Holt, Rinehart & Winston.

American Psychiatric Association. (1980). *Diagnostic and statistical manual of mental disorders* (3rd ed.). Washington, DC: Author

American Psychological Association. (1974). *Standards for educational and psychological tests*. Washington, DC: Author

Anastasi, A. (1987). *Psychological testing* (5th Ed.). New York: Macmillan.

Cronbach, L. J. (1960). *Essentials of psychological testing* (2nd Ed.). New York: Harper & Brothers.

Exner, J. E., Jr. (1991). *The Rorschach: A comprehensive system: Vol. 2. Interpretation* (2nd ed.). New York: Wiley.

Exner, J. E., Jr. (1993) *The Rorschach: A comprehensive system: Vol. 1. Basic foundations* (3rd ed.). New York: Wiley.

Exner, J. E., Jr., & Sanglade, A. A. (1991). Rorschach changes following brief and short-term therapy. *Journal of Personality Assessment, 59,* 59–71.

Freeman, F. N. (1926). *Mental tests*. New York: Houghton Mifflin.

Freeman, F. S. (1962). *Theory and practice of psychological testing* (3rd ed.). New York: Holt, Rinehart & Winston.

Garwood, J. (1977). A guide to research on the Rorschach prognostic rating scale. *Journal of Personality Assessment, 41,* 117–199.

Holzman, W. H., Thorpe, J. S., Swartz, J. D., & Herron, E. W. (1961). *Inkblot perception and personality*. Austin, TX: University of Texas Press.

Lerner, P. M. (1991). *Psychoanalytic theory and the Rorschach*. Hillsdale, NJ: The Analytic Press.

Rorschach, H. (1921). *Psychodiagnostik*. Bern, Switzerland: Bircher.

Weiner, I. B. (1993). Searching for Rorschach theory—A wild goose chase. In *Proceedings book: XIV Congress of Rorschach and projective methods* (pp. 23–32). Lisbon, Portugal: Sociedad Portugesa de Rorschach.

Weiner, I. B. (1994a). Rorschach assessment. In M. E. Maruish (Ed.) *The use of psychological testing for treatment planning and outcome assessment* (pp. 249–278). Hillsdale, NJ: Lawrence Erlbaum Associates, Inc.

Weiner, I. B. (1994b). The Rorschach inkblot method (RIM) is not a test: Implications for theory and practice. *Journal of Personality Assessment, 62,* 498–504.

Weiner, I. B., & Exner, J. E., Jr. (1991). Rorschach changes in long-term and short-term pschotherapy. *Journal of Personality Assessment, 56,* 453–465.

Zubin, J., Eron, L. D., & Schumer, F. (1965). *An experimental approach to projective techniques*. New York: Wiley.

4

Whither Goest Our Redoubtable Mentor, the MMPI/MMPI–2?

Alex B. Caldwell

Caldwell Report

and

Department of Psychiatry
Department of Psychology
University of California at Los Angeles

Four areas of MMPI use and development toward the year 2000 and beyond are discussed. First, although the MMPI–2 booklet is a clear improvement, we will continue to need to use both profiles, the MMPI–2 for normative purposes and the MMPI profile for pattern interpretation. Applying MMPI expectations to MMPI–2 profiles is a violation of Meehl's basic actuarial prediction concepts. Secondly, as psychologists begin prescribing medications, we may be able to substantially refine drug choices. Thirdly, the measurement of socioeconomic status levels appears to be the major, missing moderator variable in MMPI/MMPI–2 interpretation. Lastly, an effective and positive MMPI/MMPI–2 feedback paradigm is discussed that fits well within the managed care context.

In my inability to relocate my functioning crystal ball, I can only offer my thoughts and speculations as to the future evolution of our seasoned but ever-rejuvenated mentor. What our mentor's pleasure will be in the year 2000 and beyond cannot be foretold, but being a bit of a would-be futurist, I do have some expectations.

I will discuss four topics: (a) With which pattern do we clothe him or her, the original Minnesota Multiphasic Personality Inventory (MMPI; Hathaway & McKinley, 1967) pattern or the MMPI–2 (Butcher, Dahlstrom, Graham, Tellegen, & Kaemmer, 1989), or do we change patterns for different occasions?; (b) Can he or she guide us in choices of medications?; (c) How may paying attention to socioeconomic status (SES) moderate our perceptions of the MMPI/MMPI–2?; and (d) What roles can our mentor play on the changing stage of mental health care delivery?

MMPI VERSUS MMPI–2 PROFILE?

We have seen a steady and progressive conversion from the use of the MMPI (Hathaway & McKinley, 1967) booklet to the MMPI–2 (Butcher et al., 1989) booklet. In 1990, I (Caldwell, 1990) endorsed the latter as more user-friendly, and I continue to believe it to be (especially for younger age levels). The ongoing problem is with the choice of the MMPI versus the MMPI–2 profile to plot our scores. Edwards, Weissman, and Morrison (1993) and Humphrey and Dahlstrom (1995) showed that the raw score values between the MMPI and MMPI–2 are highly comparable, both absolutely and as to rank order correlations across the 10 scales. The T-score correspondence between the two profiles is, however, much poorer. Edwards et al. (1993) concluded: "We advocate plotting the raw scores on both sets of norms to see what different interpretations might result" (p. 1). Humphrey and Dahlstrom (1995) asserted even more strongly:

> However, when the raw scores were transformed into T scores on their respective norms, the patterning was often drastically different, indicating that the bases for clinical interpretation derived from the MMPI and the MMPI–2 profiles were sufficiently at variance to require different conclusions. Until the correlate base of the MMPI–2 is better established, it is recommended that two separate profiles be drawn, one from the original norms and the other from the restandardized norms, and that each be interpreted separately to determine their differences and similarities. (p. 428)

A rebuttal (Ben-Porath & Tellegen, 1995) was offered stressing the "failure" of Humphrey and Dahlstrom (1995) to consider Cronbach and Gleser's (1953) differentiation of shape, scatter, and elevation. I feel that the lack of appreciation of profile configurations as well as their negatively critical bias led their arguments to miss the primary importance of MMPI patterns, which has always been the central point of departure for MMPI interpretation. Especially in the normal range they were discussing, where there is by definition minimal elevation and quite limited scatter, the pattern is the whole foundation of an MMPI interpretation. The algorithms I have written to computer-generate the Caldwell Report interpretations for normal range MMPI profiles have always been more pattern-dependent and complex than the algorithms for more elevated profiles of the same code type. The point of emphasis here is that both published data and personal experience converge on the fact that the same set of raw scores produces profiles that lead to different codings of T scores and different interpretations (Humphrey & Dahlstrom, 1995) when plotted on the MMPI versus the MMPI–2 profiles. The less elevated the profile, the greater these interpretive differences.

A basic tenet of Meehl's (1954) work on actuarial prediction is that we use objective measurements to identify a relatively homogeneous group of participants. When a new participant meets the criteria for membership in this group, what we have identified as the characteristics of this group become our prediction as to the makeup and behavior of the new individual. Meehl predicted that the accuracy of these objective predictions would be better than the accuracy of predictions based on clinical judgment. The fact that this hypothesis of equal or greater accuracy for actuarial prediction over clinical judgment has since had an effectively 100% confirmation appears to be unique in the social sciences (Dawes, Faust, & Meehl, 1993; P. E. Meehl, personal communication, August 15, 1994). As Meehl (1986) summarized, "There is no controversy in social science that shows such a large body of qualitatively diverse studies coming out so uniformly in the same direction as this one" (p. 372).

A problem arises when half or even nearly 60% (Dahlstrom, 1992) of the membership of an objective group or 2-point high point code type on one profile do not belong to the same grouping on the other profile. Notably troublesome clinically are the patients who obtain less elevated 48/84 profiles on the MMPI, who show characteristic 48/84 behaviors clinically, and whose scores produce a different code on the MMPI–2. As a specific example, if a female client obtains a 26 code on the MMPI–2, we could easily assume that what we know about 26–62 subjects from standard MMPI profiles will characterize our client. However, only 31% of those women whose raw scores generate 26 or 62 codes on the MMPI–2 (Butcher et al., 1989) actually obtain this same 26–62 code when their scores are plotted on the MMPI; it turns out that our "MMPI–2 Code 26" client is more likely to obtain a 48, 46, 24, 28, or similarly coded profile on the MMPI than to obtain a 26 or 62 code; that is, MMPI–2 profiles coded 26 or 62 will more likely not code as 26 or 62 on the MMPI. To then make 26–62 predictions about our perhaps 48 subject is to violate grossly Meehl's fundamental axiom of actuarial prediction; we are predicting from a mostly different group of people to our present client. Figures 1, 2, and 3 show examples of scores that would lead to substantially different interpretations if MMPI expectations were applied to the MMPI–2 profiles.

Although the loss of accuracy due to this shift of group membership seems logically obvious, it would be difficult to demonstrate empirically because of the secondary overlap of the "correct" code type with the "incorrect" membership of the corresponding group. For example, even if our client with a 26 code on the MMPI–2 gets a 48 code on the MMPI, Scales *2* and *6* will be relatively elevated along with *4* and *8,* and the members of the MMPI–2 26–62 group who do not code as 26 or 62 on the MMPI will still tend behaviorally to overlap our original MMPI 26–62 group. This degradation of accuracy is relative. But given the general limitations on our predictive accuracy, it seems a substantial violation of principle if not also a violation of ethics to predict the behavior of an individual from a group to which he or she may well not belong or for some codes more likely does not belong.

The crux of this profile-choice issue is our continuing access to the 50-plus years of research on patterns based on the original norms, particularly given the admit-

MMPI

Female   48 62 7 * 31 " ' 90 - / 5

	L	F	K	1	2	3	4	5	6	7	8	9	0
	53	80	40	80	96	86	100	45	97	91	100	68	67
Raw Score	5	16	7	28	43	39	40	39	24	50	55	24	40

MMPI-2

Female   62 48 7 * 31 " ' 09 - / 5

	L	F	K	1	2	3	4	5	6	7	8	9	0
	57	92	32	82	99	89	94	43	100	92	94	62	63
Raw Score	5	16	7	28	43	39	40	39	24	50	55	24	40

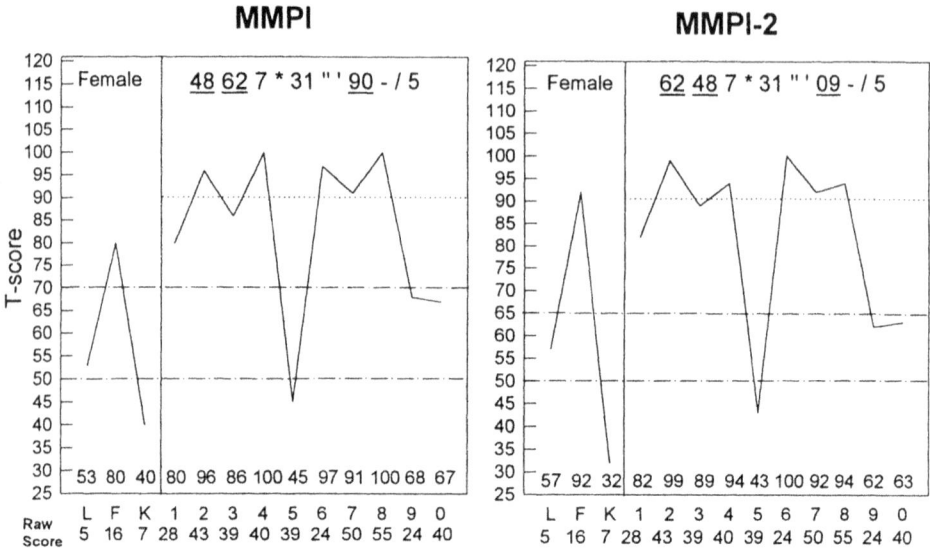

FIGURE 1   A well-defined 62 profile on the MMPI–2 that becomes a 48 profile on the MMPI norms.

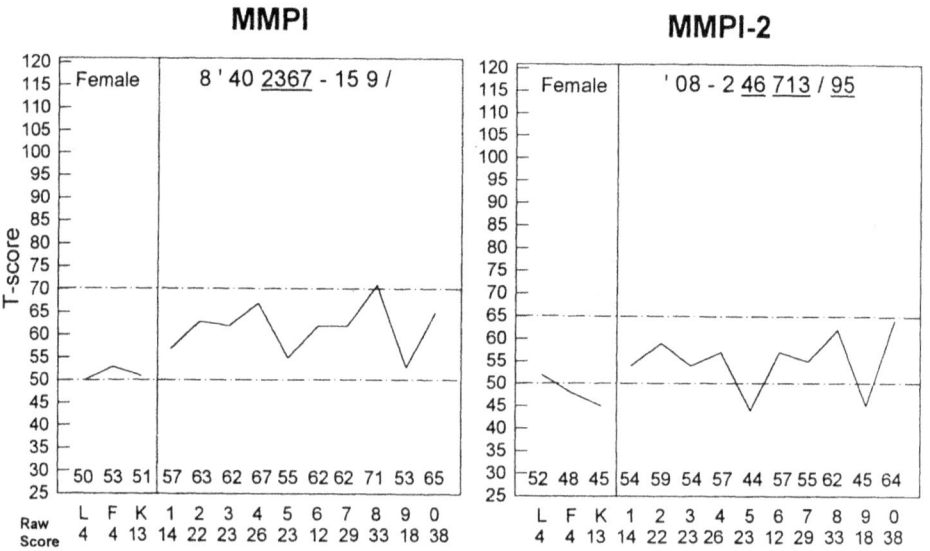

MMPI

Female   8 ' 40 2367 - 15 9 /

	L	F	K	1	2	3	4	5	6	7	8	9	0
	50	53	51	57	63	62	67	55	62	62	71	53	65
Raw Score	4	4	13	14	22	23	26	23	12	29	33	18	38

MMPI-2

Female   ' 08 - 2 46 713 / 95

	L	F	K	1	2	3	4	5	6	7	8	9	0
	52	48	45	54	59	54	57	44	57	55	62	45	64
Raw Score	4	4	13	14	22	23	26	23	12	29	33	18	38

FIGURE 2   A mixed '8–2 46 profile on the MMPI–2 that is distinctly 8'4 on the MMPI norms.

50

MMPI

MMPI-2

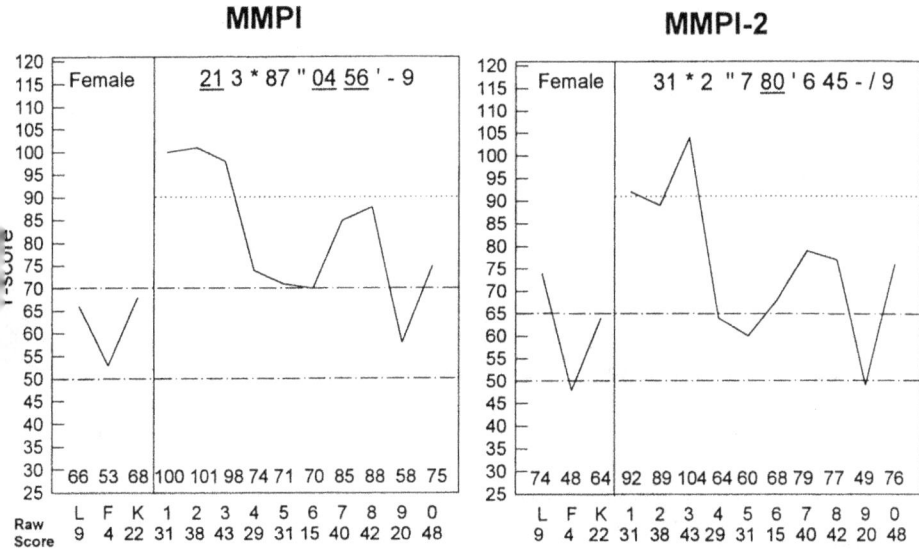

FIGURE 3   A strongly conversion-V profile on the MMPI–2 that becomes a 231* smiling depression profile on the MMPI.

tedly little code or pattern type data on MMPI–2 profiles (Butcher, Graham, & Ben-Porath, 1995). Among clinical cases, about one-third of those identified as belonging to one MMPI–2 profile code type will belong to a different MMPI code type (e.g., Butcher et al., 1989). In the normal range where pattern effects are most crucial and the effects of elevation and scatter are minimal, more than half our MMPI–2-plotted profiles belong to a different MMPI code type (Dahlstrom, 1992, reporting on the 2,600 criterion normals). Thus, any interpretation based on code type as the point of departure would change extensively.

It should be noted that normal range profiles do have a substantial frequency in patient samples. For example, of the 1,763 patient profiles from the Minnesota psychiatric inpatient population cases (Hathaway & Meehl, 1951a), from which most of the Atlas cases were drawn, 31.2% had all eight clinical scales in the normal range, although this proportion was probably inflated slightly by leniency with the number of "?" or unanswered items. For the 423 psychiatric patient cases reported in the MMPI–2 manual (Butcher et al., 1989), 21.5% were in the normal range on the MMPI–2; however, only 8% were in the normal range when plotted as MMPI profiles. These latter percentages were presumably reduced by the coding of all 10 scales and therefore counting as elevated those profiles with *Mf* or *Si* at or over *T* 70 (and the full standard deviation downward shift of Scale *5* male on the MMPI–2 norms would probably account for a considerable part of the unexpected 22% versus 8% difference between the MMPI and the MMPI–2). For an extensive review of the validity and utility of "within-normal-limits" profiles occurring in a wide variety of both patient and non-patient settings, see Duckworth and Barley (1988).

The "well defined code type" (Tellegen & Ben-Porath, 1993) is of little clinical help. If we have to throw out over half of our profiles as uninterpretable, that is, as if defined only by error variance (Ben-Porath & Tellegen, 1995), then we are trivialized if not laughed out of the clinic. The clinical predictive power (cf. Goldberg, 1965; Meehl & Dahlstrom, 1960) generated by cases from the Atlas (Hathaway & Meehl, 1951a) has never been dependent on requirements of scatter to further define our profiles. Beyond these considerations, the present and probable future pragmatic climate and limitations on financial support for large scale research on code types ("well defined" or not) are such that the great majority of interpretive studies crucial to our accumulated mass of information on the original MMPI patterns will never be repeated, especially because dissertations are not to prove what has already been tested.

One might question the utility of code type correlates based on data from 30 or more years ago (e.g., Ben-Porath & Tellegen, 1995). Scale *5,* which would be more suspect of cultural and attitudinal changes over time than any other scale, was shown by Todd and Gynther (1988) to have virtually identical correlates over a 30-year interval. If one references a current MMPI code to the Atlas (Hathaway & Meehl, 1951a), one finds striking similarities of attitude and emotional responsivity. Indeed, a current client with a 13 or 31 coded MMPI profile (Scales *1* and *3* being $T = 55$ or higher) is likely to show the idiosyncrasies of eating habits also noted 45 years ago by Hathaway and Meehl (1951b). The basic attributes of the MMPI patterns have proven remarkably stable over time.

This leaves us with a painful dilemma: What do we teach graduate students and fledgling clinicians? Obviously we cannot show them only the MMPI–2 profile; this gives them a seriously misleading map to the 50-plus years of research on the MMPI as to "similar" profiles. When we plot MMPI–2 scores on MMPI profiles, some scales such as *Pd* and *Mf* male across all elevations and *Sc* in some ranges change 10 *T*-score points or more. For example, given the routine clinical interpretation of MMPI Pd *T* scores around *T*–60, then behaviorally a *T* score of 51—or even 50!—on *Pd* on the MMPI–2 norms is already a meaningful elevation.[1] It seems equally wrong to utilize only the original MMPI pattern in teaching students, given the predominant use of the MMPI–2 booklet and the normative meaningfulness of *T*–50 on the MMPI–2 norms when used on a single scale basis.

---

[1] I am troubled by wondering how many of the volunteers for the MMPI–2 normative sample were people with mildly to moderately elevated scores on Scale *4–Pd* who were prompted by a want for self-insight and for a clearer sorting of life directions in themselves or for their spouses. A selective bias of this sort would help account for the otherwise large and never-explained shift in the norms for Scale *4.*

The only workable solution I have been able to find is the double-plotting of the MMPI–2 raw scores that has been my practice since the release date of the MMPI–2 in 1989. By putting the two profiles side by side, my colleagues and students and I can examine the contemporary MMPI–2 profile on a scale-by-scale normative basis and simultaneously access the 50-plus years of pattern research from the original MMPI profile. Unhappily, I do not see a future ending date for this practice. Even as pattern data eventually get published on the subsets of people belonging to the MMPI–2 code types, clinically we cannot afford to disregard or jettison the 50 years of research on the MMPI pattern effects. Given the relatively limited overlap of groups defined by our codes (e.g., 26–62, 48–84, elevated 13–31, etc.) on the two different profiles, the potentials for confusion are terribly great. The question, "Was that an 'MMPI 26' attribute or only an 'MMPI–2 26' attribute?" would be memory-taxing if not mind-boggling. The cleanest separation seems to be to use the MMPI–2 individual scale T scores for T–50 and standard deviation differences from it, and to use the original MMPI configuration for personality characteristic and behavioral prediction purposes.

This double-plotting has not proven difficult to defend in court. The judge and jury easily understand that test items written almost 60 years ago needed updating. They can also accept that we have 50 years of research on the patterns these scales produce on the MMPI but very little research on the different patterns that they lead to on the MMPI–2. If one were challenged, "Is there not a large quantity of research that has come out on the MMPI–2?," one could point out that there indeed is but that this research is primarily on such issues as the comparability of the two forms, assessing the validity of our results, and on all the scales that are new to the MMPI–2 revision. It has not duplicated the MMPI pattern research; nothing has been done on the MMPI–2 that is comparable to such clinically rich resources as the Atlas (Hathaway & Meehl, 1951a) or the books by Marks and Seeman (1963) and Gilberstadt and Duker (1965). Thus, in a forensic context, one can straightforwardly assert that using the MMPI–2 booklet and plotting the scores on the MMPI profile gives us the best of both worlds.

As an addendum, neither the MMPI nor the MMPI–2 samples can be justified as being even close to census representative, given the about T–55 mean elevation for normals on the original MMPI norms (Pancoast & Archer, 1989) and the large educational and socioeconomic deviation of the MMPI–2 sample (Butcher et al., 1989). Five percent of their 2,600 normative participants have less than a high school education against about 33% in the 1980 census, and 45% have graduated from college compared to only about 16% of the census population. I continue to urge strongly that the MMPI–2 norms be revised to be made census representative. This revision could be done straightforwardly by weighting the 2,600 normative participants according to census parameters of education and occupation to compensate for the major upward socioeconomic bias; or, for example, a subset of 2,000 protocols that were fitted or weighted to match the 1990—or year 2000—census might be extracted to create new norms (no changes would be required in the booklet or scoring templates, of course). Our statements about how an individual compares to people in general would carry far more weight. Our mentoring should be of, by, and for all the people.

MEDICATIONS AND THE MMPI/MMPI-2

As of this writing, the pursuit of prescription privileges for psychologists is a major issue across the country. The Department of Defense has already established a successful training program, the Psychopharmacology Demonstration Project. Whether we personally prescribe or not, it is a basic, practical question: Can psychologists bring scientific rigor, predictive accuracy, and clinical effectiveness to the selection of medications beyond what has been achieved to date?

It is my impression, shared I believe by many, that psychiatrists' drug prescription habits are often just that, that is, habits that are governed by reinforcement histories such as dramatic early career successes with particular drugs. How else do we explain the extent to which individual physicians each become dedicated to their own subset of drugs, outside of which they may only infrequently (if hardly ever) prescribe. It is true that there is a virtue in familiarity with the side effects and complications of whatever drugs one uses, many drugs are largely equivalent, and the constant changing of available drugs may be limiting on how many the prescriber knows in comfortable detail. Nevertheless, physician psychotropic prescription habits seem personal and idiosyncratic well beyond these constraints. Can we do better?

A very early study showed great promise, but more recent neurotransmitter studies using the MMPI or MMPI-2 seem remarkably absent. Halevy, Moos, and Solomon, (1965) showed a striking specificity of lowered serotonin concentrations to elevations on Scales 2-D, 7-Pt, 8-Sc, and F. The patients were given the MMPI, and blood samples were drawn at the beginning of the study or on admission to the ward (medications and other serotonin affecting agents were carefully controlled). The elevated profile on Figure 4 shows a direct correspondence to the chronic, endogenous depressions for which serotonin-enhancing drugs are maximally beneficial (although their prescriptions are hardly limited to patients with elevated 287 patterns, especially Prozac and the other selective serotonin reuptake inhibitors).

We need to test such questions as (a) how specifically and narrowly the antidepressants are focused on Scale 2-D, (b) as neuroleptics lower Scale 8-Sc, does the relief of confusion spread to a lowering of elevations on other scales, and (c) can we quantify the extent to which lithium carbonate reduces elevations on Scale 9-Ma (or Scales 2 plus 9)? Do elevations on Scale 4-Pd have an interfering effect across the board; that is, if Scale 4-Pd is substantially elevated and especially if it is among the first two or three scales in the code, are the benefits of medications

MMPI

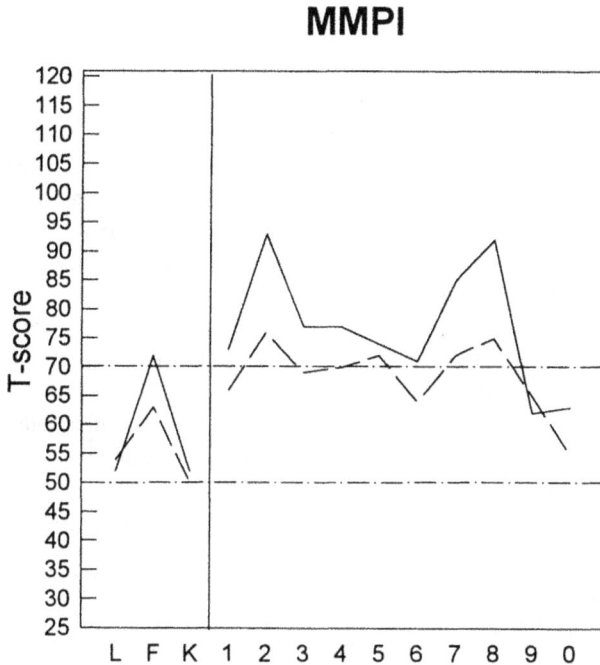

FIGURE 4   MMPI profiles of "low" and "high" serotonin groups. From *A Relationship Between Blood Serotonin Concentrations and Behavior in Psychiatric Patients* (p. 5), by A. Halevy, R. H. Moos, & G. F. Solomon, 1965, London: Pergamon Press Ltd. Copyright 1965 by Pergamon Press Ltd. Reprinted by permission.

consistently less than would otherwise be expected? What mechanisms underlie this phenomenon? Would this be relevant to issues around the overmedication of prison inmates? It is also my prediction[2] that the physiologic anchoring of Scale 6 is primarily in the momentary norepinephrine response to an attack on one's person or will, and this is why there are no satisfactory medications for treating paranoid disorders per se. Such clinical-experience hypotheses obviously need rigorous testing and—if confirmed—the attention of drug prescribers.

The MMPI/MMPI-2 also needs to be studied in relation to predicting atypical physiologic responses to medications. Having the MAC scale (MacAndrew, 1965) elevated along with some combination of Scales 2–D and 9–Ma elevated—especially all three simultaneously—seems particularly associated with such atypical reactions to chemicals of many different types. Warnings as to potentially irregular physiologic responses would be helpful in a variety of settings.

---

[2]These hypotheses are presented in detail in Caldwell (1996).

We urgently need MMPI versus neurotransmitter data of the sort generated so long ago by Halevy et al. (1965) to generate medication-specific hypotheses for clinical testing. At any time or in any context in which human neurotransmitter levels and configurations are being carefully assessed, it would be of great benefit to include concomitant MMPI–2 testing. Armed with such data, I believe that our future ability to make person-fitted prescription choices of psychotropic medications may go well beyond anything being practiced to this date. The ability to optimize the probability of prescription success is terribly important clinically. Trial and error sequences where one drug after another "does not do it" are very defeating and discouraging for the patient aside from the risks of so much medication and dosage changing. Given the current shift in mental health delivery systems toward the use of medications for anything they might benefit (whatever our convictions about such an emphasis on drugs), I believe MMPI/MMPI–2 research in this area is urgently indicated in the immediate future. If I hear our redoubtable mentor correctly, the message is that we have much medication response and neurotransmitter-by-code-type homework to do.

SES AS A KEY MODERATOR VARIABLE

Comments in test reports as to the client's SES can easily arouse a hesitation or sensitivity lest one be accused of elitism. Even affirmations of higher status (e.g., a child custody litigant) can be read as implying superiority in comparison to unspecified lower status "others." For some there may be an underlying idealism that the United States should be a relatively open and classless society without the abuses of the poor and inferior that are accepted as "the way of life" in more rigidly class-stratified societies. This remains an aspirational goal and not a realized reality.

MMPI correlations with SES have been observed since the addendum to the K factor article in which, to their initial surprise, higher SES participants had more elevated scores on their correction Scale, $K,$ than did their general normals (Meehl & Hathaway, 1946). Hathaway and Monachesi (1963), in the most extensive MMPI research project ever done on adolescence[3], found a variety of MMPI scale and pattern correlates of the educational, occupational, and residential components of

---

[3]Although the handbook (Vol 1; Dahlstrom, Welsh, & Dahlstrom, 1972) did contain adolescent normative data based in part on their ninth-grade participants, Hathaway and Monachesi never advocated utilizing separate adolescent norms. They apparently felt that the scores plotted on the traditional adult norms better characterized adolescent behavior. This is the same argument offered in the first section of this article, that is, that although the means and standard deviations of a newer set of norms (MMPI–2, adolescence, etc.) may better describe population or peer group deviations on each individual scale, the 50 years of research on the original normative patterns provide the better prediction of an individual's personality characteristics and behavior. See Greene (1991) for a detailed discussion of the contradictory data on adolescent versus adult norms and descriptors for adolescent participants.

SES. For example, lower SES was predictive of school dropout for boys and girls as well as depression in boys. Delinquency was often a compound of lower SES and *Pd,* but delinquency was clearly not limited to lower SES adolescents. Teachers overpredicted delinquency for lower SES male adolescents and underpredicted it for higher SES male adolescents; higher SES was more inhibitory of delinquency for girls than boys. They felt their data supported the "downward drift" hypothesis, that Scale *8* elevations predicted ending up in lowered SES circumstances later in life.

The most extensive analysis of the effects of SES on MMPI performance was presented in the book on American minorities by Dahlstrom, Lachar, and Dahlstrom (1986). Across the research presented, the most consistent effects were noted on Scales *F* and *8–Sc* as well as Welsh's *A* and especially Barron's *Es;* the secondarily affected scales were *K, 9–Ma,* and *0–Si.* The SES effects on these various scales were consistently independent of racial and ethnic membership. Higher SES participants also presented as having better self-management, less somatic concern, and fewer fears with some tendency toward more feminine scores on *5–Mf* in the male participants. In summarizing the MMPI assessment of mental disorders, they wrote:

> In several of the studies cited above, when samples of black and white adults were equated for the socioeconomic and other background factors, the differences between the ethnic groups in rate and severity of mental disorder were no longer detectable. That is, the overall differences between black adults (or those of other ethnic minorities) and white comparison groups appeared to reflect systematic differences in the proportion of socially disadvantaged individuals represented in each ethnic group. (p. 193)

Some of the MMPI/MMPI–2 texts have commented on the relationship of SES to Scales *F* and *K* (Friedman, Webb, & Lewak, 1989; Greene, 1991). Lower SES is characterized by more *F* and less *K,* and conversely higher SES is associated with limited scores on *F* but frequent elevations on *K.* Greene (1991) asserted:

> The interpretation of the *K* scale changes dramatically depending on the socioeconomic class and education level of the client and the setting in which the MMPI–2 is administered (e.g., personnel selection, state hospital, university). The potential impact of these factors on the *K* scale becomes even more noteworthy on the MMPI–2 because of the relatively high socioeconomic class and years of education that characterized the MMPI–2 normative group. (p. 116)

In contrast, *L* greater than *K* is more often characteristic of lower SES participants. Clinically, the *L–K* slope can be interpreted as being in part a balance between lower class, naive denial of fault versus the sophisticated minimizing of higher SES participants.

Dahlstrom and Tellegen (1993) prepared a supplement on SES for the MMPI-2 manual (Butcher et al., 1989), looking specifically at the effects of education and occupation as the primary anchors of SES; they also assessed the contributions of age, gender, and race to MMPI-2 scale variances among the criterion normals. In general, the effect of education on MMPI-2 scores was stronger than the effect of occupational levels, but the latter were consistently in the same direction. They divided education by five levels from postgraduate to less than high school. Levels of education related strongly to the validity scales. Compared to the less than high school group, the postgraduate participants' mean was about 9 T-score points higher on K (i.e., nearly one full standard deviation), just under 8 T-score points lower on F, and about 5.5 T-score points lower on L. On the K-corrected clinical scales the differences ranged from only about 4 T-score points on Hs (postgraduate partici- pants being lower) to slightly above 1 point on Scale 7. Note, however, that the most educated group had lower mean K-corrected T scores on Hs (48.95 male, 48.95 female), and their total raw scores were mostly due to $K;$ in contrast, the least educated group had higher mean T scores on Hs (53.39 male, 52.33 female), and less than half of their total raw score was from the K-correction. If one estimates the raw scores on Hs without K and plots them on the non-K-corrected norms, the T-score differences are at least twice as large (about 9 T-score points for male participants and 8 for female participants versus the K-corrected differences of 4.44 male and 3.38 female). Among other effects, therefore, the K-correction is—and always has been—compensating for the effects of SES by raising the T scores of higher SES (i.e., higher K) participants and—by adding relatively small amounts of K—lowering the T scores of lower SES participants. Without the K-correction we would see larger effects of SES on all of the K-corrected clinical scales in addition to the validity scale effects noted earlier.

Although Dahlstrom and Tellegen (1993) emphasized that most of the variance of scores is due to individual differences in personality rather than SES or the other demographic variables they analyzed, the single high-point scale effects of SES were larger. For example, Scales 1 highest male and 2 highest female, either elevated or not, or Scale 8 highest and elevated were all associated with lower educational levels, and Scales 3 highest but in the normal range male or both female and 6 highest but in the normal range for women were associated with higher educational levels. As Dahlstrom and Tellegen summarized, "the differences in mean values on the clinical scales associated with socioeconomic variations are rather small, although the differences in the distribution of salient scores (i.e., high-point codes) are more clearly in evidence" (p. 10).

Such data make it obviously relevant to ask whether a person's SES identifica- tion can be measured directly with the MMPI/MMPI-2. In this context, traditional thinking (Warner & Lunt, 1941) has conceptualized six socioeconomic classes: upper, middle, and lower, each divided into an upper and lower subclass. Concepts of these six classes have become so uniquely differentiated that one might be tempted to visualize an improbable six-modal curve. On the MMPI, SES has been scaled by Nelson (1952) based on high versus low patient scores on the Warner Index (Warner, Meeker, & Eells, 1949). In contrast to Warner's "six mode distribution," by observation the scores obtained on Nelson's Ss scale clearly fall into an at least quasi-normal distribution; indeed they appear nearly normal with a mild skew toward extreme low scores, perhaps related to the common "pathology skew" of distributions affected by extremes of psychopathology. Such a normal distribution does not, however, invalidate the descriptive meaningfulness of our traditional six levels of conceptualization, for example, "lower middle class individuals are characterized by ... ." It does, however, raise the question whether or not the attributes we assign to one or another of the six levels (e.g., emphasis on education, attitudes toward sex and religion, short-term survival versus long-term life planning, etc.) may better be conceptualized as aspects of complex subdimensions of status identification that go across all six levels rather than being discrete and unique characteristics that are limited to a single SES level.

I would propose that Nelson's (1952) Ss scale provides us with a key psychometric moderator variable that has two fundamental utilities. The first of these is the assessment of validity from Scales L, F, and K, and the second is the impact of low SES responding on Scale 8–Sc and the potentially spurious appearance of serious disturbance. Greene and Nichols (1990) found that the Ss scale correlated $-.54$ with F and $.57$ with K in a sample of 10,922 Mayo Clinic patients and $-.68$ with F and $.60$ with K in 10,524 Missouri psychiatric patient admissions. The greater correlation with F for the state hospital patients may be attributable at least in part to an attenuation of the distribution of F scores for medical patients, that is, most of the latter ($M = 5.5$ items, $SD = 4.4$) had relatively few positive F item responses in contrast to the psychiatric sample ($M = 9.8$, $SD = 7.6$). As to the use of K to measure deliberate defensiveness, Cofer, Chance, and Judson's (1949) conscious fake-good scale, Malingering positive or Mp, correlated $.42$ with K in contrast to a correlation between Mp and the Ss scale of only $.04$, these latter two correlations being identical in both of these large and quite different samples. Thus, the large contribution of the Ss scale to K ($.57$ and $.60$) is strikingly independent of the smaller but also substantial contribution of Mp to K ($.42$). The consistent elevation of K in higher SES samples thus appears primarily attributable to sophisticated but sincere responding rather than to any consistently greater defensiveness of the upper classes.

Distinguishing these two independent origins of K and F matters greatly in many contexts. In child custody and job screening assessments, one frequently gets high elevations on K. Evaluating an elevated K according to these moderator scales, it might alternatively be interpreted as deliberately faking good, as sincere upper class responding, or as a proportional summation of both. Using the Ss scale together with scales such as Mp and Wiggins' (1959) Sd as moderators thus can greatly refine our understanding of a score on K. In state, county, and Veterans Administration hospitals one gets many profiles with moderate to extreme elevations on F

as well as on such psychotic scales as 6–*Pa* and 8–*Sc*. Here the question is whether the person is (a) malingering sick in seeking admission, disability money, or other benefits; (b) making a large number of rare and atypical but sincere responses secondary to having very peculiar experiences and perhaps a major thought disorder; or (c) simply responding atypically as a function of a low SES lack of sophistication and awareness as to how others will perceive and react to his or her odd and socially unmoderated responses. Using scales such as *Ss* and *Ds* (Dissimulation; Gough, 1954) as moderators again can greatly refine our interpretation of *F* and of the *F* minus *K* difference.

A recent study (Saba, 1995) looked at a subsample of Hispanic participants in a Worker's Compensation setting all of whom had specifically been determined not to have any significant psychiatric disorder. Many of them nevertheless had elevations on Scale 8–*Sc* over *T* = 70, some being quite high. Saba's question was, what would correlate with having versus not having such spurious elevations? This "spurious 8" phenomenon is a disconcertingly frequent problem when working with this and similar subpopulations where the participants come from low (to very low) SES backgrounds and often have limited reading and educational levels. Saba included a variety of independent variables including Nelson's *Ss* scale, gender, level of education, a Short Acculturation Scale (Marin, Sabogal, VanOss-Marin, Otero-Sabogal, & Perez-Stable, 1987), an acculturative index incorporating this scale (Marin, Gamba, & Marin, 1992), job category, and country of origin. Although the correlations varied by subsamples, it was unequivocal that Nelson's *Ss* scale was the predominant predictor of spurious 8s, consistently better than the level of acculturation or the person's job, education, or country of origin.

The general argument here is that the determination of validity from Scales *L*, *F*, and *K* can be greatly facilitated by a consideration of the differential contributions of SES (as measured by the *Ss* scale) versus specific measures of conscious distortion. In this logic, SES is considered a strong but unconscious influence on the person's responding; high versus low SES participants are answering as their talents and experiences have shaped them. The interpretation of deliberate or conscious distortion is then far stronger when supported by independent measures of faking healthy, for example, *Mp*, or faking sick, *Ds*. Although obviously relevant if not at times crucial in forensic and administrative contexts, these contrasts are also noteworthy in clinical settings where one may be unsure how much genuine health and normality to attribute to a person whose profile is within the normal range or how severe a disturbance to attribute to an individual whose elevated and high-*F* profile is otherwise of marginal validity. Despite my initial hesitation to discuss SES in our MMPI and MMPI–2 reports, the clarity gained by the addition of this material to our Caldwell Report Test-Taking Attitude section has been very favorably received.

There is a problem that should be noted as to the use of *T* scores for the *Ss* scale based on the 2,600 normative participants for the MMPI–2 (see Appendix). The marked discrepancy from the U.S. census data discussed earlier produces a strongly inflated mean raw score on the 73 items that were retained from Nelson's Ss scale in the MMPI-2, and the standard deviation may be attenuated as well. In comparison to this high SES sample, everyone gets a "too low" T score on Ss. Prorating the mean raw score from the retained items to the original MMPI norms yields a T score between 62 and 63, well over a full standard deviation higher; this is the largest MMPI versus MMPI-2 T-score difference on any scale I have observed. The original MMPI mean was probably somewhat low (although Hathaway's sample was quite close to the 1930 census), but the MMPI-2 raw score mean is clearly inflated. For example, T scores less than zero should never occur but do, and scores over T-70 are virtually nonexistent but should occur. It appears that one needs to add close to 10 T-score points to the Ss scale T scores on the MMPI-2 norms, and, in particular, the deviance of low to extremely low Ss scale T scores should be underinterpreted.

In summary, the Ss scale as a measure of the person's level of socioeconomic identification appears to be a key moderator of our interpretations meriting much greater attention over the next decade. It matters greatly in the interpretation of high scores on K where degree of defensiveness is ambiguous, as well as with low scores on K where Ss is higher and adds weight to the hypothesis that the person is being excessively self-critical. It also matters for Scales F and $8-Sc$ where a quite low SES identification may lead to extensive atypical responding without a serious disorder and in the absence of any deliberate attempt to exaggerate or malinger, generating a spurious impression of a serious disturbance.

My reading of our redoubtable mentor's attitude is that the more accurate and comprehensive our information, the better determinations and interventions we will make. If moderating our interpretations according to our measure of SES improves them, then it can be hoped that our resolution is utilitarian rather than elitist.

A PARADIGM FOR THE MMPI/MMPI-2 IN TREATMENT

Use of the MMPI/MMPI-2 in the ever-engulfing arena of "managed" psychotherapy is coming to be a valuable tool in want of a paradigm for its use. By the year 2000 and beyond, it is distressingly easy to imagine very little testing of any type being done because it is not being authorized by managed care reviewers. The impact of the associated loss of quality of care provided is a potential misfortune for many clients as well as a frustrating defeat for capable providers. The only alternative, now barely glimpsed on the horizon, is the adoption of a modified Canadian-style or single-payer plan where 96% to 98% of the health care dollar goes for service in contrast to the siphoning off of 25% to 30% or more (possibly over 45%) of each mental health care dollar for the enrichment of managed health care entrepreneurs.

A natural question to ask is, what would be an optimal or ideal integration of use of the MMPI/MMPI–2 into time-limited interventions? One requirement would be that to be worthwhile within six-visits-or-less time constraints, taking the MMPI–2 would need to be integral to the intervention. Taking the inventory would be sensible or even appealing to the client based on a hope or expectation of specific benefit. It would also need to be of substantial, positive consequence or gain to a good majority if not almost all clients. More extended treatment, when indicated, would not be compromised. Finally, the procedure would be validated, but it would not require an excessive amount of training for the assessor/therapist to become proficient in providing it.

The paradigm that strikingly fits all of these requirements is that of Finn (see Finn, 1996, for a detailed instructional manual). The focus of his Therapeutic Assessment paradigm is to begin with a session reaching a mutual agreement on what questions the client wants answered by the assessment. This is a joint and collaborative enterprise, with a strong emphasis on the equalitarianism of the participants, one with questions and the other to answer them. Following test administration, scoring, and review, there is a feedback session in which the test data are focused on the pre-agreed questions. Thus, the client is an active partner rather than a passive testee, the questions have been shaped to be meaningfully assessment-answerable, and the client departs with what is typically a significant increase in clarity about him or herself. The expectation of net gain is realized within a time-limited framework. More extended subsequent therapy is in no way precluded; indeed, the relay of the results to an ongoing therapist would be mutually perceived as constructive.

An initial publication has reported clear effectiveness for this paradigm (Finn & Tonsager, 1992). Thirty-two college participants received such feedback, and 29 controls received only examiner attention as a part of being tested (both groups were from a student counseling center waiting list). Those participants receiving feedback reported a significant decline in symptomatic distress and a significant increase in self-esteem after feedback and at a 2-week follow-up. At these times they also indicated they felt more hopeful about their problems. The initial level of distress was the same for both groups and did not affect the benefit from feedback. Research is under way with tentatively greater positive benefits from this approach even as compared to active psychotherapy of at least equal time duration (S. E. Finn, personal communication, August 13, 1995).

Finn (1996) estimated that 8 to 10 hr of work under supervision is quite adequate for second-year clinical psychology graduate students to use the intervention procedure effectively. It does not require the learning of a large domain of verbal subtlety in the wording of feedback; one is not just doing a "reading" of the profile. Rather, one is focusing on the pre-agreed questions and what light the scores and their patterns reflect on the questions posed and the issues raised. As may be desired, there is additional material on MMPI/MMPI–2 feedback in the chapter by Erdberg

(1979) and the book by Lewak, Marks, and Nelson (1990). These latter sources are rich both in issues on which one might focus and in useful wordings for the context of feedback.

My intuition is that our redoubtable mentor would see no problem with the evolution of therapeutic assessment in addition to traditional clinical decision making and treatment planning. Indeed, the recent revision of the ethics of the American Psychological Association (1990) clearly endorsed increased feedback to clients from our assessments, a position with which few actively disagree but with which I think many feel uncomfortable for want of a practiced procedure. Given (a) that we have such a paradigm, (b) that it easily complies with current time constraints, (c) that "getting some answers" is practical and appealing to the testee, (d) that it has been demonstrated to be effective, (e) that it is ethically supported, and (f) that it is straightforward to learn and apply, I believe our mentor would contend that there is a compelling argument for a general increase in the therapeutic application of MMPI/MMPI–2 (and other test) feedback.

Logical, additional uses of the MMPI/MMPI–2 within the managed care arena are in the assessment of treatment efficacy and in preventive care. Given the data that longer term treatment leads to substantially better outcomes (Seligman, 1995), one could easily anticipate increasing legal challenges to the major restrictions on duration of treatment as well as legislative constraints; it may become more profitable for managed care companies to provide more extensive and effective treatment than to lose major lawsuits over insufficiently brief and standards-of-practice-violating care. Having an initial MMPI/MMPI–2 would also help to avoid misdirected treatment approaches. Another productive and cost-effective utilization of the MMPI/MMPI–2 would be in identifying those in need of preventive interventions. MMPI/MMPI–2 screening would be used to identify emotional problems prior to costly breakdowns as well as in avoiding the entrenchment and fixation of chronically dysfunctional patterns of behavior. In summary, in the absence of treatment data that is specific to research on MMPI–2 code types, and because of the enormous and comprehensive literature on the MMPI (cf. Dahlstrom, Welsh, & Dahlstrom, 1975), going from the MMPI–2 booklet to the MMPI profile stands as the optimal intervention for malpractice protection, for the evaluation of overall treatment effectiveness, and in the initiation of cost-effective preventive care interventions.

SUMMARY AND FUTURE CONSIDERATIONS

There seems to be no question that the MMPI–2 booklet is here to stay; the wordings are much more "user friendly" than those of the original MMPI, especially with young participants. As noted earlier, I strongly contend that the MMPI–2 norms need to be adjusted to match the 1990 census; given the importance of SES, we should be comparing our clients to people in general and not just to a highly educated slice of the populace. Behavioral predictions based on MMPI–2 codes that incorporate large proportions of people with different MMPI codes is a fundamental violation of Meehl's actuarial premises. Therefore, the plotting of MMPI–2 raw scores on MMPI norms in order to access the 50-plus years of research is also here to stay for a long time, as frustrating and confusing as that is in the teaching of fledgling psychologist assessors.

The hypothesis that MMPI/MMPI–2 codes correspond to specific neurotransmitter configurations (or to repetitive sequences or cascades of neurotransmitter arousal and inhibition) is a concept with far more ramifications than merely the prescription of medications discussed earlier. The link between the burgeoning field of neuroscience and its eventual elaboration of psychopathology (Caldwell, 1994) may well lie in the association of traumatic and/or repetitively threatening experiences to long-term alterations of neurotransmitter balances (and related transmission and structural effects). Not only would such knowledge greatly enhance prescription efficacy, but measurement of the return to more functional and personally gratifying homeostatic neural balances could provide a basic criterion of successful psychotherapy even in the absence of drugs. I would venture to speculate that if the MMPI/MMPI–2 is ever replaced by a test of equal or greater scope and power, the new criterion groups will be identified in part by the specificities of their concomitant neurotransmitter configurations and alterations of neural function.

Exploring the psychopathological ramifications of lower socioeconomic class membership has sociopolitical implications beyond the refining of our understanding of our clients and their life experiences. What is the impact on a person's mental health of the negative public role, economic insecurities, and limitations of opportunity associated with low SES status? Do policies that make the rich richer and the poor poorer (making the slope of the national income curve increasingly steep) have demonstrably adverse emotional effects? Conversely, would these be significantly ameliorated by policies that lead to a relatively more gradual national income slope? I believe our contribution to this as personality assessors lies in defining and elaborating the psychopathological consequences of low SES circumstances; Dahlstrom et al. (1986) is a most noteworthy start. A broader understanding of the psychopathological consequences of lower SES membership can then be of help in evaluating the tradeoffs of a variety of social and economic policies.

Lastly, psychology is currently in a distressing downswing as to the reduction of our ability to provide the capabilities we have cultivated and honed. Expanding our paradigms for active test feedback to our clients seems a straightforward adaptation to current constraints. From personal experience it is also a remarkably gratifying undertaking. When clients feel understood in ways they have never experienced, when clients find new ways to comprehend what is happening both inside and around them, and when clients feel their awareness of choices expanded as a result of our contact with them, we feel good about ourselves and our professional worth. I recommend it.

Psychologists often feel victimized because other gatekeepers (e.g., physicians or managed care operatives) refer only selectively to them or greatly limit the care they can provide. But whenever psychological and emotional issues are crucial to the management of an individual's care, I believe that the psychologist who is aided in his or her decision-making process by MMPI/MMPI–2 results (and other efficient assessments as indicated) can be a scientifically informed and uniquely focused gatekeeper. I also believe it would be to the benefit of the public as well as the autonomy of our profession for us to create and own our own mental health delivery companies. In such settings I believe psychologists with good knowledge of the MMPI/MMPI–2 or with good interpretations of it will consistently make more constructive and cost-effective treatment decisions than anyone else.

Our redoubtable mentor seems in remarkably good health for its age. It continues to offer us a rich largesse of hypotheses and information. It is up to us to expand these capabilities and their providence into the next century.

ACKNOWLEDGMENT

I thank Alice F. Chang, Grant Dahlstrom, David Nichols, Roger Greene, and two dedicated, anonymous reviewers for many helpful comments on earlier drafts of this article.

REFERENCES

American Psychological Association. (1990). Ethical principles of psychologists. *American Psychologist, 45*, 390–395.

Ben-Porath, Y. S., & Tellegen, A. (1995). How (not) to evaluate the comparability of MMPI and MMPI–2 profile configurations: A reply to Humphrey and Dahlstrom. *Journal of Personality Assessment, 65*, 52–58.

Butcher, J. N., Dahlstrom, W. G., Graham, J. F., Tellegen, A. M., & Kaemmer, B. (1989). *MMPI–2: Manual for administration and scoring.* Minneapolis: University of Minnesota Press.

Butcher, J. N., Graham, J. R., & Ben-Porath, Y. S. (1995). Methodological problems and issues in MMPI, MMPI–2, and MMPI–A research. *Psychological Assessment, 7*, 320–329.

Caldwell, A. B. (1990, August). *Measurement of the human condition.* Paper presented at the meeting of the American Psychological Association, Boston.

Caldwell, A. B. (1994). Simultaneous multilevel analysis [Commentary]. *American Psychologist, 49*, 144–145.

Caldwell, A. B. (1996). *MMPI AND MMPI–2: Scales, theory, and interpretation* [Cassette recordings]. Los Angeles: Caldwell Report.

Cofer, C. N., Chance, J. E., & Judson, A. J. (1949). A study of malingering on the MMPI. *Journal of Psychology, 27*, 491–499.

Cronbach, L. J., & Gleser, G. C. (1953). Assessing similarity between profiles. *The Psychological Bulletin, 50*, 456–473.

Dahlstrom, W. G. (1992). Comparability of two-point high-point code patterns from original MMPI norms to MMPI–2 norms for the restandardization sample. *Journal of Personality Assessment, 59,* 153–164.

Dahlstrom, W. G., Lachar, D., & Dahlstrom, L. E. (1986). *MMPI patterns of American minorities.* Minneapolis: University of Minnesota Press.

Dahlstrom, W. G., & Tellegen, A. (1993). *Manual supplement. Socioeconomic status and the MMPI–2: The relation of MMPI–2 patterns to levels of education and occupation.* Minneapolis: University of Minnesota Press.

Dahlstrom, W. G., Welsh, G. S., & Dahlstrom, L. E. (1972). *An MMPI handbook: Vol. 1. Clinical interpretation.* Minneapolis: University of Minnesota Press.

Dahlstrom, W. G., Welsh, G. S., & Dahlstrom, L. E. (1975). *An MMPI handbook: Vol. 2. Research applications.* Minneapolis: University of Minnesota Press.

Dawes, R., Faust, D., & Meehl, P. E. (1993). Statistical prediction versus clinical prediction: Improving what works. In G. Keren & C. Lewis (Eds.), *A handbook for data analysis in the behavioral sciences: Methodological issues* (pp. 351–367). Hillsdale, NJ: Lawrence Erlbaum Associates, Inc.

Duckworth, J. C., & Barley, W. D. (1988). Within-normal-limit profiles. In R. L. Greene (Ed.), *The MMPI: Use with specific populations* (pp. 278–315). Philadelphia: Grune & Stratton.

Edwards, D. W., Weissman, H. N., & Morrison, T. L. (1993). *Forensic case studies with additional data to resolve critical MMPI–2/MMPI differences.* Paper presented at the meeting of the American Psychological Association, Toronto, Canada.

Erdberg, P. (1979). A systematic approach to providing feedback from the MMPI. In C. S. Newmark (Ed.), *MMPI clinical and research trends* (pp. 328–342). New York: Praeger.

Finn, S. E. (1996). *Using the MMPI–2 as a therapeutic intervention.* Minneapolis: University of Minnesota Press.

Finn, S. E., & Tonsager, M. E. (1992). Therapeutic effects of providing MMPI–2 test feedback to college students awaiting therapy. *Psychological Assessment, 4,* 278–287.

Friedman, A. F., Webb, J. T., & Lewak, R. (1989). *Psychological assessment with the MMPI.* Hillsdale, NJ: Lawrence Erlbaum Associates, Inc.

Gilberstadt, H., & Duker, J. (1965). *A handbook for clinical and actuarial MMPI interpretation.* Philadelphia: Saunders.

Goldberg, L. R. (1965). Diagnosticians vs. diagnostic signs: The diagnosis of psychosis vs. neurosis from the MMPI. *Psychological Monographs, 79*(9, Whole No. 602), 1–28.

Gough, H. G. (1954). Some common misconceptions about neuroticism. *Journal of Consulting Psychology, 18,* 287–292.

Greene, R. L. (1991). *The MMPI/MMPI–2: An interpretive manual.* Boston: Allyn & Bacon.

Greene, R. L., & Nichols, D. (1990). [Raw scores and T-score correlation matrices for medical and psychiatric patients]. Unpublished raw data.

Halevy, A., Moos, R. H., & Solomon, G. F. (1965). A relationship between blood serotonin concentrations and behavior in psychiatric patients. *Journal of Psychiatric Research, 3,* 1–10.

Hathaway, S. R., & McKinley, J. C. (1967). *The Minnesota Multiphasic Personality Inventory* (Rev. ed.). New York: Psychological Corporation.

Hathaway, S. R., & Meehl, P. E. (1951a). *An atlas for the clinical use of the MMPI.* Minneapolis: University of Minnesota Press.

Hathaway, S. R., & Meehl, P. E. (1951b). The Minnesota Multiphasic Personality Inventory. In *Military clinical psychology* (Department of the Army Technical Manual TM 8:242; Department of the Air Force Manual AFM 160–145). Washington, DC: U.S. Government Printing Office.

Hathaway, S. R., & Monachesi, E. D. (1963). *Adolescent personality and behavior: MMPI patterns of normal, delinquent, dropout, and other outcomes.* Minneapolis: University of Minnesota Press.

Humphrey, D. H., & Dahlstrom, W. G. (1995). The impact of changing from the MMPI to the MMPI–2 on profile configurations. *Journal of Personality Assessment, 64,* 428–439.

Lewak, R. W., Marks, P. A., & Nelson, G. E. (1990). *Therapist guide to the MMPI & MMPI–2.* Muncie, IN: Accelerated Development.

MacAndrew, C. (1965). The differentiation of male alcoholic outpatients from nonalcoholic psychiatric outpatients by means of the MMPI. *Quarterly Journal of Studies on Alcohol, 26,* 238–246.

Marin, G., Gamba, R. J., & Marin, B. V. (1992). Extreme response style and acquiescence among Hispanics: The role of acculturation and education. *Journal of Cross-Cultural Psychology, 23,* 489–509.

Marin, G., Sabogal, F., VanOss-Marin, B., Otero-Sabogal, R., & Perez-Stable, E. J. (1987). Development of a short acculturation scale for Hispanics. *Hispanic Journal of Behavioral Science, 9,* 183–205.

Marks, P. A., & Seeman, W. (1963). *The actuarial description of abnormal personality: An atlas for use with the MMPI.* Baltimore: Williams & Wilkins.

Meehl, P. E. (1954). *Clinical versus statistical prediction: A theoretical analysis and a review of the evidence.* Minneapolis: University of Minnesota Press.

Meehl, P. E. (1986). Causes and effects of my disturbing little book. *Journal of Personality Assessment, 50,* 370–375.

Meehl, P. E., & Dahlstrom, W. G. (1960). Objective configural rules for discriminating psychotic from neurotic MMPI profiles. *Journal of Consulting Psychology, 24,* 375–387.

Meehl, P. E., & Hathaway, S. R. (1946). The K factor as a suppressor variable in the MMPI. *Journal of Applied Psychology, 30,* 525–564. (Reprinted in *Basic readings on the MMPI: A new selection on personality measurement,* by W. G. Dahlstrom and L. Dahlstrom, Eds., 1980, Minneapolis: University of Minnesota Press)

Nelson, S. E. (1952). The development of an indirect, objective measure of social status and its relationship to certain psychiatric syndromes (Doctoral dissertation, University of Minnesota). *Dissertation Abstracts, 12,* 782.

Pancoast, D. L., & Archer, R. P. (1989). Original adult MMPI norms in normal samples: A review with implications for future developments. *Journal of Personality Assessment, 53,* 376–395.

Saba, L. (1995). *Predictors of an elevated Scale 8 (Sc) on the MMPI, Version Hispana, in Hispanic workers.* Unpublished doctoral dissertation, Fielding Institute, Santa Barbara, CA.

Seligman, M. E. P. (1995). The effectiveness of psychotherapy: The *Consumer Reports* study. *American Psychologist, 50,* 965–974.

Tellegen, A., & Ben-Porath, Y. S. (1993). Code-type comparability of the MMPI and MMPI–2: Analysis of recent findings and criticisms. *Journal of Personality Assessment, 61,* 489–500.

Todd, A. L., & Gynther, M. D. (1988). Have MMPI Mf scale correlates changed in the past 30 years? *Journal of Clinical Psychology, 44,* 505–510.

Warner, W. L., & Lunt, P. S. (1941). *The social life of a modern community.* New Haven: Yale University Press.

Warner, W. L., Meeker, M., & Eells, K. (1949). *Social class in America.* Chicago: Science Research Associates.

Wiggins, J. S. (1959). Interrelationships among MMPI measures of dissimulation under standard and social desirability instructions. *Journal of Consulting Psychology, 23,* 419–427.

APPENDIX
Item Composition and Scoring Direction for Socioeconomic Status Scale (Ss) for MMPI-2

2	T	135	F	235	F	392	F
5	F	139	T	238	F	396	F
17	F	145	F	240	F	397	F
24	F	149	F	241	F	399	F
28	F	151	T	253	F	403	F
30	F	160	T	254	F	407	F
32	F	175	F	286	F	427	T
41	T	193	F	294	F	429	F
42	F	197	F	305	F	431	F
44	F	198	F	307	F	438	F
53	F	210	F	309	F	456	T
60	F	203	T	312	F	471	F
70	F	217	T	319	F	472	F
80	F	218	F	332	F		
83	F	220	F	333	F		
101	F	224	T	334	F		
109	F	225	F	348	F		
111	F	229	F	357	F		
119	F	232	T	362	T		
133	F	234	F	385	T		

	M	*SD*
Male	57.27	6.37
Female	56.81	6.49

Note. I thank W. G. Dahlstrom for calculation of these means and standard deviations based on the 2,600 subjects of the MMPI-2 normative sample.

5

The MCMI–III: Present and Future Directions

Theodore Millon
Harvard Medical School
and
Department of Psychology
University of Miami

Roger D. Davis
Department of Psychology
University of Miami

Both the original Millon Clinical Multiaxial Inventory (MCMI–I; Millon, 1977) and the Millon Clinical Multiaxial Inventory–II (MCMI–II; Millon, 1987) were refined and strengthened on a regular basis by both theoretic logic and research data. This aspiration has continued. The new Millon Clinical Multiaxial Inventory–III (MCMI–III; Millon, 1994) has been further coordinated with the most recent official diagnostic schema, the *Diagnostic and Statistical Manual of Mental Disorders* (4th ed., [*DSM–IV*]; American Psychiatric Association [APA], 1994) in an even more explicit way than before. Although the publication of the first version of the MCMI preceded the publication of the *DSM–IV*, its author played a major role in formulating the official manual's personality disorders, contributing thereby to their conceptual correspondence. The *DSM–III–R* (APA, 1987) was subsequently published in the same year as the MCMI–II; the inventory was modified in its final stages to make it as consonant as possible with the conceptual changes introduced in the then forthcoming official classification. The present version of the MCMI, the MCMI–III, strengthens these correspondences further by drawing on many of the diagnostic criteria of the *DSM–IV* to serve as the basis for drafting the inventory's items. This article reports on a select set of theoretical and empirical developments that are being carefully weighed for possible inclusion in future MCMIs, or as a guide in the refinement process of future MCMIs.

A brief historical review may be in order. Like the MCMI–I and MCMI–II, the MCMI–III is not cast in stone, but instead remains an evolving assessment instrument, one that will be significantly upgraded and refined to reflect substantive advances in knowledge, be it from theory, research, or clinical experience. What prompted the introduction of MCMI–III changes? First, the taxonomic theory of which the first two MCMI versions were deductive and operational measures, had undergone further developments (Millon, 1986a, 1986b, 1990). Consequently, two new MCMI personality disorder scales were introduced in the second version, and an additional personality scale was added in this most recent, or third version. Similarly, owing to its increasing importance in diagnostic work, a new clinical syndrome scale (posttraumatic stress disorder) was added to the MCMI–III. Second, there has been a continuous growth of interest in personality and its disorders. The *Journal of Personality Disorders* and the recently established *International Society for the Study of Personality Disorders* illustrate the emergence of these syndromes as a major focus for mental disorders. This surge of clinical, theoretical, and research literature reflect on the late 70s, 80s, and 90s as a time of Renaissance in personality theory and assessment (Millon, 1984, 1990). Enriched by this knowledge, much of which has been incorporated into the DSM, an increasingly solid base for making refined diagnostic decisions has been found, well beyond the literature of the late 70s and early 80s. In addition, Millon's work has led him to articulate an expanding base of diagnostic criteria and personality concepts (e.g., Millon, 1986a, 1990), much more extensive than those of earlier *DSM*s. This growing body of clinical literature provides much of the knowledge base for the MCMI–III. To the extent that *DSM–IV* also reflects these advances, its correspondence to MCMI–III has been further strengthened. Third, numerous cross-validation and cross-generalization studies have been and continue to be executed with the goal of evaluating and improving each of the several elements that embody both MCMI instruments—their items, scales, scoring procedures, algorithms, and interpretive text (see Choca, Shanley, & Van Denburg, 1992; Craig, 1993; Hsu & Maruish, 1992; Maruish, 1994). These ongoing investigations will continue to provide an empirical grounding for further upgrading of each of these components.

With the preceding information as a base, a number of changes were introduced to create the MCMI–III:

1.   One additional personality disorder scale—the Depressive Personality—has been added to the 13 that constituted the personality segment of MCMI–II. Also, a Posttraumatic Stress Disorder scale was added to the clinical syndromes group, as well as a small set of items to strengthen the utility of the Noteworthy Responses section in the areas of Child Abuse, Anorexia, and Bulimia. Modifications have been made also in procedures for correcting distortion effects (e.g., random responding, faking, denial, complaining) that simplify the scoring procedures developed in the MCMI–II.

2. To provide for additional scales and to optimize MCMI item to *DSM–IV* criteria correspondence, as well to reflect generalization studies, 95 new MCMI–III items were introduced to replace 95 extant MCMI–II items.

3. An item weighting system ranging from 1 to 3 points was introduced in MCMI–II scoring to reflect item differences in the variety and strength of their supporting validation data. In the MCMI–III, prototypal items are given a weight of 2 points; all others receive 1 point in the scoring system. Because the prototypal items demonstrate substantive, structural, and external validation on their "home" scale (Loevinger, 1957), they are given a higher weight than subsidiary items selected on the basis of external validation alone.

4. Interpretive texts were expanded and refined to reflect general advances in knowledge, changes introduced in the MCMI–III's underlying theory and the *DSM–IV*, as well as progress in treatment planning utilizing short-term and circum-scribed methods.

A principal goal in constructing the MCMI was to keep the total number of items small enough to encourage use in diverse diagnostic and treatment settings, yet large enough to permit the assessment of a wide range of clinically relevant behaviors. At 175 items, the final form is much shorter than comparable instruments, with terminol-ogy geared to an eighth-grade reading level. The majority of clients can complete the MCMI in 20 to 30 min, facilitating relatively simple and rapid administration, and minimizing client resistance and fatigue. This article reports on some of the theoretical and empirical developments that are in the pipeline for future MCMIs.

The MCMI–III consists of 24 clinical scales, as well as three "modifier" scales, Disclosure, Desirability, and Debasement, the purpose of which is to identify distorting tendencies that characterize clients and their responses. The next two sections constitute the basic personality disorder scales, essentially reflecting Axis II of the *DSM*. The first section (1 to 8B) appraises what are to be viewed as moderately severe personality pathologies, ranging from the Schizoid to the Self-Defeating (Masochistic) scales; the second section (scales S, C, and P) represents more severe personality pathologies, encompassing Schizotypal, Borderline, and Paranoid disorders. The following two sections cover several of the more prevalent Axis I disorders, ranging from the more moderate clinical syndromes (scales A to T) to those of greater severity (scales SS, CC, and PP). The division between personality and clinical disorders scales parallels the multiaxial model, with its important interpretive implications. The MCMI–III scales are presented in Table 1.

THEORETICAL DEVELOPMENTS:
ASSESSMENT OF PERSONALITY SUBTYPES

Personality disorders are best thought of as prototypes. Within each prototype, however, lie numerous variations. There is no one single schizoid or avoidant or depressive or

TABLE 1
Structure of the Millon Clinical Multiaxial
Inventory

Clinical personality patterns	
1	Schizoid
2A	Avoidant
2B	Depressive
3	Dependent
4	Histrionic
5	Narcissistic
6A	Antisocial
6B	Aggressive (Sadistic)
7	Compulsive
8A	Passive-aggressive (Negativistic)
8B	Self-defeating (Masochistic)
Severe personality pathology	
S	Schizotypal
C	Borderline
P	Paranoid
Clinical syndromes	
A	Anxiety
H	Somatoform
N	Bipolar: Manic
D	Dysthymia
B	Alcohol dependence
T	Drug dependence
R	Posttraumatic stress disorder
Severe syndromes	
SS	Thought disorder
CC	Major depression
PP	Delusional disorder
Modifying indices	
X	Disclosure
Y	Desirability
Z	Debasement
V	Validity

histrionic type, but instead, several variations, different forms in which the core or prototypal personality expresses itself. With the publication of *Disorders of Personality: DSM–IV and Beyond,* Millon and Davis (1995) elaborated a series of personality subtypes for each of the major prototypes deduced from Millon's evolutionary theory (1990). These subtypes essentially represent a reading of the modern and historical literature in convergence with clinical wisdom, cultural myth, and empirical fact. Often, they are simply mixtures of major types. The deficient conscience, fraudulent dealings, and arrogant attitude of the "Unprincipled" Narcissist, for example, is reminiscent of the con-man or charlatan, a cultural stereotype incarnated as a kind of antisocial narcissist. Likewise, the "Nomadic" Antisocial, represented as a gypsy-like roamer, vagrant, or itinerant railroad bum, existing as a scavenger at the margins of society, essentially reflects a mixture of the Schizoid and Antisocial.

In other cases, the subtypes exist at the confluence of Millon's evolutionary theory and other organizing principles. Psychodynamic thinkers, for example, have described the "Compensating" Narcissist as an individual who counteracts deep feelings of inferiority and lack of self-esteem by creating for oneself the illusion of being superior and exceptional. Similarly, the "Hypersensitive" Avoidant represents a more manifestly cognitive variant of a major type, being intensely wary and suspicious, alternately panicky, terrified, edgy and timorous, then thin-skinned, high-strung, petulant, and prickly. Table 2 lists the subtypes described by Millon and Davis (1995) for the Narcissistic Personality, along with their hypothesized MCMI–III profiles. Descriptions for the 14 personality disorders of *DSM–IV* and *DSM–III–R* are available in Millon and Davis (1995).

Besides the obvious relationship of each subtype to its cousins, all the subtypes share an important feature: Each is a statement of particular truth about the nature of the personologic landscape, a claim that the world contains such-and-such personalities in it, more by historical accident than ontological necessity. Each is a specific manifestation of a major type in the context of our particular times and culture, and if history or culture were different, then the subtypes would likely be different, also. The major prototypes, on the other hand, are, in a sense, required by the theory, just as Existence, Adaptation, and Replication are required by the laws of evolution. Although the subtypes lack the deductive inevitability of major prototypes, they nevertheless bring the major types down to a level of unparalleled descriptive specificity, and, it is hoped, proportionately increased clinical utility.

TABLE 2
Narcissistic Subtypes and Their Millon Clinical Multiaxial Inventory
(MCMI) Profiles

Elitist
    Feels privileged and empowered by virtue of special childhood status and pseudo-
    achievements; entitled facade bears little relation to reality; seeks favored and good-life;
    is upwardly mobile; cultivates special status and advantages by association. MCMI: 5
Amorous
    Sexually seductive, enticing, beguiling, tantalizing; glib and clever; disinclines real
    intimacy; indulges hedonistic desires; bewitches and inveigles the needy and naive;
    pathological lying and swindling. MCMI: 5–4
Unprincipled
    Deficient conscience; unscrupulous, amoral, disloyal, fraudulent, deceptive, arrogant,
    exploitive, a con-man and charlatan, dominating, contemptuous vindictive. MCMI: 5–6A
Compensatory
    Seeks to counteract or cancel out deep feelings of inferiority and lack of self-esteem; off-
    sets deficits by creating illusions of being superior, exceptional, admirable, noteworthy;
    self-worth results from self-enhancement. MCMI: 5–8A/2A

However, it is precisely because the subtypes are not inevitable products of the evolutionary theory that they not only bear a greater burden of validational evidence than do the major types, but also present a greater challenge for reliable and valid assessment. In particular, the issue of base rates, the prevalence of the various subtypes, is of particular importance. Because the base rates for some of the major types are quite low, the Schizoid and the Sadistic, for example, many of the subtypes are likely to be quite rare. A particular clinician, in fact, might go years between seeing a particular subtype, making such validational research almost impossible in any one clinical setting. Moreover, some subtypes may be seen quite frequently, whereas others will hardly ever be observed. All of the problems associated the prediction of low base rate phenomena, like the prediction of suicide or murder, are also problems here.

Nevertheless, several directions could be pursued in order to advance the assessment utility of the MCMI in relation to the subtypes. Millon (1995), for example, presented MCMI–III codetypes for each personality disorder subtype. Thus, on theoretical grounds, it is expected that the Unprincipled Narcissist will appear as a 5 – 6A, whereas the "Compensating" Narcissist is more likely to appear is a 5 – 8A or 5 – 2A. Such a codetype approach would seem to be the most straightforward, especially where these subtypes exist predominately as a mixture of two or more major types. In the coming years, as clinicians already skilled in Millon's theory become well enough acquainted with these subtypes to provide useful external validity ratings, studies that examine the diagnostic efficiency of these MCMI profile patterns will become possible. Not all 5 – 8A codetypes, for example, are likely to be classified as "Compensating" Narcissists. Conversely, some "Compensating" Narcissists may produce profiles other than the 5 – 8A. Eventually, the MCMI–III items most directly responsible for each subtype profile will be identified and examined against the content of the subtypes, and a feedback process will begin through which the item content of the MCMI and the content of the subtypes themselves are mutually refined. Items for future MCMI's will definitely be written with accurate classification of these subtypes in mind.

How an emphasis on personality subtypes will affect the length of the MCMI and its exact item composition, are, of course, open questions at the current time. The answers in part are dependent on the nature of the empirical problems encountered. Certainly, it would seem difficult to provide an accurate assessment of over 60 subtypes with an MCMI of only 175 items. Even if all of the MCMI items were oriented toward Axis II, that would still leave less than 3 unique items per subtype, far too few to protect discriminant validity. Fortunately, the base rates of some the major personalities, namely the Antisocial and Borderline, makes their subtypes more important than those of the Schizoid, for example. Where compromises in inventory length must be made then, they will favor the assessment of those subtypes that are most clinically relevant, at least for pencil-and-paper forms. Future computer-administered versions of the MCMI, programmed to optimize the selection of items based on the client's pattern of prior responses, need not administer an entire item bank, and are much more likely to yield highly specific, subtype-relevant information.

EMPIRICAL DEVELOPMENTS: TRAIT SUBSCALES FOR SOME FUTURE MCMI AXIS II SCALES

Psychological instruments may be interpreted at several levels. At the lowest level lie individual test items. Because any single item is too unreliable and narrow as a predictor of broader individual differences, many items are usually aggregated together to form scales. Each scale, in turn, represents only a single dimension of the total personality, and consequently, are usually examined conjointly as set, or profile configuration. Assuming test validity, and assuming that the inventory has some claim, either deductive-theoretical or inductive-statistical, as a representation of all of personality, the profile configuration essentially becomes an intervening variable for individuality.

A level of interpretation that is becoming more important in modern inventories is the personality trait. Traits are assessed at a level between what are variously called types, styles, syndromes, or higher order dimensions, and the level of individual items. Each personality disorder may be thought of as consisting of a set of such trait characteristics. Conversely, the covariation of a particular set of personality traits may be thought of as a personality disorder. There are, then, four levels of clinical interpretation within an inventory—item-level, trait-level, scale-level, and profile configuration.

Trait subscales are clinically useful. Recall that each personality syndrome is viewed in the prototypal model as a covariant attribute structure whose features, taken one by one, are neither necessary nor sufficient for the diagnosis of the syndrome. Although theoretically the most prototypal member of a syndrome possesses all its features, most individuals will not. As astute clinicians know, no two narcissistic personalities are exactly alike, no two antisocial personalities are exactly alike, and so on. In the *DSM–IV*, nine criteria are listed for the Borderline Personality Disorder, five of which are required for diagnosis. Conceivably, then, two individuals might both be diagnosed with the disorder, while having only one feature or criterion in common, allowing for considerable trait or criterion heterogeneity within any personality type. The specific personality traits that an individual possesses is of interest when we want to know what kind of schizoid the person is, what kind of dependent, and so on, a fact that is obviously relevant to the identification of adult subtypes described earlier. However, an individual may also receive specific disorder subscales in the absence of a diagnosis. Such elevations correspond to problematic trait characteristics that deserve attention but are not so pervasively expressed as to constitute full-fledged personality disorders. The *DSM* allows problematic traits to be noted on Axis II, but apparently this possibility is rarely used clinically, perhaps because the *DSM* is criterion-oriented rather than trait-oriented.

The existence of personality traits as a legitimate level of organization in human personality, and their utility in clinical interpretation, argues that they should be represented in any personality disorders inventory. Because of its relative brevity, traits have not yet been explicitly represented in the MCMI. Instead, the structure of the inventory at levels before that of syndrome or disorder has drawn on an item-weighting system informed by the strength of each item's validational data, the intrinsic interrelatedness of the personality disorders, and the prototypal structure of mental disorders generally. An item weighting system ranging from 1 to 3 points was introduced in the MCMI–II; in the MCMI–III, prototypal items are given a weight of 2 points; all others are weighted 1 point only. Because the prototypal items demonstrate substantive, structural, and external validation (Loevinger, 1957) on their "home" scale they are given a higher weight than subsidiary items selected on the basis of external validation alone. Prototypal items represent features of their respective disorders and are doubly weighted. Nonprototypal items represent features that, although not central, are nevertheless relevant to their respective disorders. Thus, an item such as "I like to be the center of attention when I'm in a group," might be weighted 2 points on the Histrionic scale, and 1 point on the Narcissistic scale.

Such multiple assignments have caused some (Wiggins, 1982) to express concern regarding the discriminant validity of the MCMI scales. Exploratory studies (Davis, 1994) with the Millon Adolescent Clinical Inventory, designed according to the 3 – 2 – 1 weighting system, show that factoring the items assigned to each MCMI personality scale separately results in brief subscales that often share over half their items. Similar results would likely emerge for the MCMI–II. In contrast, the MCMI–III personality scales were designed to be shorter, using a 2 – 1 weighting system. Factor studies currently underway reveal, not unexpectedly, that the item overlap of the resulting MCMI–III factor traits is substantially more favorable to clinical use. The results of these inductive, or "bottom-up," studies must, of course, be examined in conjunction with theoretical, or "top-down" considerations, in order to appraise their value. Of course, trait subscales need not be designed for every MCMI Axis II disorder, but might instead be constructed only for those disorders of greater clinical relevance frequently seen in clinical settings—certainly the Antisocial, Borderline, and Paranoid, and perhaps the Narcissistic and Dependent, but not, for example, the Schizoid or Sadistic.

CONJOINT DEVELOPMENT AND
REFINEMENT OF INSTRUMENTALITIES
ACROSS DIVERSE DATA SOURCES

One of the fundamental principles in instrument construction is that validity should be built into an instrument from the beginning. Loevinger (1957), Jackson (1970), and Skinner (1986) discussed test construction as an iterative three-stage process. In the first, rational stage, the content of each construct to be measured is defined as precisely as possible. Items may be written and refined by multiple so-called experts in the theory of the construct, sorted according to their discriminative characteristics, ranked in terms of difficulty level, and so on, all before being put to actual participants. In the second, internal stage, the items are given to real individuals. Various statistics are then calculated to ensure that the items tap a single dimension. Items with strong relationships to scales for which they were not intended may be deleted or reassigned. In addition, a correlation matrix of the instruments scales may be examined for anomalies and items reassigned or dropped in order to bring this pattern in line with theoretical expectations. In the third, external stage, the newly developed scales are assessed against other instruments of established reputation. Items that pass through all three stages are said to have been validated theoretically, statistically, and empirically. The Millon inventories have essentially been constructed according to this tripartite logic.

Although inventories should be constructed to mirror our expectations regarding relationships between constructs both internal and external to the instrument as precisely as possible, they should also possess a generative value. That is, an inventory should assist in the accumulation of new knowledge. If our test is intended to assess personality disorders, we might expect, for example, that individuals classified as dependent personalities will also be classified as experiencing depressive episodes more often than, say, antisocials, simply because dependents are likely to feel helpless and hopeless more often than antisocials, who take the initiative in changing their external world, albeit usually in a destructive fashion. Together, these internal–internal and internal–external expectations form a set of constraints that our inventory must be constructed to satisfy. Each such constraint is an additional point through which the instrument's predictions are triangulated with reality as it is assumed to exist. The larger this set of constraints, the better, for if the inventory can satisfy many such constraints at the beginning, then we can have greater confidence that it will meet future challenges.

Sometimes, for example, after an instrument has been constructed, certain variables about which we had no preformed ideas show a significant relationship. Perhaps in the beginning we believed that antisocial personalities should also report high family distress and a high incidence of alcoholism. Perhaps we also believed that dependents personalities should report overprotective parents and an inability to end relationships, and these expectations were built into the instrument. About the relationship between dependent personality and the incidence of alcoholism, however, we may have no expectations at all, so that the magnitude of this second relationship is "free to vary," simply because we do not know much about it, how it should be evaluated, or whether it should even exist at all. How do we evaluate this observed, but unexpected, relationship? Having constructed our instrument to satisfy multiple constraints in the form of theoretically driven expectations, we are no longer working with just any item pool. The more our test satisfies many different constraints, the greater our expectations of the generalizability of the entire system of instrumentation. Demonstrated validity in diverse areas of the nomological network becomes a promissory note that observed relationships between intervening variables elsewhere is not peculiar to their particular mode of operationalization, but is instead representative of nature's structure and, so, worthy of genuine scientific interest. In general, the more constraints an instrument satisfies at the outset, the more confidence we can have in the validity of relationships that are unanticipated.

At the current time, most psychological instruments are developed within a single data source, be it self-report, clinical ratings, observer ratings, or projective, and then validated against instruments of already established utility within that same data source. Validation against instruments from other data sources, although important, is usually secondary. Thus, a new self-report scale to measure dependency finds evidence for its validity first against other self-report dependency scales, and then, against observer ratings and projectives, and so on. Lower correlations between self-report and rated forms are attributed to method considerations, and often rightfully so. Unfortunately, this rather haphazard style of instrument development often leads to confusing results where such instruments are paired against each other in a multitrait–multimethod matrix. The narcissistic scale of a self-report instrument may correlate more highly with the histrionic rating scale, and so on. Many such mismatches are likely to be found for any given set of personality instruments, a fact that has undermined confidence in the valid assessment of personality disorders.

A much better method blurs the distinction between internal and external by viewing test construction as a system of relations or constraints to be satisfied across multiple data sources. Here, the goal is to build an entire suite of instruments informed one by the others across the entire construction process. The more data sources that can be involved, the better. For example, a self-report inventory for the personality disorders, an observer-rated version of the same inventory, and a clinical checklist would be constructed simultaneously, not one at a time. Correlation matrices between all instruments would be inspected at every stage. Thus, if during development it was found that the observer-rated narcissistic scale correlated more highly with the self-report histrionic scale than with its parallel self-report narcissistic scale, indicating a lack of convergent validity, the items from both pools would be examined, not only with regard to their content characteristics and correlation to their assigned scale, but also in terms of their cross-method correlations. Violations of multitrait–multimethod considerations would be tracked to particular items, and these would be reassigned, dropped, or rewritten. Thus, rather than being examined post hoc, multitrait–multimethod considerations become a fundamental part of the item selection process, considered from the beginning, allowing each instrument to strengthen the others. Validity is built into an entire system of instrumentation, and not simply into a single instrument. Future versions of the MCMI will are likely to be constructed in this fashion.

What are the requirements for the construction of such a test suite? The first is essentially practical, reflecting a much larger investment on the part of participants, and the need for more iterations in the development process. Both patients and their clinicians must be subjected to the agonies of providing data for a large item pool. The second is theoretical, and is the more difficult of the two, requiring expert clinical judgment concerning the constructs the test seeks to embrace. The construction process is begun knowing that correlations between like scales across diverse data sources will be less than unity, and that this reflects measurement error as it does the informational biases of the respective sources. Personalities can be expected to differ in terms of their level of self-knowledge and the extent to which they distort objective information. The egocentricity of the Narcissist and his tendency to construe reality in ways favorable to self makes him less likely than the pessimistic and self-focused Depressive to provide valid self-report information. We might conjecture, then, that the correlation between self-reported and clinician-rated Narcissistic personality is likely to be less than that between self-reported and clinician-rated Depressive personality. And this is the problem the theorist faces. Knowing that the multitrait–multimethod matrix reflects informational biases as well as measurement error, the theorist must provide a substantive framework within which to evaluate the direction and magnitude of its correlations and to determine the path in which the results are best refined. In turn, this involves knowing (a) those traits or characteristics for which each personality can typically be expected to provide valid self-report information, (b) those traits or characteristics for which each personality cannot be expected to provide such information, (c) those traits or characteristics for which clinicians can typically be expected to provide valid ratings, and (d) those traits or characteristics that, for whatever reason, clinicians will not easily be able to rate.

Unfortunately, the *DSM*'s Axis II, deliberately formulated to be atheoretical, and so existing at a descriptive rather than explanatory level, cannot provide the substantive framework necessary to guide such research. Rather than providing a coherent deductive foundation within which to ask questions about the various personalities, Axis II is best viewed as a body of descriptive material collated across several perspectives, but not really coordinated with any of them. Although the periodic table is the unique province of chemistry, the problematic behaviors that are to be carved up into diagnostic categories are often given to psychopathologists by parties whose standards are extrinsic to psychopathology as a science. Perhaps we live in a more enlightened age, but was it not so long ago that Sullivan, a founder of the interpersonal school, proposed the "homosexual personality"? Or that the "masochistic personality" came under fire as reflecting biases against women? Philosophers of science agree that the system of kinds undergirding any domain of inquiry must itself be answerable to the question that forms the very point of departure for the scientific enterprise: Why does nature take this particular form rather than some other? Why these particular diagnostic groups rather than others? One cannot merely accept any list of kinds or dimensions as given. Committee consensus is not science. Instead, a taxonomic scheme must be justified, and to be justified scientifically, it must be justified theoretically. Taxonomy and theory are intimately linked.

Item writers involved in attempts to construct a coordinated suite of multimethod instruments, future versions of the MCMI, and the Millon Personality Diagnostic Checklist (MPDC; Tringone, in press) require a strong theoretical basis on which the various personality disorders can be compared and contrasted for their manifestations across different data sources. Relevant example questions are "What traits does the narcissist possess about which he or she is likely to have self-knowledge and will admit to?," and "What traits does the narcissist possess about which he or she is unlikely to have self-knowledge?" For the authors, this basis is Millon's Evolutionary theory (Millon, 1990). Although a detailed exposition is beyond the scope of this article, the theory essentially seeks to explicate the structure and styles of personality with reference to deficient, imbalanced, or conflicted modes of ecological adaptation and reproductive strategy. Four domains or spheres in which evolutionary principles are demonstrated are labeled as Existence, Adaptation, Replication, and Abstraction. The first relates the serendipitous transformation of random or less organized states into those possessing distinct structures of greater organization; the second refers to homeostatic processes employed to sustain survival in open ecosystems; the third pertains to reproductive styles that maximize the diversification and selection of ecologically effective attributes; and the fourth concerns the emergence of competencies that foster anticipatory planning and reasoned decision making. Polarities derived from the first three phases—pleasure–pain, passive–active, and other–self, respectively—are used to construct a theoretically embedded classification system of personality disorders Personalities, which we have termed *deficient,* and which lack the capacity to experience or to enact certain aspects of the three polarities (e.g., the schizoid has a faulty substrate for both "pleasure" and "pain"); those spoken of as *imbalanced* lean strongly toward one or another extreme of a polarity (e.g., the dependent is oriented almost exclusively to receiving the support and nurturance of "others"); and those we judge as *conflicted* struggle with ambivalences toward opposing ends of a bipolarity (e.g., the passive–aggressive vacillates between adhering to the expectancies of "others" versus enacting what is wished for one's "self"). Figure 1 illustrates the place of the *DSM* personality disorders within the polarity model. These polarities lend the model a holistic, cohesive structure that facilitates the comparison and contrast of groups along fundamental axes, sharpening the meanings of the derived constructs, preventing their definitions from being co-opted by one perspective or school to the exclusion of others, and "fixing" them against construct drift.

	Existential Aim		Replication Strategy		
	Life Enhancement	Life Preservation	Reproductive Propagation		Reproductive Nurturance
				Self - Other	
Polarity	Pleasure - Pain		Self - Other		
Deficiency, Imbalance, Conflict	Pleasure - Pain - +	Pleasure Pain (Reversal)	Self - Other +	Self + Other -	Self - Other (Reversal)
Adaptation Mode		DSM Personality Disorders			
Passive: Accomodation	Schizoid / Depressive	Masochistic	Dependent	Narcissistic	Compulsive
Active: Modification	Avoidant	Sadistic	Histrionic	Antisocial	Negativistic
Structural Pathology	Schizotypal	Borderline, Paranoid	Borderline	Paranoid	Borderline, Paranoid

FIGURE 1   The polarity model.

In addition to providing a polarity model by which to derive the entire constellation of personality disorders, Millon and associates have also stressed that personality is an intrinsically multioperational construct. That is, personality disorders are not simply about behavior, or about cognition, or about unconscious conflicts, but rather, as disorders of the entire matrix of the person, embrace all of these data domains. In past (Millon, 1986a) and current writings (Millon & Davis, 1995), Millon and associates have set forth comprehensive (exhaustive of the major domains of personality) and comparable (existing at approximately equal levels of abstraction) attributes for eight functional and structural domains of the personality. Each cell of the resulting 8 × 14 Domain × Disorder matrix contains the diagnostic attribute that in the authors' judgment best captures the expression of each personality style within that particular domain (see Figure 2). The columns of the matrix suggest a comparison and contrast of the personality disorders within a particular content area, while its rows suggest a comprehensive picture of each ideal type, the total expression of each personality. The first gets at discriminate validity; the second at convergent validity.

In contrast, the criteria of the *DSM–IV* are both noncomprehensive (no real scheme through which to meaningfully distribute personality attributes has been developed) and noncomparable (the criteria run the gamut from very broad to very narrow). Noncomprehensive criteria lead to redundancies and omissions. Noncomparable criteria lead to a mixture of levels. Consider, for example, the dependent personality disorder. Criterion 1 states "Has difficulty making everyday decisions without an excessive amount of advice and reassurance from others." Criterion 2, however, says almost the same: "Needs others to assume responsibility for most major areas of his or her life." In fact, five of the eight dependent personality criteria seem oriented toward the interpersonal conduct domain, two seem oriented toward the self-image domain, and only one is concerned with cognitive style, leaving the domains of regulatory mechanisms, object representations, morphologic organization, mood/temperament, and expressive acts completely unaddressed. Consider the obsessive-compulsive personality disorder. Criterion 5 is relatively narrow and behavioral: "Is unable to discard worn-out or worthless objects even when they have no sentimental value." In contrast, criterion 8 requires more inference: "Shows rigidity and stubbornness." In fact, the inability to discard worthless objects could well be considered simply a behavioral manifestation of the trait of rigidity.

Failure to multioperationalize the personality disorders via comprehensive and comparable attributes almost certainly contributes to diagnostic inefficiency and invalidity, and provides a critique of the content validity of the *DSM–IV* criteria sets. Even more problematic, because the *DSM* is usually taken as the "gold standard" by which other measures of personality disorder are judged, and because most modern measures seek to conform to the *DSM* in some way, the degree to which these criteria sets distort the practice of modern clinical science is an open question—there is no gold standard for the gold standard. Because most test authors

	Behavioral Acts	Interpersonal Conduct	Cognitive Style	Self-Image	Object Representations	Regulatory Mechanisms	Morphologic Organization	Mood/ Temperament
Schizoid	Impassive	Unengaged	Impoverished	Complacent	Meager	Intellectualization	Undifferentiated	Apathetic
Avoidant	Fretful	Aversive	Distracted	Alienated	Vexatious	Fantasy	Fragile	Anguished
Depressive	Disconsolate	Defenseless	Pessimistic	Worthless	Forsaken	Asceticism	Depleted	Melancholic
Dependent	Incompetent	Submissive	Naive	Inept	Immature	Introjection	Inchoate	Pacific
Histrionic	Dramatic	Attention-Seeking	Flighty	Gregarious	Shallow	Dissociation	Disjointed	Fickle
Narcissistic	Haughty	Exploitive	Expansive	Admirable	Contrived	Rationalization	Spurious	Insouciant
Antisocial	Impulsive	Irresponsible	Deviant	Autonomous	Debased	Acting-Out	Unruly	Callous
Sadistic	Precipitate	Abrasive	Dogmatic	Combative	Pernicious	Isolation	Eruptive	Hostile
Compulsive	Disciplined	Respectful	Constricted	Conscientious	Concealed	Reaction Formation	Compartmentalized	Solemn
Negativistic	Resentful	Contrary	Skeptical	Discontented	Vacillating	Displacement	Divergent	Irritable
Masochistic	Abstinent	Deferential	Diffident	Undeserving	Discredited	Exaggeration	Inverted	Dysphoric
Schizotypal	Eccentric	Secretive	Autistic	Estranged	Chaotic	Undoing	Fragmented	Distraught or Insentient
Borderline	Spasmodic	Paradoxical	Capricious	Uncertain	Incompatible	Regression	Split	Labile
Paranoid	Defensive	Provocative	Suspicious	Inviolable	Unalterable	Projection	Inelastic	Irascible

FIGURE 2   Attributes within each functional and structural domain.

consider it necessary to construct their instruments in accordance with the diagnoses and criteria of the *DSM–IV*, we can conclude that almost every extant instrument that emphasizes the *DSM* is to an unknown extent contaminated by this problem, a consideration that argues strongly for the role of theory as a guide when selecting attributes, criteria, or items by which to operationalize personality disorders.

Obviously, its atheoretical shortcomings, together with its noncomprehensive and noncomparable format, makes the *DSM* difficult to regard even now as a gold standard for the MCMI–II, MCMI–III (which actually features many items as rephrases of the official criteria), and Millon Personality Diagnostic Checklist. Because of its theoretical anchoring, the MCMI and MPDC are perhaps best regarded as measures of the *DSM* constructs, but more, the "more" being the surplus meaning provided by the theory. However, as the theory continues to evolve along the lines necessary to construct a coordinated suite of instruments (of which the MCMI will be only one essential leg), the relationship between future MCMIs and the *DSM–IV* will require close consideration, and perhaps even a re-evaluation. That an atheoretical, but official, classification should act as the criterion against which a theoretically grounded system is judged can only be described as a paradox, one faced not only by integrative theorists, but by interpersonal and psychodynamic thinkers, as well.

CONCLUSIONS

Although we have chosen to review only a select set of present theoretical and empirical fronts, additional developments in the "Millonian tradition," unfortunately beyond the scope of this article, will undoubtedly influence the direction and content of future inventories, indirectly at first, but more directly as time proceeds. One of these is the formation of a Research Network to coordinate researchers interested in Millon's theory and inventories, using the rapidly developing resources of the Internet (for information, e-mail iaspp@aol.com). These advances in communications technology, with the ability, for example, to pilot large numbers of items with readily obtained, sizable samples gathered from sites as small as the individual private-practice clinician and as large as the largest hospital or university setting, will undoubtedly speed the development, validation, and coordination, of inventories of all types.

REFERENCES

American Psychiatric Association. (1987). *Diagnostic and statistical manual of mental disorders* (3rd ed., rev.) Washington, DC: Author.

American Psychiatric Association. (1994). *Diagnostic and statistical manual of mental disorders* (4th ed.) Washington, DC: Author.

Choca, J. P., Shanley, L. A., Van Denburg, E. (1992). *Interpretive guide to the Millon Clinical Multiaxial Inventory (MCMI).* Washington, DC: American Psychological Association.

Craig, R. J. (Ed.). (1993). *The Millon Clinical Multiaxial Inventory: A clinical research information synthesis.* Hillsdale, NJ: Lawrence Erlbaum Associates, Inc.

Davis, R. D. (1994). *The development of content scales for the Millon Adolescent Clinical Inventory.* Unpublished master's thesis, University of Miami.

Hsu, L. M., & Maruish, M. E. (1992). *Conducting publishable research with the MCMI–II: Psychometric and statistical issues.* Minneapolis: National Computer Systems.

Jackson, D. N. (1970). A sequential system for personality scale development. In C. D. Spielberger (Ed.), *Current topics in clinical and community psychology* (Vol. 2; pp. 61–92). New York: Academic.

Loevinger, J. (1957). Objective tests as instruments of psychological theory. *Psychological Reports, 3,* 635–694.

Maruish, M. (Ed.). (1994). *The use of psychological testing for treatment planning and outcome assessment.* Hillsdale, NJ: Lawrence Erlbaum Associates, Inc.

Millon, T. (1977). *Manual for the Millon Clinical Multiaxial Inventory (MCMI).* Minneapolis: National Computer Systems.

Millon, T. (1984). On the renaissance of personality assessment and personality theory. *Journal of Personality Assessment, 48,* 450–466.

Millon, T. (1986a) Personality prototypes and their diagnostic criteria. In T. Millon & G. L. Klerman (Eds.), *Contemporary directions in psychopathology: Toward the DSM–IV* (pp. 671–712). New York: Guilford.

Millon, T. (1986b). A theoretical derivation of pathological personalities. In T. Millon & G. L. Klerman (Eds.), *Contemporary directions in psychopathology: Toward the DSM–IV* (pp. 639–670). New York: Guilford.

Millon, T. (1987). *Manual for the Millon Clinical Multiaxial Inventory–II (MCMI–II).* Minneapolis: National Computer Systems.

Millon, T. (1990). *Toward a new personology.* New York: Wiley.

Millon, T. (1994). *Millon Index of Personality Styles (MIPS) manual.* San Antonio, TX: Psychological Corporation.

Millon, T. (1995, August). *Subtypes of the personality disorders.* Presentation given at the Conference on the Millon Inventories, Minneapolis, MN.

Millon, T., & Davis, R. D. (1995) *Disorders of personality: DSM–IV and beyond.* New York: Wiley-Interscience.

Skinner, H. A. (1986). Construct validation approach to psychiatric classification. In T. Millon & G. L. Klerman (Eds.), *Contemporary directions in psychopathology: Towards the DSM–IV* (pp. 307–330). New York: Guilford.

Tringone, R. (in press). *The Millon Personality Diagnostic Checklist.*

Wiggins, J. S. (1982). Circumplex models of interpersonal behavior in clinical psychology. In P. Kendall & J. Butcher (Eds.), *Handbook of research methods in clinical psychology.* New York: Wiley-Interscience.

6

Stability and Change in Personality Assessment: The Revised NEO Personality Inventory in the Year 2000

Paul T. Costa, Jr. and Robert R. McCrae

Gerontology Research Center
National Institute on Aging
National Institutes of Health

The Revised NEO Personality Inventory (NEO–PI–R) consists of 30 facet scales that define the broad domains of the Five-Factor Model of personality. No major revisions of the basic model are anticipated in the near future. Despite their popularity, social desirability and inconsistency scales will not be added to the NEO–PI–R because their validity and utility have not yet been demonstrated. Among possible changes are minor modifications in wording and more extensive adaptations for adolescents and for populations with low reading levels. Contextualized (e.g., work-related) versions of the instrument will be further explored. Many changes are more easily implemented on the computer than the print version of the instrument.

Standardized personality measures are generally preferred to ad hoc instruments because they are known quantities: They have published norms and an established record of reliability, validity, and predictive utility. Each widely used instrument represents an investment by the community of applied assessors who have mastered a set of constructs and accumulated their own experience with its use. All of these considerations encourage test authors and publishers to be conservative when making changes to their instruments.

However, the science of personality assessment advances and the needs of assessors change, and instruments must be adapted if they are to remain state-of-the-art. The Revised NEO Personality Inventory (NEO–PI–R; Costa & McCrae, 1992) began in 1978 as the NEO Inventory, measuring facets of Neuroticism (N), Extraversion (E), and Openness to Experience (O; Costa & McCrae, 1980). With the addition of global scales to measure the two new factors of Agreeableness (A) and Conscientiousness (C), it was published in 1985 as the NEO–PI (Costa &

McCrae, 1985). It was joined by a brief version, the NEO Five-Factor Inventory (NEO–FFI), in 1989 (Costa & McCrae, 1989), and was expanded to include facets of A and C in 1992. Each change in format allowed us to update empirical evidence on the functioning of the instrument and to enhance its utility and convenience for users.

The underlying scientific basis of the instrument—the Five-Factor Model (FFM) of personality (Digman, 1990; McCrae & John, 1992)—has not changed. Indeed, there is far more evidence of its comprehensiveness, universality, and practical relevance today than when the NEO–PI was first published. We do not imagine that the FFM is the last word in personality structure, but we do believe that it will remain the basis of personality assessment for many years.

Whether the 30 specific facets we have chosen to represent the five factors constitute the optimal set is, of course, open to debate. Different traits might have been selected (Costa & McCrae, 1995), perhaps tailored to the needs of clinicians or educators or industrial/organizational (I/O) psychologists. But without committing ourselves irrevocably to the 30 existing facets of the NEO–PI–R, we remain confident that they are a meaningful selection of traits that can profitably be used in research and practice. In consequence, we do not envision any significant changes in the structure of the NEO–PI–R in the near future.

Our intention in this article, then, is to list some potential changes that could expand application of the NEO–PI–R and enhance its utility. We hope thereby to enlist the help of researchers with special interests and test users with access to novel populations. For example, we are already indebted to colleagues around the world for translations of the NEO–PI and NEO–PI–R into a score of languages, from Icelandic to Filipino. We welcome all these contributions to the further evolution of the instrument.

Before presenting the changes we plan or hope to make, however, we devote some time to a discussion of a change we do not anticipate making, despite popular demand: the addition of validity scales to identify socially desirable and inconsistent responding. Attractive as the idea is, we remain unconvinced that such scales are effective in detecting invalid protocols, and we have no intention of including useless or misleading scales in the NEO–PI–R.[1]

THE QUESTIONABLE UTILITY OF VALIDITY SCALES

Every social scientist knows that questionnaires are fallible instruments, subject to an intimidating array of biases and distortions. Respondents may answer at random,

---

[1]Infrequency scales are sometimes successful in detecting random responding (Hough, Eaton, Dunnette, Kamp, & McCloy, 1990), but at the cost of including "trick" questions that may alienate the respondent.

or may misunderstand items, or deliberately lie, or agree indiscriminately to any assertion presented to them. Some of these biases can be induced experimentally, as dozens of studies on faking good or bad have shown (e.g., Paulhus, Bruce, & Trapnell, 1995). It would be nice to be able to identify individuals whose personality scores were inaccurate because of the influence of some bias; their results could then be discarded or adjusted. Some authors hold that it would be more than nice: Ben-Porath and Waller (1992) asserted that "detection of an attempt to provide misleading information is a vital and absolutely necessary component of the clinical interpretation of test results" (p. 24), and suggested that use of an instrument without validity scales "runs counter to the basic tenets of clinical assessment" (p. 24).

This sentiment is widely and deeply held by clinicians, so we must be clear in our response to it. Of course, clinicians ought to be concerned with the validity of results. They should not even administer questionnaires to floridly psychotic or profoundly demented or grossly uncooperative patients. They should not accept uncritically the personality profile suggested by self-reports, particularly if it conflicts with other data or their impressions of the patient. They should supplement data from self-reports with data from observers, or legal or medical records when possible. And they should consider any useful evidence that can be gained from examining the pattern of test responses. But they should not suspect, adjust, or discard scores on the basis of "validity" scales that are themselves of dubious validity and utility (McCrae et al., 1989).

The NEO–PI–R in fact includes a number of checks on the validity of responses. The most direct is a set of three questions at the bottom of the answer sheet that ask respondents if they have tried to answer honestly and accurately, responded to all statements, and entered responses in the correct spaces. Although face valid, these checks have not been empirically validated; so few respondents endorse them—usually less than 1% of volunteers—analyses are difficult. These items are intended to identify a few individuals who are frankly uncooperative. Administrators are also advised to check for missing data and not to score protocols with more than 40 missing items or facet scales with than 3 missing items. Acquiescence and naysaying can be gauged by counting *agree* and *strongly agree* responses: Normative data show that only 1% of volunteers score 150 or more on this count, and only 1% score 50 or less. There is also a check for one form of random responding, seen in repetitive strings of identical responses that probably indicate hurried responding and a lack of attention to item content (Costa & McCrae, 1992). All of these checks are performed automatically in the computer administered version of the NEO–PI–R.

Conspicuously missing are two popular validity indicators: Measures of social desirability (SD) or faking, and measures of inconsistent responding. Their omission is not an oversight; it represents our judgment that these indicators simply do not work in most situations.

Social Desirability

SD scales typically consist of items that have a clearly desirable response. We know that people who are trying falsely to appear to have good qualities will endorse many such items, and the creators of SD scales wish to infer from this that people who endorse many SD items are trying to create a good impression. That argument is formally identical to asserting that presidential candidates shake hands, and therefore people who shake hands are probably running for President.[2] In fact, there are many much more common reasons for shaking hands, and there is also a more common reason than impression management for endorsing SD items—namely, because the items are reasonably accurate self-descriptions.

How do we know they are accurate?—only by consulting an outside source, such as a peer rater. A series of studies from Dicken (1963) to Borkenau and Ostendorf (1992) showed that a variety of SD scales fail to separate invalid from valid responses. Indeed, "correcting" self-reports through the use of SD scales often reduced, rather than enhanced, their validity as assessed by an outside criterion (McCrae & Costa, 1983; McCrae et al., 1989).

Most recently, Schinka, Kinder, and Kremer (this issue) developed Positive and Negative Presentation Management scales from the NEO–PI–R item pool. Piedmont and McCrae (1996) examined these scales as moderator variables in predicting peer ratings on NEO–PI–R domains from self-reports on the same domains. Did high scorers on the two impression management scales give less valid self-reports? Not at all. In this normal, volunteer sample there was no evidence that either of the Schinka et al. scales moderated the validity of the self-reports.

It is likely that the scales do not work in normal volunteer samples because the base rate of extreme impression management is too low, and it is possible that these or other SD scales would in fact prove useful in clinical or selection settings. We encourage researchers to test SD scales in such settings using peer or clinician ratings as criteria, and we would happily add SD scales to the NEO–PI–R if the data warrant their use. In the meantime, we suggest that users of all personality inventories regard validity scales skeptically.

Inconsistency

Inconsistency is a different kind of variable, designed to detect certain kinds of random or careless responding. L. R. Goldberg (personal communication, January 25, 1995; cf. Goldberg & Kilkowski, 1985) chose pairs of NEO–PI–R items that

---

[2]The reader should consider whether a simulation study, instructing participants to pretend to be running for office and documenting their handshaking behavior, would contribute at all to the plausibility of this inference. If not, what is the utility of faking studies for the validation of SD or defensiveness scales (e.g., Stein, Graham, & Williams, 1995)?

were very similar in content and created an index of consistency by correlating, for each participant, responses to the first member of each pair with responses to the second. Consistent responding would be expected to lead to a high correlation. (A second consistency index based on items with opposite meanings was also created, and the total consistency score is the mean of the two.) Goldberg reasoned that random responding would lead to low consistency indices, and proposed to discard data from the least consistent responders.

Here, too, however, there are alternative explanations for low consistency scores. In particular, it seems likely that people who have undesirable traits may be ambivalent about admitting them, and may do so only some of the time. Their scale scores, then, would not be as high as they should be in some absolute sense, but they will still tend to be higher than those of people without undesirable traits, who consistently deny them.

This is a testable hypothesis, and it is not even necessary to go beyond self-report data to test it. Any two self-reports of the same trait should be positively correlated if respondents are providing valid data. Purely random responding, however, would lead to correlations near zero. Data from Goldberg's Eugene–Springfield Community Sample—a quasi-random sample of volunteers initially ranging in age from 18 to 85—are reported in Table 1. In this table, NEO–PI–R domain scales are correlated with corresponding factors from Goldberg's (1992) unipolar adjective markers, which had been administered 7 months earlier than the NEO–PI–R. Results for the most, middle, and least consistent responders are given in the first three columns; the fourth column shows validity coefficients for the 15% of the sample scoring lowest in consistency. As the last row of the table shows, there is some variation in consistency scores (although even the least consistent group had

TABLE 1
Convergent Correlations Between NEO Personality Inventory–Revised
Domain Scales and Goldberg Adjective Factors and Mean
Consistency in Subsamples Differing in Response Consistency

Domain/Factor	Trichotomized Consistency Index			Least Consistent[c]
	High[a]	Middle[a]	Low[b]	
N	.66	.65	.63	.66
E	.71	.62	.65	.70
O	.50	.52	.50	.49
A	.48	.55	.37	.38
C	.65	.65	.65	.58
Consistency	.75	.61	.44	.36

Note. Goldberg's Emotional Stability scale is reflected to measure Neuroticism. All correlations significant at $p < .001$.
[a]$n = 280$. [b]$n = 281$. [c]$n = 130$.

a positive mean consistency score). Declines in consistency, however, are not paralleled by declines in validity: It is apparent that all five factors show moderate to good validity in all subsamples; only for A is there a suggestion that inconsistency reduces validity slightly.

Some respondents may on occasion respond randomly, and they would presumably score high on an index of inconsistency. But most people with high inconsistency scores are not responding randomly, and much more would be lost than gained by discarding their data.

ADAPTATIONS AND IMPROVEMENTS

Some of the possible changes to the NEO–PI–R currently under consideration would consist of minor modifications requiring little or no reconceptualization on the part of the user. For example, the 60 items of the NEO–FFI are taken from among the 240 items in the full NEO–PI–R. It has been suggested to us that they be moved forward to the beginning of the questionnaire, so that respondents who fail to complete the full inventory can nevertheless be scored on the five factors. This would require a reprinting of the test booklet, but no other changes.

A few items from N, E, and O were rewritten when the Revised NEO–PI was published; eventually, other item changes will probably be necessary. For example, the Openness to Values item "I believe that the 'new morality' of permissiveness is no morality at all" is becoming dated. A review of items for content that would be inconsistent with the requirements of the Americans with Disabilities Act (ADA) found only a handful of questionable items, but at some point they might need to be changed. Any changes, of course, would be based on equivalence studies showing that the revised scales were essentially unchanged in mean levels and in construct validity.

Some test users—especially counselors and I/O psychologists with ADA concerns—may prefer an inventory that omits traits related to N. It would be possible to publish a four-factor version of the instrument to accommodate their concerns. Similarly, I/O psychologists guided by the findings of Barrick and Mount (1991) may want a scale that measures only C. Such abridged versions are currently available by special license.

Other changes would be more substantial. We have often been asked if the NEO–PI–R can be used with high school students or younger children. There is a growing body of evidence suggesting that the FFM itself is an appropriate model for the personality structure of children (John, Caspi, Robins, Moffitt, & Stouthamer-Loeber, 1994; Mervielde, Buyst, & DeFruyt, 1995), and that the five factors can be linked to traditional temperament variables (Halverson, Kohnstamm, & Martin, 1994). However, studies to date have not used the NEO–PI–R to measure the FFM in these age groups. Data from intellectually gifted sixth graders show that the NEO–FFI can be used without any adaptation in that special population

(Parker, in press). It seems likely, however, that an adapted version would be advisable for a more general adolescent population. Fairly extensive research would be needed to establish the equivalence of the adult and adolescent versions, compile age-appropriate norms, and determine the lower limits of the age range in which the questionnaire could be meaningfully used. It would also be useful to gather data on the validity of adult ratings of children using Form R of the NEO–PI–R.

Overall, the NEO–PI–R has about a sixth-grade reading level, but there are a few items, particularly in the Openness domain, that are more difficult (Schinka & Borum, 1994). Use of the NEO–PI–R with some populations, like prison inmates, can cause problems. One solution has been to offer definitions for difficult words (J. O. Casey, personal communication, August 5, 1992; Schinka & Borum, 1994). Ultimately, a simplified version of the inventory might be desirable.

Schmit, Ryan, Stierwalt, and Powell (1995) reported that the criterion-related validity of NEO–PI–R scales may be enhanced by altering the items to refer directly to the context of interest. Thus, in a study predicting grade point average, "I strive for excellence in everything I do" was changed to "I strive for excellence in everything I do at school" (Schmidt et al., 1995, p. 615). Their findings suggest that a series of inventories might be desirable, each geared to a particular setting. A simpler alteration would be to leave the items unchanged and change the instructions to the respondents, requesting that they describe themselves as they are at work, at school, with their spouse, and so on. Schmit et al. reported that these kinds of alterations leave structural properties of the test intact, but affect mean levels. Thus, research would be needed to establish appropriate norms for each different adaptation.

THE ADAPTABLE COMPUTER

An obstacle to all these changes is the inertia of printed materials. Constructing and double-checking a profile sheet to present specialized norms is a tedious business, and may well not be cost-effective if the number of potential users is small. Likewise, modifying items, even item order, in a printed item booklet is expensive. By contrast, it is relatively easy to alter software by typing in new means and standard deviations; this might even be made into an option for users who wish to heed the familiar advice to use local norms. Customized software versions of the NEO–PI–R are a realistic possibility within the next 5 years.

The NEO Software System already provides a wide range of features that are not directly or easily available to users of the hand-scored version: It calculates orthogonal factor scores, examines a variety of validity indicators, and can compare self-report and observer rating profiles for an individual, pointing out specific areas of agreement and disagreement. In the future it might offer a glossary with definitions of difficult terms; it might even assess age and reading level and choose an appropriate version of the inventory to administer. Adaptive testing (Waller & Reise, 1989), in which items are chosen to maximize accuracy and efficiency, is also a possibility with computer administration.

It is hardly a novelty to say that the technology of the future is computer-based, and that the pace of technological change is accelerating. Psychological assessors who are themselves high in Openness to Experience are likely to enjoy the next decade. For those who are less open, it is perhaps reassuring to recall that human nature itself does not change so rapidly—if at all. The five factors of personality will remain among the objects of psychological assessment for the rest of our professional lifetimes.

ACKNOWLEDGMENT

We thank Lewis R. Goldberg for providing the data analyses reported in Table 1 and for valuable comments on the article.

REFERENCES

Barrick, M. R., & Mount, M. K. (1991). The Big Five personality dimensions and job performance: A meta-analysis. *Personnel Psychology, 44,* 1–26.

Ben-Porath, Y. S., & Waller, N. G. (1992). Five big issues in clinical personality assessment: A rejoinder to Costa and McCrae. *Psychological Assessment, 4,* 23–25.

Borkenau, P., & Ostendorf, F. (1992). Social desirability scales as moderator and suppressor variables. *European Journal of Personality, 6,* 199–214.

Costa, P. T., Jr., & McCrae, R. R. (1980). Still stable after all these years: Personality as a key to some issues in adulthood and old age. In P. B. Baltes & O. G. Brim Jr. (Eds.), *Life span development and behavior* (pp. 65–102). New York: Academic.

Costa, P. T., Jr., & McCrae, R. R. (1985). *The NEO Personality Inventory manual.* Odessa, FL: Psychological Assessment Resources.

Costa, P. T., Jr., & McCrae, R. R. (1989). *The NEO–PI/NEO–FFI manual supplement.* Odessa, FL: Psychological Assessment Resources.

Costa, P. T., Jr., & McCrae, R. R. (1992). *Revised NEO Personality Inventory (NEO–PI–R) and NEO Five-Factor Inventory (NEO–FFI) professional manual.* Odessa, FL: Psychological Assessment Resources.

Costa, P. T., Jr., & McCrae, R. R. (1995). Domains and facets: Hierarchical personality assessment using the Revised NEO Personality Inventory. *Journal of Personality Assessment, 64,* 21–50.

Dicken, C. (1963). Good impression, social desirability, and acquiescence as suppressor variables. *Educational and Psychological Measurement, 23,* 699–720.

Digman, J. M. (1990). Personality structure: Emergence of the five-factor model. *Annual Review of Psychology, 41,* 417–440.

Goldberg, L. R. (1992). The development of markers for the Big-Five factor structure. *Psychological Assessment, 4,* 26–42.

Goldberg, L. R., & Kilkowski, J. M. (1985). The prediction of semantic consistency in self-descriptions: Characteristics of persons and of terms that affect the consistency of responses to synonym and antonym pairs. *Journal of Personality and Social Psychology, 48,* 82–98.

Halverson, C. F., Kohnstamm, G. A., & Martin, R. P. (Eds.). (1994). *The developing structure of temperament and personality from infancy to adulthood.* Hillsdale, NJ: Lawrence Erlbaum Associates, Inc.

Hough, L. M., Eaton, N. K., Dunnette, M. D., Kamp, J. D., & McCloy, R. A. (1990). Criterion-related validities of personality constructs and the effect of response distortion on those validities. *Journal of Applied Psychology, 75,* 581–595.

John, O. P., Caspi, A., Robins, R. W., Moffitt, T. E., & Stouthamer-Loeber, M. (1994). The "little five": Exploring the nomological network of the five-factor model of personality in adolescent boys. *Child Development, 65,* 160–178.

McCrae, R. R., & Costa, P. T., Jr. (1983). Social desirability scales: More substance than style. *Journal of Consulting and Clinical Psychology, 51,* 882–888.

McCrae, R. R., Costa, P. T., Jr., Dahlstrom, W. G., Barefoot, J. C., Siegler, I. C., & Williams, R. B., Jr. (1989). A caution on the use of the MMPI K-correction in research on psychosomatic medicine. *Psychosomatic Medicine, 51,* 58–65.

McCrae, R. R., & John, O. P. (1992). An introduction to the five-factor model and its applications. *Journal of Personality, 60,* 175–215.

Mervielde, I., Buyst, V., & DeFruyt, F. (1995). The validity of the Big-Five as a model for teachers' ratings of individual differences among children aged 4–12 years. *Personality and Individual Differences, 18,* 525–534.

Parker, W. D. (in press). An empirical typology of perfectionism. *American Educational Research Journal.*

Paulhus, D. L., Bruce, M. N., & Trapnell, P. D. (1995). Effects of self-presentation strategies on personality profiles and their structure. *Personality and Social Psychology Bulletin, 21,* 100–108.

Piedmont, R. L., & McCrae, R. R. (1996). *Are validity scales valid in volunteer samples? Evidence from self-reports and observer ratings.* Unpublished manuscript, Loyola College, Maryland.

Schinka, J. A., & Borum, R. (1994). Readability of normal personality inventories. *Journal of Personality Assessment, 62,* 95–101.

Schmit, M. J., Ryan, A. M., Stierwalt, S. L., & Powell, A. B. (1995). Frame-of-reference effects on personality scale scores and criterion-related validity. *Journal of Applied Psychology, 80,* 607–620.

Stein, L. A. R., Graham, J. R., & Williams, C. L. (1995). Detecting fake-bad MMPI–A profiles. *Journal of Personality Assessment, 65,* 415–427.

Waller, N. G., & Reise, S. P. (1989). Computerized adaptive personality assessment: An illustration with the Absorption scale. *Journal of Personality and Social Psychology, 57,* 1051–1058.

7

Future Directions for the MMPI–A: Research and Clinical Issues

Robert P. Archer

Department of Psychiatry
Eastern Virginia Medical School

The Minnesota Multiphasic Personality Inventory–Adolescent (MMPI–A; Butcher et al., 1992), released in 1992, was developed specifically for use with adolescent respondents. The purpose of this article is to offer suggestions concerning 6 areas of productive research with this instrument. These areas include studies of the utility of codetype interpretation, issues related to profile elevation in clinical samples, and the identification of criterion for evaluating the usefulness of traditional and new MMPI–A scales. Further, these research issues also include establishing the optimal age ranges for use with the MMPI–A, detecting the effects of the release of a revised instrument on clinician's test use patterns with adolescents, and evaluating the optimal methods for the use of the MMPI–A Structural Summary interpretative approach. It is noted that these research recommendations are by no means exhaustive, and that many other research areas should also be investigated in developing a comprehensive research literature for this revised instrument.

The Minnesota Multiphasic Personality Inventory–Adolescent (MMPI–A; Butcher et al., 1992), a revision of the original MMPI, was released in 1992 and designed specifically for use with adolescent respondents. The developers of the MMPI–A had the benefit of being able to examine and review the results of numerous decisions reached by the MMPI–2 Restandardization Committee ranging from important methodological issues in the development of uniform T-score transformation procedures and content scales to pragmatic topics including the placement of new scales on the MMPI–2 profile sheets. Similar to the objectives in creating the MMPI–2, a concerted effort was made to develop the MMPI–A through retaining the most useful and productive aspects of the original test instrument while also improving on several less desirable features of the MMPI. Thus, the instrument length was reduced from 556 to 478 items, and 70 items were revised or modified to simplify wording or to improve the relevance of items to adolescent life

97

experiences. For example, the item, "I liked school" was modified for the MMPI–A to, "I like school," and "In school my marks in deportment were quite regularly bad" was modified to appear as "In school my grades in classroom behavior (conduct) are quite regularly bad." In addition, a variety of new items not in the original MMPI item pool were incorporated into the MMPI–A to provide coverage of topics relevant for adolescents, including, "Sometimes I use laxatives so I won't gain weight," "My parents do not really love me," and "I am often upset by things that happen in school."

Contemporary normative data were collected for the MMPI–A based on the responses of 815 girls and 805 boys from geographically and ethnically diverse groups. The creation of these contemporary adolescent norms offered the potential to resolve the pervasive confusion spanning several decades, concerning the most appropriate norms to use in interpreting adolescent MMPI profiles. A set of 6 supplementary and 15 content scales were created and selected for the MMPI–A that held the promise of encouraging special scale research with adolescent populations. With the exception of the MAC scale (MacAndrew, 1965), MMPI special scales had received scant research attention in adolescent populations and interpretive recommendations for this age group were based almost exclusively on clinical lore rather than empirical findings. A comprehensive MMPI–A manual was created that provided substantial information on the reliability and validity of this new instrument, as well as extensive MMPI–A data from normative and clinical samples (Butcher et al., 1992). Several sources of overview and recommendations concerning interpretive practice have been provided for the MMPI–A, including Archer (1992b, 1994, 1997), Archer and Krishnamurthy (1996a), Archer, Krishnamurthy, and Jacobson (1994), Butcher and Williams (1992), and Williams, Butcher, Ben-Porath, and Graham (1992). In addition, possible directions for future MMPI–A research were identified by Archer (1992a) and methodological issues in conducting research with various forms of the MMPI, including the MMPI–A, were recently offered by Butcher, Graham, and Ben-Porath (1995).

Following the substantial amount of resources, time, and effort invested in the development of the MMPI–A, a balanced and comprehensive evaluation of the utility of this instrument will require an extended period of investigation that will undoubtedly take us into the 21st century. The purpose of this article is to update and expand the earlier discussion by Archer (1992a) to offer some suggestions concerning specific areas that may be productive in terms of this systematic evaluation. These topic areas include the following issues:

1. The utility of the codetype interpretation approach.
2. Issues related to MMPI–A profile elevation.
3. The evaluation of traditional and new MMPI–A scales.
4. Optimal age ranges for use with the MMPI–A.
5. Effects of the MMPI–A on clinicians' test use patterns.
6. The MMPI–A Structural Summary interpretive approach.

CODETYPE INTERPRETATION APPROACH

Evaluating the utility of the codetype interpretation approach for the MMPI–A requires consideration of at least three overlapping issues. These issues may be defined as the generalizability of adolescent codetype literature derived with the original form of the MMPI to the MMPI–A, the adequacy of this original literature as related to the MMPI–A, and the need for development of a new codetype literature specifically based on the revised test instrument.

The issue of codetype congruence is centrally involved in the discussion of the generalizability of the adolescent codetype literature to the MMPI–A, that is, the degree to which the accumulated MMPI literature on adolescents developed over the past 50 years is relevant and applicable to interpretation of the MMPI–A. Although the MMPI–A and the MMPI are not psychometrically equivalent forms, these instruments do share substantial psychometric overlap and a common heritage. As reported in the MMPI–A manual, the 2-point codetype congruence rates found between the MMPI and the MMPI–A for all adolescents in the normative sample was 67.8% for males and 55.8% for females, and 69.5% for males and 67.2% for females in the clinical sample (Butcher et al., 1992). However, Butcher et al. (1995) recommended that both congruence studies and correlate studies be restricted to those participants producing relatively well-defined MMPI profiles. Definition, in this context, refers to the difference between the T-score value on the lowest scale employed in a particular codetype grouping, and the next highest clinical scale in the profile. For example, the definition found for a 2-point code would be the T-score difference found between the second and third most elevated basic scale in the MMPI profile. Butcher et al. (1995) suggested that T-score differences of less than 5 points should be considered inadequate in terms of definition for meaningful analysis. If we restrict the 2-point codetype classification of adolescents reported from the MMPI–A manual to a minimum of 5 points (a procedure that results in exclusion of roughly 80% of the participants in the normative sample and 68% of participants in the clinical sample), the congruence rates for remaining protocols increase to 95.2% for male and 81.8% for female adolescents in the normative sample, and roughly 95% for boys and girls in the clinical sample (Butcher et al., 1992). These congruence data are quite similar to the 2-point codetype congruence rates reported between the MMPI and MMPI–2 for normal and clinical samples for adults. These data, in turn, would suggest that the congruence rate between the original form of the MMPI and the MMPI–A is adequate to permit the generalizability of findings from the original test form to the MMPI–A to the extent that such findings are useful and valid.

A critical component of the extensive literature developed on the original form of the MMPI with adolescents consists of the contributions of Marks, Seeman, and Haller (1974), who developed actuarial-based personality descriptors for 29 two-point MMPI codetypes. The main participant pool utilized by Marks et al. in developing these codetype descriptors involved 834 adolescents between the ages of 12 and 18 who had received at least 10 hr of psychotherapy. A detailed description of the methodological procedures used in this codetype correlate study are presented in Marks et al. (1974) and in Archer (1987, 1992b). In addition to the codetype correlates reported by Marks et al., several investigators conducted research on the clinical correlates of single or individual MMPI scales, including Hathaway and Monachesi's (1963) investigation of approximately 15,000 Minnesota adolescents in school settings in the late 1940s and 1950s; the work of Archer, Gordon, Giannetti, and Singles (1988) and Archer, Gordon, Anderson, and Giannetti (1989) in samples of adolescent inpatients; and the research by Williams and Butcher (1989a) in a sample composed predominantly of adolescent substance abusers.

Despite the fact that 2-point codetypes have been the basis of MMPI interpretation for both adults and adolescents, there is not unanimous agreement concerning the suitability of 2-point codetype interpretation for the MMPI–A. Although Marks et al. (1974) reported a richly correlated literature associated with adolescents' 2-point codes produced by adolescents in clinical settings, Williams and Butcher (1989b) found surprisingly few significant correlates associated with 2-point codes on the original form of the MMPI. Therefore, one of the fundamental questions to be answered concerning the MMPI–A involves the applicability of 2-point codetype interpretation in deriving accurate descriptors associated with adolescents' profiles. In this regard, Janus, Tolbert, Calestro, and Toepfer (1996) recently investigated the accuracy of MMPI–A codetype narratives in a sample of 134 adolescent psychiatric inpatients. The single and 2-point codetype narratives generated for each patient, from two sets of adolescent norms as well as one set of adult norms, were blindly rated along various accuracy dimensions by inpatient treatment staff. Results indicated that the MMPI–A produced higher accuracy ratings when codetype narratives were based on either the original set of adolescent norms developed by Marks and Briggs (1972) or standard MMPI–A adolescent norms than when adult K-corrected norms were used to generate codetype narratives. The study by Janus et al. is an important initial step in establishing the clinical utility of codetype interpretation with the MMPI–A.

Issues about the generalizability and applicability of the adolescent literature on the original MMPI underscore the need for new correlate research based directly on the MMPI–A and conducted in a variety of clinical settings. Unfortunately, although this research objective is relatively easy to propose, it will likely prove to be quite difficult to fulfill. As noted by Butcher et al. (1995), any reasonably comprehensive study of MMPI codetypes requires the participation of several thousand participants. The collection of adolescent MMPI data has never been an easy task and very few large-scale adolescent samples have been collected in the past 55 years. Adolescents, particularly adolescents who receive MMPI evaluations, are seldom known for their cooperative, patient, and compliant features. In addition to issues related to characteristics of adolescent psychopathology, more recent factors related to increasingly stringent informed consent procedures and escalating restrictions on psychological assessment associated with the economics of managed care may converge to further inhibit the development of a large-scale adolescent database of the type necessary for the evaluation of codetype correlates. Thus, although the ultimate resolution of the applicability of the 2-point codetype interpretation of adolescent's profiles may rest on the development of a MMPI–A correlate literature, such a codetype correlate literature is not likely to be forthcoming in the near future. Indeed, such a literature has been relatively slow in developing for the MMPI–2 (Archer, Griffin, & Aiduk, 1995).

ISSUES RELATED TO PROFILE ELEVATION

A second area of interest relates to the relatively low magnitude of MMPI–A basic scale T-score elevations that occur on this revised instrument. As noted by Archer (1984, 1987), normal range mean profiles for adolescent populations were often found on the original form of the MMPI, leading to the recommendation by Ehrenworth and Archer (1985) that T-scale values ≥ 65 be employed as the demarcation point for defining clinical range elevations when using the Marks and Briggs (1972) adolescent norms. Archer, Pancoast, and Klinefelter (1989) found that a reduction of the clinical scale T-score value from 70 to 65 to define clinical levels of symptomatology resulted in increases in test sensitivity in accurately identifying profiles produced by normal adolescents versus adolescents receiving treatment in inpatient and outpatient clinical settings. The tendency of the MMPI–A to produce even lower T scores for a given raw score value, in comparison with findings from the original MMPI using Marks and Briggs (1972) adolescent norms, may be directly related to the changes in the MMPI basic scale means and standard deviations between the two normative samples. Archer (1992b, 1997) illustrated this issue in presenting a comparison of MMPI profile elevations produced for a group of 1,032 female and 730 male adolescent psychiatric patients profiled on the traditional Marks and Briggs (1972) norms and on the MMPI–A adolescent norms. Profiles based on the MMPI–A norms were consistently lower than the original adolescent norms across all basic scales, with the MMPI–A basic scale mean T-score elevations uniformly below 60. Indeed, approximately 30% of these teenagers produced Within-Normal-Limits individual profiles defined as profiles containing no basic clinical scale T-score elevation ≥ 60. These data indicate that the MMPI–A may have significant limitations, in terms of test sensitivity, in accurately detecting the presence of significant psychopathology among adolescents.

Recently, Alperin, Archer, and Coates (1996) examined the effectiveness of a K-correction factor for the MMPI–A as a potential method of increasing test sensitivity. Specifically, the authors used the MMPI–A normative sample of 1,620 adolescents and a clinical sample of 122 adolescent inpatients to empirically develop K-weights for the MMPI–A basic scales (excluding Mf and Si) to permit the optimal prediction of normal versus clinical status for each of the eight basic clinical scales. Hit rate analyses were used to assess the degree to which K-corrected uniform T scores resulted in improvements in classification accuracy, in contrast to the standard MMPI–A non-K-corrected norms, defined in terms of accurate placement of profiles into the normative and clinical groups. Results from this study indicated that the adoption of a K-correction procedure for the MMPI–A did not result in any systematic improvement in test accuracy, and these findings did not appear to support the clinical use of a K-correction factor in interpreting MMPI–A protocols. An additional issue addressed in this study, however, concerned the relative efficacy of applying a T-score value ≥ 60 versus $T \geq 65$ as the criterion in defining MMPI–A clinical range elevations when using the standard MMPI–A norms. This latter question stems, in part, from the presence of the transitional or "gray" zone on the MMPI–A profile sheets ($T = 60$ to $T = 65$, inclusive) that serve to define a marginal range of T-score elevation. In this investigation, criteria of $T \geq 65$ produced an overall hit rate of 70% accurate identification in contrast to a 57% hit rate with the $T \geq 60$ criteria, and the former criteria also produced a more effective balance between test sensitivity (71%) and specificity (70%). These results appear consistent with the recommendation contained in the MMPI–A manual that, "a clinically significant elevation is defined as an MMPI–A T-score ≥ 65" (Butcher et al., 1992, p. 43). More research is clearly needed, however, on the important issue of the relatively low profile elevations found for the MMPI–A.

EVALUATION OF TRADITIONAL AND NEW SCALES

The developers of the MMPI–A attempted to maintain as much consistency with the original instrument as possible, and, therefore, the standard traditional clinical scales were retained with extensive item deletions limited to scales Mf and $Si,$ and extensive item composition changes occurring only for the F scale. Given the relatively limited changes in item composition for most of the MMPI–A basic scales, it would appear very unlikely that the external correlates for these clinical scales have changed substantially. Research findings by Archer and Gordon (1994) and by Williams, Ben-Porath, and Hevern (1994) further support this view by demonstrating that the minor revisions of the MMPI–A basic scale item pool did not result in significant psychometric changes in the response patterns to these items. However, the MMPI–A also includes many new scales including 15 content scales, 3 new supplementary scales, 3 Si subscales and 4 new validity scales that do not have direct counterparts on the original form of the MMPI. These new measures, particularly those MMPI–A scales that do not have direct counterparts on the MMPI–2, will require on-going validity studies in a variety of clinical populations to establish the correlate meaning of these measures.

It is clear that significant gender differences occur in item endorsement patterns of adolescents, and these differences have been reflected in separate *T*-score conversions from male and female respondents in the MMPI–A norms. For example, boys produce higher mean raw score values than girls on the *MAC–R* and *IMM* supplementary scales. The degree to which gender differences may occur in correlate patterns is currently unclear, however, and research attention should also be focused on this topic. There is a broader question, however, concerning what criterion should be standardly employed in determining whether these new scales meaningfully contribute to the MMPI–A and what criterion should be used in determining whether to create additional new scales for the MMPI–2 or MMPI–A.

Butcher et al. (1995) suggested the importance of establishing incremental validity as a means of evaluating the utility of new MMPI–2 or MMPI–A scales. Specifically, Butcher et al. recommended that data must be presented demonstrating that the new scale adds significantly to the prediction of relevant behaviors beyond levels that can be accomplished by using existing and more familiar scales or indices. Using these criterion, for example, Butcher et al. cited research findings by Ben-Porath, Butcher, and Graham (1991) supporting the use of the MMPI–2 Depression and Bizarre Mentation content scales in successfully discriminating between patients receiving diagnoses of schizophrenia and major affective disorder. Butcher et al. (1995) also noted the report by Timbrook, Graham, Keiller, and Watts (1993) concerning the apparent failure of the subtle-obvious subscales to incrementally add to the standard validity scales in the detection of individuals malingering on the MMPI–2. Pursuing this criterion for the evaluation of new scales, Archer, Elkins, Aiduk, and Griffin (1995) recently examined the incremental validity of the MMPI–2 supplementary scales in a sample of 597 adult psychiatric patients using external measures composed of other self-report instruments (including the Symptom Checklist–90–Revised) and clinician's ratings of psychopathology. MMPI–2 basic and supplementary scale data were examined through a series of hierarchical regression analyses to statistically evaluate the degree to which the supplementary scales provided incremental contributions in the prediction of variance on outcome measures. Similar research was also conducted on the same sample for the MMPI–2 content scales by Archer, Aiduk, Griffin, and Elkins (1996). These researchers concluded that the MMPI–2 supplementary and content scales generally increased, albeit modestly, the amount of variance accounted for in external criterion variables. These types of incremental validity studies also should be undertaken with the MMPI–A because, as noted by Butcher et al. (1995), incremental validity studies based on the MMPI–2 are not necessarily generalizable across settings or populations. However, a fundamental issue to be resolved in this type of research concerns the degree or relative proportion of incremental gain that should be established for a new scale in order to demonstrate efficacy. For example, in the recent incremental validity studies by Archer and his colleagues, the inclusion of MMPI–2 supplementary and content scale data to equations based on the MMPI–2 basic scales generally resulted in quite limited incremental increases, often averaging about 1% of variance in prediction to individual SCL–90–R variables and approximately 5% for clinician rating variables. Although these incremental gains met the standard statistical criterion for significance, contributions this small may or may not reflect the addition of clinically meaningful amounts of information to levels achieved solely by the MMPI–2 basic scales.

OPTIMAL AGE GROUPS

The issue of the age groups most suitable for the MMPI–A administration was subject to substantial debate within the MMPI Adolescent Project Committee, with the eventual decision to recommend the use of the instrument with adolescents ages 14 through 18, inclusive. Given that the normative samples for both the MMPI–2 and the MMPI–A include 18-year-olds, however, individuals in this age group could be potentially evaluated using either instrument. The general guideline for test selection provided in the MMPI–A Manual (Butcher et al., 1992) is to recommend the use of the MMPI–A in evaluation of adolescents living in a dependent environment (e.g., living at home and attending high school) and to employ the MMPI–2 with those adolescents who are in college, employed, or otherwise leading a more independent adult lifestyle. Although these guidelines are likely to be useful in matching a large majority of adolescents to the most appropriate form, it seems possible that some 18-year-olds will be relatively difficult to place in terms of their suitability for the MMPI–A versus MMPI–2. For example, would the MMPI–A or the MMPI–2 be most appropriate with an 18-year-old female adolescent who is attending high school while raising a 6-month-old infant and living at home with her parents?

Shaevel and Archer (1996) recently undertook an examination of the profile elevation and configuration effects of scoring 18-year-old respondents on MMPI–2 and MMPI–A norms. A series of comparisons were conducted to evaluate the degree to which identical raw scores produced similar or dissimilar T scores on both instruments, and the MMPI–A protocols of 50 18-year-olds were rescored on MMPI–2 non-K-corrected norms. Results indicated that substantial differences can occur as a result of the selection of test instrument for 18-year-olds. In general, the MMPI–2 produced lower validity scale T-score values and higher clinical scale T scores for given raw score values than the MMPI–A. These differences were found to range as large as 15 T-score points and resulted in different single scale and 2-point profiles in 34% of the cases examined in this investigation. Although more research is clearly needed on this topic, these findings indicate that the clinician's selection of MMPI instruments has important implications in terms of profile features obtained for 18-year-olds. Given this observation, a conservative recommendation would be to profile and compare the MMPI–A and MMPI–2 normative values for 18-year-olds in those relatively rare assessment situations in which the selection of the MMPI–A versus the MMPI–2 appears to be a difficult or arbitrary decision.

At the other end of the adolescent age spectrum, although the MMPI–A norms do not include adolescents below age 14, the MMPI–A manual notes that this test instrument may be administered to bright and mature adolescents as young as 12 and 13 years old. Because notable maturational differences are found between boys and girls in this age group, a relevant issue for future research concerns the degree to which gender differences may differentially affect the capacity of 12- and 13-year-old adolescents to respond meaningfully to the MMPI–A. Questions also remain, however, concerning the best way to assess whether 12-and 13-year-olds are suitable for MMPI–A administration. The original form of the MMPI required a substantial amount of cognitive maturation and reading ability for successful administration. A comprehensive evaluation recently reported by Dahlstrom, Archer, Hopkins, Jackson, and Dahlstrom (1994) indicated that the MMPI–2 and MMPI–A revisions of the original instrument did not substantially lower these administration requirements, and the average item difficulty level for all three forms of the MMPI was approximately the sixth-grade level. Both Archer (1992b) and Dahlstrom et al. (1994) have recommended administering a reading test prior to the MMPI–A when adolescents' reading comprehension is questionable, and/or requiring the respondent to read aloud and explain a sample of the more difficult items in the test booklet. Further, the *Variable Response Inconsistency* scale (*VRIN*) and *True Response Inconsistency* scale (*TRIN*), particularly *VRIN*, should prove useful in terms of detecting adolescents with inadequate reading or comprehension skills in order to meaningfully respond to the MMPI–A. Additionally, reading comprehension difficulties might be identified by the use of two experimental scales for the MMPI–A, the Items-Easy (*Ie*) and Items-Difficult (*Id*) scales developed by Krakauer, Archer, and Gordon (1993).

The *Ie* and *Id* measures are 13-item scales that contain items similar in endorsement frequency in the MMPI–A normative sample, but different in terms of reading level difficulty. By comparing the difference in raw score values between these scales, the clinician can potentially identify adolescents with deficient reading ability (*Id* > *Ie*), particularly when used in conjunction with other validity scales such as the *VRIN* scale. For example, elevated scores on the *VRIN* scale may, in combination with an acceptable difference between the *Id* and *Ie* scales (*Id* – *Ie* ≤ 1) denote a random response pattern produced by a noncooperative adolescent, whereas elevated *VRIN* scale scores in combination with elevated endorsement of the *Id* scale items in contrast to *Ie* scale items may represent a well-intentioned but deficient reader.

Overall, much more validity research is needed concerning the crucial issues of the qualifications and characteristics necessary for an adolescent to successfully complete the MMPI–A and the optimal means of detecting adolescents with significant reading deficits. Although the vast majority of validity scale research has been focused on adult populations, this issue is particularly crucial with adolescent respondents because both motivational and literary issues are particularly relevant to this age group.

CLINICIAN'S TEST USE PRACTICES

Another important issue involves the impact of the release of the MMPI–A on the test use patterns of clinicians working with adolescent clients. Archer, Maruish, Imhof, and Piotrowski (1991) conducted a national survey on the use of assessment instruments with adolescents and found that the original form of the MMPI was the third most frequently mentioned test instrument (after the Wechsler scales and the Rorschach), and was ranked sixth in frequency of psychological test usage with adolescents. These findings serve to establish a baseline from which to evaluate the effects of the MMPI–A on clinicians' practices in future surveys. For example, release of the MMPI–A may have increased the utilization of this test with adolescents because the revised instrument is perceived by clinicians as more relevant to the assessment of teenagers than the original form. Further, the release of the MMPI–A was also accompanied by the development of several computer-based test interpretation packages for this instrument that may have the effect of facilitating the use of the instrument by a broad range of clinicians.

On the other hand, the development of a separate form of the MMPI specifically for use with adolescents also resulted in increased clinician costs for test materials, scoring keys, computerized interpretation programs, and associated materials and products. Many clinicians, particularly those who only occasionally assess adolescent clients, may unfortunately elect to forego the use of the MMPI–A because of the additional expense associated with this instrument. Financial concerns may also become increasingly salient for clinicians as the effects of managed care decrease the reimbursement dollars available for many forms of psychological assessment. It should also be noted, however, that the decreasing reimbursement for psychological assessment may also serve to increase the utilization of the MMPI–A, in contrast to other instruments, because it provides a standardized method of assessing adolescents along a wide variety of dimensions of psychopathology of direct relevance to diagnostic, treatment planning, and outcome assessment issues. Thus, as the traditional multiple instrument battery requiring several hours of administration time largely disappears as a result of managed care preauthorization requirements, the MMPI–A may be seen as a particularly important element to retain in testing practices because of its relative yield of clinically rich and comprehensive information within an acceptable cost to benefit framework.

The issue of the clinical and commercial success of the MMPI–A is not only relevant to the test publishers of the MMPI, but also to publishers of other successful instruments who may be faced with decisions concerning the costs and benefits of similar revision efforts. Additionally, the release of the MMPI–A also raises questions concerning the broader issues of the commercial, scientific, and clinical usefulness of the development of other specialized forms of the MMPI for populations that may have unique characteristics. For example, given evidence that aged populations respond to the MMPI in a manner that is different than adults or adolescents, would a geriatric form of the MMPI be appropriate for future development? Given the ongoing controversy concerning racial and ethnic differences on the MMPI, are there compelling arguments to be made in favor of the development of a specialized form of the MMPI for a specific minority group? Is a specialized form of the MMPI practical, in terms of both scientific and commercial factors, in personnel selection settings? Finally, if several specialized forms of the MMPI are eventually developed, is it reasonable to expect clinicians to develop an accompanying competence in these specialized instruments and to appreciate the often subtle differences in interpretive strategy that might occur between varying test forms?

MMPI–A STRUCTURAL SUMMARY

A final issue relates to the potential utility of the MMPI–A Structural Summary as a viable means of integrating and interpreting MMPI–A scale information. In comparison to the 13 standard scales typically used with adolescents on the original form of the MMPI, the MMPI–A presents a much larger number (i.e., 69) of standardly used scales and subscales that require careful integration of extensive information derived across three separate profile sheets. This interpretation process is further complicated by the observation that there are substantial intercorrelations between the MMPI–A basic and content scales (Butcher et al., 1992) and among the content scales (Archer 1992a). For example, data from the MMPI–A normative sample indicate that MMPI–A basic scale *Hs* is highly intercorrelated with the *A–hea* content scale ($r = .91$ for boys and $r = .90$ for girls), and scores from MMPI–A basic scale *Pt* are correlated .84 for boys and .89 for girls with scores derived from the *A–anx* scale. These pairs of scales appear to provide redundant information concerning the individuals' personality status and functioning.

In a recent factor-analytic study of the MMPI–A, eight scale-level factors were identified using a principal factor analysis procedure (Archer, Belevich, & Elkins, 1994). These eight factors were derived based on the MMPI–A normative sample of 1,620 adolescents, and have recently been replicated in a clinical sample of 358 adolescents (Archer & Krishnamurthy, 1996b). The eight factors were labeled *General Maladjustment, Immaturity, Disinhibition/Excitatory Potential, Social Comfort, Health Concerns, Naiveté, Familial Alienation,* and *Psychoticism*. The MMPI–A Structural Summary (Archer & Krishnamurthy, 1994) is organized around these factor groups and is, therefore, derived purely from empirical findings regarding the relationships between, and the underlying dimensions of, the MMPI–A scales.

The MMPI–A Structural Summary contains clusters of MMPI–A scales and subscales organized within the eight factor groupings. The scales subsumed under each factor cluster are organized logically in terms of basic scales, content scales, supplementary scales, and subscale groups. Within these subgroups, the scales appear in descending order from scales having the highest to the lowest correlation with the respective factors. The structural summary also presents spaces at the bottom of each factor grouping to derive the total number or percentage of scales that show critical values for a specific factor. Empirical correlates of the MMPI–A structural summary factors have been provided by Archer and Krishnamurthy (1994) based on data concerning salient behaviors, life events, and presenting problems obtained from the 1,620 adolescents in the MMPI–A normative sample and an inpatient sample of 122 adolescent respondents. A comprehensive presentation of all significant external correlates of the structural summary factors are also provided in Appendix C of the *MMPI–A Casebook* by Archer et al. (1994). Many questions remain, however, concerning the most effective manner in which to use the Structural Summary.

A major challenge is the identification of the optimum way to utilize Structural Summary data to allow for the most accurate prediction of adolescent behaviors and characteristics. For example, Archer and Krishnamurthy (1994) noted, on a logical and rational basis, that at least half of the scales and subscales associated with a particular factor should reach critical values before the interpreter emphasizes that dimension as salient in the adolescent's personality characteristics. Further, it also seems likely that examining the specific pattern of elevated scales or subscales within a factor grouping can be useful in refining the MMPI–A interpretation for that adolescent. For example, an adolescent may produce a pattern of scale and subscale elevations on the general maladjustment (Factor 1) dimension that highlights anxiety as the primary form of distress in contrast to alienation, depression, or other components of the first factor. An additional issue relates to the feasibility of developing a configural pattern approach to the interpretation of the Structural Summary dimensions that would be analogous to the configural interpretation approach as used in deriving specific diagnostic judgments and descriptive statements for the MMPI basic scales. For example, it is possible that conduct disorder symptomatology is best identified by co-occurring elevations on the dimensions or factors of Immaturity, Disinhibition/Excitatory Potential, and Familial Alienation, although internalizing or neurotic symptomatology might be best represented by co-elevations on the General Maladjustment and Social Discomfort dimensions. Another tactic for the development of configural analysis for the MMPI–A Structural Summary might be derived from the use of cluster analysis techniques to provide empirically based categories of substantial diagnostic and clinical utility. The use of carefully designed research studies in clinical settings should allow for an adequate evaluation of these, and other, issues related to the Structural Summary.

CONCLUSION

The developers of the MMPI–A have attempted to build an instrument worthy of the proud heritage associated with the original test instrument. The future popularity and clinical utility of the MMPI–A will be determined by the degree of systematic and focused research attention devoted to this instrument. This article provides some suggestions for six broad and applied areas that might prove useful in obtaining a greater understanding of the MMPI–A. This list, however, is in no way meant to be exhaustive and there are many other areas or aspects of the MMPI–A that warrant intensive and ongoing research attention. The MMPI–A will enter the 21st century with substantial promise and potential to the extent that researchers from many perspectives and orientations contribute to building the type of rich, empirical database that was so crucial in the development of the original test instrument.

REFERENCES

Alperin, J. J., Archer, R. P., & Coates, G. D. (1996). Development and effects of a *K*-correction procedure for the MMPI–A. *Journal of Personality Assessment, 67,* 155–168.

Archer, R. P. (1984). Use of the MMPI with adolescents: A review of salient issues. *Clinical Psychology Review, 4,* 241–251.

Archer, R. P. (1987). *Using the MMPI with adolescents.* Hillsdale, NJ: Lawrence Erlbaum Associates, Inc.

Archer, R. P. (1992a). Issues in the development and use of the MMPI–A. *SPA Exchange, 2,* 1–3, 12.

Archer, R. P. (1992b). *MMPI–A: Assessing adolescent psychopathology.* Hillsdale, NJ: Lawrence Erlbaum Associates, Inc.

Archer, R. P. (1994). The Minnesota Multiphasic Personality Inventory–Adolescent. In M. Maruish (Ed.), *Use of psychological testing for treatment planning and outcome assessment* (pp. 423–452). Hillsdale, NJ: Lawrence Erlbaum Associates, Inc.

Archer, R. P. (1997). *MMPI–A: Assessing adolescent psychopathology* (2nd ed.). Mahwah, NJ: Lawrence Erlbaum Associates, Inc.

Archer, R. P., Aiduk, R., Griffin, R., & Elkins, D. E. (1996). Incremental validity of the MMPI–2 content scales in a psychiatric sample. *Assessment, 3,* 79–90.

Archer, R. P., Belevich, J. K. S., & Elkins, D. E. (1994). Item-level and scale-level factor structures of the MMPI–A. *Journal of Personality Assessment, 62,* 332–345.

Archer, R. P., Elkins, D. E., Aiduk, R., & Griffin, R. (1995). *The incremental validity of MMPI–2 supplementary scales.* Manuscript submitted for publication.

Archer, R. P., & Gordon, R. A. (1994). Psychometric stability of MMPI–A item modifications. *Journal of Personality Assessment, 62,* 416–426.

Archer, R. P., Gordon, R. A., Anderson, G. L., & Giannetti, R. (1989). MMPI special scale correlates for adolescent inpatients. *Journal of Personality Assessment, 53,* 654–664.

Archer, R. P., Gordon, R. A., Giannetti, R., & Singles, J. (1988). MMPI scale clinical correlates for adolescent inpatients. *Journal of Personality Assessment, 52,* 707–721.

Archer, R. P., Griffin, R., & Aiduk, R. (1995). MMPI–2 clinical correlates for ten common codes. *Journal of Personality Assessment, 65,* 391–407.

Archer, R. P., & Krishnamurthy, R. (1994). A structural summary approach for the MMPI–A: Development and empirical correlates. *Journal of Personality Assessment, 63,* 554–573.

Archer, R. P., & Krishnamurthy, R. (1996a). Minnesota Multiphasic Personality Inventory–Adolescent (MMPI–A). In C. S. Newmark (Ed.), *Major psychological assessment instruments* (Vol. 1, rev., pp. 59–107). Boston: Allyn & Bacon.

Archer, R. P., & Krishnamurthy, R. (1996b). *MMPI–A scale level factor structure: Replication in a clinical sample.* Manuscript submitted for publication.

Archer, R. P., Krishnamurthy, R., & Jacobson, J. M. (1994) *MMPI–A casebook.* Tampa, FL: Psychological Assessment Resources.

Archer, R. P., Maruish, M., Imhof, E. A., & Piotrowski, C. (1991). Psychological test usage with adolescent clients: 1990 survey findings. *Professional Psychology: Research and Practice, 22,* 247–252.

Archer, R. P., Pancoast, D. L., & Klinefelter, D. (1989). A comparison of MMPI code types produced by traditional and recent adolescent norms. *Psychological Assessment: A Journal of Consulting and Clinical Psychology, 1,* 23–29.

Ben-Porath, Y. S., Butcher, J. N., & Graham, J. R. (1991). Contribution of the MMPI–2 content scales to the differential diagnosis of schizophrenia and major depression. *Psychological Assessment: A Journal of Consulting and Clinical Psychology, 3,* 634–640.

Butcher, J. N., Graham, J. R., & Ben-Porath, Y. S. (1995). Methodological problems and issues in MMPI, MMPI–2 and MMPI–A research. *Psychological Assessment, 7,* 320–329.

Butcher, J. N., & Williams, C. L. (1992). *Essentials of MMPI–2 and MMPI–A Interpretation.* Minneapolis: University of Minnesota Press.

Butcher, J. N., Williams, C. L., Graham, J. R., Archer, R. P., Tellegen, A., Ben-Porath, Y. S., & Kaemmer, B. (1992). *MMPI–A (Minnesota Multiphasic Personality Inventory–Adolescent): Manual for administration, scoring, and interpretation.* Minneapolis: University of Minnesota Press.

Dahlstrom, W. G., Archer, R. P., Hopkins, D. G., Jackson, E., & Dahlstrom, L. E. (1994). *Assessing the readability of the Minnesota Multiphasic Personality Inventory Instruments—the MMPI, MMPI–2, MMPI–A* (MMPI–2/MMPI–A Test Reports No. 2). Minneapolis: University of Minnesota Press.

Ehrenworth, N. V., & Archer, R. P. (1985). A comparison of clinical accuracy ratings of interpretive approaches for adolescent MMPI responses. *Journal of Personality Assessment, 49,* 413–421.

Hathaway, S. R., & Monachesi, E. D. (1963). *Adolescent personality and behavior.* Minneapolis: University of Minnesota Press.

Janus, M. D., Tolbert, H., Calestro, K., & Toepfer, S. (1996). Clinical accuracy ratings of MMPI approaches for adolescents: Adding ten years and the MMPI–A. *Journal of Personality Assessment, 67,* 364–383.

Krakauer, S. Y., Archer, R. P., & Gordon, R. A. (1993). The development of the Items-Easy (*Ie*) and Items-Difficult (*Id*) scales for the MMPI–A. *Journal of Personality Assessment, 60,* 561–571.

MacAndrew, C. (1965). The differentiation of male alcoholic out-patients from nonalcoholic psychiatric patients by means of the MMPI. *Quarterly Journal of Studies on Alcohol, 26,* 238–246.

Marks, P. A., & Briggs, P. F. (1972). Adolescent norm tables for the MMPI. In W. G. Dahlstrom, G. S. Welsh, & L. E. Dahlstrom, *An MMPI handbook: Vol. 1. Clinical interpretation* (Rev. ed., pp. 388–399). Minneapolis: University of Minnesota Press.

Marks, P. A., Seeman, W., & Haller, D. L. (1974). *The actuarial use of the MMPI with adolescents and adults.* Baltimore: Williams & Wilkins.

Shaevel, B. S., & Archer, R. P. (1996). Effects of MMPI–2 and MMPI–A norms on T-score elevations for 18-year-olds. *Journal of Personality Assessment, 67,* 72–78.

Timbrook, R. E., Graham, J. R., Keiller, S. W., & Watts, D. (1993). Comparison of the Wiener–Harmon subtle-obvious scales and the standard validity scales in detecting valid and invalid MMPI–2 profiles. *Psychological Assessment, 5,* 53–61.

Williams, C. L., Ben-Porath, Y. S., & Hevern, B. W. (1994). Item level improvements for use of the MMPI with adolescents. *Journal of Personality Assessment, 63,* 284–293.

Williams, C. L., & Butcher, J. N. (1989a). An MMPI study of adolescents: I. Empirical validity of standard scales. *Psychological Assessment: A Journal of Consulting and Clinical Psychology, 1,* 251–259.

Williams, C. L., & Butcher, J. N. (1989b). An MMPI study of adolescents: II. Verification and limitations of code type classifications. *Psychological Assessment: A Journal of Consulting and Clinical Psychology, 1,* 260–265.

Williams, C. L., Butcher, J. N., Ben-Porath, Y. S., & Graham, J. R. (1992). *MMPI–A content scales: Assessing psychopathology in adolescents.* Minneapolis: University of Minnesota Press.

8

Prospects for the Assessment of Normal and Abnormal Interpersonal Behavior

Jerry S. Wiggins and Krista K. Trobst

Department of Psychology
University of British Columbia

The Interpersonal Adjective Scales (IAS) and the Inventory of Interpersonal Problems (IIP) are current representatives of a long-standing tradition and their use as assessment instruments is expected to become increasingly widespread in the near future and beyond. The IAS is a direct descendent of the interpersonal circumplex tradition and is characterized by an extraordinarily close relation between theory and method in the assessment of both normal and disordered personalities. The IIP stems from a more recent conceptual distinction between psychiatric symptoms and problems of living that has been linked directly to the interpersonal circumplex. This review is meant to alert clinicians to promising supplements to traditional intrapsychic and symptomatic psychodiagnostic batteries.

A decade or so ago, the *Journal of Personality Assessment* (*JPA*) published a symposium on "Interpersonal Circumplex Models: 1948–1983" (LaForge, Freedman, & Wiggins, 1985) dedicated to the late Editor, Walter Klopfer, that acknowledged "More articles dealing with the Interpersonal System have appeared in this *Journal* than in any other" (LaForge et al., 1985, p. 613). A decade or so later, *JPA* published a symposium on "The Legacy of Timothy Leary" (Strack, 1996) with contributions from the major figures associated with circumplex models during the last 30 years. That the present editors chose to include interpersonal circumplex measures in this Special Series is evidence of the uninterrupted support by *JPA* of a tradition whose future has not always been as bright as it appears to be today.

Future historians writing in *JPA*, 20 years hence, are likely to characterize the present era as one greatly concerned with structural models of dimensions of normal and abnormal behavior in general, and with the five-factor model (FFM) and interpersonal circumplex model (ICM) representations of these dimensions, in particular (e.g., Digman, 1990; Ozer & Reise, 1994; Wiggins & Pincus, 1992). The FFM has emphasized the dimensions of: (I) Surgency/Extraversion, (II) Agreeableness, (III) Conscientiousness, (IV) Neuroticism, and (V) Openness/Intellect; the ICM has emphasized the dimensions of: (a) Dominance, and (b) Nurturance.

The first two dimensions of the FFM are both substantively and empirically isomorphic with the two axes that define the ICM (McCrae & Costa, 1989; Trapnell & Wiggins, 1990). This overlap permits a convenient division of labor within a common "working model" (Wiggins, 1992) between those subscribing to factorial and circumplex models, and has led to fruitful considerations of the similarities and differences between these two representations (e.g., DeRaad, 1995; Hofstee, DeRaad, & Goldberg, 1992; Saucier, 1992; Wiggins & Trapnell, 1996). The NEO Personality Inventory–Revised is the most prominent test associated with the FFM tradition and it is described elsewhere in this Special Series (Costa & McCrae, this issue).

The Interpersonal Adjective Scales (IAS; Wiggins, 1995) and the Inventory of Interpersonal Problems (IIP; Horowitz, Rosenberg, Baer, Ureno, & Villasenor, 1988) are firmly rooted in the venerable ICM tradition and they are at the forefront of the current "back to basics" trend in the literature of personality structure and assessment that reaffirms the centrality of dispositional traits in both their adaptive and problematic manifestations (Wiggins & Pincus, 1992). The IAS consists of 64 trait-descriptive adjectives (e.g., "dominant") that respondents rate for self- or other- descriptive accuracy on an 8-point Likert scale. Responses are scored for eight categories of interpersonal traits (e.g., assured-dominant) that together form a circumplex around the coordinates of Dominance and Nurturance. The IIP consists of 127 statements of interpersonal problems (e.g., "I try to control other people too much") that respondents rate for self- or other- perceived degree of problematicity on a 5-point Likert scale. The circumplex version of this instrument (IIP–C; Alden, Wiggins, & Pincus, 1990) consists of 64 items that are scored for eight categories of interpersonal problems (e.g., domineering) that together form a circumplex around the coordinates of Dominance and Warmth.

INTERPERSONAL ADJECTIVE SCALES

Origins

The conceptual framework in which the IAS is embedded had its origins in five venerable research traditions, some of which span more than half a century: (a) the lexical tradition in personality (John, Angleitner, & Ostendorf, 1988), (b) the interpersonal theory tradition in clinical psychology and psychiatry (Kiesler, 1996), (c) the traditions of order and facet analysis (Guttman, 1966), (d) the social exchange and impression management traditions of both sociology and social psychology (Carson, 1969), and (e) the multivariate–trait tradition (Wiggins & Trapnell, 1997). As such, it has functioned both as an instrument for the psychological and clinical assessment of individuals and as a framework for integrating diverse concepts and measures from a variety of research traditions in personality, social, and clinical psychology.

Advances in Theory and Method

A distinctive feature of the IAS is the extraordinarily close relation between theory and method that has characterized that instrument from the outset. The boundaries between theory and measurement become indistinct in the geometric operationalization of concepts such as universe of content, interpersonal type, deviant disposition, similarity of persons, prototype, social exchange, and complementarity. This bidirectional influence between theory and method is also evident with respect to parameters of circumplex interpretation such as contexts, perspectives, levels of measurement, and levels of interpretations (Wiggins & Trobst, 1997). Thus, advances in conceptualization have given rise to suggested new measurement procedures, and advances in precision of measurement have served to clarify existing concepts.

Although it is now possible to provide a rigorous derivation of the interpersonal circumplex from the assumptions of a formal theory of social exchange, the original derivation of the model was more prosaic: "A close fought battle with empirical fact, not lofty considerations of logical symmetry, produced the sixteen categories. In the closing stages, the circle emerged" (LaForge, 1977, p. 8). The Interpersonal Check List (ICL; LaForge & Suczek, 1955) was a remarkable achievement for its time and perhaps only those old enough to recall the state of computers in the late 50s and early 60s can appreciate the methodological advances made during that time (e.g., LaForge, 1963). Later, using analytic procedures that now appear Jurassic in origin, Wiggins (1979) demonstrated that the variables of the ICL failed to meet certain circumplex criteria and that these criteria could best be met with truly bipolar variables within the metric of principal components analysis. It was also emphasized that the content of these bipolar variables and their interrelations were in accord with the facet-analytic formulations of social exchange proposed by Foa and Foa (1974). More recently, the IAS has been conceptualized within the broader theoretical context of the metaconcepts of agency and communion, with supportive evidence adduced from parallel constructs in evolutionary psychology, anthropology, sociology, and narrative life history, and with greater elaboration of the applications of social exchange theory and Sullivanian personality theory to the interpersonal paradigm (Wiggins & Trapnell, 1996).

Advances and Issues in Profile Analysis

The profiles associated with most objective tests of personality are convenient ways of displaying normative results obtained on component scales that have no natural ordering or conceptual significance. Thus the "conversion V" of the Minnesota Multiphasic Personality Inventory could have had a different form and been given a different label had the arbitrary ordering of scales been different (see Gurtman & Balakrishnan, 1994). In contrast, the IAS profile is an operationalization of a theory in which geometric relations among elements assume diagnostic significance. As a consequence, advances and issues in profile analysis have implications for both the construct validity and clinical utility of IAS and related instruments.

We will illustrate some of the major geometric/theoretical concepts of interpersonal assessment with reference to Figure 1, which presents the IAS profile of a 48-year-old female psychiatric inpatient who was diagnosed as Bipolar Mood Disorder, Depressive Phase. The details of this case are discussed elsewhere (Wiggins, 1995, pp. 29–32) and the present focus is on the concepts rather than their clinical significance in this particular instance.

At the bottom of Figure 1 are T scores ($M = 50$, $SD = 10$) computed with reference to an adult normative sample. The T score of 90 for the FG octant is four standard deviations (!) above the mean of the normative group. Although highly elevated, the circular profile in Figure 1 conforms generally to the characteristic configuration expected of IAS profiles. The principal elevation occurs on the defining octant (FG) with secondary elevations occurring on adjacent octants (DE, HI) and diminishing elevations to a truncated opposite octant (NO). The relative elevation of JK is a deviation from expected configuration. The mean directionality of the eight IAS vectors is an index of the overall angular location of this profile (239°) and serves to categorize this respondent as an "aloof-introverted" type. Within the FG octant, the angular location of this profile falls to the right of the prototype for this category (225°) suggesting "passive" rather than "hostile" introversion. It should be noted that the relatively highly elevated JK octant "pulls" the profile in such a direction. The arrow extending from the center of the circle to its periphery represents the vector length (VL) of this profile. VL is an index of "deviance," in both a statistical and a psychological sense. Statistically, VL is the standard deviation of scores on the eight-octant profile, expressed in T-score units (90). Psychologically, it is an index of the intensity with which a pattern of interpersonal behaviors is expressed (extreme social withdrawal).

There are a number of strong geometric and substantive assumptions involved when persons are assigned to the typological categories of the IAS and their profiles interpreted with reference to concepts such as characteristic configuration, angular location, interpersonal type, prototype, and vector length. Wiggins, Phillips, and Trapnell (1989) reported encouraging empirical support for several of the assumptions underlying these concepts. For example, they found that the characteristic configuration of IAS profiles remained the same for groups of respondents classified within each of the eight typological categories, despite the differing angular locations of profiles within each of the categories. This suggests that the principles of interpretation based on profile configuration are highly generalizable. Preliminary support was also found for the idea that IAS vector length is not a "general"

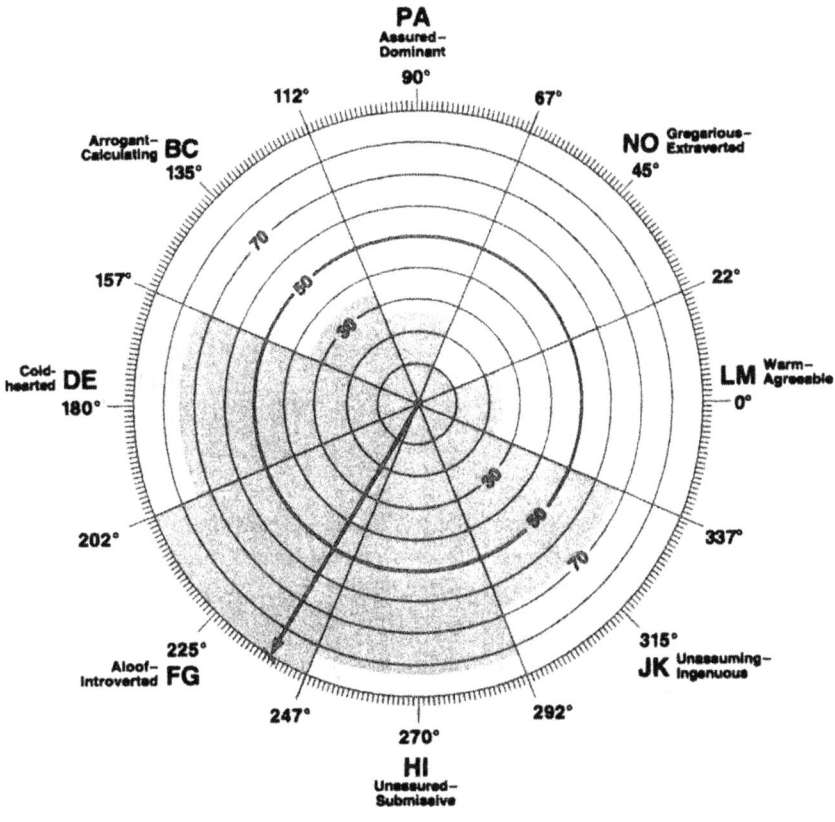

FIGURE 1 Illustrative Interpersonal Adjective Scale profile. Adapted and reproduced by special permission of the Publisher, Psychological Assessment Resources, Inc., Odessa, FL 33556, from the Interpersonal Adjective Scale–Revised by Jerry S. Wiggins, Ph.D., Copyright 1995 by PAR, Inc. Further reproduction is prohibited without permission from PAR, Inc.

measure of interpersonal problems, but rather an index of specific interpersonal problems associated with membership in a particular IAS typological category.

Although the characteristic configuration of IAS profiles is well established in groups of normal participants, it must be borne in mind that there are individual differences among participants in the extent to which this configuration holds and that such differences might have personological and/or pathological correlates.

Although it has not yet been systematically established, it would appear that deviations from characteristic configurations are much more prevalent in psychiatric populations and that such deviations may be related to concepts such as "conflict" and "ambivalence" (e.g., Kiesler, Van Denburg, Sikes-Nova, Larus, & Goldston, 1990). Gurtman (1994) developed an index of the "goodness of fit" of an interpersonal profile to any specified target profile and this index is likely to lead to a number of advances. For example, the index could be employed to assess the similarity of a given profile to normative prototypes of IAS types, to profiles of carefully diagnosed groups of patients (e.g., narcissistic personality disorder), or to any criterion group of interest.

Gurtman's profile matching procedures may be implemented with relatively available software, but it will be some time before this promising technique will be employed in clinical practice. On a brighter note, the recent availability of a commercial scoring program (Wiggins & PAR Staff, 1995) makes it possible for the clinician to obtain a profile of the kind illustrated in Figure 1 by one click of the mouse.

Applications of the IAS

General applications. Although the IAS was designed as a tool for the psychological and clinical assessment of individuals, and has proven useful in that context, the IAS circumplex has also been employed as a framework for elucidating concepts and measures from a variety of other research traditions. For example, Buss and his colleagues used their act frequency approach to specify concrete behaviors associated with IAS types (Buss & Craik, 1983), and employed this behavioral analysis to examine assortative mating (Buss, 1984) and manipulation tactics in close relationships (Buss, Gomes, Higgins, & Lauterbach, 1987). The IAS has also been employed in investigations of such topics as the constraints of agentic and communal situations on behavior (Moskowitz, 1994), complementarity (Wiggins, 1982), cross-cultural differences (Rosen, 1992), motivational orientations (Wiggins, 1980), Murray's needs (Wiggins & Broughton, 1985), nonverbal behaviors (Gifford, 1991), psychiatric diagnosis (Wiggins & Pincus, 1994), psychological androgyny (Wiggins & Holzmuller, 1978), social exchange (Wiggins & Trapnell, 1996), and the precise geometric classification of 172 scales currently used in personality, social, and clinical psychology (Wiggins & Broughton, 1991).

Assessment of personality disorders. From its inception, the interpersonal circumplex has been viewed as an alternative classification system for representing personality disorders as described in successive versions of the American Psychiatric Association's (APA) *Diagnostic and Statistical Manual of Mental Disorders* (*DSM–I;* APA, 1952; e.g., Leary, 1957), *DSM–II* (APA, 1968; e.g., Plutchik & Platman, 1977), and *DSM–III* (APA, 1980; e.g., Wiggins, 1982). This view was to some extent officially recognized in the third edition of *DSM* in which the personality disorders of Axis–II were defined in terms of maladaptive and inflexible *personality traits* (APA, 1987, p. 7). Wiggins (1987) was among the first to demonstrate the convergences among *DSM–III* conceptions of personality disorders and the normal personality dimensions of IAS. Subsequent investigations (e.g., Wiggins & Pincus, 1989) have served to clarify further the relations between Axis–II and the eight typological categories of IAS (Wiggins, 1995).

It is important to note that this recent line of investigation has been conducted within the larger framework of the FFM of personality, which provides additional information on the contribution to the classification of personality disorders of the normal personality dimensions of Conscientiousness, Emotional Stability, and Openness (Costa & McCrae, 1990; Wiggins & Pincus, 1994). A common emphasis on normal personality traits has resulted in a mutual recognition that the two models are complementary rather than competing: "The five-factor model provides a larger framework in which to orient and interpret the circumplex, and the interpersonal circle provides a useful elaboration about aspects of two of the five factors" (McCrae & Costa, 1989, p. 593). An alternative conceptual perspective is that the two factors of the interpersonal circumplex are relatively pure indicants of higher order factors, components of which can be identified in the remaining three factors of the FFM (Wiggins & Trapnell, 1996).

INVENTORY OF INTERPERSONAL PROBLEMS

Origins

The conceptual framework in which IIP is embedded had its origins in Horowitz's (1979) initial distinction between *symptoms* and *interpersonal problems.* The former (e.g., "I have difficulty sleeping") lack "an inherent conceptual organiza-tion" (Horowitz, 1979, p. 5) and may not be the principal focus of psychotherapeutic interventions. The latter (e.g., "It is hard for me to get close to people") were found to have an underlying structure "that matched the two interpersonal dimensions postulated by interpersonal theorists like Wiggins (1979) and Kiesler (1983)" (Horowitz et al., 1988, p. 888). The subsequent construction of a circumplex version of Horowitz's original instrument (IIP–C; Alden et al., 1990) confirmed the structural linkage with IAS, and the availability of two versions of the IIP increased its range of applicability. The IIP is a self-report inventory that "identifies system-atically the most common problems that people bring to treatment," specifies what "has been achieved through treatment," and helps to "differentiate between distress due to interpersonal problems and distress due to noninterpersonal problems" (Horowitz et al., 1988, p. 885). The IIP–C has the additional features of permitting the assignment of persons to typological categories and allowing the interpretation of individual profiles in the manner illustrated for IAS.

Advances in Theory and Method

Horowitz's conceptual approach to psychopathology rests on the fundamental distinctions made between: (a) interpersonal problems and interpersonal dispositions, (b) interpersonal problems and psychiatric symptoms, and (c) interpersonal distress and noninterpersonal distress (e.g., Horowitz & Vitkus, 1986; Horowitz, Weckler, & Doren, 1983). As operationalized by the IIP, interpersonal problems are interpersonal dispositions that are excessive (too much) or inhibited (too little; Pincus, 1994) and that are viewed by the respondent as distressing. Although Alden et al. (1990) found striking structural convergences between IIP–C and IAS, the precise nature of the relation between these two contexts of measurement is a topic worthy of further investigation (Wiggins & Trapnell, 1996; Wiggins & Trobst, 1997).

Horowitz and Vitkus (1986) defined a *symptom* (or syndrome) as a complex experience involving interrelated cognitive, affective, and interpersonal components. A *prototype* is a syndrome portrayed in abstract or idealized form (e.g., "lonely person") that may also be decomposed into thoughts ("Other people don't like me"), feelings ("I feel inadequate"), and interpersonal problems ("It is hard for me to make friends"). The distinction between interpersonal distress and noninterpersonal distress is operationalized in the comparison between mean scores on the IIP and mean scores on the Symptom Check List (SCL–90; Derogatis, 1977). These distinctions and the constructs that gave rise to them are embedded in the rich nomological network of interpersonal theory that permits, among other things, prediction of how "a person with a particular symptom (hence, particular interpersonal problems) tends to be drawn into particular interactions that actually sustain the symptom" (Horowitz & Vitkus, 1986, p. 444). The typology provided by the IIP–C has been shown to be congruent with the typologies developed within different conceptual frameworks such as Bowlby's (1973) attachment types (Bartholomew & Horowitz, 1991) and Weinberger's (1991) social-emotional adjustment types (Pincus & Boekman, 1995).

Advances and Issues in Profile Analysis

The major geometric/theoretical concepts of interpersonal problems assessment may be illustrated with reference to Figure 2, which presents the IIP–C profile of a 32-year-old male psychiatric outpatient who was seen for short-term intensive group psychotherapy. The details of this case are discussed elsewhere (Pincus & Wiggins, 1992, pp. 91–94) and the present focus will be on a comparison of concepts with those discussed earlier for the IAS (Figure 1).

At the bottom of Figure 2 are T scores ($M = 50$, $SD = 10$) computed with reference to an adult normative sample. The T score of 64 for the DE octant is approximately 1.5 standard deviations above the mean of the normative group.

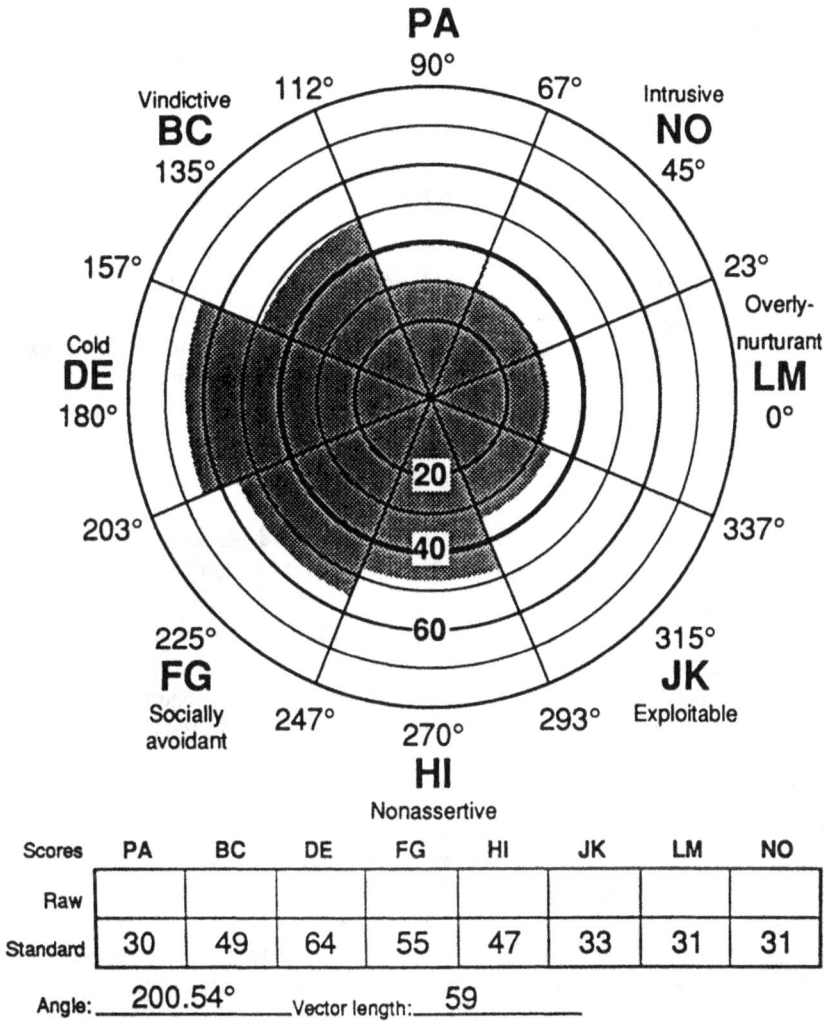

Scores	PA	BC	DE	FG	HI	JK	LM	NO
Raw								
Standard	30	49	64	55	47	33	31	31

Angle: __200.54°__ Vector length: __59__

FIGURE 2   Illustrative IIP–C profile. Reprinted from "An Expanded Perspective on Interpersonal Assessment," by A. L. Pincus and J. S. Wiggins, 1992, *Journal of Counseling and Development, 71*, p. 92. © ACA. Reprinted with permission. No further reproduction authorized without written permission of the American Counseling Association.

The profile itself is not highly elevated (vector length = 59) and it conforms reasonably well to the standard configuration expected of IIP–C profiles. The angular location of this profile (200°) categorizes this respondent as a "cold" type, but one falling very close to the boundary of the FG category of socially avoidant. Note that both the FG and HI (nonassertive) octants "pull" the profile in this direction.

The circumplexity of a set of interpersonal variables can also be evaluated graphically by plotting the correlations of each variable (ordinate) with the other variables arranged in sequence (abscissa) so that the variables appear as a set of overlapping cosine curves (Lorr & McNair, 1965; Stern, 1970; Wiggins, 1979). Gurtman (1993, 1994) recently formalized this method and developed computational procedures that allow for a useful alternative representation of interpersonal profiles. Within Gurtman's approach, the characteristic configuration of a profile is evaluated by the "best fit cosine curve" we discussed earlier. Angular location is indexed by "angle of displacement," which could also be used to evaluate distance from a prototype. Vector length is indexed by "amplitude of profile curve." Finally, Gurtman's index of "elevation" (mean level of profile) has no direct counterpart in traditional IAS circumplex profile analysis, but would appear to be especially applicable to the interpretation of IIP–C profiles, with which Gurtman has been mainly concerned.

In their factor analysis of earlier scales from the IIP, Horowitz et al. (1988) obtained a substantial "general factor" (loaded positively by all items and scales), which they interpreted as "a complaint factor, the patients' general tendency to report distress" (p. 888). A general factor was also found in the construction of IIP–C (Alden et al., 1990) and both groups of investigators 'ipsatized" their data sets prior to further analyses by expressing each participant's scale (or item) score as a deviation from that participant's mean score across all items. The interpretation of a general factor in circumplex data varies from the "g" factor in mental abilities data to the stylistic "checking factor" associated with the ICL in which participants are given the option of checking or not checking each item. The IAS, which employs an 8-point Likert format is virtually free of such a general factor (see Wiggins, Steiger, & Gaelick, 1981, for an extended treatment of this topic).

The general factor operative in IIP–C data has been shown to be substantially related to the "neuroticism" factor of the FFM (e.g., Gurtman, 1995; Soldz, 1997) and thus may be given a substantive interpretation (to the extent that the latter construct is thought to differ from "a general tendency to report distress"). Gurtman's index of "elevation" makes it possible, in principle, to interpret individual profiles with respect to this dimension. The tendency to report distress is an individual difference variable; some individuals report much distress, others little. A standardized and appropriately normed measure of this tendency would be a useful supplement to the IIP–C profile.

Applications of the IIP

General applications.   The IIP has been employed primarily in studies examining clinical issues such as the prediction of response to treatment (Alden & Capreol, 1993; Horowitz, Rosenberg, & Bartholomew, 1993; Mohr et al., 1990), the development of therapeutic alliance (Muran, Segal, Samstag, & Crawford, 1994), the interpersonal problems most discussed in treatment and those most easily treated (Horowitz et al., 1993), and projection in group counseling (Kivlighan, Marsh-Angelone, & Angelone, 1994). Interpersonal (as opposed to noninterpersonal) distress has been found to be associated with the capacity to communicate clearly about others (Horowitz, Rosenberg, & Kalehzan, 1992) and with continuation in psychotherapy (Horowitz et al., 1988). Studies have also established that different interpersonal problems are associated with different disorders (Alden & Phillips, 1990; Roberts et al., 1982).

Assessment of personality disorders.   In addition to emphasizing the inflexible and maladaptive nature of normal personality traits in the personality disorders, the DSM–III included "subjective distress" as an additional diagnostic criterion. Because the IIP–C assesses distress directly in relation to excessive or inhibited expression of trait dimensions, it should be, and in fact has been, related to DSM–III conceptions of personality disorders. For example, Pincus and Wiggins (1990) studied the relations between measures of personality disorders and the IIP–C in a college population and obtained results highly comparable to those found earlier for the IAS (Wiggins & Pincus, 1989). Soldz, Budman, Demby, and Merry (1993) replicated the results of Pincus and Wiggins (1990) in a carefully selected sample of personality disordered outpatients. Within this sample, Soldz et al. (1993) also examined the relations between personality disorders and a measure of the FFM dimensions and obtained results generally consistent with those reported in the IAS study of Wiggins and Pincus (1989). A five-factor version of the IIP–C (IIP–B5) has been developed by Pincus (1991) to include "problems" versions of the FFM factors of Neuroticism, Conscientiousness, and Openness (see also Pincus & Wiggins, 1992), and this version is currently being employed in a variety of clinical studies. A short-form version of the IIP–C (IIP–SC), useful in settings in which testing time is limited, was recently developed in an outpatient sample by Soldz, Budman, Demby, and Merry (1995). These and other recent studies (e.g., Matano & Locke, 1995) attest not only to the generalizability and clinical utility of IIP–C, but to the generalizability of the circumplex model itself across different populations and contexts of measurement (Soldz, 1997; Wiggins & Trapnell, 1996).

LOOKING FORWARD

Scholarly books often serve to define or direct a field of inquiry and Leary's (1957) canonical work clearly served both purposes. More than a decade passed before Carson's (1969) book integrated the interpersonal tradition within mainstream psychology, however, both works were likely eclipsed by Mischel's (1968) influential challenge to the entire field of personality assessment. The ensuing *l'epoque noire* of "challenge and stock taking" (Craik, 1986, p. 28) created a silence that was broken by Anchin and Kiesler's (1982) reiteration of a "gradually emerging paradigm" of human personality and psychotherapy.

We are currently witnessing a virtual explosion of high quality, edited and single-authored books on the interpersonal assessment of normal and abnormal personality that document the conceptual and empirical advances that have been made during the last decade. These books serve to inform the reader of recent developments that have been reported in a variety of standard journal outlets, as well as in new journals that have emerged during that period, such as *Psychological Assessment, Journal of Personality Disorders, Assessment,* and *Journal of Social and Personal Relationships.*

Kiesler's (1996) magisterial *Contemporary Interpersonal Theory and Research* succeeds in providing "an exhaustive coverage of contemporary interpersonal theory and research into personality, psychopathology, and psychotherapy" (p. xi) within the framework of the ICM. Plutchik and Conte's (1997) *Circumplex Models of Personality and Emotions* provides an equally comprehensive overview of the variety of utilizations of circumplex models in contemporary research. Benjamin's (1995) *Interpersonal Diagnosis and Treatment of Personality Disorders* offers a clinically rich continuation of the Sullivan–Leary tradition from the perspective of her own variant of the ICM. Further evidence of the conceptual compatibility between *DSM* personality disorders and structured measures of personality is provided in Costa and Widiger's (1994) *Personality Disorders and the Five-Factor Model of Personality,* which emphasizes the fruitfulness of combining simple structure and circumplex models in the diagnosis of these disorders. Wiggins' (1996) *The Five-Factor Model of Personality: Theoretical Perspectives* provides a forum for the interchange of ideas among major proponents of interpersonal, trait, socioanalytic, evolutionary, and lexical perspectives on personality. And finally, Strack and Lorr's (1994) *Differentiating Normal and Abnormal Personality* provides a fresh and incisive look at an ancient issue, in which interpersonal theory and methods are strongly represented.

The aforementioned listing is not claimed to be exhaustive and it is our impression from informal conversations with colleagues and publishers that there is much more "in the works." What is the significance of this embarrassment of riches that has so immeasurably enriched the canon of interpersonal assessment in the mid-1990s? In many of the works just cited, we see the careers of senior interpersonalists coming to full flower. Perhaps more important, however, are the contributions of younger clinicians, theorists, and investigators evident in these works and in numerous recent journal articles. This felicitous combination of wisdom and new technology (as the computer generation takes over) would seem to ensure an uninterrupted period of advances and consolidations within interpersonal assessment into the foreseeable future.

In these same works, we can also discern an ecumenical atmosphere in which the enforced parochialism of an earlier "dark era" has given way to an increased consideration of other methods and viewpoints, both within and outside of the interpersonal tradition. Elsewhere, McAdams (in press) shares our optimistic view of the future of trait dispositional measures, but warns that "a return to the hot rhetoric of the 1970s" might possibly occur should we "lose sight of the crucial goal of continual construct validation that empirically links traits to the prediction of behavior and the understanding of lives." The already apparent quality and sophistication of the next generation of interpersonalists would suggest that such a goal will continue to be vigorously pursued.

The end of a century has traditionally been an occasion for scholarly stock taking and for the offering of Delphic prophecies of things to come in many domains of inquiry. In our own field, the spectre of the literature on clinical prediction looms especially large when we venture forecasts of persons in general or of personality assessment psychologists in particular. Nevertheless, we cannot help but be emboldened by the remarkable resiliency and perdurability of the interpersonal circumplex tradition up to the present time. That tradition has been with us for 43 years (LaForge, Leary, Naboisek, Coffey, & Freedman, 1954) according to the received view, and for an even longer period of time (Sullivan, 1948), according to more recent evidence (Wiggins, 1996). We believe that this tradition will not only endure, but flourish, in the years to come.

ACKNOWLEDGMENTS

Krista K. Trobst now at Yale University School of Medicine, Department of Psychiatry.

This research was supported by a grant from the Social Sciences and Humanities Research Council of Canada.

We acknowledge the help and support of Maneli Badii in all phases of this project.

REFERENCES

Alden, L. E., & Capreol, M. J. (1993). Avoidant personality disorder: Interpersonal problems as predictors of treatment response. *Behavior Therapy, 24,* 357–376.

Alden, L. E., & Phillips, N. (1990). An interpersonal analysis of social anxiety and depression. *Cognitive Therapy and Research, 14,* 499–513.

Alden, L. E., Wiggins, J. S., & Pincus, A. L. (1990). Construction of circumplex scales for the Inventory of Interpersonal Problems. *Journal of Personality Assessment, 55,* 521–536.

American Psychiatric Association. (1952). *Diagnostic and statistical manual of mental disorders* (1st ed.). Washington, DC: Author.

American Psychiatric Association. (1968). *Diagnostic and statistical manual of mental disorders* (2nd ed.). Washington, DC: Author.

American Psychiatric Association. (1987). *Diagnostic and statistical manual of mental disorders* (3rd ed., rev.). Washington, DC: Author.

Anchin, J. C., & Kiesler, D. J. (1982). *Handbook of interpersonal psychotherapy.* Elmsford, NY: Pergamon.

Bartholomew, K., & Horowitz, L. M. (1991). Attachment styles among young adults: A test of a four-category model. *Journal of Personality and Social Psychology, 61,* 226–244.

Benjamin, L. S. (1995). *Interpersonal diagnosis and treatment of personality disorders* (2nd ed.). New York: Guilford.

Bowlby, J. (1973). *Attachment and loss: Vol. II. Separation, anxiety and anger.* New York: Basic Books.

Buss, D. M. (1984). Marital assortment for personality dispositions: Assessment with three different data sources. *Behavior Genetics, 14,* 111–122.

Buss, D. M., & Craik, K. H. (1983). The act frequency approach to personality. *Psychological Review, 90,* 105–126.

Buss, D. M., Gomes, M., Higgins, D. S., & Lauterbach, K. (1987). Tactics of manipulation. *Journal of Personality and Social Psychology, 52,* 1219–1229.

Carson, R. C. (1969). *Interaction concepts of personality.* Chicago: Aldine.

Costa, P. T., Jr., & McCrae, R. R. (1990). Personality disorders and the five-factor model of personality. *Journal of Personality Disorders, 4,* 362–371.

Costa, P. T., Jr., & Widiger, T. A. (Eds.). (1994). *Personality disorders and the five-factor model of personality.* Washington, DC: American Psychological Association.

Craik, K. H. (1986). Personality research methods: An historical perspective. *Journal of Personality, 54,* 18–51.

DeRaad B. (1995). The psychological approach to the structure of interpersonal traits. *European Journal of Personality, 9,* 89–102.

Derogatis, L. (1977). *SCL–90: Administration, scoring and procedures manual–I for the revised version.* Baltimore, MD: The John Hopkins Hospital.

Digman, J. M. (1990). Personality structure: Emergence of the five-factor model. *Annual Review of Psychology, 41,* 417–440.

Foa, U. G., & Foa, E. B. (1974). *Societal structures of the mind.* Springfield, IL: Thomas.

Gifford, R. (1991). Mapping nonverbal behavior on the Interpersonal Circle. *Journal of Personality and Social Psychology, 61,* 279–288.

Gurtman, M. B. (1993). Constructing personality tests to meet a structural criterion: Application of the interpersonal circumplex. *Journal of Personality, 61,* 237–262.

Gurtman, M. B. (1994). The circumplex as a tool for studying normal and abnormal personality: A methodological primer. In S. Strack & M. Lorr (Eds.), *Differentiating normal and abnormal personality* (pp. 243–263). New York: Springer.

Gurtman, M. B. (1995). Personality structure and interpersonal problems: A theoretically-guided item analysis of the Inventory of Interpersonal Problems. *Assessment, 3,* 343–361.

Gurtman, M. B., & Balakrishnan, J. D. (1994). *Circular measurement redux: The analysis and interpretation of circular interpersonal profiles.* Unpublished manuscript, University of Wisconsin at Parkside.

Guttman, L. (1966). Order analysis of correlation matrices. In R. B. Cattell (Ed.), *Handbook of multivariate experimental psychology* (pp. 438–458). Chicago: Rand McNally.

Hofstee, W. K. B., DeRaad, B., & Goldberg, L. R. (1992). Integration of the Big Five and circumplex approaches to trait structure. *Journal of Personality and Social Psychology, 63,* 146–163.

Horowitz, L. M. (1979). On the cognitive structure of interpersonal problems treated in psychotherapy. *Journal of Consulting and Clinical Psychology, 47,* 5–15.

Horowitz, L. M., Rosenberg, S. E., Baer, B. A., Ureno, G., & Villasenor, V. S. (1988). The Inventory of Interpersonal Problems: Psychometric properties and clinical applications. *Journal of Consulting and Clinical Psychology, 56,* 885–895.

Horowitz, L. M., Rosenberg, S. E., & Bartholomew, K. (1993). Interpersonal problems, attachment styles, and outcome in brief dynamic psychotherapy. *Journal of Consulting and Clinical Psychology, 61,* 549–560.

Horowitz, L. M., Rosenberg, S. E., & Kalehzan, B. M. (1992). The capacity to describe other people clearly: A predictor of interpersonal problems in brief dynamic psychotherapy. *Psychotherapy Research, 2,* 37–51.

Horowitz, L. M., & Vitkus, J. (1986). The interpersonal basis of psychiatric symptoms. *Clinical Psychology Review, 6,* 443–469.

Horowitz, L. M., Weckler, D. A., & Doren, R. (1983). Interpersonal problems and symptoms: A cognitive approach. In P. Kendall (Ed.), *Advances in cognitive-behavioral research and therapy* (pp. 81–125). London: Academic.

John, O. P., Angleitner, A., & Ostendorf, F. (1988). The lexical approach to personality: A historical review of trait taxonomic research. *European Journal of Personality, 2,* 171–203.

Kiesler, D. J. (1983). The 1982 Interpersonal Circle: A taxonomy for complementarity in human transactions. *Psychological Review, 90,* 185–214.

Kiesler, D. J. (1996). *Contemporary interpersonal theory and research: Personality, psychopathology, and psychotherapy.* New York: Wiley.

Kiesler, D. J., Van Denburg, T. F., Sikes-Nova, V. E., Larus, J. P., & Goldston, C. S. (1990). Interpersonal behavior profiles of eight cases of DSM–III personality disorder. *Journal of Clinical Psychology, 46,* 440–453.

Kivlighan, D. M., Marsh-Angelone, M., & Angelone, E. O. (1994). Projection in group counseling: The relationship between members' interpersonal problems and their perception of the group leader. *Journal of Counseling Psychology, 41,* 99–104.

LaForge, R. (1963). Research use of the ICL. *ORI Technical Report, 3*(4). Eugene: Oregon Research Institute.

LaForge, R. (1977). *Using the ICL: 1976.* Mill Valley, CA: Author.

Laforge, R., Freedman, M. B., & Wiggins, J. S. (1985). Interpersonal circumplex models: 1948–1983 (Symposium). *Journal of Personality Assessment, 49,* 613–631.

LaForge, R., Leary, T. F., Naboisek, H., Coffey, H. S., & Freedman, M. B. (1954). The interpersonal dimensions of personality: II. An objective study of repression. *Journal of Personality, 23,* 129–153.

LaForge, R., & Suczek, R. F. (1955). The interpersonal dimension of personality: III. An interpersonal check list. *Journal of Personality, 24,* 94–112.

Leary, T. (1957). *Interpersonal diagnosis of personality.* New York: Ronald.

Lorr, M., & McNair, D. M. (1965). Expansion of the interpersonal behavior circle. *Journal of Personality and Social Psychology, 2,* 823–830.

Matano, R. A., & Locke, K. D. (1995). Personality disorder scales as predictors of interpersonal problems of alcoholics. *Journal of Personality Disorders, 9,* 62–67.

McAdams, D. P. (in press). Alternative futures for the study of human individuality. *Journal of Research in Personality.*

McCrae, R. R., & Costa, P. T., Jr. (1989). The structure of interpersonal traits: Wiggins' circumplex and the five-factor model. *Journal of Personality and Social Psychology, 56,* 586–595.

Mischel, W. (1968). *Personality and assessment.* New York: Wiley.

Mohr, D. C., Beutler, L. E., Engle, D., Shoham-Salomon, V., Bergan, J., Kaszniak, A. W., & Yost, E. B. (1990). Identification of patients at risk for nonresponse and negative outcome in psychotherapy. *Journal of Consulting and Clinical Psychology, 58,* 622–628.

Moskowitz, D. S. (1994). Cross-situational generality and the interpersonal circumplex. *Journal of Personality and Social Psychology, 66,* 921–933.

Muran, J. C., Segal, Z. V., Samstag, L. W., & Crawford, C. E. (1994). Patient pretreatment interpersonal problems and therapeutic alliance in short-term cognitive therapy. *Journal of Consulting and Clinical Psychology, 62,* 185–190.

Ozer, D. J., & Reise, S. P. (1994). Personality assessment. *Annual Review of Psychology, 45,* 357–388.

Pincus, A. L. (1991, August). *Extending interpersonal problems to include the "Big Five" personality dimensions.* Paper presented at the meeting of the American Psychological Association, San Francisco.

Pincus, A. L. (1994). The interpersonal circumplex and the interpersonal theory: Perspectives on personality and its pathology. In S. Strack & M. Lorr (Eds.), *Differentiating normal and abnormal personality* (pp. 114–136). New York: Springer.

Pincus, A. L., & Boekman, L. F. (1995). Social-emotional adjustment and interpersonal problems: A circumplex analysis of the Weinberger Adjustment Typology. *Assessment, 2,* 65–80.

Pincus, A. L., & Wiggins, J. S. (1990). Interpersonal problems and conceptions of personality disorders. *Journal of Personality Disorders, 4,* 342–352.

Pincus, A. L., & Wiggins, J. S. (1992). An expanded perspective on interpersonal assessment. *Journal of Counseling and Development, 71,* 91–94.

Plutchik, R., & Conte, H. R. (Eds.). (1997). *Circumplex models of personality and emotions.* Washington, DC: American Psychological Association.

Plutchik, R., & Platman, S. R. (1977). Personality connotations of psychiatric diagnoses: Implications for a similarity model. *Journal of Nervous and Mental Disease, 165,* 418–421.

Roberts, W. R., Penk, W. E., Gearing, M. L., Robinowitz, R., Dolan, M. P., & Patterson, E. T. (1982). Interpersonal problems of Vietnam combat veterans with symptoms of posttraumatic stress disorder. *Journal of Abnormal Psychology, 91,* 444–450.

Rosen, A. S. (1992). The circle as a model for the interpersonal domain of Swedish trait terms. *European Journal of Psychology, 6,* 283–299.

Saucier, G. (1992). Benchmarks: Integrating affective and interpersonal circles with the Big Five personality factors. *Journal of Personality and Social Psychology, 62,* 1025–1035.

Soldz, S. (1997). The interpersonal circumplex as a structural model in clinical research: Examples from group psychotherapy, interpersonal problems, and personality disorders. In R. Plutchik & H. R. Conte (Eds.), *Circumplex models of personality and emotions.* Washington, DC: American Psychological Association.

Soldz, S., Budman, S., Demby, A., & Merry, J. (1993). Representation of personality disorders in circumplex and five-factor space: Explorations with a clinical sample. *Psychological Assessment, 5,* 41–52.

Soldz, S., Budman, S., Demby, A., & Merry, J. (1995). A short form of the Inventory of Interpersonal Problems Circumplex Scales. *Assessment, 2,* 53–63.

Stern, G. G. (1970). *People in context: Measuring person-environment congruence in education and industry.* New York: Wiley.

Strack, S. (Ed.). (1996). Interpersonal theory and the interpersonal circumplex: Timothy Leary's legacy. *Journal of Personality Assessment, 66,* 212–216.

Strack, S., & Lorr, M. (Eds.). (1994). *Differentiating normal and abnormal personality.* New York: Springer.

Sullivan, H. S. (1948). The meaning of anxiety in psychiatry and in life. *Psychiatry, 11,* 1–18.

Trapnell, P. D., & Wiggins, J. S. (1990). Extension of the Interpersonal Adjective Scales to include the Big Five dimensions of personality. *Journal of Personality and Social Psychology, 59,* 781–790.

Weinberger, D. A. (1991). *Social-emotional adjustment in older children and adults: I. Psychometric properties of the Weinberger Adjustment Inventory.* Unpublished manuscript, Case Western Reserve University, Cleveland, OH.

Wiggins, J. S. (1979). A psychological taxonomy of trait-descriptive terms: The interpersonal domain. *Journal of Personality and Social Psychology, 37,* 395–412.

Wiggins, J. S. (1980). Circumplex models of interpersonal behavior. In L. Wheeler (Ed.), *Review of personality and social psychology* (Vol. 1, pp. 265–293). Beverly Hills: Sage.

Wiggins, J. S. (1982). Circumplex models of interpersonal behavior in clinical psychology. In P. C. Kendall & J. N. Butcher (Eds.), *Handbook of research methods in clinical psychology* (pp. 183–221). New York: Wiley.

Wiggins, J. S. (1987, August). *How interpersonal are the MMPI personality disorder scales?* Paper presented at the meeting of the American Psychological Association, New York.

Wiggins, J. S. (1992). Have model will travel. *Journal of Personality, 60,* 527–532.

Wiggins, J. S. (1995). *Interpersonal Adjective Scales: Professional manual.* Odessa, FL: Psychological Assessment Resources.

Wiggins, J. S. (Ed.). (1996). *The five-factor model of personality: Theoretical perspectives.* New York: Guilford.

Wiggins, J. S., & Broughton, R. (1985). The Interpersonal Circle: A structural model for the integration of personality research. In R. Hogan & W. H. Jones (Eds.), *Perspectives in personality: A research annual* (Vol. 1, pp. 1–47). Greenwich, CT: JAI.

Wiggins, J. S., & Broughton, R. (1991). A geometric taxonomy of personality scales. *European Journal of Personality, 5,* 343–365.

Wiggins, J. S., & Holzmuller, A. (1978). Psychological androgyny and interpersonal behavior. *Journal of Consulting and Clinical Psychology, 46,* 40–52.

Wiggins, J. S., & PAR staff (1995). *Interpersonal Adjective Scales (IAS) scoring program.* Odessa, FL: Psychological Assessment Resources.

Wiggins, J. S., Phillips, N., & Trapnell, P. D. (1989). Circular reasoning about interpersonal behavior: Evidence concerning some untested assumptions underlying diagnostic classification. *Journal of Personality and Social Psychology, 56,* 296–305.

Wiggins, J. S., & Pincus, A. L. (1989). Conceptions of personality disorders and dimensions of personality. *Psychological Assessment, 1,* 305–316.

Wiggins, J. S., & Pincus, A. L. (1992). Personality: Structure and assessment. *Annual Review of Psychology, 43,* 473–504.

Wiggins, J. S., & Pincus, A. L. (1994). Personality structure and the structure of personality disorders. In P. T. Costa, Jr. & T. A. Widiger (Eds.), *Personality disorders and the five-factor model of personality* (pp. 73–93). Washington, DC: American Psychological Association.

Wiggins, J. S., Steiger, J. H., & Gaelick, L. (1981). Evaluating circumplexity in personality data. *Multivariate Behavioral Research, 16,* 263–289.

Wiggins, J. S., & Trapnell, P. D. (1996). A dyadic-interactional perspective on the five-factor model. In J. S. Wiggins (Ed.), *The five-factor model of personality: Theoretical perspectives* (pp. 88–162). New York: Guilford.

Wiggins, J. S., & Trapnell, P. D. (1997). Personality structure: The return of the Big Five. In R. Hogan, J. A. Johnson, & S. R. Briggs (Eds.), *Handbook of personality psychology.* Orlando, FL: Academic.

Wiggins, J. S., & Trobst, K. K. (1997). When is a circumplex an "interpersonal circumplex"? The case of supportive actions. In R. Plutchik & H. R. Conte (Eds.), *Circumplex models of personality and emotions.* Washington, DC: American Psychological Association.

PART II

Continuing Issues
in Personality Assessment

Chapters in this section address several issues that have been recurring themes, and often topics of debate, in the research and professional literature. The past decade has seen an increasing, albeit not unanimous, consensus on both the number and kinds of trait domains that are required to provide an adequate description of personality. In his review of personality theories, for example, Digman (1990) concluded that the five-factor model (as presented, for example, in the work of Costa & McCrae, 1985; Digman & Takemoto-Chock, 1981; Goldberg, 1990; and Norman, 1963, 1967) presented a set of very broad dimensions that characterize individual differences and provide a good answer to the question of personality structure. The impact of the five-factor model on personality assessment is apparent in the development of a number of instruments that now assess the five major domains, and in some cases, specific facets of these domains—a situation that poses a dilemma of choice for personality assessors and researchers looking to extract five-factor personality data from their endeavors. In the first chapter of the special section, Thomas Widiger and Timothy Trull provide a valuable review and analysis of five such instruments with the psychometric credentials that make them worthy candidates for consideration.

In the second chapter, David Nichols and Roger Greene address the issue of deception in personality assessment, using MMPI and MMPI–2 indices as operational measures of dimensions of deceptive responding. Their presentation exposes the complexity of this topic and incorporates discussion of impression-management models and research—a literature that is typically neglected in attempting to clarify validity issues in self-report responding. Clinicians will appreciate the authors' incisive parsing of possible response dynamics. Researchers, especially those conducting analog feigning studies, will likely want to make note of variables from the impression-management literature identified by the authors.

David Watson and Lee Anna Clark, in the third chapter, explore critical issues in the measurement of mood. Readers will quickly agree with their statement that the measurement of mood states has been the focus of intense research interest since the start of the decade. Using their research with the Positive and Negative Affect Schedule as a foundation point, they examine a number of important issues in mood measurement, including the nature of the domain structure, factors affecting the reliability and validity of mood measurement, and consideration of facets of mood domains.

Gregory Meyer's chapter on the integration of the MMPI–2 and Rorschach is especially timely given recent critical comments about the use of the Rorschach (e.g., Wood, Nezworski, & Stejskal, 1996). Discordant results between these two instruments, the two primary test methods of personality assessment in the field, has been puzzling and even disturbing to personality clinicians. This potential disparity in results could speak poorly of the validity of the entire endeavor of personality assessment itself. In what is likely to be a frequently cited chapter, Meyer examines the relationship of response styles across the MMPI-2 and Rorschach, and the influence of response styles on concordance between methods. His findings will undoubtedly be seen as heartening to those comitted to multiple methods of personality assessment.

In the last chapter in this part, David Faust tackles the difficult topic of the process that clinicians should rely on when faced with the task of applying scientific knowledge to clinical practice. He is very helpful in making explicit how the link between research and practice frequently is not direct, and the difficulties involved in combining the two domains are much greater than often is acknowledged. The discussion of how clinicians can go from generalizations to a particular client is particularly enlightening.

REFERENCES

Costa, P. T., Jr., & McCrae, R. R. (1985). *The NEO Personality Inventory manual.* Odessa, FL: Psychological Assessment Resources.

Digman, J. M. (1990). Personality structure: Emergence of the five-factor model. *Annual Review of Psychology, 41,* 417–440.

Digman, J. M., & Takemoto-Chock, N. K. (1981). Factors in the natural language of personality: Re-analysis, comparison and interpretation of six major studies. *Multivariate Behavioral Research, 16,* 149–170.

Goldberg, L. R. (1990). An alternative "description of personality": The Big-Five factor structure. *Journal of Personality and Social Psychology, 59,* 1216–1229.

Norman, W. T. (1963). Toward an adequate taxonomy of personality attributes: Replicated factor structure in peer nomination personality ratings. *Journal of Abnormal and Social Psychology, 66,* 574–583.

Norman, W. T. (1967). *2,800 personality trait descriptors: Normative operating characteristics for a university population.* Research Report 08310-1-T. University of Michigan, Ann Arbor, MI.

Wood, J., Nezworski, T., & Stejskal, W. (1996). The comprehensive system for the Rorschach: A critical examination. *Psychological Science, 7,* 3–10.

9

Assessment of the
Five-Factor Model of Personality

Thomas A. Widiger
Department of Psychology
University of Kentucky

Timothy J. Trull
Department of Psychology
University of Missouri

The five-factor model (FFM) of personality is obtaining construct validation, recognition, and practical consideration across a broad domain of fields, including clinical psychology, industrial–organizational psychology, and health psychology. As a result, an array of instruments have been developed and existing instruments are being modified to assess the FFM. In this article, we present an overview and critique of five such instruments (the Goldberg Big Five Markers, the revised NEO Personality Inventory, the Interpersonal Adjective Scales–Big Five, the Personality Psychopathology–Five, and the Hogan Personality Inventory), focusing in particular on their representation of the lexical FFM and their practical application.

There currently are, and probably always will be, a variety of models of personality. One model that is receiving considerable recognition (e.g., Basic Behavioral Science Task Force of the National Advisory Mental Health Council, 1996) is the lexical five-factor model (FFM) or the Big Five (Digman, 1990; Goldberg, 1993; John, 1990; Wiggins & Pincus, 1992). The FFM suggests that there are five major domains of personality: (a) Neuroticism versus Emotional Stability (or Negative Affectivity), (b) Extraversion versus Introversion (or Positive Affectivity, Surgency), (c) Conscientiousness (or Constraint), (d) Agreeableness versus Antagonism, and (e) Openness versus Closedness to Experience (or Unconventionality, Intellect). Each of these broad domains is differentiated into more specific facets. For example, Costa and McCrae (1995a) suggested that the facets of Agreeableness (vs. Antagonism) are Trust (vs. Mistrust, Suspiciousness), Modesty (vs. Arrogance), Altruism (vs. Exploitation), Compliance (vs. Oppositionalism, Aggression), Tender-Mindedness (vs. Tough-

Mindedness, Low Empathy), and Straightforwardness (vs. Deception, Manipulation).

A principal attraction of the FFM has been its empirical foundation. Most models of personality are derived from a particular theoretical perspective. Benjamin (1993), for example, emphasized early parent–child relationships that contribute to interpersonal introject dimensions of emancipation versus control and self-love versus self-attack; Cloninger and Svrakic (1994) emphasized the importance of neurotransmitter system dysregulation for the development of reward-dependent, harm-avoidant, persistent, and novelty-seeking behavior patterns and transpersonal, humanistic mechanisms for the development of self-directedness, cooperativeness, and self-transcendence; Millon and Davis (1994) emphasized evolutionary mechanisms resulting in three fundamental pleasure–pain, active–passive, and other–self functional polarities.

The lexical FFM takes a more theoretically neutral position. A criticism of the model has been the lack of a single or explicit theory for the development of the personality dispositions (e.g., Block, 1995; Butcher & Rouse, 1996; Millon & Davis, 1994), but the lexical FFM desires only to provide a reasonably comprehensive description of personality. The validity of the descriptions of personality provided by Benjamin (1993), Cloninger and Svrakic (1994), and Millon and Davis depend substantially on the validity of the respective etiological theories, and the utility of their application to a practicing clinician depends substantially on a shared, mutual theoretical perspective. In contrast, the FFM presents the traits of personality that are most important in describing oneself and others in a manner that will not favor any one particular theoretical model. This is the approach taken by the American Psychiatric Association (APA) in its development of the *Diagnostic and Statistical Manual of Mental Disorders* (4th ed.; [*DSM–IV*]; APA, 1994), recognizing (a) that the manual is to be used by clinicians with a variety of conflicting theoretical perspectives and (b) that the etiology for the various disorders is often unknown, variable, and multifactorial (Frances, Pincus, Widiger, Davis, & First, 1990). The *DSM–IV* is, at best, only partially successful in this aspiration, but it is useful and desirable for a nomenclature to attempt to be theoretically neutral.

The lexical FFM also avoids relying on the negotiations and compromises of a committee, or the brilliance and talent of a particular theorist, to identify the fundamental dimensions of personality. The derivation of the FFM dimensions is more explicitly empirical and systematic. The lexical FFM suggests that the most important personality traits will have been encoded within the natural language. Rather than look to a theorist for their discovery, look instead to human verbal behavior. "The most important differences in human transactions will come to be encoded as single terms in some or all of the world's languages" (Goldberg, 1993, p. 26). The personality traits that people have found to be most significant to consider when describing themselves and others will likely be those traits for which they have developed, across the long history of their language, the greatest number of terms to characterize these traits' various manifestations, expressions, and nuances. Systematic, objective, and comprehensive studies of the encoded language would identify the trait domains and facets that people have found to be most useful and important when trying to describe, characterize, and understand one another.

Such lexical studies have been reasonably consistent in identifying five broad domains (Digman, 1990; Goldberg, 1993; John, 1990). However, it would be premature to suggest that there is in fact a consensus regarding the FFM (Block, 1995; Costa & McCrae, 1995b; Goldberg & Saucier, 1995). There remains disagreement regarding the basic questions of the optimal number of dimensions to characterize the lexical domain, particularly as the model is applied to maladaptive personality traits (Tellegen & Waller, in press), and the optimal term(s) with which to characterize or summarize each domain and its underlying facets (e.g., Zuckerman, Kuhlman, Joireman, Teta, & Kraft, 1993).

Nevertheless, the FFM model has become so compelling that a variety of instruments have been developed, and many existing instruments have been modified, to assess the FFM. A comprehensive review of all of these measures would be beyond the scope and space limitations of this article. Our purpose is instead to review (perhaps appropriately) five alternative instruments: the Goldberg (1992) Big Five Markers, the Interpersonal Adjective Scales–Big Five (IASR–B5; Trapnell & Wiggins, 1990), the NEO Personality Inventory–Revised (NEO–PI–R; Costa & McCrae, 1992c), the Personality Psychopathology–Five (PSY–5; Harkness & McNulty, 1994), and the Hogan Personality Inventory (HPI; Hogan, 1986; Hogan & Hogan, 1992). We focus in particular on the validity of these instruments with respect to their representation of the lexical domains and with respect to their potential utility within applied settings.

GOLDBERG BIG FIVE MARKERS

Goldberg (1990, 1992) developed a series of adjective checklist markers for the FFM. These adjective checklists are available in a number of different formats. The two predominant options are a set of 100 unipolar adjectives (e.g., timid, shallow, rude, imperturbable, and demanding) and a set of 50 bipolar adjectives (e.g., timid vs. bold, angry vs. calm, and envious vs. not envious) that can be rated on a scale ranging from 1 to 9 points.

Adjective checklists are advantageous for applied settings in requiring little space or time for administration and little effort for processing. A list of 100 adjectives can be completed in just 10 to 15 min. However, a significant disadvantage of adjectives is that the intended meaning of each term can be ambiguous. "A single word allows for no context, no shading, no motivation, and no specificity" (Briggs, 1992, p. 258). Briggs, for example, noted how the term *cold* could be interpreted to mean a callous rudeness (within a domain of antagonism) or an aloof indifference (within a domain of introversion).

This difficulty is addressed somewhat by the bipolar format. For example, the meaning of *calm* is suggested in part by being placed opposite to the term *anger*. In addition, Goldberg (1992) provided two different formats for administration. One format is to provide the terms alphabetically or randomly. Another format is to organize the terms with respect to the domain from which they were obtained. For example, in this "transparent" format, Goldberg placed together the 10 bipolar pairs of silent–talkative, unadventurous–adventurous, introverted–extraverted, unenergetic–energetic, timid–bold, unsociable–sociable, inhibited–spontaneous, unenthusiastic–enthusiastic, inactive–active, and unassertive–assertive. The participant is then cued to consider these terms as belonging within some common domain. Goldberg then went further and titled this section "Introversion–Extraversion," rendering the interpretation of each bipolar pair even less ambiguous. These cues may be so transparent as to encourage response sets, but the format does diminish idiosyncratic interpretations.

The major advantage of Goldberg's (1992) scales is that they are the instruments that most strictly adhere to the goal of assessing the FFM lexical domains. The lexical FFM is an empirical effort to account for the variance among the trait terms within the language, and Goldberg attempted to reproduce explicitly and faithfully each of the five domains identified in the lexical analyses. Rather than provide a conceptual interpretation of a lexical domain, and then construct a questionnaire to assess the inferred constructs, Goldberg simply reproduced the actual lexical domain itself.

One might, of course, question whether Goldberg (1990, 1992) provided an adequate or even accurate selection of trait terms (Block, 1995; Tellegen, 1993). Goldberg himself acknowledged that there are different ways to sample the lexical universe. One approach is to provide a uniform sample of all regions, no matter the density or sparseness of the number of terms which inhabit that domain. This "uniform" approach was the method used by Wiggins (1982) in the development of the Interpersonal Adjective Scales, which sample uniformly the lexical space of interpersonal trait terms around the interpersonal circumplex. This approach is particularly useful if one wishes to place more emphasis on how the personality (interpersonal) constructs shade into and relate conceptually to one another than on their relative importance within the language for describing oneself and other persons (Saucier, 1992).

Another approach is a "representative" sampling, providing each conceptual domain with the number of adjectives that represent the density of trait terms within that region of the lexical universe. This approach would give substantially more weight to the five principal factors, although still represent the less dense regions in between. This was the earlier approach taken by Goldberg (1990). However, it is important to recognize that the five trait domains are not themselves represented equally within the English language. There appear to be more trait terms for the domain of Agreeableness than for the other four domains; there are fewer trait terms for Intellect (or Openness) and for Neuroticism than for the other three. Whereas there appear to be roughly similar frequencies of trait terms for both poles of four of the FFM domains, there are far fewer terms for low Neuroticism than for high Neuroticism (Goldberg, 1992).

A third approach to sampling, and the one used most recently by Goldberg (1992), is a "cluster" sampling, which omits the interstitial regions and represents equally each of the five primary domains. For example, each of the five factors is represented by an equal number of terms in both the unipolar and bipolar formats of Goldberg's (1992) adjective checklists. This approach is particularly useful in reliably reproducing the five-factor structure and in minimizing differences in the reliabilities of the five factors across different participant populations. However, it is worth noting that in the 100-unipolar format, there are 10 trait terms for each of the 10 poles with the exception of the domain of Emotional Instability (or Neuroticism), for which there are 14 terms to represent the pole of emotional instability and 6 terms to represent the pole of emotional stability.

Even if one accepts Goldberg's (1992) decision to use a cluster sampling, one might still question the success or accuracy of the sampling. Tellegen (1993), for example, was critical of the original sampling of the lexical universe by Allport and Odbert (1936) and Goldberg (1982, 1990). He suggested that the exclusion of such terms as *excellent, outstanding, impressive, superior,* and *flawless* (i.e., positively evaluative), and such terms as *cruel, mean, evil, awful, wicked, vicious,* and *depraved* (i.e., negatively evaluative), has resulted in a failure to recognize the presence of two additional lexical domains that would be particularly important in the description of maladaptive personality functioning. For example, it is readily apparent that many of the positively evaluative terms would be useful in characterizing narcissistic personality traits, and many of the negatively evaluative terms would be useful in characterizing antisocial/psychopathic personality traits. "Two large dimensions of Self-Evaluation [Positive Valence] and Other Evaluation [Negative Valence] can be recovered from the personality lexicon if unnecessarily restrictive exclusion criteria are not employed in the initial culling of trait terms" (Waller & Zavala, 1993, p. 131). Tellegen, Grove, and Waller (1991) also developed a provisional 161-item questionnaire (Inventory of Personal Characteristics #7; IPC7) to assess this seven-factor model. The IPC7 includes both trait terms (e.g., "quiet"; "playful"; "vicious, nasty"; and "cruel, mean") and statements (e.g., "believe that strict discipline at home would prevent most of the crime in society today" and "do things in an orderly and systematic manner"; Benet & Waller, 1995, p. 717). Initial research with the IPC7 has reproduced the seven-factor structure within other languages (Benet & Waller, 1995).

However, it should also be noted that it is difficult to evaluate the original lexical studies of Tellegen and Waller (in press), as the precise methodology and findings have remained unpublished for a number of years. Tellegen (1993) stated that "from an authoritative dictionary, we selected 400 adjectives spaced throughout the dictionary" (p. 124). In other words, there may have been no attempt to provide a comprehensive sampling of the lexical universe, as in the prior studies by Goldberg (1982, 1990). Perhaps Tellegen and Waller did not sample the lexical space in a representative fashion; one can obtain different factor structures through different representations of the lexical space (Goldberg & Digman, 1994; Saucier, 1992).

It is also reasonable to suggest that such trait terms as *cruel, mean, wicked,* and *evil* simply represent more extreme variants of FFM Antagonism and such terms as *excellent, outstanding,* and *superior* may represent extremely low Neuroticism or the facet of Arrogance within Antagonism (McCrae, 1994; Widiger & Trull, 1992). Many of the terms analyzed by Goldberg (1982, 1990, 1992) do not appear to be that much different from the terms considered by Tellegen and Waller (in press). Consider, for example, only terms beginning with the letters *a, b,* or *c* from Goldberg's (1982) original pool of 1,710 trait terms. This subset includes such terms as *abrasive, abusive, adulterous, aggressive, antisocial, bigoted, biased, blasphemous, boorish, brutal, bullish, callous, coercive, combative, cowardly,* and *cruel.* Many of these terms resemble closely Tellegen and Waller's negatively evaluative terms. The same point can be made with respect to positive evaluations. Considering again just the terms beginning with the letters *a, b,* or *c* from Goldberg's (1982) list of 1,710, there are terms like *angelic, altruistic, ascendant, benevolent, brave, bright, chic, chivalrous, clever,* and *charitable.* In fact, some of the evaluative terms identified by Tellegen and Waller were included by Goldberg (1982), such as *cruel* and *impressive.* Finally, McCrae and Costa (1995) conducted a joint analysis of the IPC7 and the NEO–PI–R and obtained a five-factor solution, although the specific associations of the positive and negative valence dimensions were not entirely consistent with these previously mentioned expectations (e.g., Positive Valence was associated with the Antagonism facet of Arrogance and the Neuroticism facet of low Self-Consciousness, but also with facets from Extraversion, Openness, and Conscientiousness).

THE NEO–PI–R

The NEO–PI–R (Costa & McCrae, 1992c) consists of 240 statements (e.g., "I often feel helpless and want someone else to solve my problems," p. 69, and "I'm a superior person," p. 72) to which the person indicates an extent of agreement on a 5-point scale. An advantage of the NEO–PI–R relative to Goldberg's (1992) scales is the differentiation of each broad domain into six underlying facets. For example, the NEO–PI–R facets of Extraversion are Warmth, Gregariousness, Assertiveness, Activity, Excitement-Seeking, and Positive Emotions. Each of the facets is assessed by eight items. There is also an informant, peer version (Form R) and a 60-item version (NEO–FFI) that lacks the facet differentiations.

"The NEO–PI–R was developed to operationalize the five-factor model of personality" (Costa & McCrae, 1992c, p. 14) and is the predominant measure of the FFM. A substantial amount of reliability and validity research has been conducted with the NEO–PI–R (Costa & McCrae, 1992c). Most important with respect to the lexical FFM, the NEO–PI–R has demonstrated consistent convergent and discriminant validity with respect to adjective checklist measures of the FFM (e.g., Goldberg, 1990, 1992; Trapnell & Wiggins, 1990), as well as indicating how alternative models of personality can be understood from the perspective of the FFM (e.g., McCrae & Costa, 1989).

The use of statements rather than adjectives is advantageous as it provides more precision and clarity for the respondent. There is much less ambiguity in the NEO–PI–R statement that "I'm known as a warm and friendly person" (Costa & McCrae, 1992c, p. 69) than in the Goldberg (1992) adjective *warm*. However, the increased precision is advantageous only if the aim is directed accurately at the target. Briggs (1992) concluded that "the NEO–PI provides a faithful representation of the five-factor model, with more precisely identified facets within each of the major domains" (p. 287). However, to the extent that the lexical FFM domains are not accurately represented by the constructs of Neuroticism, Extraversion versus Introversion, Openness versus Closedness, Agreeableness versus Antagonism, and Conscientiousness, and to the extent that each lexical domain has not been accurately described by the six respective facets, the NEO–PI–R will fail to provide an accurate operationalization of the lexical FFM (Block, 1995).

For example, McCrae and Costa (1990) identified one of the lexical domains as Neuroticism, with such facets as Anxiousness, Impulsiveness, Depression, Angry Hostility, Vulnerability, and Self-Consciousness. The interpretation of the domain as Neuroticism is shared by a number of personality researchers (Digman, 1990), and the facets of Neuroticism identified by Costa and McCrae (1995a) have demonstrated substantial construct validity. Clarkin, Hull, Cantor, and Sanderson (1993), for example, indicated how the diagnosis of borderline personality disorder, and controversies concerning its excessive prevalence and comorbidity (Widiger & Trull, 1992), can be explained when the disorder is understood as extreme Neuroticism. Others, however, suggest that a more apt label for this domain is Negative Affectivity (Tellegen & Waller, in press) and that the facet of Angry Hostility belongs within the domain of Antagonism (Zuckerman et al., 1993). Low Agreeableness, or Antagonism, does include such trait terms as *belligerence, rudeness, irritability, surliness, argumentative, combative,* and *quarrelsome* (Goldberg, 1990). Costa and McCrae (1992c), however, stated that Neuroticism Angry Hostility "represents the tendency to experience anger and related states such as frustration and bitterness" (p. 16), consistent with the construct of Negative Affectivity (Watson & Clark, 1984). In addition, "this scale measures the individual's readiness to experience anger; whether the anger is expressed depends upon the individual's level of [antagonism]" (Costa & McCrae, 1992c, p. 16). Nevertheless, this may represent an overly subtle distinction. According to the test manual, NEO–PI–R Angry Hostility correlates .47 with NEO–PI–R Antagonism (Agreeableness reverse-scored), .42 with the Antagonism facet that assesses mistrust–suspicion, and .49 with Oppositionalism–Aggression. On the other hand, the relation is even higher with NEO–PI–R Neuroticism ($r = .71$; .52 with the Neuroticism facet of Depression and .47 with Anxiousness; Costa & McCrae, 1992c). Goldberg (1992) similarly reported that NEO–PI Hostility correlated .52 with the unipolar trait markers for Neuroticism and only .26 with the trait markers for Antagonism.

Arguments have also been made against the placement of the NEO–PI–R Neuroticism facet of Impulsiveness (Hogan, 1986; Zuckerman et al., 1993). The domain of Surgency (or Extraversion) is described by Goldberg (1990) as including such trait terms as *impetuous, uninhibited, unrestrained, daring,* and *spontaneous* and the domain of Conscientiousness as including such trait terms as *negligent, inconsistent, unpredictable,* and *reckless.* Costa and McCrae (1992c), however, indicated that "NEO–PI–R impulsiveness should not be confused with spontaneity, risk-taking, or rapid decision time" (p. 16). It refers instead to a more narrowly defined inability to control urges and cravings. Costa and McCrae (1992c) included Excitement-Seeking as a facet of Extraversion and Self-Discipline as a facet of Conscientiousness. The NEO–PI–R Impulsiveness scale correlates .25 with NEO–PI–R Excitement-Seeking and –.37 with NEO–PI–R Self-Discipline, but .31 to .40 with the other five NEO–PI–R facets of Neuroticism (Costa & McCrae, 1992c). Goldberg (1992) likewise reported that NEO–PI–R Impulsiveness correlated only –.03 with the trait markers for Surgency (or Extraversion) and .37 with Neuroticism.

Despite the fact that the NEO–PI–R was derived from and developed for a largely normal range of personality functioning, its scales have related closely to various measures of maladaptive personality traits (Widiger & Costa, 1994). Butcher and Rouse (1996) suggested that "empirical research has not supported the hypothesized relationships between [the FFM] and Axis II [personality] disorders" (p. 98) but they considered only one study by Clark (1993) and did not consider many additional studies that have reported substantial relationships of the FFM with personality disorders (e.g., Clarkin et al., 1993; Costa & McCrae, 1990; Schroeder, Wormworth, & Livesley, 1992; Trull, 1992; Wiggins & Pincus, 1989). Clark and Livesley (1994) in fact concluded that their "data thus provide further support for the notion that the personality trait dimensional structure defined by the FFM is very robust and will emerge reliably as long as a broad range of personality traits are assessed" (p. 275).

Nevertheless, a limitation of a clinical application of the NEO–PI–R may be a failure to include sufficient representation of some of the more maladaptive variants of each FFM domain (Tellegen & Waller, in press; Widiger & Costa, 1994). Studies with the NEO–PI or NEO–PI–R have at times failed to confirm all of the predictions concerning the relationship of the FFM to a personality disorder due in part perhaps to a lack of sufficient representation within the NEO–PI–R of maladaptive variants. For example, only one of the eight NEO–PI–R items that assess the Conscientiousness facet of Achievement-Striving concerns excessive, maladaptive conscientiousness (i.e., "I'm something of a 'workaholic'"; Costa & McCrae, 1992c, p. 73). Workaholism is one of the *DSM–IV* diagnostic criteria for the obsessive–compulsive personality disorder, along with other indicators of excessive deliberation, dutifulness, discipline, and perfectionism. However, the other seven items from this NEO–PI–R facet scale describe an adaptive functioning (e.g., "I have a clear set of goals and work toward them in an orderly fashion"; Costa & McCrae, 1992c, p. 73). It is not surprising then for NEO–PI–R Conscientiousness to fail to correlate with measures of obsessive–compulsive personality disorder (Widiger & Costa, 1994). The one exception for the NEO–PI has been with the Millon Clinical Multiaxial Inventory (MCMI; Millon & Davis, 1994), which itself includes a number of indicators of adaptive conscientiousness within the obsessive–compulsive personality disorder item pool (Widiger & Corbitt, 1993), such as "I always make sure that my work is well planned and organized"; "I keep very close track of my money so I am prepared if a need comes up"; and "If a person wants something done that calls for real patience, they should ask me" (Millon & Davis, 1994).

The most problematic NEO–PI–R scale in personality disorder research has been NEO–PI–R Openness to Experience (e.g., Clark & Livesley, 1994; Schroeder et al., 1992; Trull, 1992). *Openness*, as originally defined by McCrae and Costa (1985b), failed to include any suggestion of maladaptivity. "Costa and I borrowed the term most directly from the work of Coan (1974), whose Experience Inventory was the starting point for the development of the Openness scales in the NEO–PI–R" (McCrae, 1994, p. 257). Coan's (1974) text concerned a discussion of the optimal personality, and openness was conceptualized by McCrae and Costa (1985b) to involve self-actualization or self-realization, as described by Rogers (1961) and Rokeach (1960), hence the facets of being open to aesthetics, values, ideas, feelings, fantasies, and actions. Costa and McCrae (1990) stated that it "seems likely that individuals can be too open" (p. 370), but it is difficult to conceptualize any clinically relevant maladaptive variants of such self-actualizing openness. In what meaningful way is one too open to aesthetics? McCrae and Costa (1985b) in fact stated that "Openness may be identified as some aspect of mental health, to be contrasted with closedness, defense, and neurosis" (p. 150).

Conventionality and unconventionality are also trait terms within the domain of Openness (Goldberg, 1982; Trapnell & Wiggins, 1990). Tellegen and Waller's (in press) identification of this domain as Unconventionality—including such traits as unusual, odd, peculiar, weird, and strange—may be more successful in characterizing extreme imagination, curiosity, and perceptivity and in accounting for such maladaptive personality traits as the odd beliefs and magical thinking of persons with schizotypal personality disorder.

INTERPERSONAL ADJECTIVE SCALES–BIG FIVE
(IASR–B5)

The IASR–B5 (Trapnell & Wiggins, 1990) is perhaps the principle alternative to Goldberg's (1990, 1992) adjective checklists. The IASR–B5 is particularly advantageous if one prefers the interpersonal circumplex (IPC) formulation of the FFM domains of Surgency (Extraversion) and Agreeableness. The IPC model of personality has generated substantial clinical interest (Benjamin, 1993; Kiesler, 1986), and a variety of studies have indicated that two of the five domains of the FFM correspond closely to a 45° rotation of the Dominance and Nurturance axes of the IPC (Hofstee, de Raad, & Goldberg, 1992; Saucier, 1992). McCrae and Costa (1989), for example, conducted a joint factor analysis of the NEO–PI (self and peer formats) and the IAS–R, which assesses eight locations around the IPC, including Assured–Dominant, Gregarious–Extraverted, Warm–Agreeable, Unassuming–Ingenuous, Unassured–Submissive, Aloof–Introverted, Cold-Hearted, and Arrogant–Calculating. All of the eight IAS–R scales loaded substantially and solely on the FFM Extraversion and Agreeableness factors (absolute factor loadings ranging from .53 to .87). The location of Extraversion versus Introversion and Agreeableness versus Antagonism within the IPC is apparent in the complementary octants at 45° to the defining IPC axes: Gregarious–Extraverted versus Aloof–Introverted and Warm–Agreeable versus Arrogant–Calculating, respectively. The elegant convergence of these two predominant models of personality provides a complementary confirmation of their validity. "The five-factor model provides a larger framework in which to orient and interpret the circumplex, and the interpersonal circle provides a useful elaboration about aspects of two of the five factors" (McCrae & Costa, 1989, p. 593).

> Although the IASR–B5 has no obvious advantage over the Goldberg (1990) adjectival scales … in providing an efficient global measure of the Big Five, the unique feature of the IASR–B5 is that it provides a highly efficient instrument for combined five-factor and interpersonal circumplex assessment. (Trapnell & Wiggins, 1990, p. 788)

The IASR–B5 will be particularly useful to clinicians and researchers who wish to consider such IPC principles as complementarity (Benjamin, 1993; Kiesler, 1986), in addition to the lexical domains of the FFM. The IPC model of personality and personality disorder suggests that specific patterns of interaction will develop depending on the persons' locations around the circumplex (e.g., hostility begets hostility, whereas dominance begets submission; Kiesler, 1986). These IPC principles are more readily assessed and tested with the IASR–B5 than with the NEO–PI–R. Both the NEO–PI–R and the IASR–B5 provide differentiations within (or between) the major lexical domains (unlike the Goldberg, 1990, 1992, adjective checklists), but the NEO–PI–R facets for Extraversion and Agreeableness were selected largely on the basis of simple structure, whereas the IAS–R scales were selected to represent equidistant locations around the circumplex (Saucier, 1992; Widiger & Hagemoser, in press). In other words, the IASR–B5 uses a uniform sampling to represent equally each of the interstitial segments between the two lexical domains of Extraversion and Agreeableness and a cluster sampling to represent the three lexical domains of Neuroticism, Openness, and Conscientiousness (Hofstee et al., 1992, extend this research to provide uniform sampling and resulting circumplexes for the other FFM axes). As a result, the 12 NEO–PI–R facets of Extraversion and Agreeableness are not equivalent to the eight octants of the IAS–R. They represent instead somewhat different slices along the circumplex, and the unique nature of the circumplex structuring of interpersonal traits (e.g., complementarity) is not readily apparent from the simple structure of the NEO–PI–R facets.

It is also useful to note that the IASR–B5 provides more depth to its assessment of the domains of Extraversion and Agreeableness than to the domains of Neuroticism, Openness, and Conscientiousness. The IASR–B5 includes 64 adjectives to assess the eight octants of the IPC, but only 60 adjectives to assess the remaining three broad domains. Facet scales for Neuroticism, Openness, and Conscientiousness are not provided, which is a substantial limitation given the importance of these facets in providing more specific distinctions (Butcher & Rouse, 1996; Costa & McCrae, 1995a; Harkness, 1992). It is informative to identify the relationship of the broad FFM domains to clinical constructs, but the utility of the FFM in everyday decisions will not become apparent without considering the more specific facets. The IASR–B5 also has the additional disadvantage of any adjective checklist in the ambiguity of the intended meaning of single trait terms. However, a glossary definition of each term is provided that can accompany the administration of the IASR–B5. For example, the ambiguous term *unabstract* is defined as "concrete, thinks in a practical, uncomplicated way."

PSY–5

One of the more recently developed measures of the FFM is the PSY–5 (Harkness, 1992; Harkness & McNulty, 1994). However, the relationship of the PSY–5 to the lexical FFM is somewhat ambiguous. On the one hand, the PSY–5 is related conceptually to the lexical FFM (Harkness & McNulty, 1994). "Markers of normal personality dimensions were included in the development of the PSY–5" (Harkness, McNulty, & Ben-Porath, 1995, p. 105). On the other hand, markers of abnormal personality functioning were given as much (if not more) emphasis than normal personality functioning.

We contend that the PSY–5 is optimized for the complementary dimensional description of the personality disorders, whereas normal sample-based five factor models do exactly what they were optimized to do: they reflect the big five vectors of personality individual differences in normal samples. (Harkness & McNulty, 1994, p. 311)

In addition, the authors emphasized differences between their FFM and those of Costa and McCrae (1992c) and Goldberg (1990, 1992), at times suggesting virtually no association; they did indicate a close relationship with the personality models of Tellegen and Waller (in press); Watson, Clark, and Harkness (1994); and Zuckerman et al. (1993).

The development of the PSY–5 proceeded through three stages. Harkness (1992) first translated the *DSM–III–R* personality disorder criteria into a lay language. Analyses of these translations yielded 39 major features (e.g., "is very self-centered and selfish, not generous" and "appears to be 'in touch with reality,'" p. 256), which related closely to the results of similar studies by Clark (1993) and by Livesley, Jackson, and Schroeder (1989). In a comparison of the 39 personality disorder features with the FFM dimensions of normal personality, Harkness noted a "strong resemblance to at least four of the Big Five" (p. 258). Harkness and McNulty (1994) subsequently combined the 39 features with 26 markers of the dimensions of personality identified by Tellegen and Waller (in press; e.g., "tends not to feel victimized, exploited, or mistreated"; "is moody, is easily irritated and upset"; and "questions authority, values rebelliousness," pp. 298–299). Analyses of these 65 features yielded the five factors of Negative Emotionality, Positive Emotionality, Aggressiveness, Constraint, and Psychoticism. Harkness et al. (1995) then conducted a systematic analysis of the revised Minnesota Multiphasic Personality Inventory (MMPI–2) item pool to develop scales for the assessment of these five constructs, yielding the PSY–5 MMPI–2 inventory.

"Although there are some surface-level similarities between the PSY–5 dimensions and [the FFM], the PSY–5 [dimensions] are likely to be mapping a different universe of psychological concepts because it originated from diagnostic criteria of nonadaptive personality" (Butcher & Rouse, 1996, p. 100). Harkness and McNulty (1994) indicated that two of the PSY–5 dimensions are virtually identical to domains of the lexical FFM: Negative Emotionality (FFM Neuroticism) and Positive Emotionality (FFM Extraversion). Harkness and McNulty, however, did suggest that PSY–5 Aggressiveness is substantially different from FFM Antagonism: "PSY–5 markers [for Aggressiveness] include features such as aggressive, cruel, violent, and enjoys frightening others" (pp. 309–310), similar to Tellegen and Waller's (in press) Negative Valence dimension. They contrasted these behaviors with the more benign Goldberg (1992) markers for Antagonism, such as rude, selfish, harsh, and uncharitable.

It is indeed the case that "PSY–5 Aggressiveness has more 'tooth and claw' than the Agreeableness dimension of the Big Five" (Harkness & McNulty, 1994, p. 309), but it may still represent a more extreme variant of Antagonism rather than a distinct domain of functioning. For example, Harkness and McNulty noted that "PSY–5 Aggressiveness maps directly onto an important model of individual differences in interpersonal behavior, the Interpersonal Circle (IPC, e.g., Wiggins, 1982; Wiggins & Pincus, 1989)" (p. 309). "Specifically, the PSY-5 Aggressiveness dimension should approximate a –.45° rotation from the dominance-submission axis" (p. 306). This is the precise location of the NEO–PI–R and Goldberg (1992) FFM Antagonism–Agreeableness dimension, as indicated in the studies by McCrae and Costa (1989), Hofstee et al. (1992), and Wiggins and Pincus (1989).

The FFM label of Antagonism does fail to convey adequately the specific and extreme facet of aggression, but a label such as Aggression will also fail to convey other facets of Antagonism, such as arrogance and mistrust. Livesley's (1990) Dimensional Assessment of Personality Pathology–Basic Questionnaire (DAPP–BQ) has a similar difficulty. Included within the DAPP–BQ is a factor scale titled Interpersonal Disesteem, which is further differentiated into subscales of Exploitation, Contemptuousness, Remorseless, Lack of Empathy, Egocentrism, Interpersonal Irresponsibility, and Sadism. Vicious sadism is perhaps inadequately described as being simply a variant of interpersonal disesteem, but sadism does appear to be within this broader domain of functioning that Livesley et al. (1989) characterized as Interpersonal Disesteem. Schroeder et al. (1992) reported that DAPP–BQ Interpersonal Disesteem correlated .70 with NEO–PI Antagonism, and a joint factor analysis of the DAPP–BQ and NEO–PI yielded a five-factor solution with Interpersonal Disesteem loading comfortably on the Antagonism dimension.

Clark, Vorhies, and McEwen (1994) reported a correlation of .58 for their Aggression scale from the Schedule for Nonadaptive and Adaptive Personality (SNAP; Clark, 1993) with NEO–PI Antagonism, and .48 with an adjective checklist for FFM Antagonism derived from Goldberg's (1982) trait markers. The SNAP is a measure of maladaptive and adaptive personality traits, derived largely from a review of personality disorder symptomatology and the Watson et al. (1994) dimensions of Negative Affectivity, Positive Affectivity, and Constraint, comparable to the development of the PSY–5 (Harkness, 1992; Harkness & McNulty, 1994). A joint factor analysis of the NEO–PI, a lexical FFM adjective checklist derived from Goldberg's (1982) trait markers, and the SNAP yielded a five-factor solution with SNAP Aggression placed comfortably within the domain of Antagonism (Clark et al., 1994). Clark and Livesley (1994) subsequently conducted a joint analysis of the SNAP, DAPP–BQ, NEO–PI, and NEO–FFI. DAPP–BQ Interpersonal Disesteem, SNAP Aggression, and SNAP Self-Centered Exploitation obtained their highest correlations with NEO–PI/NEO–FFI Agreeableness (–.73, –.65, and –.56, respectively). "Specifically, disagreeableness [is] characterized by a variety of interpersonal difficulties, including angry, rejecting, unstable, and exploitative relationships; suspiciousness and hypersensitivity toward others; and overt antisocial behaviors or conduct problems" (Clark & Livesley, 1994, pp. 270–272).

Trull, Useda, Costa, and McCrae (1995) more recently assessed the relationship of the PSY–5 with the NEO–PI and the NEO–PI–R. The highest correlations for PSY–5 Aggressiveness were with NEO–PI Agreeableness ($r = -.47$), NEO–PI–R Agreeableness ($r = -.32$), and NEO–PI–R Compliance ($r = -.39$), a facet of Agreeableness that contrasts compliance with oppositionalism and aggression. PSY–5 Aggressiveness also failed to correlate with three facets of Agreeableness: Trust (vs. Suspicion), Altruism (vs. Exploitation), and Tender-Mindedness (vs. Tough-Mindedness). Trull et al. suggested that PSY–5 Aggressiveness represents well the particular facet of Antagonism that involves physical aggression but may fail to provide sufficient representation of other maladaptive variants of Antagonism (e.g., arrogance) and maladaptive variants of Agreeableness (e.g., excessive trust, compliance, and tender-mindedness). "Low PSY–5 Aggressiveness is not indicative of high Agreeableness" (Trull et al., 1995, p. 508).

The PSY–5 dimension of Constraint is coordinated by Harkness and McNulty (1994) with the Constraint factor of Tellegen and Waller (in press) and Watson et al. (1994). They suggested that "PSY–5 Constraint is not comparable to normal sample-based Conscientiousness. ... This is not merely a difference in emphasis or extremity of markers, these are two different constructs" (Harkness & McNulty, 1994, p. 310). Yet, Watson et al. emphasized the congruence of Constraint and Conscientiousness in their integrative model: "The third higher order trait, conscientiousness or constraint, is centered around the basic issue of impulse control" (p. 26). Numerous studies have indicated substantial correspondence of Constraint with NEO–PI–R and Goldberg (1990) Conscientiousness (Clark et al., 1994; Costa & McCrae, 1992c; McCrae, 1994), including findings by Tellegen and Waller (in press) and Watson et al. (1994).

Trull et al. (1995) reported that PSY–5 Constraint correlated .37 with NEO–PI Conscientiousness and .27 with NEO–PI–R Conscientiousness. However, PSY–5 Constraint also correlated .31 with NEO–PI–R Introversion and .32 with NEO–PI–R Agreeableness. Harkness and McNulty (1994) indicated that PSY–5 "Constraint taps risk aversion, control versus impulsivity, traditional morality, rule following versus rule breaking, and criminality" (p. 310). It may then be the case that PSY–5 Constraint does represent a different organization of lexical FFM facets than is provided by Goldberg (1992) and Costa and McCrae (1992c). Trull et al. (1995) noted in particular the substantial relationship of PSY–5 Constraint to NEO–PI–R Excitement-Seeking ($r = -.40$), a facet of Extraversion. In the Harkness et al. (1995) study of the relationship of the PSY–5 to Tellegen's Differential Personality Questionnaire (DPQ; Tellegen & Waller, in press), PSY–5 Constraint correlated substantially with DPQ Constraint ($r = .57$) but also with DPQ Negative Emotionality ($r = -.15$, $p < .05$), especially the Negative Emotionality facet of Aggression ($r = -.53$, $p < .01$), with which it obtained its highest correlation for any DPQ facet scale, including all of the facets from the domain of Constraint.

Harkness and McNulty (1994) suggested that PSY–5 Psychoticism bears virtually no relationship to any FFM construct. "Psychoticism is a dramatically different construct compared to the so-called 'fifth factor' in normal population five factor models" (Harkness & McNulty, 1994, p. 310), and it "has no direct counterpart in normal sampled-based models" (Harkness et al., 1995, p. 106). Psychoticism, as defined by Eysenck (1994) within his three-factor model of personality, has been closely related to the FFM, particularly as a mixture of Antagonism and low Conscientiousness (McCrae & Costa, 1985a). Harkness and McNulty, however, noted that "although we borrowed the label from Eysenck … PSY–5 Psychoticism is entirely different from Eysenck's construct" (p. 307). PSY–5 Psychoticism concerns the extent of adequate reality testing. It "encompasses reduced reality contact, odd, unusual perception and mentation, and extensive absorption with fantasy" (Harkness & McNulty, 1994, p. 310). Trull et al. (1995) reported that PSY–5 Psychoticism correlated significantly with NEO–PI–R facets of Openness, including Openness to Fantasy (.23, $p < .001$). However, as noted earlier, NEO–PI–R Openness may lack adequate representation of excessive or maladaptive imagination and perceptivity, contributing to the failure of NEO–PI–R Openness to obtain significant positive correlations with measures of personality disorder, particularly the magical thinking, odd beliefs, and unusual perceptional experiences of persons with a schizotypal personality disorder. Costa and McCrae (1990) acknowledged that "disturbances in thinking would appear to be needed in addition to neurotic, introverted dispositions" (p. 370) to account adequately for the schizotypal personality disorder, but they suggested that "a sixth dimension of aberrant cognitions might be needed" (p. 370) rather than a revision of the construct of Openness. Tellegen and Waller (in press), on the other hand, provided a possible revision of this construct as Unconventionality, which would then adequately account for schizotypal thinking and PSY–5 Psychoticism within the lexical FFM.

In sum, the PSY–5 scales do appear to have a conceptually meaningful and often close relationship to the lexical FFM. The differences between the FFM and the PSY–5 may reflect simply the particular facets of the FFM that are emphasized within the PSY–5. In fact, the PSY–5 may be particularly useful for clinical applications of aspects of the FFM given its emphasis on the maladaptive variants. An additional advantage of the PSY–5 is that it is embedded within the MMPI–2 and the "PSY–5 scales [may then] expand the range of assessment offered by the MMPI–2" (Harkness et al., 1995, p. 112) to more general and fundamental traits of personality, in addition to its primary use as an indicator of Axis I psychopathology.

Butcher and Rouse (1996) argued "that the Five-Factor Model is too superficial for clinical assessment" (p. 87) and proposed the PSY–5 as a more viable option. However, this may reflect their preference for the MMPI–2 rather than limitations of the FFM. Ben-Porath and Waller (1992) were also critical of the application of the NEO–PI–R within clinical settings, but their criticisms involved specific concerns with the NEO–PI–R (e.g., absence of a validity scale) rather than skepti cism concerning the relevance of FFM domains (e.g., Antagonism) and FFM facets (e.g., Suspiciousness, Arrogance, and Tough-Mindedness) to the functioning of persons with mental disorders.

A potential limitation of the PSY–5, however, might be its reliance on items from the MMPI–2. It is economic to use the MMPI–2 to assess for every psychological construct of possible relevance to clinical patients, including most Axis I mental disorders, Axis II personality disorders, and fundamental traits of personality (Butcher & Rouse, 1996), but it may not be feasible or realistic to expect the MMPI–2 to be this versatile (Costa & McCrae, 1992a, 1992b). Costa, Zonderman, McCrae, and Williams (1985) indicated substantial limitations within the MMPI item pool for indicators of FFM Conscientiousness that appear to be more successfully represented within the MCMI item pool (Widiger & Corbitt, 1993). Costa et al. (1985) also noted less substantial but still significant limitations with respect to other domains of the FFM. For example, the PSY–5 may not be successful in assessing maladaptive Agreeableness (e.g., excessive compliance, gullibility, self-sacrifice, and self-effacement) by confining its representation of this domain primarily to excessive aggressiveness, and it may not be successful in assessing maladaptive closedness to experience (e.g., alexithymia, narrow-mindedness, and bigotry) by confining its representation of this domain to aberrant fantasy; imagination; and odd, peculiar experiences.

It might also be unrealistic for any self-report inventory to attempt to provide, with the same items and test instructions, an adequate assessment of fundamental traits of personality and such mental disorders as depression, anxiety, and psychosis. A variety of studies have indicated substantial distortions in persons' self-descriptions of their personality during episodes of depression, anxiety, and psychosis (Widiger & Trull, 1992), and the MMPI–2 PSY–5 may be prone to a confusion of such syndromes with premorbid or comorbid personality traits, given the expressed intention of the MMPI–2 instructions and PSY–5 items to provide an assessment of Axis I depression, anxiety, and psychosis.

HOGAN PERSONALITY INVENTORY

Hogan (1986) developed the HPI to assess the FFM from the perspective of his socioanalytic model of personality. The HPI is a 310-item inventory of trait statements with six scales to assess Adjustment (comparable to low NEO–PI–R Neuroticism), Prudence (NEO–PI–R Conscientiousness or PSY–5 Constraint), Intellectance (FFM Openness or Goldberg, 1992, Intellect), Likeability (NEO–PI–R Agreeableness), and Sociability and Ambition (NEO–PI–R Extraversion). The HPI Sociability and Ambition scales could be understood as subscales to or facets of Extraversion. The distinction between ascendance and status seeking (Ambition) versus enjoying and getting along with others (Sociability) is central to Hogan's (1983) socioanalytic theory of the self. Briggs (1992), however, suggested that HPI

Ambition may also relate to Conscientiousness (e.g., the NEO–PI–R facet of Achievement Striving), and HPI Sociability may include components of Agreeableness (e.g., ability to get along with others).

Briggs (1992) reported the correlations of the HPI and the NEO–PI with Goldberg's (1992) bipolar FFM adjective pairs. Both the HPI and the NEO–PI correlated with Goldberg's trait markers as predicted, although the findings were somewhat better for the NEO–PI, particularly with respect to their discriminant validity. For example, HPI Adjustment correlated as highly with Goldberg's Surgency scale ($r = .45$) as HPI Ambition ($r = .45$) and HPI Sociability ($r = .50$). In addition, the correlation of HPI Intellectance with Goldberg's (1992) Intellect scale was the lowest convergent validity coefficient ($r = .33$) and not quite as high as obtained with the NEO–PI Openness ($r = .42$).

Similar results have been reported by Trapnell and Wiggins (1990) with the IASR–B5 and by McCrae (1994) with the NEO–PI–R and more recently revised HPI (Hogan & Hogan, 1992). Trapnell and Wiggins (1990) reported a correlation of .44 for HPI Intellectance with IASR–B5 Openness (.67 for NEO–PI Openness) and .43 for HPI Prudence with IASR–B5 Conscientiousness (.76 for NEO–PI Conscientiousness). McCrae (1994) suggested that HPI Ambition and Likeability may be comparable to the IASR–B5 Dominance and Nurturance axes, representing approximately 45° rotations of the dimensions of Extraversion and Agreeableness. Trapnell and Wiggins (1990) also suggested that HPI Intellectance includes a number of measures of intelligence or scholastic ability (e.g., subscales for Math Ability, Good Memory, Science Ability, and School Success) rather than the personality disposition toward intellectance. Trapnell and Wiggins further suggested that HPI Prudence contains indicators of excitement-seeking (e.g., subscales for Experience-Seeking, Impulse Control, and Thrill Seeking), which both Goldberg (1990, 1992) and Costa and McCrae (1992c) place within Extraversion. Trapnell and Wiggins (1990), however, acknowledged that

> whether the traits of excitement-seeking, risk-taking, or variety-seeking are more usefully construed as subsets of extraversion, conscientiousness, or openness, respectively, or as comprising a separate domain of sensation-seeking traits having interpersonal, characterological, and cognitive aspects would seem to be an important taxonomic issue for the five-factor model. (p. 788)

It is also important to note that Hogan and Hogan (1992) recently revised the HPI. The revised HPI Prudence and revised HPI Intellectance scales appear to have increased their convergence with NEO–PI–R Conscientiousness and NEO–PI–R Openness ($r = .55$ and .50, respectively). However, McCrae (1994) also indicated that the revised HPI Ambition scale is now more highly correlated with NEO–PI–R Neuroticism ($r = -.62$) than with NEO–PI–R Extraversion ($r = .55$) due to the inclusion of subscales for the absence of depression and absence of anxiety to improve the test's predictive ability for occupational success.

In sum, the HPI does not appear to be as consistent with the lexical FFM as other measures, but it may be particularly useful in the application of FFM constructs to concerns within business, personnel, and organizational settings. In a manner analogous to the PSY–5 emphasis on maladaptive personality traits of importance in diagnosing personality disorders (Harkness & McNulty, 1994), the HPI emphasizes constructs of particular relevance to job, career, and occupational performance, including such subscales as Leadership, Competitiveness, and Mastery Motive. In addition, much of the HPI research has been confined largely to job performance predictions (e.g., correlations with supervisor ratings, commendations, number of hours absent, and revenue generated) rather than to its construct validation with respect to the FFM (Briggs, 1992; Hough, 1992). Hogan's primary objective has been to make useful predictions of importance to industrial–organizational psychology, such as the prediction of emergent leadership and effective team performance (Hogan, Curphy, & Hogan, 1994), as it is Harkness and McNulty's (1994) goal to account for the DSM–IV personality disorder symptomatology. Each has perhaps placed more emphasis on particular facets within each domain that will maximize the respective instruments' ability to make useful predictions rather than faithfully reproducing the lexical FFM domains and facets.

CONCLUSIONS AND FUTURE DIRECTIONS

The FFM is developing its construct validity and practical relevance across a broad arena of domains, including (but not limited to) industrial–organizational psychology, psychopathology, health psychology, educational psychology, and aging (Costa & McCrae, 1992c; Hogan et al., 1994; Widiger & Trull, 1992). As such, an array of instruments to assess the FFM have been and will continue to be developed. This review necessarily confined itself to only five such alternatives, but additional options include (but are not limited to) the 23 Bipolar Big Five (Duijsens & Diekstra, in press), the IPC7 (Tellegen et al., 1991), the Zuckerman–Kuhlman Personality Questionnaire (Zuckerman et al., 1993), the Structured Interview for the Five-Factor Model (Trull & Widiger, 1995), the Millon Index of Personality Styles (Millon & Davis, 1994), the Block (1961) Q-Sort, and (most important) the Five Psycho-Geometric Shapes (i.e., box, circle, triangle, rectangle, and squiggles; Dellinger, 1989).

A number of points of comparison can be made with respect to the five instruments that were reviewed. The major advantage of the Goldberg (1992) scales is the effort to provide an accurate and faithful assessment of the lexical domains in a direct, succinct, and straightforward manner. A significant advantage of the IASR–B5, relative to Goldberg (1992), is the provision of additional scales to assess the constructs of the interpersonal circumplex. The major disadvantages of the Goldberg and IASR–B5 scales are the susceptibility of adjective checklists to misinterpretation and mood state distortions, and the absence of facet scales for most (IASR–B5) or all (Goldberg) of the domains. The major advantages of the NEO–PI–R are its more precise assessment of the FFM domains and underlying facets, the empirical support for the reliability and validity of these assessments, and its application within a variety of different fields. Its major disadvantages are the absence of validity scales and its commitment to the particular constructs identified by Costa and McCrae (1992c) as being the FFM domains and facets (e.g., Openness versus Unconventionality). The major advantage of the HPI and PSY–5, relative to the NEO–PI–R, are the provision of scales that will be particularly useful or relevant within business and clinical settings, respectively. A disadvantage of both inventories, relative to the NEO–PI–R, is their failure to provide as faithful or comprehensive assessment of the FFM. This is particularly evident in the PSY–5, which may even fail to provide a comprehensive assessment of maladaptive personality traits. A concern for all of these inventories is their susceptibility to mood state distortions. This disadvantage within clinical settings will be particularly evident for the adjective checklists. The PSY–5 has the most extensive validity scales (through its inclusion within the MMPI–2) but the PSY–5 is also embedded within an inventory that uses PSY–5 items to assess for mood and anxiety disorders.

Of particular importance in future research will be direct comparisons of these alternative measures, not only with respect to their predictive validity within applied contexts (e.g., prediction of effective leadership, cardiovascular dysfunction, or psychopathic tendencies) but also their construct validity with respect to the lexical FFM. Both concerns are of substantial importance, are currently unresolved for the existing measures, and are also readily confused with one another.

Instruments that are constructed primarily or especially to serve an applied need (e.g., the HPI and PSY–5) may at times sacrifice construct validity as a measure of the lexical FFM to increase the test's utility and predictive validity. On the other hand, it is theoretically and clinically useful to recognize the place of the constructs assessed by these instruments within the context of the lexical FFM. Instruments constructed to assess the lexical FFM (e.g., Goldberg's trait markers and the NEO–PI–R) will at times fail to have as much clinical or social application, but one should not lose sight of their broader importance as a more faithful representation of the FFM.

A difficulty for all FFM instruments is the optimal characterization of each broad domain and underlying facets. One option would be to provide no name for each domain and simply identify the factors by numbers and the facets by letters, as recommended by John (1990). However, such an approach would be devoid of much theoretical or applied meaning. Nevertheless, it is important to appreciate that it would be difficult (perhaps impossible) to identify any one word to adequately represent the entire domain of behaviors that include more than 100 trait terms. Yet, the word that is chosen will have quite different implications for how the domain is understood and assessed. Digman (1990), for example, noted how the term "agreeableness ... seems tepid for a dimension that appears to involve the more humane aspects of humanity—characteristics such as altruism, nurturance, caring, and emotional support" (pp. 422–424). John (1990) likewise noted that "agreeableness is also too detached, too neutral a label for a factor supposed to capture intensely affective components, such as love, compassion, and sympathy" (p. 95). It is equally, if not more problematic, to characterize the other pole, which includes such traits as selfishness, exploitation, cruelty, viciousness, suspicion, and aggression as being simply antagonism or low agreeableness. Yet, any other single term, such as Aggressiveness (Harkness & McNulty, 1994), Likeability (Hogan, 1986), Nurturance (Wiggins, 1982), or Love (John, 1990) will be equally, if not more, inadequate and misleading. It will be important in future studies to determine whether an increase (or decrease) in predictive validity of a measure of, for example, Aggressiveness in comparison to Agreeableness reflects the inadequacy of the FFM for that particular prediction, the inadequacy of Agreeableness as the construct to represent that domain of the lexical FFM, or the inadequacy of the instrument's assessment of Aggressiveness as a facet of that domain.

REFERENCES

Allport, G. W., & Odbert, H. S. (1936). Trait-names: A psycho-lexical study. *Psychological Monographs, 47*(1, Whole No. 211).

American Psychiatric Association. (1994). *Diagnostic and statistical manual of mental disorders* (4th ed.). Washington, DC: Author.

Basic Behavioral Science Task Force of the National Advisory Mental Health Council. (1996). Basic behavioral science research for mental health. Vulnerability and resilience. *American Psychologist, 51*, 22–28.

Benet, V., & Waller, N. G. (1995). The Big Seven factor model of personality description: evidence for its cross-cultural generality in a Spanish sample. *Journal of Personality and Social Psychology, 69*, 701–718.

Benjamin, L. S. (1993). *Interpersonal diagnosis and treatment of personality disorders*. New York: Guilford.

Ben-Porath, Y. S., & Waller, N. G. (1992). "Normal" personality inventories in clinical assessment: General requirements and the potential for using the NEO Personality Inventory. *Psychological Assessment, 4*, 14–19.

Block, J. (1961). *The Q-sort method in personality assessment and psychiatric research*. Springfield, IL: Thomas.

Block, J. (1995). A contrarian view of the five-factor approach to personality description. *Psychological Bulletin, 117*, 187–215.

Briggs, S. R. (1992). Assessing the five-factor model of personality description. *Journal of Personality, 60*, 253–293.

Butcher, J. N., & Rouse, S. V. (1996). Personality: Individual differences and clinical assessment. *Annual Review of Psychology, 47*, 87–111.

Clark, L. A. (1993). Personality disorder diagnosis: Limitations of the Five-Factor Model. *Psychological Inquiry, 4*, 100–104.

Clark, L. A., & Livesley, W. J. (1994). Two approaches to identifying the dimensions of personality disorder: Convergence on the Five-Factor model. In P. T. Costa & T. A. Widiger (Eds.), *Personality disorders and the five-factor model of personality* (pp. 261–277). Washington, DC: American Psychological Association.

Clark, L. A., Vorhies, L., & McEwen, J. L. (1994). Personality disorder symptomatology from the five-factor model perspective. In P. T. Costa & T. A. Widiger (Eds.), *Personality disorders and the five-factor model of personality* (pp. 95–116). Washington, DC: American Psychological Association.

Clarkin, J. F., Hull, J. W., Cantor, J., & Sanderson, C. (1993). Borderline personality disorder and personality traits: A comparison of SCID–II BPD and NEO–PI. *Psychological Assessment, 5*, 472–476.

Cloninger, C. R., & Svrakic, D. M. (1994). Differentiating normal and deviant personality by the seven factor personality model. In S. Strack & M. Lorr (Eds.), *Differentiating normal and abnormal personality* (pp. 40–64). New York: Springer.

Coan, R. W. (1974). *The optimal personality*. New York: Columbia University Press.

Costa, P. T., & McCrae, R. R. (1990). Personality disorders and the five-factor model of personality. *Journal of Personality Disorders, 4*, 362–371.

Costa, P. T., & McCrae, R. R. (1992a). Normal personality assessment in clinical practice: The NEO Personality Inventory. *Psychological Assessment, 4*, 5–13.

Costa, P. T., & McCrae, R. R. (1992b). Reply to Ben-Porath and Waller. *Psychological Assessment, 4*, 20–22.

Costa, P. T., & McCrae, R. R. (1992c). *Revised NEO Personality Inventory (NEO–PI–R) and NEO Five-Factor Inventory (NEO–FFI) professional manual*. Odessa, FL: Psychological Assessment Resources.

Costa, P. T., & McCrae, R. R. (1995a). Domains and facets: Hierarchical personality assessment using the Revised NEO Personality Inventory. *Journal of Personality Assessment, 64*, 21–50.

Costa, P. T., & McCrae, R. R. (1995b). Solid ground in the wetlands of personality: A reply to Block. *Psychological Bulletin, 117*, 216–220.

Costa, P. T., Zonderman, A. B., McCrae, R. R., & Williams, R. B. (1985). Content and comprehensiveness in the MMPI: an item factor analysis in a normal adult sample. *Journal of Personality and Social Psychology, 48*, 925–933.

Dellinger, S. (1989). *Psycho-geometrics: How to use geometrics psychology and influence people*. Englewood Cliffs, NJ: Prentice Hall.

Digman, J. M. (1990). Personality structure: Emergence of the five-factor model. *Annual Review of Psychology, 41*, 417–440.

Duijsens, I. J., & Diekstra, R. F. W. (in press). The 23BB5: A new bipolar Big Five questionnaire. *Journal of Personality and Individual Differences*.

Eysenck, H. J. (1994). Normality-abnormality and the three-factor model of personality. In S. Strack & M. Lorr (Eds.), *Differentiating normal and abnormal personality* (pp. 3–25). New York: Springer.

Frances, A. J., Pincus, H. A., Widiger, T. A., Davis, W. W., & First, M. B. (1990). DSM–IV: Work in progress. *American Journal of Psychiatry, 147*, 1439–1448.

Goldberg, L. R. (1982). From ace to zombie: Some explorations in the language of personality. In C. D. Spielberger & J. N. Butcher (Eds.), *Advances in personality assessment* (Vol. 1, pp. 203–234). Hillsdale, NJ: Lawrence Erlbaum Associates, Inc.

Goldberg, L. R. (1990). An alternative "description of personality": The Big Five factor structure. *Journal of Personality and Social Psychology, 59*, 1216–1229.

Goldberg, L. R. (1992). The development of markers of the Big Five factor structure. *Psychological Assessment, 4*, 26–42.

Goldberg, L. R. (1993). The structure of phenotypic personality traits. *American Psychologist, 48*, 26–34.

Goldberg, L. R., & Digman, J. M. (1994). Revealing structure in the data: Principles of exploratory factor analysis. In S. Strack & M. Lorr (Eds.), *Differentiating normal and abnormal personality* (pp. 216–242). New York: Springer.

Goldberg, L. R., & Saucier, G. (1995). So what do you propose we use instead? A reply to Block. *Psychological Bulletin, 117,* 221–225.

Harkness, A. R. (1992). Fundamental topics in the personality disorders: Candidate trait dimensions from lower regions of the hierarchy. *Psychological Assessment, 4,* 251–259.

Harkness, A. R., & McNulty, J. L. (1994). The Personality Psychopathology Five (PSY–5): Issue from the pages of a diagnostic manual instead of a dictionary. In S. Strack & M. Lorr (Eds.), *Differentiating normal and abnormal personality* (pp. 291–315). New York: Springer.

Harkness, A. R., McNulty, J. L., & Ben-Porath, Y. S. (1995). The Personality Psychopathology Five (PSY–5): Constructs and MMPI-2 scales. *Psychological Assessment, 7,* 104–114.

Hofstee, W. K. B., de Raad, B., & Goldberg, L. R. (1992). Integration of the Big Five and circumplex approaches to trait structure. *Journal of Personality and Social Psychology, 63,* 146–163.

Hogan, R. (1983). Socioanalytic theory of personality. In M. M. Page (Ed.), *1982 Nebraska symposium on motivation: Personality—current theory and research* (pp. 55–89). Lincoln: University of Nebraska Press.

Hogan, R. (1986). *Hogan Personality Inventory manual.* Minneapolis, MN: National Computer Systems.

Hogan, R., Curphy, G. J., & Hogan, J. (1994). What we know about leadership. Effectiveness and personality. *American Psychologist, 49,* 493–504.

Hogan, R., & Hogan, J. (1992). *Hogan Personality Inventory manual.* Tulsa, OK: Hogan Assessment Systems.

Hough, L. M. (1992). The "Big Five" personality variables-construct confusion: Description versus prediction. *Human Performance, 5,* 139–155.

John, O. P. (1990). The "Big Five" factor taxonomy: Dimensions of personality in the natural language and in questionnaires. In L. A. Pervin (Ed.), *Handbook of personality: Theory and research* (pp. 66–100). New York: Guilford.

Kiesler, D. J. (1986). The 1982 interpersonal circle: An analysis of DSM-III personality disorders. In T. Millon & G. Klerman (Eds.), *Contemporary directions in psychopathology: Toward DSM–IV* (pp. 571–597). New York: Guilford.

Livesley, W. J. (1990). *Dimensional Assessment of Personality Pathology–Basic Questionnaire.* Unpublished manuscript, University of British Columbia, Vancouver, Canada.

Livesley, W. J., Jackson, D. N., & Schroeder, M. L. (1989). A study of the factorial structure of personality pathology. *Journal of Personality Disorders, 3,* 292–306.

McCrae, R. R. (1994). Openness to experience: Expanding the boundaries of Factor V. *European Journal of Personality, 8,* 251–272.

McCrae, R. R., & Costa, P. T. (1985a). Comparison of EPI and psychoticism scales with measures of the five-factor model of personality. *Personality and Individual Differences, 6,* 587–597.

McCrae, R. R., & Costa, P. T. (1985b). Openness to experience. In R. Hogan & W. H. Jones (Eds.), *Perspectives in personality* (Vol. 1, pp. 145–172). Greenwich, CT: JAI.

McCrae, R. R., & Costa, P. T. (1989). The structure of interpersonal traits: Wiggins' circumplex and the Five-Factor Model. *Journal of Personality and Social Psychology, 56,* 586–595.

McCrae, R. R., & Costa, P. T. (1990). *Personality in adulthood.* New York: Guilford.

McCrae, R. R., & Costa, P. T. (1995). Positive and negative valence within the Five-Factor Model. *Journal of Research in Personality, 29,* 443–460.

Millon, T., & Davis, R. D. (1994). Millon's evolutionary model of normal and abnormal personality: Theory and measures. In S. Strack & M. Lorr (Eds.), *Differentiating normal and abnormal personality* (pp. 79–113). New York: Springer.

Rogers, C. R. (1961). *On becoming a person: A therapist's view of psychotherapy.* Boston: Houghton Mifflin.

Rokeach, M. (1960). *The open and closed mind.* New York: Basic Books.

Saucier, G. (1992). Benchmarks: Integrating affective and interpersonal circles with the Big-Five personality factors. *Journal of Personality and Social Psychology, 62,* 1025–1035.

Schroeder, M. L., Wormworth, J. A., & Livesley, W. J. (1992). Dimensions of personality disorder and their relationships to the Big Five dimensions of personality. *Psychological Assessment, 4,* 47–53.

Tellegen, A. (1993). Folk concepts and psychological concepts of personality and personality disorder. *Psychological Inquiry, 4,* 122–130.

Tellegen, A., Grove, W. M., & Waller, N. G. (1991). *Inventory of Personal Characteristics #7.* Unpublished materials, University of Minnesota, Minneapolis, MN.

Tellegen, A., & Waller, N. G. (in press). Exploring personality through test construction: Development of the Multidimensional Personality Questionnaire. In S. R. Briggs & J. M. Cheek (Eds.), *Personality measures: Development and evaluation* (Vol. 1). Greenwich, CT: JAI.

Trapnell, P. D., & Wiggins, J. S. (1990). Extension of the Interpersonal Adjective Scales to include the Big Five dimensions of personality. *Journal of Personality and Social Psychology, 59,* 781–790.

Trull, T. J. (1992). DSM–III–R personality disorders and the Five Factor Model of personality: An empirical comparison. *Journal of Abnormal Psychology, 101,* 553–560.

Trull, T. J., Useda, J. D., Costa, P. T., & McCrae, R. R. (1995). Comparison of the MMPI-2 Personality Psychopathology Five (PSY-5), the NEO-PI, and the NEO-PI-R. *Psychological Assessment, 7,* 508–516.

Trull, T. J., & Widiger, T. A. (1995). *Structured Interview for the Five-Factor Model (SIFFM).* Unpublished manuscript, University of Missouri, Columbia.

Waller, N. G., & Zavala, J. D. (1993). Evaluating the Big Five. *Psychological Inquiry, 4,* 131–134.

Watson, D., & Clark, L. A. (1984). Negative affectivity: The disposition to experience aversive emotional states. *Psychological Bulletin, 96,* 465–490.

Watson, D., Clark, L. A., & Harkness, A. R. (1994). Structures of personality and their relevance to psychopathology. *Journal of Abnormal Psychology, 103,* 18–31.

Widiger, T. A., & Corbitt, E. M. (1993). The MCMI–II personality disorder scales and their relationship to *DSM–III–R* diagnosis. In R. Craig (Ed.), *The Millon Clinical Multiaxial Inventory: A clinical research information synthesis* (pp. 181–201). Hillsdale, NJ: Lawrence Erlbaum Associates, Inc.

Widiger, T. A., & Costa, P. T. (1994). Personality and personality disorders. *Journal of Abnormal Psychology, 103,* 78–91.

Widiger, T. A., & Hagemoser, S. (in press). Personality disorders and the interpersonal circumplex. In R. Plutchik & H. R. Conte (Eds.), *Circumplex models of personality and emotions.* Washington, DC: American Psychological Association.

Widiger, T. J., & Trull, T. J. (1992). Personality and psychopathology: An application of the Five-Factor Model. *Journal of Personality, 60,* 363–393.

Wiggins, J. S. (1982). Circumplex models of interpersonal behavior in clinical psychology. In P. Kendall & J. N. Butcher (Eds.), *Handbook of research methods in clinical psychology* (pp. 183–221). New York: Wiley.

Wiggins, J. S., & Pincus, H. A. (1989). Conceptions of personality disorder and dimensions of personality. *Psychological Assessment, 1,* 305–316.

Wiggins, J. S., & Pincus, H. A. (1992). Personality: Structure and assessment. *Annual Review of Psychology, 43,* 473–504.

Zuckerman, M., Kuhlman, D. M., Joireman, J., Teta, P., & Kraft, M. (1993). A comparison of three structural models for personality: The Big Three, the Big Five, and the Alternative Five. *Journal of Personality and Social Psychology, 65,* 757–768.

10

Dimensions of Deception in Personality Assessment: The Example of the MMPI–2

David S. Nichols
Oregon State Hospital–Portland

Roger L. Greene
Pacific Graduate School of Psychology

The topic of deception in personality assessment is discussed along a number of dimensions relevant to clinical practice. The dimensions described are consistency versus accuracy of item endorsement, simulation versus dissimulation, generic versus specific deception, crude versus sophisticated deception, intentional versus nonintentional deception, self-deception versus impression management, and selectivity versus inclusiveness, as these may be encountered using the revised version of the Minnesota Multiphasic Personality Inventory. The emphasis is placed on deceptive strategies as operations as distinct from the traditional categories of response style such as social desirability. Directions for future research are indicated.

A primary role for clinicians is the assessment and treatment of mental disorders based on information gained from self-report inventories such as the revised Minnesota Multiphasic Personality Inventory (MMPI–2). However, self-report is not always an accurate reflection of the patient's actual attitudes and problems. Despite long-standing concerns about the accuracy of self-report, attempts to identify sources of inaccuracy are comparatively recent. Systematic study and classification of issues in the accuracy of self-report was initiated by Cronbach's (1946, 1950) reviews of research demonstrating the existence of stylistic consistencies (response styles) in the endorsement of test items that could undermine the influence of substantive variances in personality scales, with a corresponding deleterious effect on their predictive validity. These demonstrations inaugurated a burgeoning of research and controversy on response styles in the decades of the

1950s and 1960s that focused on putative deficiencies in the MMPI. In the succeeding quarter century, interest and investigation of response styles have waned, but controversy continues to the present day (Block, 1990; Edwards, 1990). Although Cronbach (1950) hinted that response styles might admit of substantive interpretation as personality traits, the response style research of the 1950s and 1960s focused on the theory and methodology of personality measurement that rarely trickled down to the domain of pragmatic concerns characterizing the day-to-day activities of clinicians. Clinicians are less concerned with the canons and pitfalls of psychological measurement as such; they are more concerned with the features of individual test performance that may compromise personality description and clinical prediction. In this context, clinicians attend to response styles not as conceptual categories (e.g., acquiescence, nay saying, or social desirability) but as operations utilized by the individual (e.g., faking bad, faking good, overreporting, underreporting, lying, malingering, responding defensively).

Reflecting the pragmatic concerns of clinicians, *deception* is used as an umbrella term for a variety of operations described next. In keeping with the likelihood that some forms of deception operate outside of awareness, deception is to be understood in its descriptive, not its evaluative, aspect. That is, the emphasis is on test-taking operations (forms of deception) that may have the effect of misleading clinicians, regardless of whether such operations are intentional.

We explicate the subject of deception in relation to self-report personality inventories and propose a reconceptualization of deception in clinical personality assessment. Although terms such as *validity* and *response style* are reasonably well understood within the field of personality assessment, this reconceptualization is necessary because their degree of conceptual overlap and appropriate range of application have been subject to confusion in particular circumstances, especially in the understanding and description of the individual case. For example, Scales *L, F,* and *K* of the MMPI–2 traditionally have been classified as validity scales. Yet these scales almost invariably come up in MMPI–2 discussions of deception. The question is whether they are validity scales, measures of deception, or both.

We make a distinction between consistency and accuracy of item endorsement before examining the issue of deception, because persons must endorse the items consistently before the discussion of deception is relevant. Only after the consistency of item endorsement has been established does it become possible to assess whether the person attempted to be deceptive in endorsing the items on the MMPI–2, the method(s) used to be deceptive, and the effects of this deception on the test findings. This reconceptualization of deception is made by highlighting (a) the difference between concealing what one believes to be true (dissimulation) and displaying what one believes to be false (simulation); (b) crude versus more sophisticated attempts to deceive; (c) generic versus specific deception; (d) intentional versus nonintentional deception; (e) self-deception versus impression management; and (f) inclusiveness versus selectivity in item endorsement.

INCONSISTENCY VERSUS INACCURACY

Nichols, Greene, and Schmolck (1989) developed a distinction between the concepts of consistency and accuracy of item endorsement in part on the grounds that the assessment of the consistency of the individual protocol is necessary before the standard clinical scales can be interpreted. A description of the endorsement of items as deceptive is unwarranted unless the items have been read and understood well enough for deceptive operations to have come into play. The distinction advanced by Nichols et al. (1989) was that between a content-nonresponsive (CNR) approach to endorsing items, and content-responsive faking (CRF). CNR occurs when the items are endorsed randomly, whereas in CRF, various deceptive strategies may be adopted to frustrate the purposes of assessment and mislead the clinician, such as grossly overreporting or underreporting symptoms and complaints. All CRF strategies depend on the items being endorsed consistently if the effort to deceive the clinician is to succeed.

In the MMPI environment, information about response consistency was gathered from two measures: the Test–Retest Index (T–R; Buechley & Ball, 1952; Greene, 1979) and the Carelessness Scale (*CLS*; Greene, 1978). These measures consisted of pairs of identical (T–R) or semantically similar (*CLS*) items. Because T–R and *CLS* did not survive the restandardization of the MMPI, two new consistency measures were devised for the MMPI-2: the Variable Response Inconsistency Scale (*VRIN*)—which, like *CLS*, consists of semantically similar pairs of items—and the True Response Inconsistency Scale (*TRIN*), consisting of item pairs that are opposite in content but keyed in the same direction. *VRIN* is most sensitive to response inconsistency when the percentages of true and false responses are similar or diverge only moderately, whereas *TRIN* is most sensitive to response inconsistency when the percentages of true and false responses are widely divergent.

DISSIMULATION VERSUS SIMULATION

The distinction between dissimulation and simulation rests on whether one seeks to mask actual traits, attitudes, and dispositions or to mimic such attributes when these are felt to be descriptively inaccurate.

Individuals may conceal certain attributes they believe to be descriptive of their behavior and personality (i.e., they may try to dissimulate). Such concealment is typically undertaken with reference to some tangible or anticipated threat of rejection by a mental health practitioner, potential employer, or a judge rendering a determination of child custody. The strategy of dissimulation can be applied to both the underreporting and overreporting of psychopathology. When the characteristics being concealed are socially undesirable or psychopathological, we speak of underreporting (being defensive or faking good). In underreporting, individuals seek to conceal indications of emotional distress, attitudinal deviance, and behavioral undercontrol by masking symptomatic or otherwise psychopathological characteristics. When the characteristics being concealed are socially desirable or nonpsychopathological, we speak of overreporting (exaggerating or faking bad). In overreporting, persons seek to mask their personal resources for coping and adjustment in order to avoid creating the impression of a capacity to respond adaptively to stresses. Thus, persons may seek to conceal their capacity to struggle against symptomatic expression, to combat the deleterious influences of symptoms on functioning, to create perspective and order in experience, and to accept support and assistance from others.

Persons also may try to simulate characteristics that they feel may not be descriptive of themselves. Such simulation typically is undertaken in mental health settings in which symptoms and problems are exaggerated as a communication of desperation (the "cry for help"), in disability and insurance compensation proceedings to support a claim of injury or disability, and in forensic settings to support a plea of insanity or diminished capacity. As in the case of dissimulation, a strategy of simulation also can be applied to both underreporting and overreporting of psychopathology. In underreporting, persons seek not to conceal adjustment or psychopathology, but to simulate freedom from any concerns about their personal adjustment or any form of psychopathology. They may endorse items not merely to conceal symptoms and maladjustment, but to assert a degree of soundness, virtue, prudence, strength, and well-being that is, if anything, superior to "normal" levels. In overreporting, persons simulate psychopathology by endorsing items considered to represent, not normal levels of stress and maladjustment, but the extremes of social deviance and mental disorder.

In underreporting as a result of dissimulation, persons are trying to conceal any indication of emotional distress, whereas in underreporting as a result of simulation, they are trying to assert superior adjustment. In overreporting as a result of dissimulation, persons conceal their resources for coping with their problems, whereas as a result of simulation, they report extreme levels of psychopathology and emotional distress.

GENERIC VERSUS SPECIFIC DECEPTION

Persons may dissimulate or simulate characteristics that can range from a rather generic description of psychopathology at one extreme (e.g., typified by instructions for persons to "fake bad" without further specification) to a very specific set of idiosyncratic behaviors at the other. As a rule, generic deception is readily detected by a number of MMPI–2 scales including F, $F - K$ (Gough, 1950), and Gough's (1954) Dissimulation scale (Ds). On the other hand, persons may discern an advantage to the dissimulation or simulation of specific traits or behaviors such as fearfulness, lethargy, suspiciousness, pain or other somatic problems, rebellious-ness, laziness, hostility, passivity, rule-breaking, excitement, or any other of hundreds of individual areas of item content that may leave few, if any, traces and may therefore be all but undetectable. This strategy is one that, to the best of our knowledge, has not been described in the literature of the MMPI/MMPI–2. An example, based on simulation, illustrates the endorsement of a specific area of item content as a decoy (Bell & Whaley, 1991) to arrest and divert the clinician's attention toward a result consonant with the person's purposes and to move the clinician toward a premature or erroneous conclusion. One of us, David S. Nichols, recalls a very disorganized inpatient with persecutory ideation who was committed following an altercation with her landlord. She produced a protocol with extremely elevated scores on scales composed of somatic content. Once her mental status had improved, she confided a dread of being seen as having a psychiatric disorder and had endorsed numerous somatic complaints in the hope that she would be trans-ferred to a medical hospital. This type of deceptive strategy is exemplified by a significantly elevated scale(s) that is strikingly inconsistent with the person's history or background. One approach to its assessment would be through the examination of scales with common item content. For MMPI–2 scales grouped on this basis, reference may be made to the MMPI–2 Structural Summary (Nichols & Greene, 1995).

Another approach is suggested by the tendency of scores on the subtle compo-nents of the basic MMPI–2 scales to increase as the endorsement of obvious items decreases, or vice versa, the so-called paradoxical effect (e.g., Burkhart, Christian, & Gynther, 1978). More detailed discussion of focused dissimulation or simulation is beyond the scope of this article, but a review of the paradoxical effect has appeared recently in Hollrath, Schlottmann, Scott, and Brunetti (1995). Reference to scale-by-scale differences in the endorsement of obvious–subtle items may provide cues to such focused strategies. For example, the respondent wishing specifically to simulate depression might produce a pattern of scores in which the subtle components are higher than their obvious counterparts for all scales except Depression.

In an evolving area of research investigating whether persons may be able to simulate specific mental disorders, several studies have made disorder-specific criteria available to the participants who are then instructed to malinger: borderline personality disorder (Sivec, Hilsenroth, & Lynn, 1995; Wetter, Baer, Berry, & Reynolds, 1994; Wetter, Baer, Berry, Robison, & Sumpter, 1993), closed head injury (Lamb, Berry, Wetter, & Baer, 1994), paranoia (Sivec, Lynn, & Garske, 1994), posttraumatic stress disorder (Fairbank, McCaffrey, & Keane, 1985; Wetter et al., 1993), schizophrenia (Rogers, Bagby, & Chakraborty, 1993; Wetter et al., 1993), and somatoform disorders (Sivec et al., 1994). Two generalizations can be made of this series of studies. First, validity indicators usually have good success at detecting those disorders such as schizophrenia (Rogers et al., 1993) and borderline personality disorder (Sivec et al., 1995; Wetter et al., 1994) that are characterized by extensive and severe psychopathology. The specific scale or index that is most successful varies by study as does the optimal cutting score. Second, persons who are instructed to simulate a specific disorder that is characterized by circumscribed and less severe psychopathology are both able to do so and are fairly difficult to detect (Lamb et al., 1994; Wetter et al., 1993), although success in this form of deception may owe as much or more to schooling in the nature and function of validity indicator as to schooling in a particular disorder.

CRUDE VERSUS SOPHISTICATED DECEPTION

Successful dissimulation or simulation requires that persons endorse items at odds with the true nature of the characteristics to be masked or mimicked, respectively, and that the consequences of these activities do not produce test scores or patterns that are recognizably false. Consideration of the degree of success achieved in the efforts to simulate a mental disorder or dissimulate its absence inevitably raises questions about the person's familiarity with the test instrument, including its scoring methods and norms, and, absent significant familiarity, the general intellectual and test-taking resources that the person brings to the task. Although discussion of the influence of the person's "test wisdom" for a specific personality test on the accuracy of item endorsement is beyond the scope of this article, we address the influence of certain general assets that the person may bring to the task of deception in personality testing and their bearing on the detection of deceptive motivation.

We distinguish between methods of deception that are relatively crude, in which persons' test-taking skills are unrefined and their execution of the deception is clumsy, and those that are relatively sophisticated, in which persons possess sufficient insight, knowledge, or experience of the test situation to execute a plan of deception smoothly. The origins of sophistication may range widely, from a factual foreknowledge of response style indicators whether gained through conversation with others who have completed the MMPI–2 or a formal preadministration orientation to the test and the purposes of the MMPI–2 evaluation, to an educated appreciation of the role and training of the clinical psychologist. Some persons may even be perceptive enough to recognize patterns within the test items.

Whether persons adopt a strategy of simulation, dissimulation, or some combination of the two, the success of their efforts to shape the attitudes and opinions of the clinician is of more than casual interest to both parties. For the person, success in applying the chosen strategy(ies) is measured primarily by progress toward whatever goal the deception was thought to be instrumental in achieving. In some cases success may be measured in the narcissistic gain of "putting one over" on the clinician. In either event, the success of the strategy depends on the clinician's failure to detect its operation or inability to compensate for it. For the clinician, success in detecting persons' attempts at deception provides an opportunity to better understand their personality and adjustment and their desire to influence the assessment. If deception is detected easily, the clinician may consider factors such as subnormal intelligence, naivete, cultural marginalization, cognitive rigidity, and impaired social reality testing. The clinician also may seek to develop inferences about persons' adaptation outside the assessment setting, and these inferences will shape and be shaped in turn by the analysis of other MMPI–2 scales and indices. If the clinician deems the strategy a sophisticated one, detects it only with difficulty, or is unable to detect a deceptive strategy, the clinician may be justified in drawing more favorable inferences about the persons' adaptation, such as those reflecting intellectual complexity, alertness, cognitive flexibility, sophistication, discernment, and sensitivity to nuance.

On the MMPI/MMPI–2, most of the items with psychopathological content are keyed for the true response. The only exception to this generalization are the items with primarily somatic content; these items are mostly keyed false. Thus, one indicator of an artless approach to deception is a very high proportion of true responses (*True* %) when persons wish to display psychopathology (simulation) or a very high proportion of false responses (*False* %) when the object is to mask it (dissimulation). High *True* % tends to produce extremely high elevations on Scales *F*, *6*, *8*, and *9*, with Scales *1*, *2*, and *3* ranging low. High *False* % strongly elevates Scales *L*, *F*, *K*, *1*, *2*, *3*, *4*, and *8*, with no low ranging scores save perhaps Scale *9*. On the MMPI–2, some degree of deception is suggested whenever *True* % reaches a level of 60, and whenever *False* % reaches a level of 70.

Another crude strategy involves the diffuse or general endorsement of psychopathology and results in unusually high mean profile elevation. Like a high *True* % value, a high average elevation for the eight basic clinical scales (Scales *1–4* and *6–8*) is an indication that pathological item content has been endorsed indiscriminately. Mean elevation (ME) has previously been discussed by Levitt and Gotts (1995) as a validity indicator. They pointed out the difficulty of obtaining an ME of 75 without widespread elevations among the clinical scales. For normals, ME is typically in a range of 45–55*T*. For general psychiatric in- and outpatients, the range is 55–65*T*. The profiles of even the most severely distressed psychiatric patients (e.g., *2–8/8–2* and *8–6/6–8* profiles) rarely exceed an ME of 80*T*, and even at this level, all of the basic scales are likely to exceed 65*T*, with a consequent breakdown in what might be called "profile coherence." That is, the respondent's portrayal of symptomatology becomes so diffuse that the profile tends to deviate from the typical pattern of two or three distinct high points, three or four intermediate elevations, and one or two distinct low points. An ME exceeding 85*T*, therefore, suggests a degree of overinclusiveness in the endorsement of psychopathology that is consistent with a crude attempt to simulate mental disorder. Protocols in which the ME exceeds 80*T* and *True* % exceeds 60 provide strong indication of a crude deceptive strategy. Dependable indicators of the contrasting sophisticated strategy for mimicking psychopathology are unclear at this time. But this should not be taken to mean that sophisticated efforts to deceive will inevitably succeed in leading the clinician to confirm mental disorder, disability, or diminished capacity on the basis of test performance. In most cases, scales such as F, Psychiatric F ($F[p]$; Arbisi & Ben-Porath, 1995), and Ds, perform well in the detection of simulated psychopathology, regardless of whether the approach is crude or not. But it is difficult not to believe that in some cases, and perhaps a significant number of them, sophisticated simulation may go undetected. And, in general, it appears that these instances of successful simulation cannot be attributable solely to a lack of test expertise on the part of the clinician but in many instances will be the result of extraordinary preparations by respondents—preparations that may include immersion in the relevant literature, actual practice with the test, and even direct or indirect consultation with experts.

The tactics and techniques employed to mask psychopathology and maladjustment may also be seen as falling on a gradient of relative crudeness versus sophistication. The Lie (L) scale affords the most ready example of a crude masking technique. As a scale of improbable virtues, it lends itself to persons who wish to display a virtuous persona in the hope that subjectively felt moral flaws and failings will go undetected. The crudeness of the L method of simulating adjustment is in the fact that the items reflect virtues that few are expected to endorse as valid self-descriptors, virtues that, by common knowledge, are honored more in the breach than in the observance.

Another crude masking technique involves the avoidance of items reflecting activity in emotional life such as interest and a feeling of engagement; a sense of energy and excitement; and the pleasures of interaction, social involvement, and the assertion of one's individuality. In some persons, the denial or admission of symptoms may be secondary to the wish to convey that it is an attenuated subjectivity that experiences them. Welsh's (1956) Repression (R) performs as a measure of this dimension. Here a deceptive end is achieved by masking personal resources that, if admitted, would suggest a reservoir of adaptive capacity that could be brought to bear in the interest of adjustment. Because the items of R deny the presence and operation of a rather wide range of mostly positive emotional resources, high scores reflect the inhibition, constriction, or immobilization of vital emotionality, thereby creating an impression of helplessness; of one from whom little can be expected. Despite the availability of scores on R for nearly 40 years, and their regular inclusion in automated MMPI-2 reports, this scale remains underresearched and poorly understood, particularly in relation to concepts with which it could be hypothetically associated such as alexithymia, negativism, and emotional numbing.

The K scale was devised, in part, as a means of detecting a more sophisticated form of dissimulation that might well go undetected by L (Meehl & Hathaway,

1946), and many scales have been developed subsequently to afford the interpreter perspective on the performances of more sophisticated respondents, including the new Superlative Self-Presentation scale (*S*) of Butcher and Han (1995).

INTENTIONAL VERSUS NONINTENTIONAL DECEPTION

In the discussion thus far, we have tended to frame deception as a process that persons undertake intentionally in order to achieve desired outcomes that, in principle, could be articulated. However, both the revelation and concealment of symptoms and maladjustment may be unintended. Just as ego-syntonic, delusional ideation may lead the otherwise defensive paranoid to inadvertently display suspiciousness on some of the more pathological items on the Paranoia (*Pa*) or Cynicism (*CYN*) scales, it could be said that ego-syntonic defensive ideation may lead the person with a relatively positive and cooperative attitude toward the assessment to inadvertently conceal areas of maladjustment or concern. In both cases, crucial elements of the deceptive process may operate out of awareness and therefore outside the conscious control of the person. The support of habitual or long-cherished self-attributions, the maintenance and protection of self-esteem, the occasion of dissonance between an habitual view of one's good adjustment and emergent evidence to the contrary, or even the reflex of giving oneself the benefit of reasonable doubts may operate in the person's interaction with test items in the absence of any conscious desire to frustrate the purposes of testing or to mislead the clinician.

Experience with various empirically developed scales such as the MacAndrew Alcoholism scale (*MAC-R*; MacAndrew, 1965) and the Overcontrolled Hostility scale (*O-H*; Megargee, Cook, & Mendelsohn, 1967) suggests that persons' awareness of their motives and dispositions is often incomplete, unformulated, and even inaccessible to introspection. Similarly, persons' ability to discern the meaning and implications of the items of the MMPI–2 varies not only with their wishes and attitudes, but with the items themselves, which differ in degrees of subtlety, desirability, and ambiguity. As a consequence, responses to the items will be determined in part by persons' self-conscious or deliberate desire to communicate, or not to communicate, certain symptoms, complaints, facts, feelings, and attitudes, but also by dispositions that are tacit and inadvertent—more global, inchoate, and distant from conscious awareness and control.

SELF-DECEPTION VERSUS IMPRESSION MANAGEMENT

Factor studies of various measures of self-favorable responding to the MMPI have repeatedly produced findings indicating that defensiveness cannot be subsumed under a single dimension. In Wiggins' (1964) analysis and extension of these reports, he distinguishes between *Alpha* (Block, 1965), a dimension consistent with Edwards' (1957) interpretation of faking good on personality inventories without special instructions to do so (p. 57), and *Gamma,* which Wiggins (1964) interpreted as "social desirability role-playing" (p. 555). Expanding on Wiggins' analysis, Paulhus (1984, 1986) proposed a two-factor model of social desirability responding that distinguishes between self-deception, the tendency to bias inventory responses brought about by the person's belief that such responses are true and justified, and impression management (other-deception), a self-conscious and deliberate attempt to tailor responses so as to create a favorable impression and mislead the clinician in the direction of an overly benign personality description from test results.

   Gamma has been labeled variously as a "lying" (Edwards, Diers, & Walker, 1962), "propagandistic bias" (Damarin & Messick, 1965) and "impression management" (Paulhus, 1984, 1986), and these labels converge on the theme of a self-conscious, or intentional, motivation to promote a favorable impression of the self. As Paulhus (1986) noted, this dimension has been understood as (a) strategic simulation, in which the person enacts a socially desirable role as a means of gaining power or advantage over a particular target, (b) a motive, to attain admiration, affection, or approval, and (c) a skill that allows one to successfully calibrate self-presentation to ambient social exigencies in order to achieve a state of appropriate and harmonious integration within the stream of interaction.

   A series of analyses of 11 noncollege samples by Nichols and Greene (1988) supported Paulhus' distinction, with the *Alpha* dimension best marked by Edwards' Social Desirability (*SD*), with loadings averaging .91 across samples. The *Gamma* dimension was most clearly marked by Wiggins' (1959) Social Desirability (*Sd*) and Cofer, Chance, and Judson's (1949) Positive Malingering (*Mp*), with average loadings across samples of .92 and .85, respectively.

   Although large effect sizes have been found for *Mp* and *Sd* (Baer, Wetter, & Berry, 1992), these scales remain underexplored in research and clinical practice. Their loss of items in the transition to the MMPI–2 (seven each) should not be an impediment to such exploration, as both have performed well in their attenuated versions (Baer, Wetter, Nichols, Greene, & Berry, 1995).

   Research designs that evaluate the comparative performance of various measures of impression management within specific populations, like those recently reported by Otto, Lang, Megargee, and Rosenblatt (1988) and by Baer et al. (1995), provide the best evidence of incremental validity and the most reliable guidance for clinical practice with these scales. The recent research showing that nondepressed individuals harbor not fewer but more illusory self-attributions than depressed individuals (e.g., Lewinsohn, Mischel, Chaplain, & Barton, 1980) calls into question long-held views about the supposed virtues of realism in self-perception. Indeed, Greene, Davis, and Welch (1989) found that low scorers on one measure of self-deception (*SD*) were more likely to be rated as anxious and depressed than high scorers.

Much investigation into the motives, styles, contexts, and consequences of self-deception will be required before a meaningful set of classifications relevant to the tasks of personality assessment can be achieved. For now, the distinction between benign and malignant forms of self-deception is too hazy to allow confident judgments without reference to data external to the MMPI–2.

SELECTIVITY VERSUS INCLUSIVENESS

The task of completing the MMPI–2 is one in which persons must make decisions not only about the kinds of symptoms and attitudes to be communicated to the clinician, but also about their range. For example, persons wishing to convey information about the depressive state they are experiencing have a very broad range of items from which to choose in conveying the description of this subjective state as they uniquely experience it and its consequences in their life. The items available for endorsement in the person's effort to delimit the depressive state as it is experienced are by no means confined to those contained in Scale 2 (*D*) and the Depression content scale (*DEP*), but are also included in significant numbers among the other clinical scales (e.g., *3* [*Hy*], *4* [*Pd*], *6* [*Pa*], *7* [*Pt*], *8* [*Sc*], *0* [*Si*]), and among many of the content scales (e.g., *ANX, OBS, LSE, SOD, WRK, TRT*). In the attempt to convey the person's experiences, some items will be endorsed as distinctly germane to their symptomatic description, items having certain semantic and structural characteristics that in their topical, intensity, and durational aspects may be deemed descriptively on the mark and experientially central. For the majority of items, however, the fit between item and experience will be more tenuous. In one case, the name given to the symptom may fail to achieve precise subjective resonance or semantic recognition (e.g., blue, restlessness, regret); in another, the tense will be wrong; in still another, the intensity implied will be excessive (or insufficient); and in a fourth, the temporal or frequency characteristics of the item will seem a poor match. For the majority of items, then, endorsement may be best considered a threshold phenomenon for which overreporting and underreporting can be seen as limiting cases, one dependent on persons' estimate of the goodness of the items' fit to their subjective experience, their need or desire to convey this experience to the clinician, or a combination of these.

In this context, the report of symptoms via the MMPI–2 can be seen as falling along a gradient that is anchored at one end by standard measures of generalized or indiscriminate underreporting, extending into a range wherein symptoms are reported in a highly selective and discriminating fashion. This range yields, in turn, to a range in which the endorsement threshold is sufficiently low to result in a less discriminating, more inclusive report of symptoms. It terminates in a range traditionally anchored by measures of generalized or indiscriminate overreporting. It is important to note that the intermediate ranges of the gradient just described—ranges that may conveniently be called *selective* and *inclusive,* respectively—should not be considered in the same light (that of inaccuracy) as its extremes. Rather, performances in these intermediate ranges can be, and traditionally have been, considered acceptably accurate and interpretable. Although the distinction between selective and inclusive styles of symptomatic presentation has not been noted previously in the MMPI/MMPI–2 literature, there are reasons to suppose that these styles may correspond to differences in their respective empirical correlates, diagnostic handling, clinical management, and response to treatment. For example, selective reporters of psychopathology may be less confused and distractible, enjoy greater cognitive control, may be more committed to working to alleviate the symptoms they have gone to such trouble to delineate, and be more articulate in describing and discussing their symptoms than inclusive reporters. Such an advantage might lead to more accurate diagnosis, more efficient and appropriate treatment selection, more active collaboration with treatment personnel, fewer treatment trials, and better and more rapid therapeutic outcomes.

There are two measures on the MMPI–2 that, in combination, provide some indication of the person's orientation to conveying symptoms. The value determined by the average elevation (ME) of the basic eight clinical scales (*1–,4 6–9*) less the value for the proportion of items endorsed true (*True* %) can serve as a crude index of selectivity versus inclusiveness, with values in the range of 23 to 40 indicating selectivity and values from 5 to 22 indicating a trend toward overinclusiveness. Values within the selective range suggest that although the person is sufficiently symptomatic to produce an elevated profile, the endorsement of false-keyed, correction, and subtle items, along with the moderated endorsement of true-keyed items, have contributed to the production of that elevation. Because most of the somatic content on the MMPI–2 is false keyed, this index would perform poorly among somatoform profiles. An alternate and possibly superior index is the total T score difference on the Obvious minus the Subtle subscales (see Greene, 1991), with values in a range from 30 to 90 marking a relatively selective area of this range and values from 90 to 150 marking a relatively inclusive range of symptomatic report. It should be emphasized that this discussion of selective versus inclusive responding, in general, and the suggestions for the assessment of these styles of response, in particular, are offered for the purpose of stimulating discussion and investigation. The clinical application of the indexes described at this time is premature.

A NOTE ON "LYING"

Weil (1989) told of a jealous father who would interrogate his son about the mother's visitors during the day while the father was at work. If the son reported that no one had visited, the father beat him. To avoid these beatings, the son soon resorted to confabulating reports for his father (pp. 205–207).

We often make clinical judgments about the reliability of the reports our patients make to us without much consideration for the patient's own experience of truth and falsehood. Yet Weil's example shows that the truth is not always a paying proposition. Like other response classes, the truth may bring more grief than reward, and it can be important for the clinician to appreciate what life has taught the patient about truth and falsity, about lying and fessing up.

The Lie scale (*L*) of the MMPI was composed from an earlier set of items written by Hartshorne and May (1928) for their studies of deceit in children. But in labeling the scale as he did, Hathaway was not after the patient's attitudes toward truth versus lying. Rather he merely wished to provide several opportunities for the patient to claim "extremely good and rare human qualities which it is statistically absurd to suppose will all or in large part [apply to anyone]" (Meehl & Hathaway, 1946, p. 530). Among the 15 items of *L*, only 1 takes as its subject the truth itself: 41, "I do not always tell the truth." Yet there are at least 8 other items (26, 81, 269, 284, 383, 418, 433, and 434) that have content addressing attitudes toward truth and deception. In a sample of 3475 psychiatric inpatients and outpatients, coefficient alpha is .59 for this nine-item Lying scale, an acceptable value for a scale of this length. In the same sample, the Lying scale is correlated inversely with *L* (–.47) and *Pa3* (–.62; Moral Virtue), respectively, and positively with the MMPI–2 Cynicism (*CYN*) content scale (.64), indicating that the high Lying scorer views others as comparably lacking in veracity.

Both *L* and the Lying scale are likely to vary inversely with educational level and socioeconomic status. But whereas *L* reflects one's level of fear of criticism or moral judgment, the Lying items get at the respondent's pragmatic conception of truth. Has telling the truth proven to be a successful strategy, even when some potential reward for not doing so has been apparent? Or, have its costs tended to outweigh its benefits? And we may further ask, what kind of world is it for one for whom the truth seems not to work very well?

Consider the differences among four hypothetical patients, each having one of these four patterns of scores of *L* and the Lying scale: High Low, High High, Low High, and Low Low. The High Low combination suggests an individual who claims the moral high ground in all of the areas covered in *L* and, if for no other reason but the sake of consistency, places truth-telling high on his or her scale of values. The Low High combination covers the opposite, immoral trend. But what of High High and Low Low? The High High combination would seem to reflect qualities of both naiveté concerning what constitutes a realistic portrayal of virtues in this culture and an unusually timid, harm-avoidant approach to discourse, wherein truth-telling is seen as a kind of provocation for the punitive hostility of others. Note that it is not only authority that is in question in the Lying items—it is people in general. The Low Low scorer has the courage of his or her lack of conviction, conveying that, whereas one may abjure faultless manners in the comfort of one's own home, gossip, procrastinate, enjoy obscenity, get angry at times, vote in spite of ignorance, or act from competitive motives, a sense of honor requires that one admit such failings with a degree of candor that many would find coarse, excessive, and even paradoxically self-serving!

SUMMARY

The multifaceted nature of deception in personality assessment has been illustrated with reference to a number of dimensions, most of which are described for the MMPI–2. At the present time, most of the dimensions discussed are not sufficiently well understood and require further clinical observation and research inquiry. It is nevertheless clear that the concept of deception in personality assessment is one bearing a level of complexity that has been largely unforeseen. As a result, the opportunities for confounding among these dimensions in previous investigations of deception has made their results difficult to interpret. Although the advances made in the study of deception over the past 50 years have been considerable, further clarification of the dimensions and operations of deception will make unprecedented demands on the acuity of clinicians and the ingenuity of researchers through the year 2000 and beyond.

ACKNOWLEDGMENTS

We thank Mary Beth Grabon and David R. Strong for discussions of some of the issues presented here and for access to their unpublished materials, and two anonymous reviewers for their helpful comments on the article.

REFERENCES

Arbisi, P. A., & Ben-Porath, Y. S. (1995). An MMPI-2 infrequent response scale for use with psychopathological populations: The Infrequency-Psychopathology scale F(p). *Psychological Assessment, 7,* 424–431.

Baer, R. A., Wetter, M. W., & Berry, D. T. R. (1992). Detection of underreporting of psychopathology on the MMPI: A meta-analysis. *Clinical Psychology Review, 12,* 509–525.

Baer, R. A., Wetter, M. W., Nichols, D. S., Greene, R. L., & Berry, D. T. R. (1995). Sensitivity of MMPI–2 validity scales to underreporting of symptoms. *Psychological Assessment, 7,* 419–423.

Bell, J. B., & Whaley, B. (1991). *Cheating and deception.* New Brunswick, NJ: Transaction.

Block, J. (1965). *The challenge of response sets.* New York: Appleton-Century-Crofts.

Block, J. (1990). More remarks on social desirability. *American Psychologist, 45,* 1076–1077.

Buechley, R., & Ball, H. (1952). A new test of "validity" for the group MMPI. *Journal of Consulting Psychology, 16,* 299–301.

Burkhart, B. R., Christian, W. L., & Gynther, M. D. (1978). Item subtlety and faking on the MMPI: A paradoxical relationship. *Journal of Personality Assessment, 42,* 76–80.

Butcher, J. N., & Han, K. (1995). Development of an MMPI-2 scale to assess the presentation of self in a superlative manner: The S scale. In J. N. Butcher & C. D. Spielberger (Eds.), *Advances in personality assessment* (Vol. 10, pp. 25–50). Hillsdale, NJ: Lawrence Erlbaum Associates, Inc.

Cofer, C. N., Chance, J. E., & Judson, A. J. (1949). A study of malingering on the MMPI. *Journal of Psychology, 27,* 491–499.

Cronbach, L. J. (1946). Response set and test validity. *Educational and Psychological Measurement, 6,* 475–494.

Cronbach, L. J. (1950). Further evidence on response sets and test design. *Educational and Psychological Measurement, 10,* 3–31.

Damarin, F., & Messick, S. (1965). *Response styles as personality variables: A theoretical integration of multivariate research* (Research Bulletin 65–10). Princeton, NJ: Educational Testing Service.

Edwards, A. L. (1957). *The social desirability variable in personality assessment and research.* New York: Dryden.

Edwards, A. L. (1990). Construct validity and social desirability. *American Psychologist, 45,* 287–289.

Edwards, A. L., Diers, C. J., & Walker, J. N. (1962). Response sets and factor loadings on sixty-one personality scales. *Journal of Applied Psychology, 46,* 220–225.

Fairbank, J. A., McCaffrey, R. J., & Keane, T. M. (1985). Psychometric detection of fabricated symptoms of posttraumatic stress disorder. *American Journal of Psychiatry, 142,* 501–503.

Gough, H. G. (1950). The F minus K dissimulation index for the MMPI. *Journal of Consulting Psychology, 14,* 408–413.

Gough, H. G. (1954). Some common misconceptions about neuroticism. *Journal of Consulting Psychology, 18,* 287–292.

Greene, R. L. (1978). An empirically derived MMPI carelessness scale. *Journal of Clinical Psychology, 34,* 407–410.

Greene, R. L. (1979). Response consistency on the MMPI: The TR index. *Journal of Personality Assessment, 43,* 69–71.

Greene, R. L. (1991). *The MMPI-2/MMPI: An interpretive manual.* Boston: Allyn & Bacon.

Greene, R. L., Davis, H. G., & Welch, S. M. (1989, August). *Clinical correlates of self-deception and impression management on the MMPI.* Paper presented at the 97th annual convention of the American Psychological Association, Atlanta.

Hartshorne, H., & May, M. A. (1928). *Studies in deceit.* New York: Macmillan.

Hollrath, J. L., Schlottmann, R. S., Scott, A. B., & Brunetti, D. G. (1995). Validity of the MMPI subtle items. *Journal of Personality Assessment, 65,* 278–299.

Lamb, D. G., Berry, D. T. R., Wetter, M. W., & Baer, R. A. (1994). Effects of two types of information on malingering on the MMPI-2: An analogue investigation. *Psychological Assessment, 6,* 8–13.

Levitt, E. E., & Gotts, E. E. (1995). *The clinical application of MMPI special scales* (2nd ed.). Hillsdale, NJ: Lawrence Erlbaum Associates, Inc.

Lewinsohn, P. M., Mischel, W., Chaplain, W., & Barton, R. (1980). Social competence and depression: The role of illusory self-perceptions? *Journal of Abnormal Psychology, 89,* 203–212.

MacAndrew, C. (1965). The differentiation of male alcoholic outpatients from nonalcoholic psychiatric outpatients by means of the MMPI. *Quarterly Journal of Studies on Alcohol, 42,* 238–246.

Meehl, P. E., & Hathaway, S. R. (1946). The K factor as a suppressor variable in the MMPI. *Journal of Applied Psychology, 30,* 525–564.

Megargee, E. I., Cook, P. E., & Mendelsohn, G. A. (1967). Development and validation of an MMPI scale of assaultiveness in overcontrolled individuals. *Journal of Abnormal Psychology, 72,* 519–528.

Nichols, D. S., & Greene, R. L. (1988, March). *Adaptive or defensive: An evaluation of Paulhus' two-factor model of social desirability responding in the MMPI with non-college samples.* Paper presented at the 23rd annual symposium on Recent Developments in the Use of the MMPI, St. Petersburg Beach, FL.

Nichols, D. S., & Greene, R. L. (1995). *MMPI-2 Structural Summary interpretive manual*. Odessa, FL: Psychological Assessment Resources.

Nichols, D. S., Greene, R. L., & Schmolck, P. (1989). Criteria for assessing inconsistent patterns of item endorsement on the MMPI: Rationale, development, and empirical trials. *Journal of Clinical Psychology, 45,* 239–250.

Otto, R. K., Lang, A. R., Megargee, E. I., & Rosenblatt, A. I. (1988). Ability of alcoholics to escape detection by the MMPI. *Journal of Consulting and Clinical Psychology, 56,* 452–457.

Paulhus, D. L. (1984). Two-component models of socially desirable responding. *Journal of Personality and Social Psychology, 46,* 598–609.

Paulhus, D. L. (1986). Self-deception and impression management in test responses. In A. Angleitner & J. S. Wiggins (Eds.), *Personality assessment via questionnaires: Current issues in theory and measurement* (pp. 143–165). Berlin: Springer-Verlag.

Rogers, R., Bagby, R. M., & Chakraborty, D. (1993). Feigning schizophrenic disorders on the MMPI-2: Detection of coached simulators. *Journal of Personality Assessment, 60,* 215–226.

Sivec, H. J., Hilsenroth, M. J., & Lynn, S. J. (1995). Impact of simulating borderline personality disorder on the MMPI-2: A cost-benefits model employing base rates. *Journal of Personality Assessment, 64,* 295–311.

Sivec, H. J., Lynn, S. J., & Garske, J. P. (1994). The effect of somatoform disorder and paranoid psychotic role-related dissimulations as a response set on the MMPI-2. *Assessment, 1,* 69–81.

Weil, J. L. (1989). *Instinctual stimulation of children: From common practice to child abuse, Vol. 2: Clinical cases.* Madison, CT: International Universities Press.

Welsh, G. S. (1956). Factor dimensions *A* and *R.* In G. S. Welsh & W. G. Dahlstrom (Eds.), *Basic readings on the MMPI in psychology and medicine* (pp. 264–281). Minneapolis: University of Minnesota Press.

Wetter, M. W., Baer, R. A., Berry, D. T. R., & Reynolds, S. K. (1994). The effect of symptom information on faking on the MMPI-2. *Assessment, 1,* 199–207.

Wetter, M. W., Baer, R. A., Berry, D. T. R., Robison, L. H., & Sumpter, J. (1993). MMPI-2 profiles of motivated fakers given specific symptom information: A comparison to matched patients. *Psychological Assessment, 5,* 317–323.

Wiggins, J. S. (1959). Interrelationships among MMPI measures of dissimulation under standard and social desirability instructions. *Journal of Consulting Psychology, 23,* 419–427.

Wiggins, J. S. (1964). Convergences among stylistic response measures from objective personality tests. *Educational and Psychological Measurement, 24,* 551–562.

11

Measurement and Mismeasurement of Mood: Recurrent and Emergent Issues

David Watson and Lee Anna Clark
Department of Psychology
University of Iowa

The "affective explosion" in psychology has led to tremendous advances in mood measurement. Mood ratings reflect a hierarchical structure consisting of two broad dimensions—Positive Affect and Negative Affect—and multiple specific states. Brief scales have been developed that reliably assess Positive and Negative Affect across different populations and time frames, in both between- and within-subject data. We examine controversies related to (a) the content of these higher order scales and (b) the independence of Positive and Negative Affect. Regarding the latter, we show that Positive and Negative Affect scales remain largely independent across a wide range of conditions, even after controlling for random and systematic error. Finally, there remains little consensus regarding the lower order structure of affect. This lack of a compelling taxonomy has substantially slowed progress in assessing mood at the specific affect level.

Psychology first discovered behavior, then embraced cognition, and finally in the 1980s recognized the central importance of affect in human experience. This belated acknowledgment prompted an ongoing explosion of research related to mood and emotionality. Indeed, a PsycLIT database survey of articles published in the 3-year period from 1992 to 1994 revealed 1,857 articles with the keywords "mood" or "emotion." This upsurge in research, in turn, has led to a growing need for reliable and valid measures to assess affect-related constructs. In this article we focus specifically on issues related to the measurement of subjectively experienced mood. As we discuss, although some problems and controversies remain, mood researchers have made great progress in the development of precise and valid measures, particularly at the general factor level.

THE HIERARCHICAL STRUCTURE OF MOOD

At first glance, mood assessment may appear to be a formidable and daunting enterprise. One obvious problem is that mood ratings require respondents both to quantify subtle changes in their own internal experience—which they may or may not be able to do with much precision—and to report these changes honestly and accurately—which they may or may not be inclined to do. Fortunately, although mood measurement is by no means error-free (as we discuss in some detail subsequently), these problems have not proven insurmountable; in fact, we later review considerable evidence demonstrating the construct validity of affect self-ratings.

A more vexing problem concerns the nature and scope of the moods to be sampled. The list of potentially relevant mood states is enormous: How does one decide which to assess? As discussed elsewhere (Watson & Clark, 1991, 1992a), mood researchers have addressed this problem in two basic ways. One old and prominent approach—which is closely linked to classical emotion theory—emphasizes the importance of discrete, specific types of affect, such as anxiety, hostility, depression, and joy. In support of this view, researchers repeatedly have identified well-defined content factors reflecting discrete types of affect; moreover, very similar factors—including fear, anger and sadness—have emerged consistently across different studies (e.g., McNair, Lorr, & Droppleman, 1971; Watson & Clark, 1994b; Zuckerman & Lubin, 1985). Furthermore, measures of these discrete affects show good convergent and adequate discriminant validity, thereby establishing the viability of the underlying specific affect constructs (see Bagozzi, 1993; Berenbaum, Fujita, & Pfennig, 1995; Diener, Smith, & Fujita, 1995; Watson & Clark, 1992a).

Nevertheless, the limitations of this approach also have become increasingly apparent. The most serious problem is that measures of different affects tend to be strongly and systematically interrelated. Specifically, people who experience significant levels of one type of negative affect (e.g., fear) also tend to report elevated levels of other negative moods (e.g., anger, sadness); similarly, individuals who report one type of positive feeling (e.g., energy) report many others (e.g., interest, joy) as well. Watson and Clark (1992a), for instance, reported strong correlations among measures of fear, sadness, guilt, and hostility in several studies that included both self- and peer-rated affect. Similarly, using both self- and informant data, Diener et al. (1995) found that scores on various negative affects (fear, shame, anger, sadness) were strongly interrelated, as were measures of two different positive affects (love, joy). Indeed, multitrait–multimethod analyses consistently demonstrate much stronger evidence for nonspecificity (i.e., significant correlations among measures of different, similarly-valenced affects) than for specificity (i.e., unique relations between measures of the same target affect) in mood data (for discussions of this issue, see Bagozzi, 1993; Berenbaum et al., 1995; Watson & Clark, 1992a).

This enormous nonspecificity demonstrates that mood can be characterized by a much smaller number of general dimensions. In response to this evidence, mood researchers increasingly have turned to the second basic approach, namely, dimensional models. Although earlier models often posited three major dimensions (e.g., Engen, Levy & Schlosberg, 1958), the accumulating evidence gradually has led to a general consensus that two broad factors constitute the basic dimensions of affect (e.g., Diener et al., 1995; Feldman, 1995; Larsen & Diener, 1992; Russell, Weiss, & Mendelsohn, 1989; Tellegen, 1985; Watson & Tellegen, 1985). We discuss these "Big Two" dimensions shortly, but first we want to emphasize that these two basic approaches—dimensions and discrete affects—are not incompatible or mutually exclusive; rather, they essentially reflect different levels of a single, integrated hierarchical structure (see Berenbaum et al., 1995; Diener et al., 1995; Watson & Clark, 1992a; Watson & Tellegen, 1985). That is, each of the higher order dimensions can be decomposed into several correlated yet ultimately distinct affective states, much like a general factor of personality (e.g., neuroticism) can be subdivided into several narrower components or "facets" (e.g., anxiety, vulnerability). In this hierarchical model, the lower level reflects the unique descriptive/explanatory power of the individual discrete affects (i.e., specificity), whereas the general dimensions reflect their shared, overlapping qualities (i.e., nonspecificity).

As noted earlier, both specificity and nonspecificity can be demonstrated in the same set of data, although evidence for the latter tends to be somewhat stronger. Moreover, as we have argued elsewhere (Watson & Clark, 1992a), both levels of this hierarchical structure must be assessed for a complete and comprehensive exploration of mood. However, very different issues are involved in assessing general versus specific types of affect. Consequently, we examine the two levels of the hierarchical structure separately, starting with the general, higher order level.

THE "BIG TWO" OF AFFECT

The Two-Factor Structure of Affect

What are the general dimensions that underlie mood ratings? Two alternative conceptualizations—which essentially represent rotational variants of one another—have played a particularly prominent role in the literature (Feldman, 1995; Larsen & Diener, 1992; Mayer & Gaschke, 1988; Watson & Tellegen, 1985). First, many researchers advocate an approach based on dimensions that are usually labeled *Pleasantness versus Unpleasantness* (i.e., the extent to which one is generally feeling good vs. bad) and *Activation or Arousal* (i.e., the extent to which one is feeling engaged or energized) (Feldman, 1995; Larsen & Diener, 1992; Russell et al., 1989). These dimensions originally were identified in non-self-report data such as studies of facial and vocal emotional expressions and semantic analyses of mood terms (see Russell, 1980). However, it subsequently was found that

Pleasantness and Activation typically emerged as the first two unrotated factors in analyses of self-rated mood as well (Feldman, 1995; Russell, 1980; Watson & Tellegen, 1985). In light of this evidence, several researchers have championed this model as a basic organizing scheme for mood research (see Feldman, 1995; Larsen & Diener, 1992; Russell et al., 1989).

The second prominent scheme focuses on the dimensions that reliably emerge after an orthogonal, simple structure rotation of affect self-ratings. These are factors typically labeled *Negative Affect* and *Positive Affect.* The Negative Affect dimension represents the extent to which one is nonspecifically experiencing a negative or aversive mood, such as feelings of nervousness, sadness, irritation, guilt, contempt, or disgust. In contrast, Positive Affect reflects the extent to which one is experiencing a positive mood, such as feelings of joy, interest, energy, enthusiasm, or alertness. Note that unlike the Pleasantess/Activation model, this scheme makes a fundamental distinction between positive and negative affective experience; indeed, because it is based on an orthogonal rotation (in which the factors are constrained to be uncorrelated), this conceptualization posits that variations in positive and negative mood are largely independent of one another. We explore this point in detail in a later section.

An extensive body of evidence supports this particular two-factor scheme. Positive and Negative Affect consistently emerge as major factors across different descriptor sets, time frames, response formats and rotational schemes, and in both within- and between-subject analyses (Mayer & Gaschke, 1988; Meyer & Shack, 1989; Tellegen, 1985; Watson, 1988; Watson & Tellegen, 1985; Zevon & Tellegen, 1982). Cross-cultural replicability also has been demonstrated in Japan (Watson, Clark, & Tellegen, 1984), Israel (Almagor & Ben-Porath, 1989), and Russia (Balatsky & Diener, 1993). Thus, the structure's robustness is impressive.

We focus our discussion on Positive and Negative Affect, rather than Pleasantness and Activation, for three closely related reasons. First, although the latter model has been a dominant force in non-self-report data, it has been less popular and influential in the self-report literature, which is our central concern. Second, mood researchers have devoted far more attention to the assessment of Positive and Negative Affect than to the measurement of Pleasantness and Activation. In this regard, it is noteworthy that several reliable and valid measures of Positive and Negative Affect have been developed (for a comparative analysis, see Watson, 1988). In contrast, the Pleasantness/Activation model has produced only one systematic, well-validated self-report measure in recent years: the Affect Grid (Russell et al., 1989), which uses a single item to measure both dimensions. Finally, because they have received the bulk of the attention, the Positive and Negative Affect dimensions (and the scales developed to assess them) also have been the focus of the greatest concern and controversy. Consequently, by focusing on this model we can examine several unresolved theoretical issues and ongoing empirical controversies.

Measuring Positive and Negative Affect

As mentioned earlier, many different measures have been developed to assess the higher order Positive and Negative Affect dimensions. Watson (1988) examined the psychometric properties of several 4- to 10-item scales, including those created by Bradburn (1969), Diener (e.g., Diener & Emmons, 1984; Diener & Iran-Nejad, 1986), and Stone (e.g., Kennedy-Moore, Greenberg, Newman, & Stone, 1992; Stone, 1987). Most of these measures (the most notable exception being the 5-item scales developed by Bradburn, 1969) had acceptable internal consistency reliabilities—with coefficient alphas generally in the .75 to .90 range—as well as excellent convergent validity, with convergent correlations generally ranging from .70 to .90. Thus, researchers wishing to measure these constructs apparently can choose from a number of reasonably good alternatives. However, the discriminant validity of the scales (i.e., the correlation between Negative and Positive Affect) varied widely; thus, the selection of a particular measure can have potentially important consequences. We return later to this issue of discriminant validity.

To establish the construct validity of these general mood measures more fully, we now discuss their psychometric properties in more detail, drawing on the data we have collected using our own scales, which comprise the Positive and Negative Affect Schedule (PANAS; Watson, Clark, & Tellegen, 1988). The original PANAS contains 10-item Negative and Positive Affect scales. The terms comprising Negative Affect are afraid, ashamed, distressed, guilty, hostile, irritable, jittery, nervous, scared, and upset. The Positive Affect scale consists of active, alert, attentive, determined, enthusiastic, excited, inspired, interested, proud, and strong. The terms can be used with several different time frames (e.g., how one feels right now, how one has felt over the past few weeks). In each case, respondents rate the extent to which they have experienced each term on a 5-point scale ranging from 1 (*very slightly or not at all*) to 5 (*extremely*).

Watson et al. (1988) reported data establishing the reliability and validity of the PANAS scales. Specifically, they conducted a series of analyses on six large data sets, with sample sizes ranging from 586 to 1,002; respondents rated themselves on the 60-item mood questionnaire created by Zevon and Tellegen (1982), which contains all 20 PANAS descriptors. These data sets differed only in the rated time frame; specifically, respondents rated how they felt "right now (that is, at the present moment)" (Moment instructions), "today" (Today), "during the past few days" (Past Few Days), "during the past few weeks" (Past Few Weeks), "during the past year" (Past Year), and "in general, that is, on the average" (General).

The PANAS scales showed excellent internal consistency in all six data sets. Specifically, the coefficient alphas for the Negative Affect scale ranged from .84 to .87, whereas those for Positive Affect ranged from .86 to .90. We have since extended these data by including two additional time frames in which respondents rated how they had felt "during the past week" (Past Week) and "during the past month" (Past Month); these new instructions yielded comparable reliability estimates (see Watson & Clark, 1994b, Table 4). These data clearly demonstrate that with relatively few items, one can create reliable, internally consistent measures of Positive and Negative Affect.

Watson et al. (1988) also examined the key issue of factorial validity—that is, whether the PANAS scales accurately captured the underlying general Positive and Negative Affect factors. To investigate this issue, they subjected the ratings in each of the six data sets to a principal factor analysis (squared multiple correlations in the diagonal). Two dominant factors emerged in each solution and were rotated using varimax. Each of these solutions generated two sets of factor scoring weights that were used to compute regression-based estimates of the underlying general factors. Watson et al. then correlated these estimated factor scores with the PANAS scales in each data set. These results established that the PANAS scales were excellent measures of their target factors. Specifically, the PANAS Positive Affect scale had correlations ranging from .89 to .95 with the Positive Affect factor scores, and from –.02 to –.17 with the Negative Affect factor. Conversely, the PANAS Negative Affect scale had correlations ranging from .91 to .93 with scores on the Negative Affect factor, and from –.09 to –.18 with the Positive Affect factor. Thus, the PANAS scales provide highly accurate measures of their target constructs.

One very important implication of these data is that affective structure is highly stable across varying temporal instructions. That is, the fact that the PANAS scales correlated .89 and greater with their target factors in every sample indicates that the same factors emerged in all six data sets (and, hence, in six different time frames). Watson (1988) conducted further analyses confirming that this two-factor structure is highly robust across different time frames.

We subsequently have extended these validity data substantially by conducting a parallel series of analyses using (a) a different set of mood descriptors (i.e., the 60 terms comprising the Expanded Form of the PANAS, or PANAS–X; see Watson & Clark, 1994b), (b) two additional time frames (Past Week and Past Month), (c) a nonstudent sample, and (d) within-subject data. As before, the ratings in each data set were subjected to a principal factor analysis; two dominant factors emerged in each case and were rotated using varimax rotation. These solutions were used to create regression-based factor scores, which then were correlated with the PANAS scales.

These new analyses involved 13 additional data sets. Eleven were traditional between-subject samples in which large numbers of respondents were assessed on a single occasion. Eight of the data sets were collected from students at Southern Methodist University (SMU); they differed only in the rated time frame (e.g., Moment, Today, General). Two additional samples consisted of University of Iowa students who rated themselves using Past Few Days and General instructions. The 11th sample was composed of Dallas-area adults who rated their mood using Past Week instructions. Sample sizes ranged from 289 to 1,657 (see Table 1), with a combined sample size of 8,685.

Correlations between the resulting factor scores and the PANAS scales are reported in Tables 1 (Positive Affect scale) and Table 2 (Negative Affect scale); these are displayed in the columns marked "Regular PANAS" (we consider alternative versions of the scales in a subsequent section). The results closely replicate those reported by Watson et al. (1988). Note that the convergent correlations invariably are extremely high, ranging from .90 to .95 for Positive Affect (median = .93) and from .92 to .95 for Negative Affect (median = .94). As before, the discriminant correlations generally are quite low, ranging from −.02 to −.28 (median = −.10) for Positive Affect and from .00 to −.16 (median = −.05) for Negative Affect. Thus, these data again demonstrate that (a) the PANAS scales are excellent measures of the underlying factors, (b) their factorial validity is essentially unaffected by the time frame or the nature of the sample, and (c) the underlying two-factor structure is itself highly robust across different populations and temporal instructions.

TABLE 1

Analyses of Positive Affect: Correlations Between Alternative Versions of the PANAS Scale and Regression-Based Scores on the First Two Varimax Factors in Between- and Within-Subject Data

Sample/ Rated Time Frame	No. of Observations	P Factor Correlations			N Factor Correlations		
		Regular PANAS	Bipolar PANAS	PANAS Plus	Regular PANAS	Bipolar PANAS	PANAS Plus
Between-subject analyses							
SMU students							
Moment	1,027	.94	.90	.97	−.02	−.15	−.09
Today	1,007	.95	.88	.97	−.05	−.23	−.10
Past Few Days	289	.93	.85	.97	−.01	−.25	−.08
Past Week	1,278	.94	.84	.97	−.09	−.28	−.15
Past Few Weeks	678	.92	.77	.96	−.09	−.34	−.14
Past Month	1,006	.94	.83	.96	−.12	−.34	−.15
Past Year	315	.90	.79	.95	−.17	−.39	−.19
General	1,657	.93	.84	.97	−.10	−.30	−.13
Iowa students							
Past Few Days	502	.93	.82	.95	−.19	−.39	−.23
General	598	.91	.81	.93	−.17	−.33	−.24
Dallas-area adults							
Past Week	328	.92	.80	.94	−.28	−.47	−.31
Within-subject analyses							
SMU students							
Moment	10,169	.93	.94	.93	−.20	−.19	−.28
Today	11,322	.90	.89	.91	−.23	−.27	−.31

Note. PANAS = Positive and Negative Affect Schedule; P Factor = Positive Affect Factor; N Factor = Negative Affect Factor; SMU = Southern Methodist University.

TABLE 2
Analyses of Negative Affect: Correlations Between Alternative Versions
of the PANAS Scale and Regression-Based Scores on the First Two Varimax
Factors in Between- and Within-Subject Data

Sample/ Rated Time Frame	No. of Observations	*N Factor Correlations*			*P Factor Correlations*		
		Regular PANAS	*Bipolar PANAS*	*PANAS Plus*	*Regular PANAS*	*Bipolar PANAS*	*PANAS Plus*
Between-subject analyses							
SMU students							
Moment	1,027	.94	.90	.95	−.05	−.12	−.12
Today	1,007	.94	.91	.96	.00	−.11	−.05
Past Few Days	289	.95	.92	.96	−.01	−.14	−.05
Past Week	1,278	.94	.90	.95	−.03	−.19	−.10
Past Few Weeks	678	.93	.88	.95	−.08	−.24	−.12
Past Month	1,006	.95	.90	.96	−.05	−.20	−.09
Past Year	315	.92	.88	.94	−.05	−.19	−.13
General	1,657	.93	.88	.95	−.01	−.13	−.05
Iowa students							
Past Few Days	502	.94	.88	.95	−.16	−.32	−.21
General	598	.94	.90	.95	−.04	−.18	−.10
Dallas-area adults							
Past Week	328	.93	.89	.95	−.15	−.28	−.21
Within-subject analyses							
SMU students							
Moment	10,169	.89	.85	.90	−.16	−.16	−.21
Today	11,322	.89	.85	.90	−.18	−.26	−.25

Note. PANAS = Positive and Negative Affect Schedule; N Factor = Negative Affect Factor; P Factor = Positive Affect Factor; SMU = Southern Methodist University.

The final two samples represent within-subject analyses in which respondents rated themselves repeatedly over a large number of occasions. The first sample consisted of 226 SMU undergraduates who rated their current, momentary mood over a 1- to 2-month period ($M = 45.0$ assessments per respondent). The participants completed one mood assessment per day, at different times of day; these times varied according to a prearranged, randomized schedule. The second sample was composed of 254 SMU students who rated their mood on a daily basis (using Today instructions) over a 1- to 2 month-period ($M = 44.6$ assessments per respondent); all ratings were made in the evening to provide a reasonable estimate of the respondents' mood over the day. All participants in both samples completed a minimum of 35 individual mood assessments.

The ratings in each sample were standardized on a within-subject basis (i.e., each person's responses were converted to standard scores). This procedure eliminates all interindividual variability, so that subsequent analyses reflect only within-subject variation; this, in turn, permits one to examine all of the ratings from each of the respondents in a single analysis. Accordingly, the standardized data in each sample were subjected to separate principal factor analyses; this is essentially equivalent to factoring each respondent's data separately and then averaging the resulting solutions. Paralleling the between-subject data, two large factors were extracted in each sample and rotated using varimax rotation. Finally, the resulting solutions were used to create regression-based factor scores on the underlying Positive and Negative Affect dimensions.

Correlations between these factor scores and the PANAS scales also are presented in Tables 1 and 2. These data closely replicate the between-subject results and again demonstrate the factorial validity of the PANAS scales. Once again, the convergent correlations were invariably high (range = .89 to .93) and the discriminant coefficients were consistently low (range = −.16 to −.23). Consequently, we see clear evidence that the PANAS scales accurately capture the major dimensions underlying both interindividual and intraindividual affective experience. In addition, these data further establish the generality and robustness of affective structure. In this case, it is especially noteworthy that the same basic structure—at least at the general factor level—emerges in both between-subject and within-subject analyses. This has important implications that we consider subsequently.

CURRENT CONTROVERSIES IN THE ASSESSMENT OF POSITIVE AND NEGATIVE AFFECT

Content-Related Issues

We hope to have convinced the reader that (a) self-rated mood is characterized by two large and highly robust dimensions that reliably emerge across a wide range of conditions and (b) it is possible to construct brief scales that accurately capture these dimensions. Viewed from this perspective, it might seem that researchers have resolved the major issues related to the assessment of mood at the major factor level. Regrettably, this is not quite the case. Several key points remain unresolved and at least somewhat controversial.

Researchers have raised three basic concerns regarding the content of these general factor scales. The first is that the content of these scales is overinclusive, specifically, that many of the commonly used scales include terms that do not clearly represent emotions (for discussions of this issue, see Clore, Ortony, & Foss, 1987; Diener et al., 1995; Larsen & Diener, 1992; Morgan & Heise, 1988). Diener et al. (1995), for instance, expressed concern that the PANAS Positive Affect scale contains terms such as strong, active, and alert that "are not considered by many theorists to represent emotions" (p. 131). This issue is complicated by the fact that the definition of emotion is itself controversial (see Ekman & Davidson, 1994), so that it is not entirely clear which terms do—or do not—represent emotions.

Nevertheless, it surely is true that most of the commonly used general factor scales—including the PANAS—contain terms that do not clearly refer to emotions.

This criticism would be compelling if one accepts the argument that mood measurement should be restricted to descriptors that clearly reflect emotions. That is, this argument is based on the assumption that mood research should use emotion theory as its underlying conceptual/assessment framework, and that the ultimate goal of mood research is to assess the experiential component of the basic emotions. In our own research, however, we never have viewed this as a desirable goal. In fact, as we have argued elsewhere (see Watson & Clark, 1994a), we believe that emotion theory offers a poor model for mood research. Briefly put, the problem is that emotions occur as fleeting and highly intense episodes, whereas the bulk of waking life is spent in longer lasting, low- to medium-intensity states (e.g., Diener & Iran-Nejad, 1986; Watson, 1988). Consequently, most of everyday life is spent in mood states that do not clearly correspond to classic emotions.

Furthermore, our respondents appear to make no real distinction between "emotional" and "nonemotional" terms. For example, we consistently find that ratings of happy, joyful, active, and alert are strongly positively intercorrelated, even though the first two terms may reflect emotions, whereas the latter two may not. Note, moreover, that because they are strongly correlated with terms that clearly represent emotions, the inclusion of these nonemotional descriptors changes neither the fundamental nature nor the external correlates of the scales—it simply expands the pool of candidate items to facilitate the construction of highly reliable measures.

For these reasons, we do not believe that the inclusion of nonemotional terms represents a serious problem in general factor mood scales, such as the PANAS. We acknowledge, however, that researchers interested in measuring emotions per se are better advised to use instruments that are more closely tied to emotion theory, such as Izard's Differential Emotions Scale (DES; Izard, Dougherty, Bloxom, & Kotsch, 1974; see also Izard, Libero, Putnam, & Haynes, 1993).

A second (and very understandable) concern involves the unipolar nature of these general factor scales. Positive and Negative Affect typically have been described as bipolar dimensions, especially in the seminal papers in this literature (see Watson & Tellegen, 1985; Zevon & Tellegen, 1982). Zevon and Tellegen (1982), for instance, emphasized that "the opposing ends of the two broad dimensions are both associated with adjectival descriptors" (p. 112) and, therefore, that Positive and Negative Affect are *"descriptively bipolar"* (p. 112). Similarly, Watson and Tellegen (1985) clearly characterized these dimensions as bipolar (see especially their Figure 1), with terms reflecting fatigue (e.g., drowsy, sleepy, sluggish) and serenity (e.g., calm, relaxed) defining the low ends of Positive and Negative Affect, respectively. Recently, however, several writers have pointed out that the PANAS scales (and, indeed, virtually all of the commonly used measures of these dimensions) contain only the high-end markers and include no terms assessing fatigue and serenity (Larsen & Diener, 1992; Mossholder, Kemery, Harris, Armenakis, & McGrath, 1994; Nemanick & Munz, 1994). These authors have questioned the validity of these general factor scales, arguing quite plausibly that unipolar scales cannot validly assess bipolar dimensions.

Why were descriptors reflecting fatigue and serenity excluded from the PANAS scales? The reason is that it is important to maximize both convergent and discriminant validity in constructing general mood scales. In practical terms, this translates into selecting descriptors that consistently show strong loadings on one factor and near-zero loadings on the other (see Watson et al., 1988). However, terms reflecting fatigue and serenity tend to be factorially complex, with significant loadings on both Positive and Negative Affect. Consequently, including these terms failed to enhance the psychometric properties of the PANAS scales; in fact, in certain instances the inclusion of these terms lessened the reliability and validity of the scales.

Moreover, it became that unipolar scales were quite capable of measuring the underlying dimensions. For example, as we already have shown, the PANAS scales correlate extremely strongly with Positive and Negative Affect factor scores in both within- and between-subject data, and across a wide range of temporal instructions. Nevertheless, one still might wonder whether bipolar scales would show somewhat better convergent and/or discriminant validity. To examine this issue, we constructed a "bipolar" form of the PANAS. To create a bipolar Positive Affect scale, we reverse-keyed the four terms comprising the Fatigue scale of the PANAS–X (drowsy, sleepy, sluggish, tired) and added them to the 10 high-end descriptors. In parallel fashion, we constructed a bipolar Negative Affect scale by reverse-keying the three descriptors comprising the PANAS–X Serenity scale (at ease, calm, relaxed) and adding them to the 10 high-end terms. We then correlated these bipolar scales with the Positive and Negative Affect factor scores in the 13 data sets that were described earlier.

These correlations also are displayed in Tables 1 and 2 (in the columns headed "Bipolar PANAS"). The regular, unipolar PANAS scales clearly outperform their bipolar counterparts. In virtually every instance the regular PANAS scales show better convergent and discriminant validity than these bipolar measures. The data for the Positive Affect scales are especially striking. Across the 13 data sets, the unipolar scale has median convergent and discriminant correlations of .93 and –.12, respectively; in sharp contrast, the corresponding values for the bipolar scale are .84 and –.30, respectively. On the basis of these data, we believe that unipolar scales provide superior assessment of the underlying factors and we do not recommend the use of bipolar scales for this purpose.

However, we still are left with an enigma: How can unipolar scales assess bipolar dimensions with such fidelity? The answer is that these dimensions actually are not strongly or clearly bipolar, especially in between-subject data. In this regard, the distinction between within- and between-subject data may be crucial. An inspection of Table 1 indicates that the bipolar Positive Affect scale performed nearly as well as the regular PANAS scale in the within-subject analyses, but fared rather poorly in the between-subject data. This pattern suggests that the bipolar scheme emphasized in early conceptualizations of the constructs (e.g., Watson & Tellegen, 1985; Zevon & Tellegen, 1982) more accurately reflects within-subject than between-subject data, which makes sense in that these early conceptualizations were based heavily on analyses of within-subject data.

To investigate this issue further, we conducted additional analyses in our two large within-subject samples. The data in each sample were analyzed in three different ways. First, as before, we standardized the ratings on a within-subject basis, thereby eliminating all of the between-subject variance. We then correlated scores on the regular PANAS scales with the Fatigue and Serenity scales of the PANAS–X; note that this essentially is equivalent to computing separate, within-subject correlations for each respondent and then averaging the resulting values.

Second, we standardized the ratings on an assessment-by-assessment basis; that is, we separately standardized the data from each respondent's first assessment (Assessment #1), each respondent's second assessment (Assessment #2), and so on. Because relatively few individuals completed more than 45 momentary mood assessments, these analyses were restricted to the first 45 assessments from each respondent in the Moment data (total $N = 10,036$, $M = 223.0$ respondents per assessment); for similar reasons, we used only the first 42 assessments from each respondent in the Daily data (total $N = 10,536$, $M = 250.9$ respondents per assessment). Again, we correlated the resulting scores on the same four scales; note that this is essentially equivalent to computing separate between-subject correlations for Assessment 1, Assessment 2, and so on, and then averaging the resulting values. Thus, these analyses characterize the same data at the nonaggregated (i.e., single assessment) between-subject level.

Finally, we computed overall average Positive Affect, Negative Affect, Fatigue, and Serenity scores for each respondent across the entire rating period. Paralleling the other analyses, we then correlated these average scores. Note that these analyses now characterize the same data at an aggregated (i.e., multi-assessment) between-subject level.

These analyses provide a particularly elegant comparison of within-versus between-subject data, in that they are based on the same ratings collected from the same respondents, and so control for many potential confounds. The resulting correlations are presented in Table 3, and they strikingly document the changes that occur as one moves from within- to between-subject analyses. Looking first at the data for Fatigue, one sees that it is primarily a marker of low Positive Affect in the within-subject analyses ($rs = -.62$ and $-.41$ in the Moment and Daily data, respectively), comparably related (but in opposite directions) to the two scales in the nonaggregated between-subject analyses, and essentially a marker of high Negative Affect in the aggregated between-subject data ($rs = .48$ and $.65$ in the

Correlations of General Positive and Negative Affect
With the Fatigue and Serenity Scales of the PANAS–X
in Within- and Between-Subject Analyses

	Fatigue		Serenity	
Analysis	Positive Affect	Negative Affect	Positive Affect	Negative Affect
Moment ratings				
Within-subject analyses				
Mean r	−.62	.26	.21	−.43
Between-subject analyses				
Mean nonaggregated r	−.41	.32	.36	−.28
Aggregated r	.08	.48	.59	.07
Daily ratings				
Within-subject analyses				
Mean r	−.41	.30	.37	−.48
Between-subject analyses				
Mean nonaggregated r	−.30	.41	.39	−.38
Aggregated r	−.03	.65	.44	−.22

Note. PANAS–X = Expanded Form of the Positive and Negative Affect Schedule. Moment data are based on 10,169 (within-subject), 10,036 (nonaggregated between-subject), and 226 (aggregated between-subject) observations. Daily data are based on 11,323 (within-subject), 10,536 (nonaggregated between-subject), and 248 (aggregated between-subject) observations.

Moment and Daily samples, respectively). Similarly, Serenity correlates more highly with Negative Affect in the within-subject analyses ($rs = -.43$ and $-.48$ in the Moment and Daily data, respectively) but is more strongly—and positively—related to Positive Affect in the aggregated between-subject analyses ($rs = .59$ and .44, respectively). Overall, consistent with our earlier suggestion, we see clear evidence of bipolarity in the within-subject data, but very little evidence of it in the aggregated between-subject analyses. Before leaving these results, we should note that this weak bipolarity in the between-subject data may be attributable to an acquiescence response bias (Green, Goldman, & Salovey, 1993), an issue we examine in a later section.

On the basis of these data, it appears that the original bipolar formulation works reasonably well in within-subject analyses (the data in the Moment sample are particularly impressive), but that the Positive and Negative Affect dimensions are, at best, weakly bipolar in between-subject data. These results strengthen our belief that unipolar scales provide the easiest, clearest, and most robust assessment of the underlying dimensions.

The third content-related concern—which has been specifically directed toward our PANAS scales—is that these scales fail to include any terms related to happiness (e.g., happy, joyful) and sadness (e.g., sad, depressed; for a discussion, see Larsen & Diener, 1992). The argument is that because happiness and sadness seem to be central to the experience of positive and negative mood, respectively, the exclusion of these terms seriously compromises the validity of these general factor scales. In a related vein, it has been suggested that the variance attributable to happy and sad affect is not well-captured in the PANAS scales. For instance, Larsen and Diener (1992) suggested that the exclusion of sadness terms from the Negative Affect scale "implies that the dimension labeled Negative Affect, as well as the PANAS N[egative] A[ffect] scale, does not include certain emotions that many psychologists and most naive subjects consider to be quite central to subjectively unpleasant experiential states" (p. 29).

In fact, the exclusion of these terms does not substantially compromise the construct validity of the PANAS scales. The reason is that these are general factor scales that assess the shared component common to many specific types of affect. For example, the PANAS Positive Affect scale taps the shared, overlapping variance that is common to positive mood descriptors such as alert, enthusiastic, and interested, as well as happy. Because of this, variance attributable to specific descriptors can be well-captured in the scales, even if the descriptors themselves are omitted. To demonstrate this key point, we computed correlations between the PANAS scales and (a) the 5-item Sadness scale from the PANAS-X (consisting of alone, blue, downhearted, lonely, sad) and (b) a 4-item Happiness scale (consisting of cheerful, delighted, happy, joyful) in the 13 previously described data sets. Note that these Sadness and Happiness scales contain no overlapping terms with the PANAS scales.

The relevant correlations are reported in Table 4. These data clearly show that Happiness is strongly related to Positive Affect: Across the 13 data sets, the correlations range from .64 to .78, with a median value of .73. Similarly, Sadness is strongly linked to Negative Affect; across the 13 samples, the correlations range from .56 to .74, with a median value of .69. Thus, happy and sad affect are well-captured in the Positive and Negative Affect scales, respectively, of the PANAS.

These data lead to a further question, however: If happiness and sadness are strongly related to Positive and Negative Affect, why were descriptors reflecting these important affects omitted from the PANAS scales? The answer is that terms reflecting happy and sad affect tend to be moderately negatively correlated with one another, a point we discuss in more detail in a later section. Indeed, as is also shown in Table 4, the correlation between the Happiness and Sadness scales ranged from –.28 to –.52 across the 13 samples, with a median value of –.41. Consequently, including such terms would have raised the correlation between the scales and lessened their discriminant validity.

Still, one could argue that this decrease in discriminant validity might be offset by an even larger increase in convergent validity. To examine this issue,

TABLE 4
Correlations Among Measures of Sadness, Happiness,
and General Positive and Negative Affect

Sample/ Rated Time Frame	No. of Observations	Happiness– Positive Affect	Sadness– Negative Affect	Happiness– Sadness
Between-subject analyses				
SMU students				
Moment	1,027	.73	.68	−.37
Today	1,007	.75	.69	−.30
Past Few Days	289	.67	.73	−.28
Past Week	1,278	.74	.69	−.42
Past Few Weeks	678	.71	.69	−.35
Past Month	1,006	.76	.74	−.32
Past Year	315	.64	.63	−.41
General	1,657	.70	.67	−.32
Iowa students				
Past Few Days	502	.75	.73	−.48
General	598	.65	.67	−.43
Dallas-area adults				
Past Week	328	.78	.73	−.52
Within-subject analyses				
SMU students				
Moment	10,169	.77	.56	−.42
Today	11,322	.72	.57	−.50

Note. SMU = Southern Methodist University.

we created augmented "PANAS Plus" scales that added happiness and sadness descriptors to the regular PANAS scales. Specifically, we added the four terms from our ad hoc Happiness scale to Positive Affect, and three terms from the PANAS–X Sadness scale (blue, downhearted, sad) to Negative Affect. We then correlated these augmented scales with the Positive and Negative Affect factor scores in the 13 data sets.

These correlations also are displayed (in the "PANAS Plus" columns) in Tables 1 and 2. When compared to the regular PANAS scales, these augmented versions do, in fact, show better convergent validity, as well as poorer discriminant validity, but in both cases the change is slight. Specifically, the regular PANAS Positive Affect scale had median convergent and discriminant correlations of .93 and −.12, respectively; adding in the happiness-related terms yielded corresponding values of .96 and −.15, respectively. Similarly, the regular PANAS Negative Affect scale had median convergent and discriminant correlations of .94 and −.05, respectively; adding in the sadness descriptors produced corresponding values of .95 and −.12, respectively. Not surprisingly, this decrease in discriminant validity was paralleled by an increased correlation between the scales. Across the 13 samples, the correlation between the regular PANAS scales ranged from $-.02$ to $-.38$, with a median value of $-.16$; in contrast, the PANAS Plus scales had correlations ranging from $-.11$ to $-.47$, with a median value of $-.23$.

These data suggest that adding in happiness and sadness descriptors might lead to a slight enhancement of convergent validity without seriously damaging the discriminant validity of the scales; accordingly, researchers wishing to maximize the former might consider including such terms. We also should note, however, that this incremental validity might result simply from the increased length of the scales, and that it might be possible to obtain even better results (i.e., increased convergent validity without decreased discriminant validity) by adding terms reflecting other types of content. For our current purposes, however, the key point is that happy and sad affect are well-captured by the PANAS scales; consequently, the essential nature of these scales remains the same regardless of whether happy and sad descriptors are included or excluded.

On the Independence of Positive and Negative Affect

The PANAS scales are based on a structure that reflects two fundamental psychometric principles. The first is that affects with same valence (e.g., nervous vs. angry; enthusiastic vs. happy) tend to be substantially positively intercorrelated. This principle—which forms the justification for combining disparate positive and negative mood descriptors into broad, general scales—has been amply documented and is noncontroversial. The second principle is that oppositely valenced affects (e.g., nervous vs. enthusiastic) tend to be only weakly negatively correlated with one another. In contrast to the first, this second principle—which forms the justification for separating positive and negative descriptors into distinct measures—has been the subject of considerable argument and controversy. We now consider three major controversies concerning the apparent independence of positive and negative mood.

First, various researchers have argued that this apparent independence may reflect the use of improper or inappropriate response formats. Meddis (1972) offered the earliest challenge of this sort. Meddis was particularly critical of a 4-point response format (*definitely do not feel, cannot decide, feel slightly, definitely feel*) that was widely used in early studies of mood, and that still is being employed in some contemporary research. Meddis maintained that this format is problematic for two reasons. First, it is asymmetric—that is, it contains two categories of endorsement (feel slightly, definitely feel) but only one of nonendorsement (definitely do not feel). Second, the "cannot decide" option is ambiguous and does not clearly fall between definitely do not feel and feel slightly. Meddis argued that these problems might serve to weaken the size of observed negative correlations. Furthermore, he showed that when these problems were corrected, stronger negative correlations were obtained between opposite mood terms.

Meddis' assertions initially caused great concern among mood researchers, because they suggested that response formats exerted an enormous—and perhaps highly artifactual— influence on mood ratings. However, when Russell (1979) attempted to replicate Meddis' findings, he concluded that this problematic format "contributes at most a modest bias" (p. 350). Moreover, other investigators found that the structural/psychometric properties of mood ratings actually were highly robust across different response formats (Hendrick & Lilly, 1970; Thayer, 1986). In a similar vein, Watson and Tellegen (1985) demonstrated that clearly identifiable Positive and Negative Affect factors emerged using formats that were not subject to Meddis' criticisms. Consequently, these format-related problems cannot account for the observed independence between positive and negative mood.

Warr, Barter, and Brownbridge (1983) proposed another format-based explanation for this observed independence. They noted that most of the widely used instruments ask respondents to rate the extent to which they experienced each term (e.g., not at all to extremely), which does not require them to make any logical or empirical connection between positive and negative moods. For instance, over a period of a few weeks, individuals may well experience prolonged episodes of both joy and sadness, and so could rate themselves as being relatively high in both moods. Obviously, this would serve to weaken the observed correlations between positive and negative mood states. However, with a "frequency" format, respondents rate what proportion of a specified time period they experience each term (e.g., none of the time to most of the time), so that an increment in one affect implies a decrement in others. Consequently, Warr et al. (1983) argued that stronger (negative) correlations between positive and negative mood might emerge using a frequency format, and they presented some preliminary support for their assertions.

Watson (1988) subsequently subjected the issue to a more exhaustive test, collecting mood ratings (using Past Few Weeks time instructions) from two large student samples. The ratings in one group used an extent format, whereas those in the other were based on a frequency format. The results showed that response format influenced the strength of the relation between negative and positive mood, but the effect was rather small. Most notably, the correlation between the PANAS scales was −.16 (representing 3% shared variance) in the extent ratings, and still only −.28 (reflecting 8% shared variance) in the frequency ratings. On the basis of these data, we must conclude that format-based explanations cannot account for the observed independence of positive and negative mood.

A second challenge to independence involves the rated-time sample. Diener and Emmons (1984) reported data from four studies in which respondents rated their mood across different time frames or time intervals. On the basis of these data, they concluded that

The relation between positive and negative affect depends on the time period being considered. Positive and negative affect states do vary inversely, but only over short time spans; the two are unlikely to occur together within the same person at the same moment. (p. 1114)

Diener and Emmons's (1984) data seemed to suggest that affective structure was unstable across different time frames, such that independent Positive and Negative Affect factors would only emerge using longer, more traitlike temporal instructions (e.g., Past Month, Past Year, General ratings; for discussions, see Diener & Emmons, 1984; Green et al., 1993; Watson, 1988).

However, data we presented earlier indicate that affective structure is highly robust across different time frames (e.g., Tables 1 and 2). Moreover, Watson (1988) presented evidence demonstrating that the correlation between positive and negative mood does not vary as a function of the rated time frame. Similarly, Table 5 presents correlations between the PANAS scales in eight large between-subject data sets (with a combined sample size of 14,463). All of the respondents were SMU undergraduates; the samples differ only as a function of the temporal instructions that were used to generate the ratings. Once again, there obviously is no tendency for the correlation between Positive and Negative Affect to decline as the rated time frame lengthens. In fact, the two weakest associations are observed in the Moment ($r = -.06$) and Today ($r = -.05$) ratings, whereas the strongest correlation ($-.23$) is observed in the Past Year data.

How, then, can we explain Diener and Emmons' (1984) data? A close examination reveals that few of their data were based on a direct manipulation of the rated time frame, and these involved relatively small samples and only a few time frames (see their Study 2). Instead, most of their evidence consisted of analyzing intensive

TABLE 5
Correlations Between the PANAS Positive
and Negative Affect Scales as a Function
of the Rated Time Frame

Rated Time Frame	N	NA–PA r
Moment	2,213	−.06
Today	1,664	−.05
Past Few Days	1,577	−.17
Past Week	1,521	−.14
Past Few Weeks	2,076	−.13
Past Month	1,006	−.15
Past Year	964	−.23
General	3,622	−.13

Note. PANAS = Positive and Negative Affect Schedule; NA = Negative Affect; PA = Positive Affect.

within-subject data sets in various ways, similar to the findings we presented in Table 3. Specifically, they showed that average within-subject correlations (which were based on single assessments of momentary or daily mood) between Positive and Negative Affect were moderately negative, but that aggregated between-subject correlations (which necessarily reflect a greater number of assessments and, hence, more extensive time samples) tended to be weakly negative or even slightly positive.

This is an important finding, but on reflection one can see that these analyses are ambiguous and confound two different effects. That is, in comparing within-subject to aggregated between-subject data, one is simultaneously (a) moving from within- to between-subject data (the "subject effect") and (b) aggregating across a greater number of assessments (an "aggregation effect"). These effects can be disentangled by conducting nonaggregated between-subject analyses, paralleling those reported in Table 3. Note that comparing within-subject data to nonaggregated between-subject data allows one to model the subject effect (i.e., within- versus between-subject data are compared at the same level of nonaggregation), whereas the difference between the nonaggregated and aggregated between-subject data permits one to quantify the aggregation effect (i.e., between-subject data are compared at different levels of aggregation). Therefore (paralleling our earlier analyses of fatigue and serenity), we again analyzed our two large within-subject samples in three different ways, in this case focusing on the correlation between the PANAS scales.

These correlations are reported in Table 6. Several aspects of these data are noteworthy. First, we see clear evidence of a subject effect; specifically, a comparison of the within-subject and nonaggregated between-subject data indicates an 8% drop in shared variance in both the Moment (from 9% to 1%) and Daily (from 12% to 4%) ratings. Second, we do see some evidence of a modest aggregation effect: The correlations move from being weakly negative in the nonaggregated between-subject data to being weakly/moderately positive in the aggregated data. Finally, and most important, the scales are relatively independent of one another in all of the analyses. Indeed, even the within-subject analyses indicate only 9% (Moment data) and 12% (Daily data) shared variance between Positive and Negative Affect.

In summary, the data indicate that Positive and Negative Affect scores are relatively independent (a) across a wide range of temporal instructions, (b) in both within- and between-subject analyses, and (c) in both nonaggregated and aggregated data. Therefore, it appears that this independence actually is highly robust across different time samples.

The third major challenge is that the apparent independence of Positive and Negative Afffect is artifactual and reflects the operation of systematic measurement errors, such as response sets and rating biases (for discussions, see Diener et al., 1995; Green et al., 1993; Tellegen, Watson, & Clark, 1994). Mood researchers have been particularly concerned with the acquiescence response bias, which can be defined as "an individual-difference variable to agree or disagree with an item

TABLE 6
Correlations Between the PANAS Positive and Negative
Affect Scales in Within- and Between-Subject Analyses

Analysis	Moment Ratings	Daily Ratings
Within-subject analyses		
Mean r	−.30	−.34
Between-subject analyses		
Mean nonaggregated r	−.09	−.19
Aggregated r	.32	.06

Note. PANAS = Positive and Negative Affect Schedule. Moment data are based on 10,169 (within-subject), 10,036 (nonaggregated between-subject), and 226 (aggregated between-subject) observations. Daily data are based on 11,323 (within-subject), 10,536 (nonaggregated between-subject), and 248 (aggregated between-subject) observations.

regardless of its content" (Russell, 1979, p. 346). In mood rating scales, acquiescence would be reflected in a tendency for respondents to prefer certain numbers over others, regardless of item content. For instance, some respondents might prefer to use lower numbers (i.e., 1s or 2s), whereas others might be prone to higher, more extreme ratings (i.e., 4s or 5s). It must be emphasized that this potential problem is by no means limited to mood measurement, nor is there any reason to believe that mood ratings are especially susceptible to it; indeed, very similar arguments have been raised in other assessment areas as well (e.g., Wiggins, 1973).

Although mood researchers have been aware of the potential problem of response biases for some time (see, for example, Bentler, 1969; Diener & Emmons, 1984; Russell, 1979, 1980), this issue has resurfaced recently because of an influential article by Green et al. (1993). Green et al. offered a bold and clear challenge, stating:

> In our view, the independence of positive and negative affect is a statistical artifact. The conclusion that positive and negative affect are largely uncorrelated fails to take account of the errors of measurement that arise in mood assessment. ... When one adjusts for random and systematic error in positive and negative affect, correlations between the two that at first seem close to 0 are revealed to be closer to −1.00 and support a largely bipolar structure. (p. 1029)

Green et al. (1993) then proceeded to report results from several studies that seemingly confirm their bold assertion. Most notably, after controlling for both random and systematic (i.e., acquiescence) measurement error, they obtained corrected correlations between positive and negative mood of −.84, −.84, −.91, and −.87 in four different analyses! These values obviously reflect a very strong degree of bipolarity and apparently establish the validity of their bold claim.

These results are interesting, but taken alone they are misleading and fail to prove the validity of Green et al.'s (1993) argument. The problem is that Green et al.

specifically examined happy and sad affect, rather than the broader range of content assessed in the PANAS scales. As we already have seen, terms reflecting happiness and sadness do tend to be moderately negatively correlated. Indeed, according to the two-factor structure outlined by Watson and Tellegen (1985), happiness and sadness are predicted to be negatively correlated and strongly bipolar, even before correcting for random and systematic error. This was, in fact, exactly what Green et al. (1993) found. Specifically, in these same four analyses, the mean uncorrected correlations (after r to z transformation) between their positive and negative mood measures were $-.53$, $-.56$, $-.61$, and $-.53$, respectively. In fact, in their first analysis, Green et al. reported that simply summing the observed measures into aggregate scores yielded a raw, uncorrected correlation of $-.72$. Consequently, Green et al. did not show that near-zero uncorrected correlations mask corrected coefficients that are close to -1.00; rather, they simply demonstrated that measures that already are bipolar in raw, uncorrected data become even more strongly bipolar after controlling for random and systematic error. These data do establish an effect due to measurement error, but it is much more modest than Green et al. claim.

Green et al. (1993) apparently were aware that it was problematic to use happy and sad affect to explore the issue of independence, because they conducted one final analysis using "items derived from the PANAS" (p. 1037). Not surprisingly, this analysis yielded substantially weaker evidence of bipolarity. The raw correlations ranged from $-.11$ to $-.47$, with a mean value of only $-.31$; this increased to $-.58$ after controlling for random and systematic error. These data are difficult to interpret, however, because Green et al. actually used bipolar mood scales that contained content not found in the PANAS (e.g., "feeling very focused and 'on task'," "had trouble paying attention," "feel 'calm, cool, and collected'," "feeling calm and relaxed") and that likely influenced the magnitude of these correlations significantly (see Tellegen et al., 1994). Consequently, these findings do not suggest the magnitude of the corrected correlations that might be obtained using the PANAS. Nevertheless, they again indicate that measurement error influences the bipolarity of affect ratings to some extent.

As we have seen, Green et al.'s (1993) data are suggestive but not definitive. Fortunately, this issue has been examined further in two subsequent studies. First, Tellegen et al. (1994) created brief measures of Positive Affect, Negative Affect, happiness, and sadness. Consistent with the findings of Green et al. (1993), happiness and sadness already were strongly related in the raw data, with uncorrected correlations ranging from $-.47$ to $-.61$. Controlling for random error raised the correlation to $-.73$, and further controlling for acquiescence increased it to $-.92$. In other words, scales that already were strongly bipolar in raw data (displaying from 22% to 37% shared variance) showed even greater bipolarity after eliminating both random and systematic error (85% shared variance). In sharp contrast, the uncorrected correlations between Positive and Negative Affect ranged from $-.12$ to $-.25$; controlling for random error increased the correlation to only $-.28$, and further controlling for acquiescence raised it to only –.43. In other words, scales that were largely independent in raw data (showing from 1% to 6% shared variance) remained only moderately related (18% shared variance) even after eliminating both random and systematic error.

Diener et al. (1995) extended these findings by examining the relation between four negative affects (fear, anger, sadness, shame) and two positive affects (love, joy) using three different types of data (self-ratings, aggregated daily ratings, informant ratings). Their results closely replicated the Positive Affect–Negative Affect findings of Tellegen et al. (1994). Specifically, the raw correlations between global positive and negative mood ranged from .04 to –.28, indicating that they were largely independent before correction; after controlling for error, the latent correlation between positive and negative mood still was only moderate (–.44, reflecting 19% shared variance). Thus, the results of both studies again suggest that measurement error exerts a moderate influence on bipolarity.

Note that all of these results were derived from between-subject analyses in which structural modeling was used to eliminate the influence of error. There is, however, a very different way to examine the possible influence of response biases such as acquiescence. As was noted earlier, acquiescence is defined as an individual difference variable—that is, it reflects a consistent tendency for respondents to use ratings differently. Accordingly, its influence is necessarily confined to between-subject analyses in which the ratings of one individual are compared to those of another. The problem of acquiescence therefore can be bypassed completely by conducting within-subject analyses of individual respondents.

Thus, the strength of the acquiescence bias can be estimated by comparing correlations derived from between- and within-subject analyses, as we already have done in Table 6. The reader will recall that we observed an 8% drop in shared variance in moving from the within- to the nonaggregated between-subject analyses, which again suggests that systematic error exerts a moderate influence on bipolarity. However, recall that the PANAS scales were only moderately correlated with one another, even in the within-subject analyses (mean $rs = -.30$ and $-.34$ in the Moment and Daily data, respectively). Taken together with the results of the earlier studies, we can conclude that random and systematic error exert a significant influence on the bipolarity of affect ratings, but that Positive and Negative Affect remain distinct, separable, and only moderately correlated even after controlling for such error. In light of these data, we continue to believe that the most sensible assessment approach is to measure positive and negative mood separately.

Validity of Self-Rated Affect

This detailed discussion of measurement error might lead some readers to question the validity of mood ratings altogether. However, in response, we reiterate that error is a universal problem in assessment, and that there is no evidence that self-rated affect is especially susceptible to either random or systematic error. Moreover, an accumulating body of data clearly supports the construct validity of self-rated affect. For instance, trait affect measures are strongly stable over intervals of several months and display substantial levels of stability over retest intervals as long as 7 to 9 years (e.g., Izard et al., 1993; Watson & Clark, 1994b; Watson & Walker, 1996). Furthermore, trait affect ratings show strong convergence with the general personality traits of Neuroticism and Extraversion (e.g., Tellegen, 1985; Watson & Clark, 1994b). For example, Meyer and Shack (1989) reported that self-rated Positive and Negative Affect correlated .66 and .63 with Extraversion and Neuroticism, respectively. Similarly, averaging across four samples, Watson and Clark (1992b) found that the PANAS Negative Affect scale correlated .58 with various measures of Neuroticism, and that the Positive Affect scale correlated .58 with Extraversion.

In addition, self-rated affect displays significant convergent validity in relation to non-self-report data. Clark and Watson (1991), for instance, reviewed evidence from several studies reporting significant correlations between self-rated affect and clinicians' ratings of psychopathology. In a related vein, several studies have demonstrated a significant level of convergence between self-rated and informant-rated affect (e.g., Diener et al., 1995; Watson & Clark, 1991, 1994b). Thus, the available data firmly establish the construct validity of self-reported affect; consequently, although error remains a perennial concern, affect self-ratings can be used with confidence.

ASSESSING MOOD AT THE LOWER ORDER LEVEL

The Taxonomic Problem

Despite some lingering concerns and unresolved issues, mood researchers clearly have made enormous strides in measuring mood at the general factor level, with most investigators agreeing that the higher order level is characterized by two broad dimensions. Moreover, reliable and valid measures of these general factors have been developed and are now widely used.

However, the situation is quite different at the lower order, specific affect level. In fact, although researchers continue to be quite interested in studying mood at this level, our review of the literature suggests that little psychometric progress has been made in recent years. In our view, the most significant barrier to improved assessment continues to be the lack of a compelling taxonomy at the lower order level. That is, even after decades of study, mood researchers still show little consensus regarding the basic states that must be included in a complete and comprehensive investigation of mood. Without an organizing taxonomic scheme, it is impossible to determine whether existing instruments assess mood in a valid and comprehensive manner.

We can illustrate this problem by examining the scales included in four prominent multiaffect inventories: the DES (Izard et al., 1974, Izard et al., 1993), the Multiple Affect Adjective Check List–Revised (MAACL–R; Zuckerman & Lubin, 1985), the Profile of Mood States (POMS; McNair et al., 1971), and our own PANAS–X (Watson & Clark, 1994b). A comparison of these inventories indicates two basic points of consensus. First, all of these instruments contain scales assessing the basic negative affects of fear/anxiety, sadness/depression, and anger/hostility. Second, they all include at least one measure of positive mood.

Beyond this modest consensus, these inventories show substantial discrepancies. First, the number of component scales varies widely, with the DES and PANAS–X providing much more differentiated assessment (12 and 11 scales, respectively) than the POMS and MAACL–R (6 and 5 scales, respectively). Moreover, the focus of their content differs dramatically. For instance, the DES assesses nine different negative moods (Fear, Anger, Disgust, Contempt, Inward Hostility, Sadness, Guilt, Shame, Shyness) and only two types of positive mood (Interest, Enjoyment), whereas the PANAS–X includes only five negative affects (Fear, Hostility, Sadness, Guilt, Shyness) but three different positive mood scales (Joviality, Self-Assurance, Attentiveness). To some extent, this differential focus simply reflects the fact that these inventories assess affect with varying degrees of specificity. For example, whereas the DES places descriptors of anger, disgust, and contempt into three distinct scales, the PANAS–X combines them in a single measure of Hostility. It is noteworthy, however, that each of the instruments also appears to contain unique content that is not well-captured by any of the others. That is, only the DES contains a measure of Shame, only the POMS assesses Confusion-Bewilderment, only the MAACL–R measures Sensation Seeking, and only the PANAS–X includes an index of Serenity. Consequently, although there is much overlap, each of these inventories apparently assesses a somewhat different domain of content.

How does one choose among these disparate measures? This question would be relatively easy to answer if we had a compelling lower order taxonomy; in this case, one simply would need to determine how well the psychometric structure of each instrument captured the underlying taxonomy of the domain. In the absence of any clear structural consensus, however, all one can do is evaluate the measures according to the classic psychometric criteria of reliability and validity. Unfortunately, because very few studies have directly compared the psychometric properties of two or more of these instruments under controlled conditions, the available evidence is less than definitive. Nevertheless, we briefly review the key issues of (a) internal consistency reliability and (b) discriminant validity, for which the data are relatively good.

Internal Consistency of Specific Affect Scales

All of these instruments were created using factor analysis, so that one would expect their component scales to be internally consistent. However, this issue is complicated by the fact that conventional indices of internal consistency—such as KR– 20 and coefficient alpha—are a function of two different parameters: the number of scale items and the average intercorrelation among the items (for a discussion, see Clark & Watson, 1995). This point becomes particularly salient when examining the DES, which contains very brief (3-item) scales. Indeed, Izard et al. (1993, Table 1) found that the coefficient alphas of the DES scales varied widely and that several of them failed to achieve generally accepted standards for establishing reliability (i.e, .65 for Surprise, .62 for Shyness, .60 for Shame, .56 for Disgust). Again, considering the brevity of the DES scales, these data are hardly surprising; nevertheless, they indicate that it may be desirable to lengthen some of these weaker measures to enhance their reliability.

In contrast, the scales included in the other inventories generally show very high levels of internal consistency. For instance, McNair et al. (1971, Table 8) reported KR–20 reliabilities ranging from .84 to .96 for the six POMS scales in two different samples. Similarly, Zuckerman and Lubin (1985, Tables 9 and 10) presented data indicating that four of the MAACL–R scales (Anxiety, Depression, Hostility, Positive Affect) consistently showed adequate reliabilities in both state and trait data, with coefficient alphas typically falling in the .70 to .90 range. However, the 12-item Sensation Seeking scale produced coefficient alphas ranging from .49 to .81 in state ratings, and from only .07 to .63 in trait ratings. On the basis of these data, it appears that the scale needs additional work; consequently, it should be used with considerable caution.

Finally, Table 7 reports coefficient alphas for the 11 lower order scales of the PANAS–X (these data are adapted from Watson & Clark, 1994b, Table 12). The values shown are median reliability estimates computed across 11 samples (nine student, one adult, one psychiatric patient). The individual sample sizes ranged from 107 to 1,657, with a combined sample size of 8,194; the respondents completed the scales using one of eight different time frames. These data demonstrate that the longer (i.e., 5- to 8-item) PANAS–X scales all are highly reliable, with median values ranging from .83 (Self-Assurance) to .93 (Joviality). Moreover, the shorter (i.e., 3- and 4-item) scales also yield consistently good reliability estimates, with values ranging from .76 (Serenity) to .88 (Fatigue). Thus, similar to the POMS and the MAACL–R (with the exception of Sensation Seeking), the PANAS–X provides a reliable assessment of mood at the specific, lower order level.

Discriminant Validity of Specific Affect Scales

Because of the underlying influence of the higher order dimensions (which is manifested in strong intercorrelations among similarly valenced affects), discrimi-

TABLE 7
Internal Consistency Reliabilities of the Lower Order Scales
in the Expanded Form of the Positive and Negative Affect Schedule
(PANAS–X)

Scale	Sample Items	Coefficient alpha[a]
Fear (6)	frightened, scared, nervous	.87
Sadness (5)	sad, blue, lonely	.87
Guilt (6)	guilty, ashamed, angry at self	.88
Hostility (6)	angry, disgusted, scornful	.85
Shyness (4)	shy, bashful, timid	.83
Fatigue (4)	sleepy, sluggish, drowsy	.88
Joviality (8)	happy, enthusiastic, energetic	.93
Self-assurance (6)	proud, confident, daring	.83
Attentiveness (4)	alert, concentrating, determined	.78
Serenity (3)	calm, relaxed, at ease	.76
Surprise (3)	surprised, amazed, astonished	.77

Note. The number of items comprising each scale is shown in parentheses.
[a]Median values computed across 11 samples (total N = 8,194; adapted from Watson & Clark, 1994b, Table 12).

nant validity has been a perennial problem in the assessment of mood at the lower order level. As noted earlier, although adequate discriminant validity has been demonstrated in many instances, the evidence for scale specificity is modest at best (see Bagozzi, 1993; Berenbaum et al., 1995; Watson & Clark, 1992a). The original MAACL (Zuckerman & Lubin, 1965)—which contained scales assessing Anxiety, Depression, and Hostility—was the most notorious manifestation of this specificity problem. The MAACL scales typically displayed intercorrelations ranging from .70 to .90 and, moreover, tended to produce identical patterns of results (see Gotlib & Meyer, 1986; Zuckerman & Lubin, 1985). To their credit, Zuckerman and Lubin recognized the magnitude of the problem and sought to improve scale differentiation in the MAACL–R. They clearly have succeeded in doing so, although it must be noted that these correlations remain rather high. An inspection of the data presented by Zuckerman and Lubin (1985) indicates that the correlations among the MAACL–R negative affect scales are .61 (Anxiety vs. Depression), .61 (Anxiety vs. Hostility), and .62 (Depression vs. Hostility; these are weighted mean correlations—after r to z transformation—of the data reported in Zuckerman & Lubin, 1985, Table 2).

Watson and Clark (1994b) examined the convergent and discriminant validity of corresponding scales from the POMS (Tension–Anxiety, Depression–Dejection, Anger–Hostility) and PANAS–X (Fear, Sadness, Hostility), using data collected from 563 students (Past Few Weeks instructions). Cross-instrument scales assessing the same target affect were strongly convergent, with correlations of .85 (Fear vs. Tension–Anxiety), .91 (Sadness vs. Depression–Dejection), and .85 (Hostility vs. Anger–Hostility). With regard to discriminant validity, the correlations among the three PANAS–X scales ranged from .49 to .61 ($M = .56$), whereas those among the POMS scales ranged from .63 to .69 ($M = .66$). These mean discriminant correlations differed significantly from one another ($p < .01$, two-tailed); it therefore appears that these PANAS–X scales provide a more differentiated assessment of essentially the same content domain.

We have partially replicated these results using the fear/anxiety and sadness/depression scales in two new samples. The respondents were SMU students ($N = 516$) and Dallas-area adults ($N = 328$), both of whom rated their mood using Past Week instructions. Consistent with our earlier results, the weighted mean correlation between the POMS Tension–Anxiety and Depression–Dejection scales (.69) was significantly higher than that between PANAS–X Fear and Sadness (.59; $p < .01$, two-tailed).

These data demonstrate that the discriminant validity of scales can vary widely, even when they purportedly assess the same basic affect. Consequently, scale specificity should be a key consideration in selecting a multiaffect inventory. Unfortunately, with the exception of these POMS–PANAS–X analyses, there are few good data that directly compare the discriminant validity (and more generally, the construct validity) of alternative instruments. The collection of such comparison data should be a priority in future research.

The Necessity of Multiaffect Assessment

Our examination of the lower order level has focused exclusively on multiaffect inventories such as the DES, POMS, and PANAS–X. However, measures assessing single mood states (e.g., the state anxiety scale of the State–Trait Anxiety Inventory [STAI]; Spielberger, Gorsuch, Lushene, Vagg, & Jacobs, 1983) also have played a prominent role in the literature for decades. Some of these measures show admirable psychometric properties, and we emphasize that there is nothing intrinsically wrong with developing and using such scales. As we discuss elsewhere (see especially Watson & Clark, 1992a), however, these scales have encouraged the unfortunate practice of studying single affective states—such as anxiety or depression—in isolation. The problem with the single-affect approach is that despite their relatively narrow content, these scales are not pure or unambiguous measures of their target constructs. They invariably will be substantially correlated with measures of other, similarly valenced affects and, therefore, will be saturated with variance attributable to the underlying higher order dimensions. For example, studies have consistently shown that the STAI state anxiety scale is strongly correlated with measures of sadness/depression and anger/hostility, and that it is a strong marker of the general Negative Affect factor (e.g., Gotlib, 1984; Watson &

Clark, 1992a). Consequently, unless one assesses several different types of negative mood and the general Negative Affect factor, it is impossible to determine whether any observed effects reflect (a) the specific influence of anxiety, (b) the confounding role of some other lower order affect (e.g., depression), or (c) the hidden contribution of the underlying general factor. In other words, specific, lower order relations cannot be demonstrated in isolation but require multiaffect assessment to tease out these various possibilities.

For this reason, we strongly recommend that mood researchers routinely assess a broad range of both negative and positive moods. Which specific mood states should be included? Certainly, a comprehensive assessment should include scales assessing fearful/anxious, sad/depressed, and angry/hostile mood, as well as some type of positive affect. Beyond these minimal guidelines, the answer to this question must await further clarification of the lower order structure of affect. This remains a crucial topic for future research.

ACKNOWLEDGMENTS

We thank David Weise for his assistance in the preparation of this chapter, and Auke Tellegen for his helpful comments on an earlier version of the chapter.

REFERENCES

Almagor, M., & Ben-Porath, Y. (1989). The two-factor model of self-reported mood: A cross-cultural replication. *Journal of Personality Assessment, 53,* 10–21.

Bagozzi, R. P. (1993). An examination of the psychometric properties of measures of negative affect in the PANAS-X scales. *Journal of Personality and Social Psychology, 65,* 836–851.

Balatsky, G., & Diener, E. (1993). Subjective well-being among Russian students. *Social Indicators Research, 28,* 21–39.

Bentler, P. M. (1969). Semantic space is (approximately) bipolar. *Journal of Psychology, 71,* 33–40.

Berenbaum, H., Fujita, F., & Pfennig, J. (1995). Consistency, specificity, and correlates of negative emotions. *Journal of Personality and Social Psychology, 68,* 342–352.

Bradburn, N. M. (1969). *The structure of psychological well-being.* Chicago: Aldine.

Clark, L. A., & Watson, D. (1991). Tripartite model of anxiety and depression: Psychometric evidence and taxonomic implications. *Journal of Abnormal Psychology, 100,* 316–336.

Clark, L. A., & Watson, D. (1995). Constructing validity: Basic issues in objective scale development. *Psychological Assessment, 7,* 309–319.

Clore, G. L., Ortony, A., & Foss, M. (1987). The psychological foundations of the affective lexicon. *Journal of Personality and Social Psychology, 53,* 751–766.

Diener, E., & Emmons, R. A. (1984). The independence of positive and negative affect. *Journal of Personality and Social Psychology, 47,* 1105–1117.

Diener, E., & Iran-Nejad, A. (1986). The relationship in experience between various types of affect. *Journal of Personality and Social Psychology, 50,* 1031–1038.

Diener, E., Smith, H., & Fujita, F. (1995). The personality structure of affect. *Journal of Personality and Social Psychology, 69,* 130–141.

Ekman, P., & Davidson, R. J. (Eds.). (1994). *The nature of emotion: Fundamental questions.* New York: Oxford University Press.

Engen, R., Levy, N., & Schlosberg, H. (1958). The dimensional analysis of a new series of facial expressions. *Journal of Experimental Psychology, 55,* 454–458.

Feldman, L. A. (1995). Valence focus and arousal focus: Individual differences in the structure of affective experience. *Journal of Personality and Social Psychology, 69,* 153–166.

Gotlib, I. H. (1984). Depression and general psychopathology in university students. *Journal of Abnormal Psychology, 93,* 19–30.

Gotlib, I. H., & Meyer, J. P. (1986). Factor analysis of the Multiple Affect Adjective Check List: A separation of positive and negative affect. *Journal of Personality and Social Psychology, 50,* 1161–1165.

Green, D. P., Goldman, S. L., & Salovey, P. (1993). Measurement error masks bipolarity in affect ratings. *Journal of Personality and Social Psychology, 64,* 1029–1041.

Hendrick, C., & Lilly, R. S. (1970). The structure of mood: A comparison between sleep deprivation and normal wakefulness conditions. *Journal of Personality, 38,* 453–465.

Izard, C. E., Dougherty, F. E., Bloxom, B. M., & Kotsch, W. E. (1974). *The differential emotions scale: A method of measuring the subjective experience of discrete emotions.* Unpublished manuscript, Vanderbilt University, Nashville, TN.

Izard, C. E., Libero, D. Z., Putnam, P., & Haynes, O. M. (1993). Stability of emotion experiences and their relations to traits of personality. *Journal of Personality and Social Psychology, 64,* 847–860.

Kennedy-Moore, E., Greenberg, M. A., Newman, M. G., & Stone, A. A. (1992). The relationship between daily events and mood: The mood measure may matter. *Motivation and Emotion, 16,* 143–155.

Larsen, R. J., & Diener, E. (1992). Promises and problems with the circumplex model of emotion. In M. S. Clark (Ed.), *Review of personality and social psychology: Emotion* (Vol. 13, pp. 25–59). Newbury Park, CA: Sage.

Mayer, J. D., & Gaschke, Y. N. (1988). The experience and meta-experience of mood. *Journal of Personality and Social Psychology, 55,* 102–111.

McNair, D. M., Lorr, M., & Droppleman, L. F. (1971). *Manual: Profile of mood states.* San Diego, CA: Educational and Industrial Testing Service.

Meddis, R. (1972). Bipolar factors in mood adjective checklists. *British Journal of Social and Clinical Psychology, 11,* 178–184.

Meyer, G. J., & Shack, J. R. (1989). The structural convergence of mood and personality: Evidence for old and new directions. *Journal of Personality and Social Psychology, 57,* 691–706.

Morgan, R. L., & Heise, D. (1988). Structure of emotions. *Social Psychology Quarterly, 51,* 19–31.

Mossholder, K. W., Kemery, E. R., Harris, S. G., Armenakis, A. A., & McGrath, R. (1994). Confounding constructs and levels of constructs in affectivity measurement: An empirical investigation. *Educational and Psychological Measurement, 54,* 336–349.

Nemanick, R. C., Jr., & Munz, D. C. (1994). Measuring the poles of negative and positive mood using the Positive Affect Negative Affect Schedule and the Activation Deactivation Check List. *Psychological Reports, 74,* 195–199.

Russell, J. A. (1979). Affective space is bipolar. *Journal of Personality and Social Psychology, 37,* 345–356.

Russell, J. A. (1980). A circumplex model of affect. *Journal of Personality and Social Psychology, 39,* 1161–1178.

Russell, J. A., Weiss, A., & Mendelsohn, G. A. (1989). Affect grid: A single-item scale of pleasure and arousal. *Journal of Personality and Social Psychology, 57,* 493–502.

Spielberger, C. D., Gorsuch, R. L., Lushene, R., Vagg, P. R., & Jacobs, G. A. (1983). *Manual for the State–Trait Anxiety Inventory (Form Y).* Palo Alto, CA: Consulting Psychologists Press.

Stone, A. A. (1987). Event content in a daily survey is differentially associated with concurrent mood. *Journal of Personality and Social Psychology, 52,* 56–58.

Tellegen, A. (1985). Structures of mood and personality and their relevance to assessing anxiety, with an emphasis on self-report. In A. H. Tuma & J. D. Maser (Eds.), *Anxiety and the anxiety disorders* (pp. 681–706). Hillsdale, NJ: Lawrence Erlbaum Associates, Inc.

Tellegen, A., Watson, D., & Clark, L. A. (1994, August). Modeling dimensions of mood. In L. A. Feldman (Chair), *Mood: Consensus and controversy.* Symposium presented at the Annual Convention of the American Psychological Association, Los Angeles.

Thayer, R. E. (1986). Activation-Deactivation Check List: Current overview and structural analysis. *Psychological Reports, 58,* 607–614.

Warr, P., Barter, J., & Brownbridge, G. (1983). On the independence of positive and negative affect. *Journal of Personality and Social Psychology, 44,* 644–651.

Watson, D. (1988). The vicissitudes of mood measurement: Effects of varying descriptors, time frames, and response formats on measures of positive and negative affect. *Journal of Personality and Social Psychology, 55,* 128–141.

Watson, D., & Clark, L. A. (1991). Self- versus peer-ratings of specific emotional traits: Evidence of convergent and discriminant validity. *Journal of Personality and Social Psychology, 60,* 927–940.

Watson, D., & Clark, L. A. (1992a). Affects separable and inseparable: On the hierarchical arrangement of the negative affects. *Journal of Personality and Social Psychology, 62,* 489–505.

Watson, D., & Clark, L. A. (1992b). On traits and temperament: General and specific factors of emotional experience and their relation to the five-factor model. *Journal of Personality, 60,* 441–476.

Watson, D., & Clark, L. A. (1994a). Emotions, moods, traits, and temperaments: Conceptual distinctions and empirical findings. In P. Ekman & R. J. Davidson (Eds.), *The nature of emotion: Fundamental questions* (pp. 89–93). New York: Oxford University Press.

Watson, D., & Clark, L. A. (1994b). *Manual for the Positive and Negative Affect Schedule (Expanded Form).* Unpublished manuscript, University of Iowa, Iowa City.

Watson, D., Clark, L. A., & Tellegen, A. (1984). Cross-cultural convergence in the structure of mood: A Japanese replication and a comparison with U. S. findings. *Journal of Personality and Social Psychology, 47,* 127–144.

Watson, D., Clark, L. A., & Tellegen, A. (1988). Development and validation of brief measures of positive and negative affect: The PANAS scales. *Journal of Personality and Social Psychology, 54,* 1063–1070.

Watson, D., & Tellegen, A. (1985). Toward a consensual structure of mood. *Psychological Bulletin, 98,* 219–235.

Watson, D., & Walker, L. M. (1996). The long-term stability and predictive validity of trait measures of affect. *Journal of Personality and Social Psychology, 70,* 567–577.

Wiggins, J. S. (1973). *Personality and prediction: Principles of personality assessment.* Reading, MA: Addison-Wesley.

Zevon, M. A., & Tellegen, A. (1982). The structure of mood change: An idiographic/nomothetic analysis. *Journal of Personality and Social Psychology, 43,* 111–122.

Zuckerman, M., & Lubin, B. (1965). *Manual for the Multiple Affect Adjective Check List.* San Diego, CA: Educational and Industrial Testing Service.

Zuckerman, M., & Lubin, B. (1985). *Manual for the MAACL–R: The Multiple Affect Adjective Check List Revised.* San Diego, CA: Educational and Industrial Testing Service.

12

On the Integration of
Personality Assessment Methods:
The Rorschach and MMPI

Gregory J. Meyer

Department of Psychology
University of Alaska Anchorage

Despite being the most studied and used personality assessment tools, data from the Rorschach and MMPI generally disagree (Archer & Krishnamurthy, 1993a, 1993b). Independence is proposed to result from at least 3 factors: (a) the methods tap unique levels of personality, (b) personality has a complex organization, and (c) response styles generate considerable method variance that must be considered in nomothetic research. These ideas led to 5 hypotheses, each of which received support. Rorschach and MMPI response styles are uncorrelated, although response styles are quite consistent within a method family. MMPI–2 and Rorschach constructs of dysphoria, psychosis, or wariness are uncorrelated when response styles are ignored. However, robust convergent validity is evident when patients have similar response styles on each method (e.g., for dysphoria, $M r = .59$) and dysphoria is expressed in opposing ways on each method when response styles are discordant (i.e., $M r = -.54$). Data from the latter analyses were correlated with genuine clinical phenomena and implications were discussed for clinical practice and research.

The Minnesota Multiphasic Personality Inventory (MMPI/MMPI–2; Butcher, Dahlstrom, Graham, Tellegen, & Kaemmer, 1989) and the Rorschach Inkblot Method are the two most intensively researched, most commonly taught, and most frequently used personality assessment tools (Archer & Krishnamurthy, 1993b; Lubin, Larsen, & Matarazzo, 1984; Piotrowski & Keller, 1992; Piotrowski & Zalewski, 1993). Befitting this status, Parker, Hanson, and Hunsley's (1988) meta-analytic review demonstrated both measures have substantial reliability and good convergent validity when research is conducted with a sound theoretical or empirical rational.

Although it would seem that psychologists could be content knowing the core measures in the field are reliable and valid, this is not yet the case. After reviewing

44 studies examining MMPI and Rorschach intercorrelations, Archer and Krishnamurthy (1993a, 1993b) demonstrated the tests generally disagree. At best, a minimal relation exists between similarly named MMPI and Rorschach variables. Why these measures give disparate views of personality has become a significant conundrum for the field of assessment. Archer and Krishnamurthy (1993a) encouraged clinicians who are confronted with Rorschach and MMPI discrepancies to "make the clinical decision to emphasize certain aspects of test findings, while suppressing results from other sources of test data" (p. 138). To guide decisions about which data should be emphasized, clinicians were encouraged to "consider the relative reliability and validity of the specific data sources" (p. 138) in order to suppress that which was least reliable and valid. Such recommendations would be most appropriate if one method was clearly superior to the other.

However, if Parker et al. (1988) are correct and each tool is equally valid and reliable, such guidelines will not be sufficient. Instead, it becomes important to articulate why Archer and Krishnamurthy's findings should emerge as they do. This article will propose several clinical and methodological reasons for Rorschach and MMPI disagreement and present data demonstrating convergent validity when these factors are considered. As a starting point, however, it is useful to define the major differences between these two measures.

RORSCHACH AND MMPI DIFFERENCES

Historical precedent has left us with the terms *objective* to describe the MMPI and *projective* to describe the Rorschach. These terms are misnomers that obscure rather than clarify. In particular, they imply the MMPI is factual and precise, while suggesting the Rorschach is subjective or nonfactual. In actuality, both should be considered factual but imprecise measures of personality, each of which is adept at quantifying particular kinds of personality constructs (Meyer, 1996). More accurate terms with fewer untoward connotations are "self-assessment" to describe the MMPI and "performance-based" to describe the Rorschach.

Table 1 outlines some of the primary distinctions between the self-assessment/MMPI and performance-based/Rorschach methods. At the risk of being simplistic, some of the most obvious differences relate to the nature of the tasks. The MMPI lays out clear directions for how the task should be completed, and the task itself is familiar to anyone who has attended grammar school and completed a paper-and-pencil test. The MMPI also gives the patient only three response options (i.e., true, false, or no response). In contrast, the Rorschach presents stimuli that most people have never encountered before and only provides minimal structure. The expectations are ambiguous, consisting simply of the question "What might this be?," and each patient has extensive latitude for responding.

TABLE 1
Distinctions Between the Self-Assessment/MMPI
and the Performance-Based/Rorschach Methods
of Personality Assessment

Characteristics of the Self-Report Method	*Characteristics of the Rorschach Method*
1. Expectations are well-defined.	1. Expectations are minimally defined.
2. Stimuli are familiar.	2. Stimuli are novel.
3. Narrow range of response options.	3. Wide range of response options.
4. Task requires patient to consider self, decide if traits are characteristic, decide how to present self, and then indicate decisions on paper.	4. Task requires patient to formulate perceptions, decide which perceptions to articulate to the examiner, and then respond to further questions.
5. Administration and scoring require minimal skill.	5. Administration and scoring require considerable skill.
6. Patients are assumed to use a similar benchmark for deciding if trait is characteristic of themselves.	6. Examiner provides stable benchmark for classifying patient characteristics.
7. Measure completed alone.	7. Measure completed with an examiner.
8. Requires an in vitro description of personal characteristics.	8. Requires an in vivo demonstration of personal characteristics.
9. At best, raw data is dependent on conscious awareness and complexity of self-representations.	9. At best, raw data is dependent on engagement with the task and ability to articulate perceptions and their determinants.
10. Dissimulation and impression management affect reported symptoms.	10. Dissimulation and impression management affect engagement with task.
11. Better tool for obtaining information about specific overt symptoms, events, and experiences.	11. Better tool for assessing personality predilections which may or may not be evident in overt behavior or consciousness.

Other differences relate to what a patient must do to complete the measure. Self-assessments require patients to think about themselves, decide if certain attributes are characteristic of them, decide if they want to share this information, and then report their decisions on a piece of paper. The Rorschach requires that patients sit down with an examiner, look at 10 inked cards, formulate perceptions of what each stimulus looks like, decide if they want to share this information, articulate some responses to the examiner, and then respond to further questions during the inquiry stage.

Because the task demands are quite different, it should not be surprising if the Rorschach and MMPI obtain qualitatively different types of information. Nor should it be surprising if this information is subject to unique sources of bias and influence.

One differential source of influence is the skill required to administer and score the measures. Although considerable skill is needed to develop the items that form any self-assessment scale (as with any Rorschach scale), only minimal skill is required to administer and score a self-assessment measure. A much greater level of sophistication is necessary to accurately perform these functions with a Rorschach. The examiner must be relatively neutral; create a cooperative working alliance; know how to encourage or constrain a patient giving too few or too many responses; know the cue words that indicate an inquiry question is necessary; know how to effectively frame inquiry questions to address specific issues; and know how to accurately classify the where, what, and why of the patient's perception.

Another source of influence concerns who has greater responsibility for organizing the test data. With a self-assessment measure, each patient must accurately understand the items and all patients must use roughly equivalent mental benchmarks for deciding whether each characteristic is "mostly true" or "mostly false." With the Rorschach, responsibility for accurately decoding and consistently classifying each response is in the hands of the examiner, who again requires substantial skill to do this properly.

A third differential influence is the "interpersonalness" of each task. All self-report instruments are completed in private and do not require active interaction with an examiner. The Rorschach, on the other hand, requires consistent interaction. As such, the interpersonal dynamics of both the patient and the examiner are much more important to the completion of the Rorschach (see Schafer, 1954). Some patients may respond better to an MMPI because they prefer having control over what they disclose or because they prefer to communicate their personal attributes in a private and somewhat more anonymous fashion. Other patients may respond better to a Rorschach because they need the interpersonal structure of the task or because they are more comfortable working with someone rather than in isolation.

A fourth difference relates to the demands placed on participants. Self-assessments require patients to make personal judgments about each item in order to provide a description of what they are like. Consequently, the raw information obtained from an MMPI is very dependent on the quality of their conscious self-schema. For this information to be accurate, patients must be insightful, must not have strong emotional conflicts that result in obscuring defenses, and must have stable, well-articulated, and well-differentiated understandings of themselves.[1] The

---

[1]As David Nichols, Radhika Krishnamurthy, and a helpful reviewer noted, some MMPI experts would dispute this characterization, pointing to the empirical construction of the basic scales, the presence of subtle items, the research documenting scale correlates, and the configural approach to interpretation as evidence the MMPI yield is not limited to consciously accessible information. I am not trying to suggest otherwise. Rather, my point is simply that patient responses to all items, subtle or otherwise, are dependent on their conscious understanding of themselves. This does not mean clinical inferences are limited to the consciously bound raw information provided by patients. Clinicians can certainly infer beyond what patients consciously recognize or deliberately intend to communicate.

Rorschach does not require a patient to directly communicate personal knowledge. Rather, it requires patients to behaviorally perform. As such, it elicits a demonstration of personal characteristics, rather than a description of them (see Miller, 1987), which makes it more akin to intelligence or neuropsychological tests than to the MMPI. On the Rorschach, information is gleaned from subtle differences in what perceptions are articulated, their location, the manner in which they are described, and the qualities of ink described as giving rise to them. Although patients completing a Rorschach consistently judge the adequacy of their responses and inhibit or censor certain perceptions, because most information is obliquely obtained through nonobvious scoring categories, the information is not necessarily filtered through the patient's self-schema nor dependent on conscious awareness (see Bornstein, Rossner, Hill, & Stepanian, 1994).[2] Simultaneously, however, Rorschach scores are quite dependent on the ability of patients to spontaneously engage with the task and articulate responses. Cognitive and emotional difficulties that interfere with verbal articulation, behavioral spontaneity, or task engagement compromise score accuracy, and these confounds find no substantial parallel on a self-assessment measure.

Both methods are also subject to conscious efforts at impression management, although the nature of these influences differ. For self-assessments, patients must be willing to accurately share what they know to be true about themselves. Of course, some may decide not to do this and may pervasively deny unseemly traits, deny a circumscribed domain of characteristics (e.g., hearing voices), overemphasize problems in a selected area of symptomatology, or pervasively endorse pathology. Somewhat similar strategies can be taken with the Rorschach, such that patients can pervasively inhibit all kinds of responses, selectively censor certain classes of responses (e.g., those with sexual content), selectively emphasize certain kinds of responses, or pervasively respond to the task with dramatic and intense perceptions. However, because it is generally not clear how responses will be scored, efforts at impression management are more of a gamble with the Rorschach than the MMPI.

Finally, because of the foregoing, each method differs with respect to the information it can deliver under optimal circumstances. Self-assessments can be very effective when obtaining information about specific symptoms or experiences, whereas the Rorschach can be very effective when obtaining information about

---

[2]At times, even content with obvious personal relevance is articulated to the inkblots without the patient's awareness, as some patients experience their perceptions as external "facts" rather than personal productions. A particularly vivid example occurred with a patient hospitalized because of increasing homicidal impulses toward his wife. Shortly after admission he denied any homicidal ideation and wished to be discharged. However, when he was subsequently tested he reported Card II of the Rorschach looked like two men giving each other a high-five while stomping on a uterus that had blood shooting out of it. Despite his protests to the contrary, it required few inferential steps to conclude he was still preoccupied with hostile, aggressive, and domineering impulses toward women.

underlying personality characteristics, propensities, and mental representations. Consider questions related to hallucinations, suicidal plans, phobic fears, compulsive checking, or difficulty with early morning awakening. It does not matter how many Rorschach scores are considered, an examiner will never know the extent of these problems unless the patient is given a task like the MMPI that asks about them directly and then quantifies the responses. On the other hand, consider questions like the extent to which a patient perceives external events in a conventional fashion, has a psychic environment populated with nonhuman characters, has ideas that become illogical and inappropriately fused together in the absence of clear external structure, implicitly envisions interactions as destructive and conflictual, or is prone to focus on idiosyncratic details within the environment. It does not matter how many MMPI scores are considered; an examiner will never be able to quantify these characteristics unless the patient's behavior is observed in a controlled and normed setting like the Rorschach.

In summary, the strength of the MMPI is that it can quickly obtain specific symptomatic information and yield a portrait of the patient from the patient's perspective. Its limitations stem from its reliance on the patient to make sense of all the items and convey information to the examiner accurately and honestly. The strength of the Rorschach is that it requires a behavioral demonstration of personal characteristics, rather than a simple description. As such, it is able to obtain information that the patient may not be cognizant of and can do this to some extent despite a conscious effort not to reveal certain attributes. Limitations include the fact that scores are dependent on open engagement with the task and the ability to articulate perceptions.

Given all these differences, one reason MMPI and Rorschach scales are not strongly correlated may be because the methods are really measuring quite different things. In the past, psychology's propensity to apply the same term to two very different things has been termed the *jingle fallacy,* which stands in contrast to the *jangle fallacy* or our equally strong propensity to use different terms to describe what is actually the same thing (cf. Block, 1995). With the Rorschach and MMPI, a jingle fallacy emerges when we use the generic term *depression* to refer to the MMPI's Depression Content Scale and also the Rorschach Depression Index (*DEPI*). Depression on the MMPI is really depression as it is consciously understood and deliberately reported by the patient. Depression on the Rorschach is really depression as it is manifest in implicit perceptual propensities and qualities of verbal articulation. These should not be considered equivalent.

Just as MRI and PET scans provide distinct information about brain functioning, and optical and infrared telescopes provide distinct information about galaxies, MMPI and Rorschach scores ought to capture unique information about personality. It is curious, however, that personality research has developed such strong expectations for two very different tools to yield quite similar information. Rather than appreciating Rorschach and MMPI differences, the field often seems stuck on the goal of demonstrating both methods provide redundant information. This expectation probably has roots in Campbell and Fiske's (1959) pioneering work on test validity.

THE MULTITRAIT–MULTIMETHOD MATRIX

Campbell and Fiske's (1959) article on convergent and discriminant validity has had a broad impact on psychology, being the most frequently cited publication in the history of the *Psychological Bulletin* (Sternberg, 1992). In formulating what they termed the multitrait–multimethod (MTMM) matrix, Campbell and Fiske laid out a technique that would assist in determining the validity of psychological tests. They believed this test-focused procedure would be a necessary element in the process of explicating the nomological network that supports the construct validity for a test (Cronbach & Meehl, 1955). Campbell and Fiske's reasoning was quite straightforward: If a test is to be considered valid, it should display convergent and discriminant validity. It should be highly correlated with scales of the same construct obtained from an independent method of measurement and it should be uncorrelated with theoretically independent constructs—especially when those independent constructs are quantified by the same method of measurement.

Although they did not explicate the terminology, Campbell and Fiske's MTMM matrix presupposed three components that sum to form any observed test score: (a) actual measurement of the intended construct; (b) systematic measurement error, or the consistent but erroneous measurement of unintended factors; and (c) random measurement error, or the irregularities arising from specific content, settings, occasions, or subject states that cause scores to fluctuate over theoretically independent measurements.

To the extent observed scores are determined by actual measurement of the intended construct rather than systematic or random error, Campbell and Fiske reasoned that two independent methods of measuring the same construct should display strong convergent validity. It is this reasoning that has apparently led to the expectation that unique methods of assessment should provide redundant information. However, Campbell and Fiske (1959) also discussed caveats regarding convergent validity coefficients. Two issues they mentioned are quite relevant for understanding the lack of association between MMPI and Rorschach scores. The first concerns the nature of the constructs we try to measure in personality assessment, whereas the second was a major thrust of their article and concerns the pervasive influence of method variance.

Personality Constructs

A critical requirement for the MTMM matrix is that constructs must be uniformly expressed across levels of personality. Uniformity is essential because it allows the construct to be equally measurable by all methods of assessment. Campbell and Fiske (1959) cautioned researchers about assuming this requirement has been met. In fact, they noted how a failure to demonstrate convergence across methods could lead to a refined understanding of the personality construct, rather than to the criticism or abandonment of a test.

Unfortunately, when a test does not display convergent validity, the test is generally considered suspect, not the construct. For instance, if depression scales from the MMPI and another self-report test have strong convergent validity but neither set of measures correlate with the *DEPI,* then the Rorschach scale is considered dubious rather than our notions regarding depression. The underlying assumption is that people who appear depressed on one method should also appear depressed on all other methods. This assumption, however, is grounded in a one-dimensional view of human nature that holds it is impossible for people to be "depressed" and "not depressed" at the same time. Superficially, this belief is logical and it is true in a strict sense if depression is defined as the specific behavioral symptoms contained in the *Diagnostic and Statistical Manual of Mental Disorders* (4th ed. [*DSM–IV*]; American Psychiatric Association, 1994). However, this belief does not always conform to clinical reality.

Not only can patients appear depressed on one test and not another because of motivated distortions, but more important, a variety of clinical conditions can be identified that exemplify how affective states and psychiatric symptoms are not unitary across levels of personality. Identifying such conditions necessarily requires a more psychodynamic view of personality and psychopathology (e.g., Gabbard, 1990). For instance, consider patients with somatization, conversion, or somato-form pain disorders. Most of these people are not consistently aware of the distress, dysphoria, or psychic conflict that accompanies their condition and their underlying emotional discomfort is rarely expressed through direct and overt dysphoric symptomatology. Thus, patients with these difficulties will generally not report depression on the MMPI (nor a structured interview). However, depression may well emerge on Rorschach-derived scores if the method can truly assess underlying personality dynamics and propensities.

Many other kinds of patients (and nonpatients) protect their self-image and conscious experience from emotional distress by using defenses of denial, repres-sion, intellectualization, splitting, and/or projection. Some have conditions where their overt symptoms can be understood as compensatory defenses for opposing unconscious needs or feelings. People with these difficulties may not consciously recognize or "own" their troubling affects, even though these emotional states are still part of their underlying psychological experience. For example, the grandiosity and excessive need for admiration displayed by the narcissistic patient can be understood as defensive counter-reactions to the underlying feelings of inadequacy, shame, and inferiority that are intolerable for the patient to bear consciously (Kohut, 1971, 1984). The grandiosity implicit in paranoid ideas of reference can serve as compensation for underlying feelings of inadequacy, whereas paranoid beliefs that harm and danger are ever-present in the environment can reflect underlying anger that has been disavowed and projected externally (Akhtar, 1990). The schizoid individual who overtly expresses minimal affect and little or no desire for social engagement can often be understood as having a defensive counter-reaction to acutely sensitive emotional reactions and powerful desires for warm, close, fusing interpersonal relationships (Akhtar, 1987; Gabbard, 1990; Guntrip, 1968).

Although not exhaustive, the foregoing illustrates several conditions that should create disparities when data are obtained from different methods of personality assessment. If the MMPI can provide valid data drawn from conscious self-aware-ness and verbally mediated self-representations and if the Rorschach can provide valid data about tacit self- and other-representations; unreflected upon modes of perceiving the world; and underlying feelings, conflicts, and dynamics, then these methods should disagree when they are assessing the kinds of clinical conditions described earlier. Therefore, a second reason why the MMPI and Rorschach disagree is because certain clinical conditions can force the scores to go in opposite directions when each test is accurately measuring what it should.

Method Variance

In their original work, Campbell and Fiske (1959) noted how intrinsic features of any measurement tool interfered with the ability to accurately quantify a targeted construct. These method factors were understood as pervasive confounds affecting all tests, including the halo effect in observer ratings, apparatus factors in studies with laboratory animals, and so on. Method variance is a major component of systematic measurement error and is evident in a MTMM matrix when there is poor convergent validity across methods and poor discriminant validity within a method. Of importance, Campbell and Fiske (1959) observed that method factors typically account for a greater proportion of variance in test scores than the actual traits the tests are designed to measure. When observed scores are determined more by the systematic error of method variance than by the intended construct, personality research is obviously compromised.

All of the factors discussed in Table 1 can contribute to method variance. For instance, unskilled examiners can generate considerable systematic error in Ror-schach scores, as can poor reading comprehension in MMPI scores. However, it is useful to expand on some common individual differences that generate method variance because these response style factors are ubiquitous in clinical settings.

When completing the MMPI, some patients are situationally guarded, nondis-closing, and consciously responding to items in a socially desirable fashion (Style 1–M). Others are characterologically defended, lacking insight and self-awareness, and unable to accurately describe themselves. These patients are prone to portray themselves as overly virtuous or ideal and to have minimal awareness of affective distress (Style 2–M). Others are quite open, insightful, and forthcoming about their problems or lack thereof (Style 3–M). Still others are situationally dramatic in their presentation and strive to portray themselves in an unrealistically pathological fashion (Style 4–M). Finally, other patients are characterologically fragile, self-critical, or hypersensitive to distress. They will persistently—but honestly—think of their personality glass as half-empty rather than half-full, and experience themselves in an overly pathological and symptomatic light (Style 5–M).

A similar range of response styles are readily observed with the Rorschach. Some patients are situationally quite constricted and leery about what information will be obtained from them. They offer few responses, minimal investment in the task, resistive inquiry, and minimal determinant articulation (Style 1–R). Others have similar overt behaviors, although the root cause is very different, emanating from genuinely limited or impoverished internal resources and bewilderment with the abstractness or complexity of the task (Style 2–R). Other patients are articulate, strive to work cooperatively with the examiner, maintain active engagement with the task and spontaneously give responses, articulate determinants, and synthesize blot locations in accordance with their internal predilections (Style 3–R). Still others consciously strive to be dramatic, exhaustive, creative, or shocking in their responses to the test. Consequently, they appear very engaged and generate many structurally complex, synthesized responses (Style 4–R). Finally, some other patients also appear highly engaged with the task, producing lengthy and complex protocols. However, their engagement is driven by an unconscious propensity to unload chaotic internal states, as if the task opens their fragile psychological boundaries and unleashes a stream of emotionally laden perceptions (Style 5–R).

Even though MMPI and Rorschach scores can demonstrate validity in nomothetic research, four of these five response styles infuse observed scale scores with an extensive degree of systematic error—positive error when scores are inflated (Styles 4 and 5) and negative error when scores are deflated (Styles 1 and 2). Furthermore, even though these types of error are not mutually exclusive, they can emerge from two very different sources: either from genuine aspects of character or from manipulated forms of communication (also see Paulhus, 1984, 1986). That is, positive or negative systematic error can be due to authentic features of a patient's intrinsic states and traits (i.e., Styles 2 and 5) or to conscious efforts that are designed to convey a particular message or achieve a desired end (i.e., Styles 1 and 4).

In clinical practice, it is clear these different response styles affect the validity of obtained scores. A built-in strength of the MMPI is that it contains scales to assess these forms of systematic error. Although a T score of 40 on Scale 2 generally suggests energetic optimism and cheerful self-confidence, the meaning of this score can be quite different depending on other features of the profile. When L, F, and K and Scales 1, 2, and 3 each have a "V" rather than caret shape, the T score of 40 on

Scale 2 really means the patient has significant struggles with underlying depressive issues, even though these are consciously disavowed and contributing to a somatoform condition (e.g., Greene, 1991).

Less attention has been paid to response styles on the Rorschach. However, in their classic work on *Psychodiagnostic Testing*, Rappaport, Gill, and Schafer (1968) labeled the disengaged or constricted approach *coarctated* and labeled the engaged approach *dilated.* They saw this dimension of responding to the test as one of the most central dimensions to consider when interpreting a protocol. Their reasoning was similar to the conventional wisdom found with an MMPI; they believed the meaning of a score elevation was altered depending on whether the protocol was coarctated or dilated.

In applied practice, clinicians can recognize validity does not reside solely within a particular test scale or index, but rather is also a function of how patients interact with the task. Thus, clinicians can derive some accurate inferential knowledge about a patient when considering overall MMPI or Rorschach profiles, although this same knowledge cannot be gained by considering single scale elevations that disregard response styles. Nomothetic research, on the other hand, must typically disregard the configural and contextual information that alerts clinicians to response style influences and modifies the meaning of scale scores. This is because statistics are generally calculated from scales considered in isolation. Such an approach implicitly assumes validity is solely a function of test scales. These nonveridical data points must then bear the burden of demonstrating validity for the scale, for the test as a whole, and for the conceptual reasoning that would accompany skilled use of the instrument. Such an approach is part of the reason why it is generally impossible to separate method variance from trait variance when conducting nomothetic research (also see Cronbach, 1995).

To what extent do response styles affect observed scores on the MMPI and Rorschach? Consistent with Campbell and Fiske's (1959) observation, the first and largest dimension within each test can be considered a response style dimension (Edwards & Edwards, 1991; Meyer, 1992a, 1992b). The first MMPI dimension generally accounts for about 50% of the total test variance, and about 75% to 80% of the common variance (Edwards & Edwards, 1991).[3] The first Rorschach dimen-

---

[3]The first dimension of the MMPI is more typically given a trait interpretation rather than a method interpretation. As a trait it is considered a dimension of negative affectivity or distressed emotionality (e.g., Johnson, Butcher, Null, & Johnson, 1984). Although it would be clinically and theoretically important to try to disentangle where response styles end and negative affectivity begins, it may be impossible to accomplish and is certainly beyond the scope of this article. Suffice it to say that this dimension responds to three very different but deeply intertwined qualities. The first concerns the authentic but objectively inaccurate experience that some people have regarding their own level of disturbance (Styles 2 and 5). The second concerns conscious efforts to under- or over-report psychic problems (Styles 1 and 4). The third concerns the theoretically "accurate" trait information that could be quantified by this dimension (approximated by Style 3).

sion typically accounts for about 30% of the total variance in test scores, and about 50% of the common variance (Meyer, 1992a, 1992b). Although it is not possible to specify what proportion of each dimension may be due exclusively to method variance rather than intended trait variance, it is clear response styles have a pervasive influence on each test.

Disregarding response styles is not so problematic when research is conducted within a single assessment method. In fact, a rosier picture is obtained under these circumstances because response styles should be consistent within a method family and falsely magnify convergent validity coefficients. That is, the systematic error generated by response styles will consistently sweep scores for a construct higher (or lower) than they should be, causing the validity coefficients for two tests to be artificially inflated.

It seems unlikely, however, that response styles will operate in a consistent fashion across different methods of assessment. The factors that make someone report unrealistically virtuous ideas about him or herself on a self-report questionnaire are probably not the same factors that make someone constricted when sitting down with an examiner to articulate what ambiguous inkblots look like. Therefore, a third reason why we have not found convergent validity between the MMPI and Rorschach is because response styles operate independently on each test and tend to obscure the true extent of construct overlap.

Implications

To summarize, several reasons have been proffered as to why seemingly similar MMPI and Rorschach scales do not correlate with each other. A primary reason may be the scales actually measure different constructs, despite similar names. A second reason may be a function of personality complexity. For many clinical conditions, there should be a disparity between those characteristics that are consciously recognized or deliberately reported and those characteristics that are present on a more implicit level of personality. Finally, because response styles have a significant impact on the scores obtained from both methods, these factors may obscure the true extent of construct convergence when methods are as different as the MMPI and Rorschach.

Taking these ideas into account led to the following hypotheses: (a) the MMPI and Rorschach are sufficiently distinct so that response styles should be uncorrelated across methods; (b) response styles should be highly correlated when different tests come from the same method family; (c) consistent with previous research, no substantial correlations should be evident between theoretically similar Rorschach and MMPI–2 scales when response styles are ignored; (d) rather than fighting the confounding effects of method variance, if the analysis is limited to patients with similar response styles on each method, there should be strong positive correlations between Rorschach indices and corresponding scales from the MMPI–2; and (e) there should be strong negative correlations between Rorschach indices and corresponding MMPI–2 scales when patients display discordant response styles on each method.

METHOD

Participants

As part of a hospital-based psychological testing program, 370 patients completed both an MMPI–2 and Rorschach. However, 8 participants were excluded from the analyses; 2 appeared to complete their MMPI–2 in a random fashion (i.e., [F + Fb]/2 T score > 115 and $VRIN$ T score > 80) and 6 had Rorschach protocols of questionable utility (i.e., R < 12, or R = 12 or 13 and $Lambda$ > .50). For the single analysis within the self-report method family, data were obtained from 283 patients who had completed an Millon Clinical Multiaxial Inventory (MCMI–II; Millon, 1987) and an MMPI–2. For the primary sample of 362 patients, 52% were psychiatric inpatients, 30% were psychiatric outpatients, 15% were general medical patients, and 3% were drawn from other settings. The average age of the sample was 34.9 (SD = 11.5, range = 17 to 72); 55% were women; 60% were White, 32% African American, 4% Asian, and 4% other.

Measures

All Rorschachs were either administered by myself or by a student in training with me. I scored all protocols according to Comprehensive System guidelines (Exner, 1993), and most were also scored by a trainee, with discrepancies resolved through discussion. Reliability for this database was calculated across 63 protocols and found to be satisfactory. Percentage of exact agreement between myself and an independent coder was determined across the following categories: location and space (94%), developmental quality (88%), movement (90%), shading and achromatic color (94%), color (95%), form-dominance of determinants (89%), color shading or shading blends (97%), all determinants exact (74%), form quality (82%), pairs (95%), content (85%), popular (97%), organizational activity (88%), special scores that form the weighted sum of six special scores (82%), and other special scores (88%). All MMPI–2s or MCMI–IIs were administered at roughly the same time as the Rorschach and computer-scored by National Computer Systems (NCS). Scores were obtained from the NCS files except for 4 patients who had only MMPI–2 profile sheets available.

Dependent variables were considered in three content clusters: affective distress, psychotic processes, and wary interpersonal suspiciousness. Rorschach measures of emotional distress included the Depression Index (*DEPI*) and the Suicide

Constellation (*S–CON*). MMPI–2 variables included Scale 2, Scale 7, Depression (*DEP*), Anxiety (*ANX*), and the Negative Emotionality/Neuroticism scale from the Personality Psychopathology Five (*PSY–5–Neg*; Harkness, McNulty, & Ben-Porath, 1995). Despite real differences in the constructs being measured by these two methods, I believed that fairly strong construct overlap was still present.

The Rorschach measure of psychotic processes was the Schizophrenia Index (*SCZI*), whereas MMPI–2 measures included Scale 8, Bizarre Mentation (*BIZ*), and the Psychoticism scale from the *PSY–5* (*PSY–5–Psy*; Harkness et al., 1995). I believed these cross-method constructs had moderate correspondence.

The Rorschach measure of interpersonal wariness was the Hypervigilance Index (*HVI*). The MMPI–2 does not have any scales that measure interpersonal wariness in a way that is parallel to the *HVI*'s construct of emotional detachment combined with heightened alertness and extensive processing of environmental cues. Nonetheless, a range of MMPI–2 scales were selected, each of which address an oblique manifestation of the Rorschach construct. The MMPI–2 measures included Scale 6, Cynicism (*CYN*), Social Discomfort (*SOD*), and the Inability to Disclose component of the Negative Treatment Indicators Scale (*TRT2*; Ben-Porath & Sherwood, 1993). I believed these constructs would have mild cross-method correspondence.

Total scores were used for Rorschach scales and non-K-corrected raw scores were used for MMPI–2 scales. Rorschach distributions were approximately normal, with no scale having skew or kurtosis values exceeding |0.86|. Several MMPI–2 variables (i.e., *PSY–5–Psy, PSY–5–Neg, ANX,* and *BIZ*) had skew or kurtosis values exceeding |1.0|, but no values exceeded |4.0| and all variables were retained for the correlational analysis.

Procedures

Welsh's Anxiety Scale (*A*) was designed to quantify the first MMPI factor. To assess its adequacy, I conducted a principal components analysis of this scale along with the MMPI–2 basic, validity, and content scales. Using 470 participants from the full database, the first unrotated component accounted for 51.3% of the total variance (the second, third, fourth, and fifth components accounted for 11.7, 5.9, 4.1, and 3.7% of the total variance, respectively). As expected, this dimension was defined by the *A* scale, which had a loading of .95. These findings indicate *A* is a good measure of the MMPI–2's huge first factor.

The first factor from the Rorschach has been termed *Response Articulation* in the past (Meyer, 1992b), although I now consider *Response–Engagement (R–Engagement)* or response complexity to be more accurate descriptors. Previously, a formula for calculating *R–Engagement* was derived from a large sample of college students (Meyer, 1992b) using z scores with the following weights: .436(color shading blends) + .372(*FY*) + .325(*FC'*) + .3(*FC*) + .3(*CF+C*) + .29(shading blends) + .29(*m*) + .29(*R*) + .27(*S*) + .24(*FM*) + .22(*FV*) + .21(*W*) + .19(*MOR*) + .18(*M*) –

.24(*Lambda*). To assess the adequacy of this scale, I conducted a principal components analysis of this variable along with other nonredundant scores for location,
developmental quality, determinants, form quality, and special scores. Using 430
participants from the full database, the first unrotated component accounted for
23.4% of the total variance (the second, third, fourth, and fifth components
accounted for 8.9, 4.8, 4.4, and 3.5% of the total variance, respectively). As
expected, this dimension was most strongly defined by the *R–Engagement* scale,
which had a loading of .96. These findings indicate this scale is a good measure of
the Rorschach's large first factor.

Using 316 participants, the first MCMI–II factor accounted for 57% of the total
test variance (the second, third, fourth, and fifth components accounted for 17.9,
7.6, 6.2, and 3.2% of the total variance, respectively). This factor was most strongly
defined by the *Disclosure* validity scale, which had a factor loading of .98.[4]

For the MMPI–2, participants were considered openly responsive (Style 4–M
or 5–M) if they scored in the upper third of the *A* distribution (i.e., > 21), and
considered defensively constricted (Style 1–M or 2–M) if they scored in the lower
third (i.e., < 11). Using these criteria, 126 participants were considered expressive,
whereas 124 were considered constricted. For the Rorschach, participants were
considered openly responsive (Style 4–R or 5–R) if they scored in the upper third
of the *R–Engagement* distribution (i.e., > .728), and were considered guardedly
constricted (Style 1–R or 2–R) if they fell in the lower third of this distribution (i.e.,
< –1.103). Using these criteria, there were 121 participants classified as openly
responsive on the Rorschach and 121 participants classified as constricted. Examining response styles across methods, 87 participants adopted the same style on
both the MMPI–2 and Rorschach (i.e., openly responsive on both, *n* = 46, or
defensive on both, *n* = 41), whereas 78 participants adopted discordant response
styles across methods (openly responsive Rorschach and constricted MMPI–2, *n*
= 35, or constricted Rorschach and expressive MMPI–2, *n* = 43).

RESULTS

The first hypothesis proposed response styles on the Rorschach and MMPI would
be independent. Table 2 demonstrates this hypothesis was supported. Whether
operationally defined by the *A* and *R–Engagement* scales, or by factor scores
derived in this sample, the MMPI's first factor is uncorrelated with the Rorschach's
first factor (*r*s = .10 and .04, respectively). Secondarily, it was expected that other
response style indicators from the MMPI–2 (i.e., *L, F, K,* and *Fb*) and Rorschach
(i.e., *R* and *Lambda*) would be unrelated. The data in Table 2 support this hypothesis
as well, as these scales have an average correlation of .01.

---

[4]Factor solutions for each of these analyses are available on request.

TABLE 2
Correlation Between Rorschach Scales of Response Style
and MMPI-2 Scales of Response Style

	MMPI–2 Scale					
Rorschach Scale	A	1st Fact	F	Fb	L	K
R–Engagement	.10	.05	.05	.02	–.10	–.02
1st Factor	.08	.04	–.09	.02	–.01	.04
R	.05	.02	.02	.01	–.07	.00
Lambda	.05	.09	.06	.08	.09	–.11*

Note. R–Engagement refers to the first principal component of the Rorschach using factor scores derived from a sample of college students (Meyer, 1992b). *1st Factor* refers to the same dimension quantified by factor scores derived from the present sample. *1st Fact* refers to factor scores for the first principal component of the MMPI–2 derived from the present sample. $N = 362$ for all correlations except those with Fb, where $N = 359$.

*$p < .05$.

TABLE 3
Correlation Between MMPI–2 Scales of Response Style
and MCMI–II Scales of Response Style

	MMPI–2 Scale					
MCMI–II Scale	1st Factor	A	F	Fb	L	K
1st Factor	.85*	.78*	.68*	.73*	–.44*	–.76*
Disclosure	.80*	.74*	.64*	.67*	–.44*	–.74*
Debasement	.87*	.85*	.69*	.80*	–.39*	–.68*

Note. *1st Factor* refers to factor scores on the first unrotated principal component derived from the present sample. $N = 283$ for all correlations.

*$p < .001$.

The second hypothesis stated response styles should be strongly correlated within the same method family. This hypothesis was tested by correlating the first factor from the MMPI–2 with the first factor from the MCMI–II and also by correlating the L, F, Fb, and K validity scales from the MMPI–2 with the *Disclosure* and *Debasement* validity scales from the MCMI–II. These correlations are presented in Table 3. In contrast to the previous analysis, the first dimension of the MMPI–2 is strongly correlated with the first dimension of the MCMI–II ($r = .85$). Furthermore, the clinically derived indicators of response style from each test are also strongly related, having an average correlation of .63. Table 3 also indicates the clinical markers of response style from one test are strongly correlated with the first component from the other test. For instance, the MMPI–2's first factor is correlated with the MCMI–II *Debasement* and *Disclosure* scales at magnitudes of .87 and .80, respectively. These findings offer additional support for considering each test's first factor to be largely determined by response styles.

The third hypothesis postulated that there would be no association between Rorschach and MMPI scales of similar constructs when response styles were disregarded. This hypothesis was also supported. As can be seen in Table 4, despite considerable statistical power, there are no non-zero correlations between MMPI–2 and Rorschach scales of emotional distress. The average convergent validity coefficient for this construct is –.006. Turning to scales of psychosis and wariness, there are again no salient correlations, although one low magnitude coefficient is statistically significant in each case. Nonetheless, the general pattern is clear. For all practical purposes, when one disregards response styles in a heterogeneous sample, MMPI and Rorschach scales of affective distress, psychotic processes, and interpersonal wariness are unrelated.

The fourth hypothesis stated Rorschach and MMPI scales of similar constructs should be positively correlated when the analysis is limited to those participants who display the same type of response style on both assessment methods. Table 5 presents the results of this analysis. It can be seen there is substantial overlap between scores of emotional discomfort when patients have similar response styles on both methods. In general, the Rorschach's *DEPI* and *S–CON* correlate with MMPI–2 scales in the range of .55 to .65 (*M* = .594). A similar pattern of strong positive correlations is apparent when the constructs of psychosis and interpersonal wariness are examined. The Rorschach Schizophrenia Index now correlates in the range between .45 and .55 with corresponding MMPI–2 scales. The correlations for wariness are a bit more variable, although still substantial (*M r* = .37). Overall, these data indicate that under some circumstances, strong convergent validity can be demonstrated for these very different methods of assessment.

The fifth hypothesis stated scales of similar constructs should be negatively correlated when patients displayed different response styles on each method. The correlations for this analysis are presented in Table 6. The data clearly support the hypothesis for the construct of emotional distress, as these correlations cluster around a magnitude of –.55. Similar, but less pronounced disparities were evident for the constructs of psychosis and interpersonal wariness. The Rorschach Schizophrenia Index was negatively correlated with each of its corresponding MMPI–2 scales, although the findings were not statistically significant using the more conservative two-tailed rejection region. Negative correlations of slightly larger magnitude (*M* = –.28) were observed when the *HVI* was examined in relation to MMPI–2 scales of interpersonal wariness. The findings are certainly most robust for the construct of depression, although the general pattern supports the hypothesis that constructs will be negatively correlated across methods when patients display opposing response styles on each method.

TABLE 4

Disregarding Response Styles: Correlation Between Rorschach and MMPI–2
Scales in Three Content Areas When Response Styles Are Ignored

	Affective Distress		Psychosis		Wariness	
MMPI–2 Scales	Rorschach DEPI	Rorschach S–CON	MMPI–2 Scales	Rorschach SCZI	MMPI–2 Scales	Rorschach HVI
Scale 2	−.09	−.05	Scale 8	.15*	Scale 6	.15*
Scale 7	.00	−.01	BIZ	.09	CYN	−.07
DEP	.01	−.00	PSY–5–Psy	.09	SOD	.04
ANX	.02	.04			TRT2	.08
PSY–5–Neg	−.00	.02				

Note. DEPI = Depression Index; S–CON = Suicide Constellation; SCZI = Schizophrenia Index; HVI = Hypervigilance Index; DEP = Depression Content Scale; ANX = Anxiety Content Scale; PSY–5–Neg = Personality Psychopathology Five Negative Emotionality/Neuroticism Scale; BIZ = Bizarre Mentation Content Scale; PSY–5–Psy = Personality Psychopathology Five Psychoticism Scale; CYN = Cynicism Content Scale; SOD = Social Discomfort Content Scale; TRT2 = Inability to Disclose component of the Negative Treatment Indicators Content Scale. N = 362 for Scales 2, 6, 7, and 8; N = 359 for Content Scales; N = 358 for PSY–5 scales.
*p < .01.

TABLE 5
Similar Response Styles: Correlation Between Rorschach
and MMPI–2 Scales in Three Content Areas When Response Styles
Are Similar on Each Assessment Method

	Affective Distress		Psychosis		Wariness	
MMPI–2 Scales	Rorschach DEPI	Rorschach S–CON	MMPI–2 Scales	Rorschach SCZI	MMPI–2 Scales	Rorschach HVI
Scale 2	.42**	.50**	Scale 8	.54**	Scale 6	.45**
Scale 7	.62**	.67**	BIZ	.46**	CYN	.22*
DEP	.66**	.63**	PSY–5–Psy	.48**	SOD	.38**
ANX	.61**	.62**			TRT2	.44**
PSY–5–Neg	.59**	.62**				

Note. DEPI = Depression Index; S–CON = Suicide Constellation; SCZI = Schizophrenia Index; HVI = Hypervigilance Index; DEP = Depression Content Scale; ANX = Anxiety Content Scale; PSY–5–Neg = Personality Psychopathology Five Negative Emotionality/Neuroticism Scale; BIZ = Bizarre Mentation Content Scale; PSY–5–Psy = Personality Psychopathology Five Psychoticism Scale; CYN = Cynicism Content Scale; SOD = Social Discomfort Content Scale; TRT2 = Inability to Disclose component of the Negative Treatment Indicators Content Scale. n = 87.
*p < .05. **p < .001.

TABLE 6
Different Response Styles: Correlation Between Rorschach
and MMPI–2 Scales in Three Content Areas When Response Styles
Are Discordant Across Both Assessment Methods

Affective Distress			*Psychosis*		*Wariness*	
MMPI–2 Scales	*Rorschach DEPI*	*Rorschach S–CON*	*MMPI–2 Scales*	*Rorschach SCZI*	*MMPI–2 Scales*	*Rorschach HVI*
Scale 2	−.51**	−.43**	Scale 8	−.22	Scale 6	−.22
Scale 7	−.59**	−.57**	BIZ	−.16	CYN	−.38*
DEP	−.55**	−.52**	PSY–5–Psy	−.20	SOD	−.23*
ANX	−.56**	−.57**			TRT2	−.27*
PSY–5–Neg	−.56**	−.57**				

Note. DEPI = Depression Index; *S–CON* = Suicide Constellation; *SCZI* = Schizophrenia Index; *HVI* = Hypervigilance Index; *DEP* = Depression Content Scale; *ANX* = Anxiety Content Scale; *PSY–5–Neg* = Personality Psychopathology Five Negative Emotionality/Neuroticism Scale; *BIZ* = Bizarre Mentation Content Scale; *PSY–5–Psy* = Personality Psychopathology Five Psychoticism Scale; *CYN* = Cynicism Content Scale; *SOD* = Social Discomfort Content Scale; *TRT2* = Inability to Disclose component of the Negative Treatment Indicators Content Scale. $n = 78$.
$*p < .05.$ $**p < .001.$

Additional Analyses

MTMM matrices were constructed in order to place the previous monotrait-heteromethod convergent validity findings within a broader context. Tables 7, 8, and 9 present a condensed matrix of the correlations observed when response styles are ignored, similar, and discordant, respectively. Stronger evidence for convergent validity is indicated when test scales also display discriminant validity, or no relation with theoretically independent constructs. It is easiest to examine discriminant validity when constructs should be fully independent (i.e., $r = 0$), because then any empirical overlap can be attributed to systematic error. However, when the constructs should overlap—when affective distress should be associated with interpersonal cautiousness, for instance—it is more difficult to determine the extent to which method variance is confounding genuine trait variance.

Within a MTMM matrix, evidence for discriminant validity is obtained from three sources. The first is discriminant validity within a single method. This information is derived from the italicized heterotrait-monomethod coefficients given in each table. Although the values "wobble" a bit moving from table to table, there is consistently much more overlap among the three constructs when they are measured by the MMPI. For instance, in Table 7 the weighted average correlation among the different constructs is .57 for the MMPI–2 and .32 for the Rorschach. In Table 9 the values are .68 for the MMPI–2 and .26 for the Rorschach. The stronger correlations among the MMPI scales probably reflect the larger and more pervasive

TABLE 7

Disregarding Response Styles: An Averaged Multitrait–Multimethod
Summary Matrix on the Relation Between Rorschach
and MMPI–2 Scales of Affective Distress, Psychotic Processes,
and Interpersonal Wariness

	Rorschach Constructs			MMPI–2 Constructs		
	Distress	Psychosis	Wariness	Distress	Psychosis	Wariness
R–Distress	(.58)					
R–Psychosis	.24**	—				
R–Wariness	.34**	.43**	—			
M–Distress	−.01	.11*	.10	(.81)		
M–Psychosis	−.02	.11*	.02	.63**	(.79)	
M–Wariness	.01	.09	.02	.54**	.54**	(.36)

Note. R–Distress = Rorschach emotional distress, reflecting the average correlates of the Depression Index and the Suicide Constellation; R–Psychosis = the Rorschach Schizophrenia Index; R–Wariness = the Rorschach Hypervigilance Index; M–Distress = MMPI–2 emotional distress, reflecting the average correlates of Scale 2, Scale 7, the Depression and Anxiety Content Scales, and the Negative Emotionality/Neuroticism Scale; M–Psychosis = MMPI–2 psychosis, derived from the average correlates of Scale 8, the Bizarre Mentation Content Scale, and the Psychoticism Scale; M–Wariness = MMPI–2 interpersonal wariness, reflecting the average correlates of Scale 6, the Cynicism and Social Discomfort Content Scales, and the Inability to Disclose scale. Values within parentheses are "reliability" coefficients reflecting the average of the monotrait-monomethod correlations, coefficients in bold are convergent validity coefficients (monotrait-heteromethod), italicized coefficients are heterotrait-monomethod discriminant validity correlations, and underlined coefficients are heterotrait-heteromethod discriminant validity correlations. N = 362 for Scales 2 and 7; N = 359 for Content Scales, N = 358 for PSY–5 scales.
  *$p < .05$. **$p < .001$.

impact of response styles on the MMPI, which cause almost all scales to vary together and make it more difficult to discriminate appropriately among constructs.

Evidence for discriminant validity is also obtained when the bolded convergent validity coefficients are larger than the italicized heterotrait–monomethod coefficients. Examining Table 8, it is clear this criterion is not met if the bolded convergent validity coefficients are compared to the MMPI–2's italicized discriminant validity coefficients. Because response styles make it difficult for the MMPI to discriminate among constructs, they also make it difficult for the MMPI to demonstrate differentiated convergent validity. However, the picture is better when the contrast is with the Rorschach's discriminant validity correlations. Table 8 indicates affective distress can be differentiated from other Rorschach constructs, although psychosis has difficulty in this regard and wariness cannot. The final source of evidence for discriminant validity is obtained when the bolded convergent validity coefficients are larger than the underlined heterotrait-heteromethod coefficients found in the

TABLE 8
Similar Response Styles: An Averaged Multitrait–Multimethod
Summary Matrix on the Relation Between Rorschach
and MMPI–2 Scales of Affective Distress, Psychotic Processes,
and Interpersonal Wariness

	Rorschach Constructs			MMPI–2 Constructs		
	Distress	*Psychosis*	*Wariness*	*Distress*	*Psychosis*	*Wariness*
R–Distress	(.60)					
R–Psychosis	*.42**	—				
R–Wariness	*.46**	*.45**	—			
M–Distress	**.59***	.48*	.57*	(.86)		
M–Psychosis	.47*	**.49***	.36*	.68*	(.82)	
M–Wariness	.47*	.41*	**.37***	.60*	.60*	(.42)

Note. R–Distress = Rorschach emotional distress, reflecting the average correlates of the Depression Index and the Suicide Constellation; R–Psychosis = the Rorschach Schizophrenia Index; R–Wariness = the Rorschach Hypervigilance Index; M–Distress = MMPI–2 emotional distress, reflecting the average correlates of Scale 2, Scale 7, the Depression and Anxiety Content Scales, and the Negative Emotionality/Neuroticism Scale; M–Psychosis = MMPI–2 psychosis, derived from the average correlates of Scale 8, the Bizarre Mentation Content Scale, and the Psychoticism Scale; M–Wariness = MMPI–2 interpersonal wariness, reflecting the average correlates of Scale 6, the Cynicism and Social Discomfort Content Scales, and the Inability to Disclose scale. Values within parentheses are "reliability" coefficients reflecting the average of the monotrait-monomethod correlations, coefficients in bold are convergent validity coefficients (monotrait-heteromethod), italicized coefficients are heterotrait-monomethod discriminant validity correlations, and underlined coefficients are heterotrait-heteromethod discriminant validity correlations. $N = 87$.
*$p < .001$.

same row and column. Here again the analysis in Table 8 provides evidence supporting the discriminant validity of affective distress, but marginal evidence for psychosis, and nonsupporting evidence for wariness. Undoubtedly, the validity coefficients for the wariness construct are attenuated by the diverse MMPI–2 scales used to operationally define this construct.

Overall, although convergent validity can be demonstrated for MMPI and Rorschach constructs under certain conditions, the findings indicate discriminant validity is more difficult to attain. This appears to be a particular problem for the MMPI because method variance seems to cause poor discrimination among constructs and also hamper cross-method validation.

I also examined whether response styles could be treated as a single uniform dimension. If so, one could statistically partial response style effects from the scale scores and anticipate positive cross-method validity coefficients. However, after partialling first-factor variance from each scale, there was no evi-

TABLE 9
Different Response Styles: An Averaged Multitrait–Multimethod
Summary Matrix on the Relation Between Rorschach
and MMPI–2 Scales of Affective Distress, Psychotic Processes,
and Interpersonal Wariness

	Rorschach Constructs			MMPI–2 Constructs		
	Distress	*Psychosis*	*Wariness*	*Distress*	*Psychosis*	*Wariness*
R–Distress	(.67)					
R–Psychosis	*.13*	—				
R–Wariness	*.31***	*.40****				
M–Distress	**−.54****	−.25*	−.39***	(.88)		
M–Psychosis	**−.44****	**−.19**	−.27*	.71***	(.84)	
M–Wariness	−.41***	−.20	**−.28***	.68***	.64***	(.53)

Note. R–Distress = Rorschach emotional distress, reflecting the average correlates of the Depression Index and the Suicide Constellation; R–Psychosis = the Rorschach Schizophrenia Index; R–Wariness = the Rorschach Hypervigilance Index; M–Distress = MMPI–2 emotional distress, reflecting the average correlates of Scale 2, Scale 7, the Depression and Anxiety Content Scales, and the Negative Emotionality/Neuroticism Scale; M–Psychosis = MMPI–2 psychosis, derived from the average correlates of Scale 8, the Bizarre Mentation Content Scale, and the Psychoticism Scale; M–Wariness = MMPI–2 interpersonal wariness, reflecting the average correlates of Scale 6, the Cynicism and Social Discomfort Content Scales, and the Inability to Disclose scale. Values within parentheses are "reliability" coefficients reflecting the average of the monotrait–monomethod correlations, coefficients in bold are convergent validity coefficients (monotrait–heteromethod), italicized coefficients are heterotrait–monomethod discriminant validity correlations, and underlined coefficients are heterotrait–heteromethod discriminant validity correlations. $N = 78$.
*$p < .05$. **$p < .01$. ***$p < .001$.

dence for convergent validity across methods. For the constructs of affective distress, psychosis, and wariness, the convergent correlations averaged −.02 (range −.12 to .07). When a variable quantifying the interaction of Rorschach and MMPI–2 response styles was also partialed, convergent correlations remained at zero ($M = -.02$, range −.11 to .07).

DISCUSSION

This study tested five hypotheses, four of which were strongly supported and one which was partially supported. The large degree of variance in Rorschach scores that can be attributed to response styles is uncorrelated with the extensive variance in MMPI scores that can be attributed to response styles. As such, those factors that leave patients openly responsive or inhibited on the Rorschach are independent of those factors that leave patients openly responsive or defensive on the MMPI.

Independence across methods stands in contrast to response style consistency within a method family. Not only is the primary dimension from the MMPI–2 strongly related to the primary dimension from the MCMI–II ($r = .85$), but the clinical validity indicators from one test are highly related to the primary dimension from the other test, having an average cross-test correlation of |.72|. The latter findings provide strong support for interpreting the very large first dimension from each test as an index of response styles.

Because response styles have a pervasive but independent effect on MMPI and Rorschach scores, they were expected to obscure empirical construct overlap. Supporting this hypothesis, when response styles were ignored in this heterogeneous sample, Rorschach and MMPI–2 scales assessing similar constructs were unrelated. Convergent validity coefficients for measures of emotional distress, psychotic propensity, and interpersonal wariness had an average magnitude of .03. These data strongly support the conclusions reached by Archer and Krishnamurthy (1993a, 1993b) and suggest each method provides unique information. Although the Rorschach and MMPI may aspire to quantify the same general constructs (e.g., depression), the constructs that are actually measured are different entities.

Perhaps, however, there is not evidence for convergent validity because one method yields meaningless data. Those who are in the habit of dismissing the Rorschach may have been tempted to view the preceding results in this fashion. To counter such a view, this study also proposed two patterns of convergent validity that should be evident under restricted conditions.

Even though there are good reasons to believe Rorschach-derived constructs emerge from underlying or implicit propensities while MMPI-derived constructs emerge from conscious self-schema, I anticipated there would still be sufficient overlap among constructs to observe some degree of heteromethod validity when response styles were controlled. As expected, for those patients who had parallel response styles on each method, similar constructs were strongly correlated. The average validity coefficient was .59 for emotional distress, .49 for psychotic processes, and .37 for the broadly defined construct of interpersonal wariness and mistrust. Thus, certain kinds of people have rather similar scores across methods of assessment. Consistent with expectations, the effect is most pronounced for dysphoria and least pronounced for wariness.

However, the preceding analyses did not remove the influence of method variance. In fact, my attempt to equalize response style influences by using partial correlations failed. Thus, even though response styles can be expressed as variation along a single dimension, this indicates they are not a linear function of personality characteristics. Rather, response styles probably emerge from categorically distinct "types" of patients who differ qualitatively in their characterological disturbance and/or motivated desire to bias the data in a particular fashion.

The strategy taken in the convergent validity analysis was to leave method and trait variance confounded while intentionally equalizing response styles. In essence, the question addressed by the analysis was: If we hold response styles constant across methods—as is always the case when analyses are conducted with two self-report inventories or two observer rating scales—will there be convergent validity? Clearly, the data answer this question in the affirmative.

At the same time, the resulting validity coefficients should not be considered precise quantifications of the extent to which both methods actually measure their intended constructs. The validation goal articulated by Campbell and Fiske (1959) was to demonstrate convergent validity despite unique forms of method variance confounding the correlations. This study does not achieve that goal. Furthermore, because method variance was deliberately equalized, one could argue the observed coefficients may simply reflect manipulated method variance, rather than overlap due to genuine trait variance.

Before considering this issue in more detail, it is important to recognize the same confound always exists when convergent validity is examined between two tests drawn from within the same method family. However, in these instances, error due to method variance is more frequently overlooked. Validity coefficients between conceptually similar scales from the MMPI and another self-report inventory are often viewed as bona fide evidence of the extent to which scales are measuring similar constructs. This is not true. Presumably, some part of the obtained correlation reflects a common construct. However, one can never determine how much of the validity coefficient is due to genuine trait variance and how much is due to the artificial inflation generated by self-report method variance.

Nonetheless, it is still important to consider how matching on response styles may have affected the data in this study. Even though the first factor from the MMPI–2 and the first factor from the Rorschach were initially uncorrelated (see Table 2), selecting the upper and lower thirds on these dimensions forces the primary factors to be correlated ($r = .70$ in the matched group, $r = -.77$ in the discordant group). Consequently, it also forces any scales that are correlated with these dimensions to be correlated in the subsequent analysis. So the question then becomes, "To what extent are the convergent correlations in Tables 5 and 6 larger than would be predicted simply from matching subjects on the upper and lower thirds of each first factor?" To determine how much of a correlation was injected into the analysis by these selection procedures, a formula from the factor analytic literature was modified to suit the current circumstances. Briefly, the formula provides the expected correlation for two variables, each of which load separately on two correlated factors.[5] Once the expected degree of correlation between each MMPI and Rorschach variable is calculated, the expected value can be subtracted

---

[5]The formula is as follows: (correlation of MMPI–2 variable x with the MMPI–2's first factor) × (correlation of Rorschach variable y with the Rorschach's first factor) × (correlation between Rorschach and MMPI–2 first factors within the selected subset of participants) = expected correlation for variables x and y. Thanks again to James Wood for providing this formula and for developing and running the Monte Carlo trials reported later.

from the observed correlation to obtain a residual. This residual correlation reflects the extent of construct overlap remaining after first-factor variance is removed. In each instance the residual correlations were lower than those reported in Table 5, although they remained of substantial magnitude. The average values for dysphoria, psychosis, and wariness were .29, .25, and .20, respectively.

There would not be a downside to this psychometric correction if one could confidently attribute all first-factor variance to response styles, rather than to actual trait variance. Because this is not the case, however, the residual correlations provide an underestimate of construct overlap. Nonetheless, as an estimated floor value, they provide a better coefficient for bracketing the true extent of construct overlap than the null coefficients obtained when response styles are ignored.

As a second internal check, a small Monte Carlo study was performed to estimate the impact of the selection procedures. This analysis generated two random, uncorrelated variables to represent each method's first factor. Subsequently, linear equations were used to generate simulated variables that represented each of the MMPI scales and Rorschach indices. Each simulated variable was designed to correlate properly with its "first factor" and to have the correct amount of random error variance. This simulated data was then partitioned in the same fashion as in this study (i.e., groups of simulated subjects were selected for analysis if they fell in the upper or lower third of the simulated first-factor distributions). Subsequently, each of the simulated "MMPI" and "Rorschach" variables were correlated with each other. This procedure was repeated 10 times to create 10 separate simulated data sets and 10 sets of resulting correlations. The results were then pooled to provide another estimate of the association that should be expected from the matching procedure. Although 10 runs does not provide an optimal parameter for the estimated correlations, it provided a workable approximation. As with the formula-based approach, residual correlations were created by subtracting the pooled expected values (derived from the Monte Carlo runs) from each of the observed correlations. As before, this approach treats all first-factor variance as error variance, which is not strictly warranted. Nonetheless, the results were essentially the same. Within each content domain, the residuals were substantially higher than would have been expected from mere artifact.[6]

Another way to address the meaningfulness of the correlations in Table 5 is to use external criteria to determine whether substantive traits are being measured by these coefficients. Optimally, one could correlate the MMPI and Rorschach scores from these patients with gold-standard criteria that quantify the constructs of affective distress, psychosis, and interpersonal wariness. Unfortunately, such criteria are not available. Nonetheless, coarse external data on patient characteristics can be considered.

---

[6]Because these correction procedures have other heuristic applications, more detailed findings will be presented in a forthcoming article.

TABLE 10
Diagnoses Indicating Severe Mood, Psychotic, or Personality
Disturbances for Each of the Groups Defined by the First Factors
From the MMPI–2 and Rorschach

	Rorschach Group			
	Open/Engaged		Guarded/Defended	
MMPI–2 Group	n	%	n	%
Open/Engaged	29/29	100.0[a]	25/26	96.2
Guarded/Defended	11/13	84.6	9/21	42.9[a]

Note. Diagnoses indicating a severe mood, psychotic, and/or personality disturbance included the *Diagnostic and Statistical Manual of Mental Disorders* (4th ed.) codes of 295.xx, 296.xx, 297.xx, 298.xx, 301.0, 301.22, or 301.83.
[a]Denotes the two groups hypothesized to display a differential pattern of diagnoses; χ^2 $(1, N = 50) = 18.78, p = .000015; r = .61$.

DSM diagnoses can characterize affective distress, psychosis, and wary suspiciousness to some extent, although these are fairly crude criteria, particularly for the construct of wariness. Nonetheless, Table 10 presents data on participants who had received an externally derived diagnosis from inpatient treatment teams indicating a severe mood, psychotic, and/or personality disturbance (i.e., *DSM–IV* codes of 295.xx, 296.xx, 297.xx, 298.xx, 301.0, 301.22, or 301.83).[7] Data for all four MMPI–2 and Rorschach patterns are presented, although the hypothesis focused on the contrast between the groups that displayed a similar response style on both methods. A chi-square with Yates correction revealed that those patients who scored high on the first factor from both methods were diagnosed with a severe disturbance significantly more often than those patients who scored low on the first dimension of both measures ($p = .000015$; effect size expressed as $r = .61$). These findings support the notion that genuine trait variance is being quantified by the convergent validity coefficients presented in Table 5.

Although hypotheses were not developed for the other two groups in Table 10, these groups do not differ in their diagnostic frequency, $\chi^2(1, N = 39) = 0.41, p = .52$. Importantly, however, this argues against the skeptical position that it is the MMPI in isolation that is the workhorse pulling the preceding analysis. If the Rorschach was immaterial, the guarded MMPI–engaged Rorschach group should have had a much lower frequency of these diagnostic codes.

The final hypothesis for this study anticipated negative correlations between Rorschach and MMPI constructs when patients displayed opposing response styles

---

[7]Outpatients were excluded from this analysis because they are typically diagnosed by a single clinician rather than a treatment team. Had I included their data in the analyses, the results would have actually been more robust.

on each method. This hypothesis was also supported, although the effect was clearly stronger when measures were targeting a broad construct of negative affectivity (M $r = -.54$), rather than psychosis ($M r = -.19$) or wariness ($M r = -.27$). In fact, when residual correlations were calculated by subtracting the extent of correlation expected from the matching procedure, the average lower boundary coefficient for estimating construct correspondence remained salient for dysphoria ($-.24$), while it was small for psychosis ($-.11$) and trivial for wariness ($-.04$).

Negative cross-method correlations were expected for two clinical reasons. First, some patients were expected to have discrepant scores if they intentionally manipulated their data. Second, and more important, patients were expected to have disparities because personality characteristics are not always organized in a uniform fashion across levels of awareness. Some patients were expected to have idealized conscious beliefs about their personal attributes that would be very different from their underlying dynamics. Others were expected to genuinely report their psychic distress on the MMPI but to have characterological limitations that precluded behavioral engagement with the Rorschach. Given this is a psychiatric sample, I expected that which was denied or defended against on one method of assessment would be evident on the alternative method, as long as the patient remained openly responsive or engaged on the alternative method.

The results indicate my hypothesis was not sufficiently differentiated. The pattern does not hold across all constructs. In retrospect, this makes considerable sense. Character defenses are most often in place to ward off troubling and disruptive affective states, not to keep psychotic operations or wary hypervigilance out of awareness (e.g., Gabbard, 1990; Shedler, Mayman, & Manis, 1993; Watson & Clark, 1984). Thus, the differential support for dysphoria is most likely because affective discomfort is more heavily defended against than other constructs.

When clinicians are confronted with conflicting data on how extensively depressed a patient is, at least two possibilities must be considered. First, the communication factors that may have lead to disparities should be evaluated (Response Styles 1 and 4). This would be a primary consideration when there is some external incentive to appear healthier or more pathological than is actually true (e.g., custody evaluations, insanity defenses, etc.), as these motivations should have a particular influence on MMPI data (cf. Bornstein et al., 1994). One should also consider these factors when an unusual interpersonal dynamic may have produced a situationally guarded Rorschach protocol (e.g., an examiner who generates unusual defensiveness in a patient, etc.).

The second reason some patients present with opposing response styles on the MMPI and Rorschach is because of characterological defensive structures (Styles 2 and 5). Under these circumstances, method variance becomes synonymous with trait variance because intrinsic characteristics related to the management of negative affect actually produce the response styles. Because these patients are more important to consider for construct validity, each pattern of scores will be discussed in turn.

The first pattern consists of patients who are openly responsive on the MMPI (Styles 3–M or 5–M) but guarded or constricted on the Rorschach (Style 2–R). Many patients like this will accurately convey their emotional distress on the MMPI but not engage with the Rorschach for one of several reasons. Some may have genuinely impoverished coping resources, whereas others may be chronically guarded in an interpersonal context. Other patients, particularly those with anxiety driven problems, may defensively inhibit spontaneity and produce constricted Rorschachs because they are defended against the in vivo experience of the distress they carry with them, unwilling or unable to engage with the troubling percepts that jump out at them on the inkblots, even though they are quite able to talk about their affective distress in a more detached or abstract fashion. Finally, some patients may be so depressed they are simply unable to muster the energy and effort that is required to engage with the Rorschach and articulate many responses and determinants, although they remain capable of describing themselves on the MMPI.

Although these suppositions refer to dynamic operations and focused characteristics more than *DSM* diagnoses, patients with this MMPI–Rorschach pattern should generally receive diagnoses indicating chronic interpersonal guardedness (i.e., *DSM–IV* codes 295.3, 297.1, or 301.00), anxiety driven problems (i.e., 300.01, 300.21, 300.22, 300.3, or 300.02), or severe and immobilizing depression (i.e., 296.23, 296.24, 296.33, 296.34, 296.53, 296.54, 296.63, or 296.64). Consistent with this expectation, inpatients who were open and forthcoming on the MMPI–2 but constricted on the Rorschach had a greater frequency of these diagnoses (18 of 26, or 69.2%) compared to patients with the opposing pattern of scores (4 of 13, or 30.8%), although this result was not quite statistically significant, $\chi^2(1, N = 39) = 3.77, p = .052$; effect expressed as $r = .31$.

The other pattern consists of patients who are engaged with the Rorschach (Styles 3–R and 5–R) but defended on the MMPI (Style 2–M). Most of these patients genuinely need to see themselves as being as virtuous, ideal, and emotionally healthy as they report on their MMPI, despite the fact they are often beset by considerable underlying psychological distress. As before, affective distress can no longer be considered a single global construct that encompasses conscious as well as underlying experiences. Rather, affective distress is bifurcated. It is disavowed and defended against at the level of conscious awareness but quite evident and pressing in less consciously mediated behaviors.

Some of the psychological conditions that should give rise to this pattern of scores include conversion or somatoform disorders, masked depressions, or one of the many disorders that are characterized by defensive self-idealization and/or grandiosity, such as bipolar disorder (in a hypomanic to manic state); delusional disorder; or hysterical, narcissistic, antisocial, obsessive, or paranoid personality disorder. Considering only inpatients with an externally derived diagnosis, Table 11 presents data on the proportion who received one of these diagnoses for each of the four cross-method patterns (*DSM–IV* codes of 300.81, 300.11, 316.0, 307.8,

TABLE 11
Diagnoses Indicating the Defensive Protection of Conscious
Awareness From Affective Distress for Each Group Defined
by First Factors From the MMPI-2 and Rorschach

| | *Rorschach Group* | | | |
| | *Open/Engaged* | | *Guarded/Defended* | |
MMPI-2 Group	*n*	*%*	*n*	*%*
Open/Engaged	2/29	6.9	1/26	3.8[a]
Guarded/Defended	7/13	53.8[a]	11/21	52.4

Note. Diagnoses indicating a defensive protection against affective distress included the *Diagnostic and Statistical Manual of Mental Disorders* (4th ed.) codes of 300.81, 300.11, 316.0, 307.8, 307.89, 300.7, 311, 301.0, 301.7, 301.4, 301.5, 301.81, 296.4x, and 297.1.

[a]Denotes the two groups hypothesized to display a differential pattern of diagnoses; χ^2 $(1, N = 39) = 10.40, p = .00126; r = .52$.

307.89, 300.7, 311, 301.0, 301.7, 301.4, 301.5, 301.81, 296.4x, and 297.1). Although data for all four groups are presented, the hypothesis focused on the contrast between the groups that displayed discordant response styles across methods. A chi-square with Yates correction revealed that those patients with defended MMPI-2s and engaged Rorschachs were significantly more likely than patients with the opposing pattern to be diagnosed with a condition where conscious awareness is protected from underlying affective distress ($p = .00126$; effect size expressed as $r = .52$). Although not an a priori hypothesis, those who were defended on both methods also received one of these diagnoses significantly more often than those who were open on both methods, $\chi^2(1, N = 50) = 10.84, p = .00099$; effect size expressed as $r = .47$.

A Rorschach skeptic may take the full array of findings in Table 11 as an indication the MMPI tells the full story because the diagnostic pattern is similar whenever there is a guarded or defended MMPI profile. However, this is not the case. Because these patients are expected to defend against underlying depression, depression should not be evident on their MMPI although it should be present on Rorschach depressive indices. Thus, the MMPI should not quantify the full scope of their condition. As anticipated, the seven patients carrying such diagnoses who were defended on the MMPI-2 yet still engaged with the Rorschach had an average *T* score of 44.1 across the five MMPI-2 scales of affective distress. No patient had a *T* score greater than 59 on any scale. However, these patients had an average *DEPI* value of 5.14, and 57% were above the critical *DEPI* value of 5. Thus, the Rorschach can be sensitive to the underlying distress of these patients in a manner that the MMPI cannot.

Similar clinical observations can be made when considering the 11 patients who were guarded or constricted on both methods and also received a diagnosis indicating defenses against underlying affective distress. They had an average T score of 46.7 on the five MMPI–2 scales of dysphoria. Two patients had a T score greater than 64 on Scale 2 because they endorsed many somatic items, but no patient had a T score exceeding 58 on any of the four remaining scales. It may be recalled that a constricted Rorschach can be the result of intrinsic deficiencies that preclude engagement with the task. Exner (1993) conceptualized these deficiencies as leading to a form of helplessness-based depression, which is measured by the Coping Deficit Index. This ineffectual form of depression differs from the implicit, cognitive-affective depression measured by the *DEPI* and *S–CON*. When both forms of depression are considered, 64% of the patients receiving these diagnoses exceeded the critical cutoff score for at least one of these Rorschach indices. Again, the Rorschach captured some of the underlying distress that theoretically should be present in these patients, even though this was not quantified by the MMPI.

Overall, the diagnostic data indicate genuine clinical phenomena are being captured by the negative convergent validity coefficients given in Table 6. The findings are particularly impressive because the *DSM* diagnoses are coarse and global indicators, rather than focused criteria evaluating dynamics and defenses.

CONCLUSIONS

Several general conclusions emerge from this research. First, researchers and clinicians should adjust their conceptualization of the constructs being measured by each method so it remains clear that they are distinct latent entities. One way to facilitate this process is to develop more differentiated scale terminology. Although somewhat cumbersome, even a procedure as simple as attaching the name of the method to the name of the scale would have beneficial effects, as it is much less likely that the construct measured by the Performance-Derived Rorschach *DEPI* would become confused with the construct measured by the Self-Report-Derived MMPI–2 *DEP* Scale. Second, psychologists should recognize the limitations of each assessment method and appreciate each method's distinct range of effectiveness. Both methods can provide useful information about clinical constructs, although the data indicate neither method can consistently illuminate the full scope of any construct (see Meyer, 1996). Under optimal circumstances, the MMPI reveals what a patient understands about him or herself and is willing to convey, whereas the Rorschach reveals underlying characteristics and propensities as they are manifest through the articulation of subtle perceptual qualities. Third, because MMPI and Rorschach data are globally independent, a personality assessment would be incomplete if it relied on only one method of assessment. Thus, clinicians should competently use at least both of these measures when conducting a broad personality assessment.

Clinicians must obviously consider a range of extra-test information when sorting through Rorschach and MMPI data, perhaps particularly when confronted with cross-method discrepancies. Even in this study, which grossly simplified the issues by selecting patients with well-defined response styles, many different reasons were postulated for observing the four basic patterns of test scores. In actual practice, the complexity of the issues increases significantly. Previously, Archer and Krishnamurthy (1993a) encouraged clinicians to suppress the least reliable or valid piece of data when confronted with cross-method discrepancies. This advice is similar to the instruction many clinicians receive in training to place the greatest interpretive confidence in those findings that emerge on several different measures. Although both guidelines can certainly be appropriate at times, they offer an incomplete solution to the problem of cross-method disagreement. In fact, these suggestions can be problematic even when there is cross-method agreement, as the agreement may be due to the confluence of communication-driven response styles that inaccurately drive observed scores on both methods higher (or lower) than is true. A better solution then may be to reconceptualize the role of the clinician in personality assessment.

One vision of the assessor's role is to tally scores, ratios, and indices from one or more tests. These scores can then be taken to a cookbook for amplification or entered into a computer for an expert's descriptive report. The distillation from this process are statements about personality along with some diagnostic impressions and treatment implications. Contradictory pieces of information can be handled by omitting less frequently mentioned descriptions, or by selecting information that fits with the assessor's impression of the patient from observation or interview. Within this model, the assessor can begin to think he or she has sampled a relatively large domain of personality because most cookbooks and computer summaries are not shy about providing comments about many facets of functioning. However, the assessor in this scenario is essentially a technician who happens to work with testing information. He or she needs very little clinical acumen, minimal understanding of the strengths and limitations of each testing measure, minimal diagnostic skills, and essentially no advanced training.

The data presented here argue against this vision and instead suggest the assessor needs to be highly skilled and capable of bringing clinical acumen; integrative conceptual abilities; and extensive knowledge of tests, assessment methodology, and psychopathology to bear on each patient being evaluated. He or she must recognize what type of information each method can reveal under optimal circumstances, while also having a realistic appreciation of what information cannot be quantified. When using different methods, the assessment clinician must work to create a sophisticated portrait of the patient that makes use of all data—even when the methods are superficially discrepant, as it is just such disagreements that often provide a richer understanding of defensive structures and struggles to adapt.

Because clinical validity does not reside solely within the scales of an instrument, and because all measures are inherently limited, the clinician should not try to decide which scale or method is the most accurate in some ultimate sense. Rather, the goal should be to figure out what conditions in nature are most likely to give rise to the observed pattern of scores across all methods. This means assessment clinicians must develop a range of inferences that could explain the pattern of scores on all tests. Once this is done, these inferences need to be compared to the clinician's knowledge of psychopathology and understanding of the many complex ways people are actually put together. Through a process of successive approximation, and incorporating as much additional information as possible while still staying true to all of the test data, the clinician must then prune and shape test-derived inferences, terminating the process when an understanding of the data comes into sharper focus but before inferences extend beyond what the data will support. At times, the reasoning associated with this process should even generate impressions of the patient that are at odds with those drawn from an interview or history. If tests can truly provide nontrivial information then, at times, they should provide knowledge that is not obvious from other sources. If the alternative is to only report findings that are consistent with impressions derived from an interview or behavioral observations, then there is really no point to embarking on testing in the first place.

To achieve the skills discussed earlier, additional training beyond that offered in most graduate schools and internships will probably be necessary. However, relevant data indicate clinicians have trouble making the kinds of complex judgments that would be required by an assessment clinician even after advanced training (e.g., Dawes, 1994; Meehl, 1954). At least in part, Dawes attributed this difficulty to the fact that clinicians generally do not receive immediate feedback about their judgments and decisions. Consequently, it may be most important for assessment clinicians to consistently discuss test-based impressions with patients and openly solicit feedback about what seems accurate and inaccurate in order to critically evaluate the reasoning that led to particular conclusions (see Finn, 1996).

Finally, these data speak to the need for nomothetic research that more accurately incorporates the type of complex idiographic reasoning that would accompany skilled use of the MMPI and Rorschach in clinical practice (Meyer, 1996). In particular, the pervasive impact of response styles must be built into the planning and implementation of research. Although a fair amount of attention has been given to malingering on the MMPI, more MMPI research is needed on the intrinsic characteristics that lead to response styles and more research is needed to explore how response styles moderate external validity coefficients. Parallel research designed to achieve a better understanding of these factors on the Rorschach would also be quite beneficial.

ACKNOWLEDGMENTS

I am grateful to David S. Nichols, Radhika Krishnamurthy, Rhonda R. Dallas, and two anonymous reviewers for their constructive comments on an earlier draft of this chapter. I am also indebted to James M. Wood for his helpful comments and for his consistent challenges to the data presented here. I am also thankful to him for suggesting a formula to correct potential method artifacts and for designing and implementing the Monte Carlo trials reported in this chapter.

A version of this chapter using smaller samples was presented at the Annual Meeting of the Society for Personality Assessment, Chicago, April, 1994; and at the 29th Annual Symposium on Recent Developments in the Use of the MMPI-2, Minneapolis, MN, May 1994.

REFERENCES

Akhtar, S. (1987). Schizoid personality disorder: A synthesis of developmental, dynamic, and descriptive features. *American Journal of Psychotherapy, 41,* 499–518.

Akhtar, S. (1990). Paranoid personality disorder: A synthesis of developmental, dynamic, and descriptive features. *American Journal of Psychotherapy, 44,* 5–25.

American Psychiatric Association. (1994). *Diagnostic and statistical manual of mental disorders* (4th ed.). Washington, DC: Author.

Archer, R. P., & Krishnamurthy, R. (1993a). Combining the Rorschach and the MMPI in the assessment of adolescents. *Journal of Personality Assessment, 60,* 132–140.

Archer, R. P., & Krishnamurthy, R. (1993b). A review of MMPI and Rorschach interrelationships in adult samples. *Journal of Personality Assessment, 61,* 277–293.

Ben-Porath, Y. S., & Sherwood, N. E. (1993). *The MMPI-2 Content Component Scales: Development, psychometric characteristics, and clinical application.* Minneapolis: University of Minnesota Press.

Block, J. (1995). A contrarian view of the five-factor approach to personality description. *Psychological Bulletin, 117,* 187–215.

Bornstein, R. F., Rossner, S. C., Hill, E. L., & Stepanian, M. L. (1994). Face validity and fakability of objective and projective measures of dependency. *Journal of Personality Assessment, 63,* 363–386.

Butcher, J. N., Dahlstrom, W. G., Graham, J. R., Tellegen, A., & Kaemmer, B. (1989). *Manual for the restandardized Minnesota Multiphasic Personality Inventory: MMPI-2. An administrative and interpretive guide.* Minneapolis: University of Minnesota Press.

Campbell, D. T., & Fiske, D. W. (1959). Convergent and discriminant validation by the multitrait–multimethod matrix. *Psychological Bulletin, 56,* 81–105.

Cronbach, L. J., & Meehl, P. E. (1955). Construct validity in psychological tests. *Psychological Bulletin, 52,* 281–302.

Cronbach, L. J. (1995). Giving method variance its due. In P. E. Shrout & S. T. Fiske (Eds.), *Personality research, methods, and theory: A festschrift honoring Donald W. Fiske* (pp. 145–157). Hillsdale, NJ: Lawrence Erlbaum Associates, Inc.

Dawes, R. M. (1994). *House of cards: Psychology and psychotherapy built on myth.* New York: Free Press.

Edwards, L. K., & Edwards, A. L. (1991). A principal-components analysis of the Minnesota Multiphasic Personality Inventory factor scales. *Journal of Personality and Social Psychology, 60,* 766–772.

Exner, J. E., Jr. (1993). *The Rorschach: A comprehensive system: Vol. 1. Basic foundations* (3rd ed.). New York: Wiley.

Finn, S. E. (1996). Assessment feedback integrating MMPI-2 and Rorschach findings. *Journal of Personality Assessment, 67,* 543–557.

Gabbard, G. O. (1990). *Psychodynamic psychiatry in clinical practice.* Washington, DC: American Psychiatric Press.

Greene, R. L. (1991). *The MMPI-2/MMPI: An interpretive manual.* Boston: Allyn & Bacon.

Guntrip, H. (1958). *Schizoid phenomena, object-relations, and the self.* New York: International University Press.

Harkness, A., McNulty, J., & Ben-Porath, Y. (1995). The Personality Psychopathology Five (PSY–5): Constructs and MMPI-2 scales. *Psychological Assessment, 7,* 101–114.

Johnson, J. H., Butcher, J. N., Null, C., & Johnson, K. N. (1984). Replicated item level factor analysis of the full MMPI. *Journal of Personality and Social Psychology, 47,* 105–114.

Kohut, H. (1971). *The analysis of the self: A systematic approach to the psychoanalytic treatment of narcissistic personality disorders.* New York: International Universities Press.

Kohut, H. (1984). *How does analysis cure?* Chicago: University of Chicago Press.

Lubin, B., Larsen, R. M., & Matarazzo, J. D. (1984). Patterns of psychological test usage in the United States: 1935–1982. *American Psychologist, 39,* 451–454.

Meehl, P. E. (1954). *Clinical versus statistical prediction: A theoretical analysis and a review of the evidence.* Minneapolis: University of Minnesota Press.

Meyer, G. J. (1992a). Response frequency problems in the Rorschach: Clinical and research implications with suggestions for the future. *Journal of Personality Assessment, 58,* 231–244.

Meyer, G. J. (1992b). The Rorschach's factor structure: A contemporary investigation and historical review. *Journal of Personality Assessment, 59,* 117–136.

Meyer, G. J. (1996). The Rorschach and MMPI: Toward a more scientifically differentiated understanding of cross-method assessment. *Journal of Personality Assessment, 67,* 558–578.

Miller, S. B. (1987). A comparison of methods of inquiry: Testing and interview contributions to the diagnostic process. *Bulletin of the Menninger Clinic, 51,* 505–518.

Millon, T. (1987). *Manual for the Millon Clinical Multiaxial Inventory–II* (MCMI–II; 2nd ed.). Minneapolis, MN: National Computer Systems.

Parker, K. C. H., Hanson, R. K., & Hunsley, J. (1988). MMPI, Rorschach, and WAIS: A meta-analytic comparison of reliability, stability, and validity. *Psychological Bulletin, 103,* 367–373.

Paulhus, D. L. (1984). Two-component models of socially desirable responding. *Journal of Personality and Social Psychology, 46,* 598–609.

Paulhus, D. L. (1986). Self-deception and impression management in test responses. In A. Angleitner & J. S. Wiggins (Eds.), *Personality assessment via questionnaires: Current issues in theory and measurement* (pp. 143–165). Berlin: Springer-Verlag.

Piotrowski, C., & Keller, J. W. (1992). Psychological testing in applied settings: A literature review from 1982–1992. *The Journal of Training and Practice in Professional Psychology, 6,* 74–82.

Piotrowski, C., & Zalewski, C. (1993). Training in psychodiagnostic testing in APA-approved PsyD and PhD clinical psychology programs. *Journal of Personality Assessment, 61,* 394–405.

Rappaport, D., Gill, M. M., & Schafer, R. (1968). *Diagnostic psychological testing* (Rev. ed.). New York: International Universities Press.

Schafer, R. (1954). *Psychoanalytic interpretation in Rorschach testing: Theory and application.* New York: Grune & Stratton.

Shedler, J., Mayman, M., & Manis, M. (1993). The *illusion* of mental health. *American Psychologist, 48,* 1117–1131.

Sternberg, R. J. (1992). *Psychological Bulletin*'s top 10 "hit parade." *Psychological Bulletin, 112,* 387–388.

Watson, D., & Clark, L. A. (1984). Negative affectivity: The disposition to experience aversive emotional states. *Psychological Bulletin, 96,* 465–490.

13

Of Science, Meta-Science, and Clinical Practice: The Generalization of a Generalization to a Particular

David Faust

Department of Psychology
University of Rhode Island

Although science is the most powerful method for advancing knowledge and scientific and statistical formalisms are generally much sounder than impressionistic judgment, advanced methodological training (as it is presently comprised) is often of little direct use to practicing clinicians. Practitioners should be able to identify grossly deficient knowledge claims and clear scientific winners, but beyond this, the trick usually is to determine which scientific authority or authorities on whom to depend, a decision task that is ultimately to be tackled through the type of meta-scientific studies that Faust and Meehl have proposed. In applying scientific knowledge, the clinician usually must choose between the generalization of a scientific generalization to a particular versus the application of a clinical generalization to a particular. Determining the relative power of scientific generalizations developed outside, versus clinical generalizations developed within the setting of application, can be very difficult, and there are few established guides. A more advanced science of generalization, another meta-scientific problem, would allow sounder predictions about application to new domains and could greatly aid the practitioner.

When the answer is known a problem is usually easy. What is difficult is when we have to guess. Formulating guesses in a manner that maximizes the chances of being correct can be among the most demanding intellectual and methodological challenges. And it is this type of task that almost always faces the clinical practitioner, whether engaged in treatment or assessment.

Many proposals for the "scientist-practitioner" suggest that with a little hard work and perhaps some patching up in one or another domain, a comfortable and productive synthesis can ensue. I would suggest instead that the application of science to practice in psychology is mainly a problem of the type just noted, that is, of making decisions under conditions of uncertainty, or formulating statistical inferences or probability judgments. In turn, the judgments or statistical inferences that are needed in this domain raise deep and complex problems that cannot be resolved without making headway with certain methodological and meta-scientific (i.e., science of science) tasks. In this article I flesh out some of these issues and discuss some possible approaches that might aid progress.

It will not be argued here whether scientific method and knowledge have the potential to help, or can be of immediate help, within some areas of psychology. This would seem to be a foregone conclusion. For example, if we want to know whether a certain characteristic is statistically aberrant, it is hard to argue against representative sampling. Rather, the questions that will occupy us are how to apply methodological knowledge to clinical practice and how to decide when to defer to scientific research over clinical impression, the latter being a broader and more qualitatively diverse variant of the question about when to rely on clinical versus actuarial judgment (Dawes, Faust, & Meehl, 1989; Meehl, 1954/1996).

The problem domain to be considered is that in which choices matter. For example, if whatever ails the patient is untreatable or if all treatment options are equal, accuracy of decisions is moot. In many instances, choices that would seem to make a large difference (e.g., selection of alternate therapy modality) do not, but in many other cases differences are of a magnitude that justify our close attention (e.g., ECT versus talk therapy).

OVERVIEW OF CLINICAL VERSUS
ACTUARIAL JUDGMENT

Clinical versus actuarial judgment and meta-science will be referred to frequently, and brief explanation of both is in order. *Clinical judgment* means judgment in the head. Although the judgment may incorporate various types of information and knowledge, including scientific findings and guides, the act of data combination or integration is ultimately subjective. In the *actuarial judgment* method, data combination is both set and based on empirical relations. Being set or automatic means that, given the same data, the method will always reach the same conclusion. To be actuarial, a method must meet both conditions. Many computerized interpretive programs are not based strictly on empirical frequencies and hence are not actuarial.

To illustrate the two methods, if a baseball scout obtains ratings of batting, hitting, throwing, and character, he may combine this information in his head, which is a clinical approach. If, instead, he consults tables that contain data on such ratings of players and their ultimate success or outcome and thereby obtains a probability statement that the player will make the majors, he is using an actuarial method. With actuarial methods, data combination might involve looking up numbers on simple frequency charts or can become much more sophisticated, utilizing, for example, multiple regression formulas. The distinction between the two methods does not involve the form of input data. If subjective ratings or impressions are coded, they can be included in actuarial methods, whereas "objective" data can be interpreted clinically, as might occur when a practitioner formulates a conclusion based on test scores.

The question that originally interested Meehl (1954/1996) was how the two methods would fare in an equal race, that is, when both were provided with the same information. Over the years, there have been well over 100 comparisons of the two methods, which have covered very diverse diagnostic and predictive domains. Although there have been quite a few ties, in almost every case in which a difference has occurred, the actuarial or statistical method has beaten the clinical method, sometimes by a wide margin. Many of the reasonable objections raised to the earlier findings (e.g., that clinicians in the studies were not the most expert, were seemingly handicapped by limited data, or performed less familiar judgment tasks) have been examined and countered; to date, alteration of these conditions has not changed outcomes (see Dawes et al., 1989; Grove & Meehl, 1996). Unfortunately, certain negative, unjustified implications are sometimes drawn from these studies: that clinicians should exhibit blind and unaltering adherence to actuarial outcomes, or that clinicians do not make useful observations or have unique skills.

OVERVIEW OF META-SCIENCE

Meta-science refers to the science of science. Although scientific method offers many forms of help to the knowledge seeker, it provides limited formal assistance or few systematic methods to aid in higher level decisions and data integration activities, such as determining the most suitable topic for study, predicting the productivity of research efforts, evaluating theories, or anticipating the long-term fate of scientific ideas. There are many prescriptive guides, suggestions, or rules of thumb for conducting research or evaluating scientific products. These rules of thumb for higher level scientific judgments are usually proffered by practicing scientists, or by historians or philosophers of science.

In most cases, following or violating these rules does not guarantee a certain outcome, and rather they are linked probabilistically to success and failure. For example, although scientists disregard powerful negative evidence at their peril, there are instances in the history of science in which doing so did not preclude success. These guides and suggestions often point in different directions or are inconsistent with one another. For example, a theory might have excellent predictive power but very limited breadth. As such, the scientist often must select one guide or set of guides over the other(s).

The database for these evaluative methods or rules of thumb frequently rests on some variant of the case study method. One examines episodes in the history of science and attempts to abstract normative guides. Such a database is inadequate when indicators are probabilistic and frequently inconsistent. For example, although there have been cases in which parsimony was a better predictor of a theory's fate than formal explanatory power, the key question is just how often this occurs, for example, is it 1%, 5%, or 75%? In a probabilistic problem domain, supportive instances can be found for almost any claim, but this helps very little in developing accurate or representative frequencies. When faced with a choice under uncertain conditions, knowing such odds might well provide important pragmatic guidance to the practicing scientist.

There is limited agreement about scientific prescriptions and guides, and little precise knowledge about their probabilistic relations with outcome. These problems are especially serious precisely because the indicators tend to be inconsistent and because we want to determine how they work when combined in various ways. Clearly, this is a task for representative sampling, in this case of scientific episodes. A large database on scientific episodes now exists, thanks in particular to Sulloway's (1996) efforts. However, there have been very few attempts to perform representative sampling in this domain. Despite the remarkable overall success of science, general impressions about the accuracy or power of scientific guides currently rest on very weak and selective bases and, hence, are likely to stray considerably from the optimum. Various approaches can be used to obtain representative samples, which should allow us to develop far more solidly founded guides and begin to resolve disputes and questions about the relative merits of prescriptive advice. These and related types of formal study of scientific episodes and events can be labelled *meta-scientific research* (Faust & Meehl, 1992).

One example of a potential index for evaluating the status of theories incorporates Popper's notion of riskiness (see Faust & Meehl, 1992; Meehl, 1992). In essence, one considers the range of possible outcomes, the capacity to predict outcome absent the theory, and the match between prediction and outcome. One then cumulates results across experiments. For example, in the not-so-atypical psychology experiment, there are only two possible outcomes (Variable A will or will not be significantly related to Variable B), and one often does not need the background theory to make the prediction. In contrast, if we are trying to determine how many molecules fit within a certain space, the range of possible outcomes is enormous, and our capacity to predict the answer absent a theory is nil. Thus, when we find minimal difference between predicted and obtained outcome, the theory earns some real money in the bank.

Faust and Meehl have proposed various indices of scientific status, described methods for developing and testing them, and discussed means for attacking some of the practical and theoretical problems facing the potential meta-scientist (Faust,

1984; Faust & Meehl, 1992; Meehl, 1990, 1992, 1993). The program is one of applying more powerful analytic methods in order to appraise the status of higher-level judgments or prescriptions about scientific method and evaluation.

SCIENCE AND PRACTICE

It is widely assumed that the application of scientific knowledge and method enhances clinical activities, this being the justification, beyond turning out practicing scientists (which usually does not happen anyway), for devoting so much educational time to research mastery. Guides or prescriptions for combining practice with science are often very broad; for example, keep up with the research and use the best-validated methods, be skeptical and rigorous in your thinking, and test your ideas. It is somehow as if learning about science and clinical practices, infusing the value and desire of combining the two, and providing general guidelines is enough. It will be argued that it is not nearly enough and that: (a) applying scientific method to practice is anything but direct or easy, especially given psychologists' typical training; (b) applying scientific knowledge to practice often posses a difficult choice between the generalization of a research generalization to a particular (patient) versus the application of a clinical generalization to a particular; (c) there is often limited guidance offered or available for the integration of these two domains; and (d) the formulation of better advice will require progress in science and especially meta-science.

Methodological Knowledge

I have separated science into method and knowledge derived from that method, and start with the former. The typical clinical psychologist has learned a good deal about research design in the social sciences and statistical analysis. Beyond this, background knowledge and training in scientific methodology is highly variable. Some individuals have familiarity with basic methods in hard sciences and know what a well-developed theory looks like, but many do not (which must be one reason we too often hear that psychology is not all that different from physics or engineering).

Further, whether or not it was labelled as such, during their training clinical psychologists are taught a philosophy of science or epistemic guides. This philosophy comes in different forms and addresses methods of knowing. Many students are taught old school philosophies, such as operationalism or positivism, approaches that were in large part rejected by mainstream philosophers of science years ago. Others are taught relativism, commonly accompanied by the suggestion that the positivists were intellectually mediocre and narrow-minded individuals. Many students are taught that the philosophy of science starts and ends with Kuhn

(1970), and are not informed about the serious deficiencies of his work or that it is widely criticized by philosophers and historians of science.

Often what is taught is not explicit philosophy of science but epistemological rules of thumb, which are described as guides, principles, or adages. For example, "Look for horses and not zebras upon hearing hoofs," could be viewed as endorsing one facet of parsimony. These guides come in many forms and address everything from micro- to macro-issues. Examples might include: "Focus on one or a few areas in which you can gain real expertise." "Broaden your knowledge base because it will increase your creativity." "Explicit criteria are [are not] really important." "Prediction [fruitfulness] is the most important quality for a theory." "Try to reduce [or eliminate] excess theorizing." "You can never get directly from the facts to the theory so 'excess' theorizing is inevitable and may not be a problem at all." Of course, the list could go on and on.

These types of guides should not be conceptualized as rules. For example, we would not say, "There is no instance in the history of science in which a theory that was weak on prediction turned out to be superior." They are characteristics or strategies that presumably increase the chances of success. In most cases, there is little quality information about the strength of association between them and scientific success. For example, just how strong a predictor of scientific success is reducibility, parsimony, or formal explanatory power? Even if one eliminates direct contradictions, standing on these indicators or guides often conflict, and thus one must have an approach for making selections in the face of inconsistencies. Faust and Meehl (Faust & Meehl, 1992; Meehl, 1992) have argued that current methods for evaluating such prescriptions or guides are weak, and that more rigorous approaches and representative sampling are needed to obtain sounder knowledge and to allow more accurate appraisal of prescriptive proposals. It will subsequently be argued that some of the things we would like to know in order to better integrate science and practice will require these types of meta-scientific studies.

Methodological knowledge to help the clinician conduct research.   A goal of the clinical psychologist's scientific training is to provide the tools needed to conduct research. Recognizing that most practitioners will not do so, one might ask what the practitioner who knows scientific method is to do when he arrives at the clinic on a Thursday morning to find a patient complaining that the therapy approach being used so far is going nowhere? We certainly do not expect the practitioner to go out and conduct a study comparing the effectiveness of that approach with others when used among similar patients. (I realize the clinician could consult available research, but in this section we are dealing with methodo-logical skills and will discuss the application of scientific knowledge later.) As almost anyone involved in psychotherapy outcome research would tell that clinician, a good deal of money and dozens of research projects often yield little insight into effective therapy practice.

Methodological knowledge to help in applying assessment and treatment methods. Much of research design, statistics, and epistemic rules of thumb do not translate in any direct or obvious way to clinical practice, and much of what psychologists were taught or is communicated about the matter is misdirected. Let us take two very different examples, starting with the typical discussion of differences between test scores. The Wechsler Adult Intelligence Scale–Revised (Wechsler, 1981) will be used because of its status in the field. Pages 34 to 35 of the test manual discuss whether differences in Verbal and Performance IQ scores reach "statistical significance" and set relatively stringent thresholds (e.g., .05), presumably to avoid false-positive errors. Many manuals and texts use such an approach and terminology when discussing test score differences.

In psychological studies, significance testing is intended to appraise research hypotheses. A low probability is selected because it is generally considered a far worse error to accept something as scientifically "established" when it is false than vice versa. If the level of support is not quite sufficient, the study can be replicated. Now, this was not exactly what Fisher had in mind, and a technology for assessing pragmatic outcomes has been coopted by psychology as an approach for testing theories. As such individuals as Meehl (1978, 1990, in press) and Schmidt (in press) pointed out, classic significance testing has serious, if not fatal, shortcomings for appraising theories, in no small part because the hurdle it provides is so flabby or weak, and a radical overhaul is needed.

Thus, we start with a method designed for a technological purpose. We contort the method into a procedure for testing theories in psychology, even though it appears to have major deficiencies for this purpose. We then take the very questionable rationale and thinking that underlie its application to testing theories and apply it to a very different type of task, that of determining whether two test scores are different, as if this were like determining whether Smith's theory of introversion predicts that male and female participants will obtain different scores on some measure of joke-telling ability.

In psychological assessment, although we also may be asking whether Score A differs from Score B, it is not to test some substantive theory in a context in which false-positive errors are considered the far greater sin, rather it is to guide pragmatic decision making. In turn, a threshold model in which one decides "yea" or "nay" ill-suits a task in which the aim is to formulate the most accurate probability statement possible and then, considering costs and benefits of potential outcomes, to decide accordingly. At times, this means acting as if something is different, even if the odds are relatively small. Suppose, for example, a false-positive identification is minimally harmful but a false-negative identification is potentially disastrous (e.g., a dementing condition that can be reversed by a fairly benign treatment if caught early). Let us further assume for the purposes of this example that Verbal-Performance discrepancies are a valid indicator of the condition. Should we now say that the test data argue against assuming the condition is present because the chances are only 94 in 100, or even just 40 in 100, that the difference is a true one versus a statistical artifact?

As a contrasting example, we hear repeatedly that various scales of the Minnesota Multiphasic Personality Inventory (MMPI-2; Butcher, Dahlstrom, Graham, Tellegen, & Kaemmer, 1989) are seriously flawed because of their heterogeneity and should be subdivided. However, suppose one is dealing with an informative diagnosis, such as sociopathy, in which most of the important inferences that can be drawn from test performance rest on classification into that category, and which itself is best decided by the overall score. There are obviously some entities with genotypic similarities and phenotypic differences such that heterogeneous scales can be most effective because they cast a broad net. It may matter little exactly where on the net examinees are caught, so long as they are caught at some place or places. For the matters of clinical interest, it might make little difference whether the elevation came about more so due to items bearing on anti-authority attitudes than social imperturbability because, in either case, that individual is unlikely to be cured by talk therapy or might not be someone with whom the therapist should run up a large unpaid bill.

As these examples are intended to show, the guidance that is provided for applying scientific method to the clinic is frequently misguided. The link between the two is often not at all clear or direct and calls for considerable adjustment and adaptation, which would seem to require, at minimum, familiarity with: (a) research design and analysis, (b) some basic philosophy of science, (c) clinical practice, and (d) research on clinical judgment and decision making. One would not expect even highly capable students to work out much of this problem on their own.

The exact connection between scientific methodology and practice also remains, in large part, a problem to be worked out (see more later). Epistemologic rules of thumb are often bets with uncertain odds and provide limited basis for resolving the many situations in which guides conflict. It is fine to say that well-conducted science is epistemologically superior to subjective judgment. However, much finer distinctions are frequently needed, and the advice that we give, in many cases, is really just a crude guess or a subjective impression about a scientific matter.

There is methodological knowledge that can be of immediate assistance to practitioners. In particular, decision researchers have uncovered various principles (which could be considered methodological dictates) that can increase judgmental accuracy. For example, judgments should be adjusted in relation to base rates, predictions should be no more extreme than the variables on which they are based, and redundant information contributes much less (if anything) to predictive accuracy in comparison to nonredundant information (for a discussion of these and other guides, see Faust & Nurcombe, 1989; Faust & Willis, in press). If one prefers, such knowledge could be considered technological rather than methodological. This technology, although not perfected, is readily available and, if mastered, almost certain to increase accuracy.

The rationale or starting point for decision methods is often a negative, or an awareness of some limitation (as was the case with the formulation of scientific method). The central theme is usually something like, "Trust science or scientific method rather than your own judgment," which is hardly flattering to the clinician. Corollaries include, "Clinical impressions are often wrong," and, "Your experience often misleads you and does not necessarily increase your accuracy."

A healthy respect for the ease with which our impressions can fool us, and awareness of the serious restrictions in the human capacity to integrate complex data should encourage the use of helpful decision aids. However, given stated rationales, which may challenge highly valued beliefs, the unfortunate and destructive result may be that the rest of the message involving corrective steps of guides is never heard. It is not surprising that in return many clinical faculty fill students with contrary messages or that clinicians communicate such with each other. For example, for each time the researcher says, "Be skeptical about learning from experience," the student is perhaps twice as likely to hear, "Experience is the best guide"; and for every time the researcher says, "Do not believe or trust what you see," the student hears, "Trust what your gut tells you."

Methodological knowledge to help one become an effective consumer of research. A major rationale for teaching scientific method is so that clinicians can be intelligent consumers of new knowledge claims and, in particular, new treatment and assessment methods. The practitioner is expected to check on the merits of knowledge claims for herself and not accept matters on authority. Clinicians are to live as rugged individuals, and should not allow others to tell them what to think. But should practitioners try to assess knowledge claims for themselves, and how realistic is it to expect that they will be able to do so, given the range of activities in which they engage, the amount of information that is available, and the increasingly technical and specialized nature of research and method in psychology?

Suppose you are seeing your local doctor, a very bright Harvard graduate, for an unusual infection that has not responded to four different medications. While waiting in his office you happen to pick up a copy of the *New England Journal of Medicine,* in which a world authority on infectious disease is reporting on a new antibiotic that seems to cure the very problem you have. After you excitedly pass the news on, should the physician's response be, "Well, the report seems promising, and although I've only had one course in infectious diseases and am unfamiliar with much of the methodology used in the field, I've got to get the raw data and check out the analysis so that I can decide for myself."? And if the practitioner actually does so and comes to a different conclusion, whose opinion should you trust?

There might be the occasional instance in which your physician happened to be correct, but it is very likely to be the exception. When the aim is to maximize the chances of being correct, the best strategy in this type of circumstance seems clear—defer to the far better qualified individual (although by "qualifications" I am not necessarily referring to professional credentials, such as board certification, which may have limited relation to accuracy in soft sciences such as psychology). Further, in cases of disagreement, one typically lacks a procedure that will help very much in identifying instances in which the inferior authority or source is right, because this would usually require knowledge or a method that is superior to the one that the leading individual is already using.

What are the chances the everyday practitioner has access to such remarkable information or strategies? Consequently, the proper approach is nearly always to defer to the person with the best overall track record. How often is this going to be the practitioner analyzing a body of research, especially when practitioners often deal with a wide array of patients, conditions, and issues? Even if clinicians could regularly analyze or reanalyze scientific data and research bearing on their practices (which seemingly would leave time for little else), is this likely to be the optimal strategy for reaching correct conclusions? Rather, the heart of the problem is to identify the source on which one should rely, that is, who is most likely to be correct (another task for meta-science).

The idea that the scientist-practitioner, or, as I would prefer, the scientific-practitioner (because I do not embrace the grand notion that performing research makes one a more effective healer), should reach his own conclusions and not simply take things on authority is commonly articulated in too broad a manner. The appropriate strategy depends in part on the status of knowledge claims, and in particular whether: (a) they are weak, despite possible assertions or superficial appearances to the contrary, or only gross judgments about level of support are needed; (b) finer judgments about level of support are required or the scientific community is deeply divided on an issue; or (c) there is a clear scientific winner.

Many knowledge claims lack decent credentials, and practitioners should be able to make some reasonable appraisal about level of support and recognize quackery. Many aspects of formal scientific appraisal exceed common knowledge and are counterintuitive, thereby necessitating the acquisition of some generic skills for evaluating the strength of evidence. We want practitioners to understand the rationale underlying certain methodological principles and know how to apply them. Examples might include, "Initial studies often produce inflated estimates of efficacy, a point to be kept in mind when comparing new approaches to older and more thoroughly tested ones," or, "Lacking a sample of individuals without the condition, one cannot determine whether the sign or indicator is truly associated with the condition, because it simply may be common among individuals—both positive and negative instances of the sign and condition are necessary to appraise co-variation."

In many cases, the scientific-practitioner could simply operate by the dictum: If there is little or no scientific evidence for a proposed method, then, when available, I should almost always defer to methods for which there is at least a modicum of supportive scientific evidence. Although it would seem straightforward to appreciate and enact this guideline, many practitioners violate it regularly. This is shown, for example, by the minimal—and even negative—correlation between the popularity of psychological tests and their demonstrated validity (e.g., see Kennedy, Faust, & Willis, 1995). Even among many individuals with extensive research training, there appears to be an insufficient grasp of the epistemological advantages that scientific method provides over anecdotal evidence or case study.

In distinguishing between levels of scientific support, one wonders how someone operating with a few basic rules of thumb or meta-scientific guides would stack up against individuals with extensive research training. For example, suppose we gave individuals some way to rank order level of support along a scale that included about seven basic categories of the following type: anecdotal evidence only, controlled studies providing more supportive than negative results, and diversity of controlled studies across diverse settings yielding consistently supportive results.

Such guides would miss numerous exceptions, but it is not frivolous to ask whether someone operating from generalizations of this type, especially more refined ones derived through proper meta-scientific analyses, might beat an individual making individualized judgments, even should that person have advanced scientific training. The question is whether, for each incorrect conclusion that is fixed by calling exceptions to the general rule in individual instances, there will be more than one correct conclusion spoiled. It might seem ludicrous to think that a few global rules could achieve such success, but a lesson to be taken from the research on clinical versus actuarial judgment is that generalizations can achieve surprising predictive power and often equal or beat individualized judgments, especially when the latter lack strong foundations.

Whatever the outcome of such studies, the practitioner who can make basic distinctions between claims with and without scientific backing and in level of support is sure to benefit, for often this is all that is needed. Individuals could learn to master these distinctions with far less scientific training than the average clinical psychologist receives. It is not clear just how far such global judgmental skills would get us, but as I argue later, when distinctions become more difficult, it is doubtful that even a highly trained "scientist-practitioner" is best off trying to reach his own conclusions. We need to determine the point at which additional scientific training produces limited gains, at least for appraising research evidence in domains in which one must make selections to guide practice. I predict, especially if decent global principles can be developed and students can be lead to internalize the epistemic advantages of science over impression, that the point of diminishing returns occurs much earlier than is commonly assumed.

In other cases, research has produced a clear winner or powerful support for a proposition. For example, there is now overwhelming evidence that psychotherapy produces better overall outcomes than no treatment (Lambert & Bergin, 1994; Smith, Glass, & Miller, 1980). When there are clear winners, and even acknowledging that such conclusions are not flawless, encouraging practitioners to perform their own reviews and reach their own conclusions would usually seem counterproductive. For if they do so and come to the contrary conclusion, they typically will be wrong. Rather, the clinician's job is to keep abreast of the clear winners that emerge, and to not be mislead on that score, especially by those unfamiliar with the evidence.

The third basic circumstance is one in which there are scientific competitors but no clear winner, and in fact no gross or relatively obvious differences in level of support, thereby calling for finer and more difficult judgments. Unfortunately, this seems to be the modal situation in psychology. There is often deep division among researchers, no clear superiority in the evidentiary bases of either side and, not uncommonly, no side with strong supportive evidence but rather a mishmash of evidence running in all directions.

If scientific study has yet to resolve an issue, how is the clinician to jump into the fray and accomplish the task, and what sense does it make to tell the practitioner to reach his own conclusions? The goal is not to reach an independent conclusion, but the right conclusion, and such contrasting purposes often call for differing actions. We have a practitioner who probably must direct much of her activities to clinical work, is faced with scientific disagreements in many areas pertinent to her practice, has nowhere near the time to review the primary literature across these domains, and may well be at a disadvantage in comparison to individuals who have spent years gaining knowledge and technical expertise in very specific areas of study. The clinician, who needs to be a jack of many trades, is to settle scientific disputes that masters of specific trades cannot decide. Resolving research conundrums is mainly a task for the scientific community, and in general the clinician's better course of action is to defer to the right authority. The problem is to identify which authority that might be.

This is one area in which professional organizations can greatly aid practitioners, especially if they do not act out of self-interest. For example, some of the presidential task forces of the American Psychological Association have labored long and hard to develop accurate summaries of scientific status in one or another area (e.g., Grove et al., in preparation).

Even given extensive resources and first-rate minds, predicting the fate of scientific ideas can be very difficult, especially when they are in a relatively early stage of development, indicators are inconsistent, or comparisons are seemingly close. Improving our abilities to do so is ultimately a task for meta-science. To the extent we can develop methods to identify the winners in scientific debates sooner or more accurately, the better the opportunity practitioners will have to integrate science and practice.

Of interest, in at least two of the three domains we have discussed, including situations in which there is a clear scientific winner or in which judgments about level of scientific support go beyond coarse distinctions, the clinician is probably better off figuring out which authority to defer to rather than trying to figure things out for herself. Across all three domains, it is unclear whether the clinician's high level of methodological training really provides much of an advantage, and in fact it might even encourage independent thinking and decisions in situations in which the probability of a correct conclusion is greatly enhanced by deferring to authority. Extensive scientific training might allow a high-level critique in a few select domains, but most clinicians have relatively general practices, and it is not clear that some advantage is gained by undertaking independent analyses of the literature rather than simply having some way of identifying those on whom to depend.

Perhaps all of this seems blasphemous to those deeply invested in science (which I am) and the scientist-practitioner model, for it is often thought that the scientific attitude is incompatible with dependence on authority. However, even for full-time scientists, it is more realistic to ask when, under what circumstances, and to whom they will defer. For example, a scientist working on a new approach to a very resistant problem is probably better off thinking independently for the most part and maintaining a high level of skepticism. In contrast, a scientist extending the application of a powerful and well-corroborated theory is unlikely to benefit if she decides to reanalyze the major background studies. Philosophers as diverse as Polanyi (1966) and Russell (1948) acknowledged the need for investigators to depend on scientific authority in many instances, because it is not feasible, or even always desirable, to analyze the data for oneself. Indeed, it would represent remarkable arrogance to believe that one could do a better job analyzing data than anyone else in every area pertinent to one's basic or applied scientific activities. The problem of determining when to rely on authority and what authorities to rely on are, again, issues for meta-science, but until more formal analyses are conducted, such choices will depend mainly on subjective judgment. For example, when analyzing work on a new topic, we really do not know the extent to which we should look at a scientist's past track record (play these prior odds) or rely solely on the merits of the present product.

Application of Knowledge

Generalizations and particulars.   Scientists uncover things of potential use to practitioners. In psychology, new forms of knowledge usually take the form of generalizations, often of a fairly crude type that admit to many exceptions. For example, a study might show that 75% of individuals who obtain highly elevated scores on Scale *4* of the MMPI meet diagnostic criteria for antisocial personality disorder. Or a researcher might develop a multiple regression formula that identifies brain damage in 70% of cases. Such a formula is a type of generalization, because it specifies that we will treat all people who share certain characteristics alike, for example, that we will classify all individuals who score at or greater than .50 on the Halstead–Reitan Impairment Index (Reitan & Wolfson, 1993) as falling within the brain-damaged range. At this point in our scientific development, our discoveries rarely lead to universals or laws or more powerful formalisms, such as Maxwell's mathematization of the electromagnetic field or Kepler's laws of planetary motion. Rather, we typically uncover generalizations of modest predictive power. This is not to belittle this accomplishment, for the subject matter in psychology is often extremely difficult; it may require great ingenuity to uncover and develop predictive variables, and in many instances these generalizations do achieve a very meaningful boost in accuracy.

Although generalizations seemingly must include at least one particular, they ignore some or most particulars. For example, the one particular might be whether the individual scored above 70 on Scale *4* of the MMPI. Or we might have a decision rule that incorporates multiple scores on psychological tests and a variety of sociodemographic variables. For example, Heaton, Grant, and Matthews's (1991) normative system provides a summary index of performance across a neuropsychological battery, which is adjusted for age, education, and gender. Thus, the classification or generalization that stems from this index considers an individual's particulars on a range of variables. Particulars may be ignored because they have been found to be nonpredictive, or because they have not been studied and their effects are unknown.

One could argue that such "particulars" could be further differentiated, because, for example, all individuals of one or the other gender cannot be lumped together. I am not asserting that particular or individuating information, as the terms are being used here, necessarily means atomistic, but only that some type of particularization or subdivision is being made, or that all individuals are not being treated alike. Just how far such subdividing should proceed does not bear on our topic, for I am merely indicating that generalizations ignore some or most particulars.

Given the modest success of many generalizations in psychology, there is an inherent belief that further predictive variables are out there but have not yet been found. In principle, if the universe is orderly and events have causes, we should be able to do a lot better than the 60% or 70% or 80% accuracy that we tend to achieve through our best generalizations in psychology. It would seem to follow that we are missing some of the predictive variables and that the task is to identify and incorporate them into our decision methods.

Whether this is the proper analysis of the problem is questionable. We often reach a ceiling in accuracy once we combine an astonishingly small number of variables, such as three or four, assuming they are the best ones available and minimally redundant; adding more variables or further particulars frequently does little or nothing for us (Dawes et al., 1989; Faust, 1984). Further particulars often do not help because they are redundant with other predictors, or because weak predictors usually will not increase accuracy when combined with stronger predictors (see Goldberg, 1991).

Further, validity coefficients seem to have shown little gain in psychology over the last three or four decades. Although we have greatly expanded the range of matters on which we can achieve some degree of predictive accuracy, the absolute level of accuracy seems to have approached an upper boundary in many areas. If the feat were simply to uncover new predictive variables to add to existing predictors, these types of results should not occur. For we have in fact identified many new predictive variables or additional particulars that we can incorporate into decision procedures, but the gains in incremental validity have been limited. In many areas of psychology in which we have already achieved modest predictive success, one can conjecture that uncovering new predictive variables or further particularizing our predictions and proceeding as we otherwise would is unlikely to get us very far. Rather, the problem may have much more to do with the nature of the subject matter, the precision of measurement, and especially the state of our theories and understanding.

Generalization of a scientific generalization to a particular versus applying a clinical generalization to a particular.   A scientific generalization the clinician is thinking of applying usually has been developed in some other setting. There typically will be contrasts, some of them salient, between the setting(s) of development and the clinician's setting. As such, the clinician is dealing with the possibility of generalizing a scientific generalization to a new situation, which will be represented as SG→G. In addition, in the instant case, the clinician is not applying the scientific generalization to his patients as a group but to a particular patient. This will be represented as SG→G→P, or the generalization of a scientific generalization to a particular.

The clinician will almost inevitably be struck by possible contrasts between the particular patient and those in the original group. Suppose the scientific generalization is, "70% of patients who obtain elevated scores on Scales *1* and *3* of the MMPI and a score that is at least 10 points lower than either on Scale *2* meet diagnostic criteria for somatization disorder." The clinician will probably be aware of various ways in which the particular patient might differ from those in the majority, or diagnostic group, or of alternate factors that could explain the patient's results. For example, the patient may be scheduled for a medical test the next day to rule out a serious condition. (Parenthetically, what might be less obvious is that the individuals who comprised the diagnostic group in the background studies, and from whom the modal description emerged, were not all the same either, and that whatever individual differences they might have had were not influential enough to keep them from obtaining high 1-3, low 2 MMPI profiles. The differences between the patient and the research sample are likely to be much more salient than the differences among participants within the research group, because studies often focus on within-group commonalties and texts frequently emphasize common features or prototypes.)

In addition to research, the clinician has her own experiential base to draw from, which includes similar patients seen across similar settings or in the current setting of application. The clinician is consequently often in a position to move directly from a generalization founded on her experience to the particular patient. This will be represented as CG®P, or the application of the clinician's generalization to the particular. In judgment tasks of the type being addressed, all other things being equal, it is advantageous to bypass an inferential link, because each part of the chain is probabilistically connected to the next part and each step therefore adds error. We will do better depending on Fred to guess the specific contents of a box, if his inferences are right 75% of the time, than we would if we depend on Mary to tell us what Fred said if Mary is right only 75% of the time when reporting on Fred's statements.

The conclusions drawn from these two methods, or from SG→G→P versus CG→P, will sometimes match, in which case no choice is necessary. In other cases the two methods will lead to opposing conclusions, and one or the other must be selected. If the first method indicates that a child has been sexually abused and the second that she has not, one cannot select both outcomes.

A subtle facet of this problem also needs to be considered. In essence, studies on clinical versus actuarial judgment compare generalizations to individualized judgments. In many of these studies, after obtaining a derivation sample, the actuarial method is then applied to a new group of participants, but the participants are drawn from the same setting or general population as the derivation sample; in contrast, the clinician often judges a set of cases that come from a setting other than his own. As a result, the relative situation with inferential links is reversed. The actuarial method or generalization is applied directly (SG→P), and the clinician must apply (generalize) whatever generalizations he has formed to a different sample (CG→G→P). Stated differently, the homecourt advantage is reversed. One could conjecture that due to this reversal (which I do not believe has ever been described in the literature), studies on actuarial judgment might tend to overrepresent the advantage of scientific generalizations and actuarial methods over clinical judgment. The very tentative nature of this conjecture should be emphasized, and it will be analyzed further later.

When a clinician selects between a scientific generalization and her own judgment, we are not dealing with a difference of the magnitude, say, of building a rocket using the major manufacturer's blueprints versus experimenting with one's own untested design. In more advanced sciences, there is often a massive difference between the results achieved via formal scientific theory versus subjective judgment. In contrast, in psychology, we often deal with generalizations that might achieve between 60% to 80% accuracy. Further, the transfer of these generalizations from the settings of development to the clinician's practice is most likely to reduce accuracy.

In studies comparing clinical and actuarial judgment, ties or relatively small differences are not at all uncommon (although when differences occur they almost always favor the actuarial method; Dawes et al., 1989; Sawyer, 1966). When one considers the frequency of ties or modest differences, together with the possible alteration in results that might occur were one to shift the homecourt advantage back to the clinician, the argument for clinical generalization gains further momentum.

Possible misimpressions. I want to try to correct any misimpressions that might have resulted from the text thus far. First, although circumstances have been identified that might have inflated the relative advantages of actuarial methods and scientific generalizations in comparison to clinical judgment, I am merely attempting to frame a problem and examine current conditions of application. Identifying a possible flaw in some of the studies on the topic should not be taken as affirmative evidence for clinical judgment, nor does it negate, or give cause to dismiss, the voluminous evidence on this matter that favors the actuarial method. Second, I believe unequivocally that scientific method is a far sounder method for deriving knowledge than subjective observation. That certainly does not mean that research findings are always right and observations always wrong, although we lack dependable means for identifying when the exceptions occur. Third, description and prescription should not be confused. To describe current circumstances and possible difficulties involved in applying science to practice should not be confused with a normative or prescriptive position. I believe that the application of scientific knowledge and method has major potential advantages, although much needs to be worked out about this interface.

Comparing the success of SC→G→P to CG→P. If we now ask how well the practitioner fares depending on clinical generalizations in comparison to scientific generalizations and actuarial methods, the answer is: probably not as well, and quite possibly not nearly as well, as she might think. Studies suggest that health care providers, including psychologists, are pervasively overconfident (see Faust, 1984, 1989). Due to various factors, the frequency with which our clinical judgments seem to be confirmed typically surpasses our true rate of accuracy, thereby unduly bolstering confidence. For example, no matter whether a patient complaining of subtle memory problems is told he has normal human failings or disorder, he is likely to agree, and yet the clinician cannot be correct in both instances. Of course, if we overestimate our accuracy, we are prone to overestimating our success relative to other methods.

Additionally, local norms often turn out to be less helpful than is commonly assumed, due to such problems as obtaining a representative sample and developing or incorporating independent means for determining true status or outcome. Any advantages that might accrue can be easily negated if the method for gathering local "norms" is imprecise, as is the case with subjective or clinical impression.

Considerable research also raises serious questions about the presumed benefits of experience on diagnostic and predictive accuracy. For example, Spengler, White, and Aegisdottir's (1995) exhaustive meta-analysis suggests that clinical experience may produce only a minor, or even negligible, gain in predictive accuracy. (See Faust, 1991; Faust & Ackley, in press, for an analysis of problems in learning from clinical experience.) As such, one must question whether the clinician's experience with a local sample or seemingly comparable patient groups typically produces generalizations or conclusions that are very powerful, how frequently misimpressions are formed instead, and how often prior belief and ideology contaminate observations.

Also favoring the other side of the ledger, actuarial methods sometimes beat the clinician by a wide margin, and many studies that have produced ties or less impressive effects involve weaker methods. Further, although one might think that a considerable advantage is accrued by optimally weighting variables, and that this edge is likely to be diminished or lost as one moves across settings, such weighting is usually not that important in the first place, and shifts in assigned weights often make little difference in predictive power (Dawes, 1979; Dawes & Corrigan, 1974; Dawes et al., 1989; Wilks, 1938). One can also point to studies on clinical versus actuarial judgment in which practitioners performed tasks for which they claimed a high level of competence or without the homecourt advantage being reversed—clinicians worked in their own settings with their own populations—without any change in overall outcomes.

Finally, the clinician can frequently find studies with populations that match her own on at least broad features (e.g., outpatient mental health clinic) and, as discussed, we may need to consider fewer particulars than we commonly assume when making predictions. Further, it is often fairly easy to alter actuarial methods in accord with changes in settings. One of the possible differences we would worry about the most is a dramatic change in base rates. A clinician with local knowledge might beat a powerful actuarial method that was aligned with very different base rates, but the advantage will almost surely be negated or reversed once simple adjustments in the procedure are made.

Application of Scientific Knowledge: Summation and Further Reflections

Review of literature and armchair analysis will only get us so far. It remains the case that, at present, the differences in success achieved through scientific generalizations and actuarial methods versus clinical judgment are often modest, and the shift in the inferential homecourt advantage generally works against the clinician in the context of research and for him in the context of practice. It would be helpful to clarify the possible impact of this inferential shift through meta-analysis.

Clinicians' objections to the use of science in practice may often strike the researcher as misinformed or as excuse making, but compelling questions and arguments can be raised. Suppose the clinician says:

> You have criticized my use of subjective judgment, but the alternative you suggest does not eliminate the need to depend on the very same methods you decry. Surely you would agree that across all of the domains in which I work, the application of current scientific knowledge will not always produce superior overall results in comparison to reliance on my own decisions. After all, consider all of the ties in the research on clinical and actuarial judgment, the possible subtle disadvantages that at least some of the comparisons may have created for the clinician, and the substantial differences that may exist between settings in which methods are developed and in which I must apply them. Given how often I must make decisions under conditions in which I should have serious concerns about the generalization of research, I require guidance and systematic methods for determining the likelihood or extent of generalization. I know you appreciate this problem, because you warn about the limits of generalization in almost every one of your publications and call for more research. When I press you on this, you admit that there are no formal methods for predicting the extent of generalization and that we are left in essence to do the very thing that you are criticize, that is, formulate a subjective impression (about generalization). If your advice forces me to do the very thing you tell me not to do, maybe the problem is not mine alone.

There are indeed some deep methodological and meta-scientific problems that are far from settled, and it is no easy task under these circumstances to decide when to rely on the generalization of a scientific generalization to a particular over the application of a clinical generalization to a particular.

A SCIENCE OF GENERALIZATION

Assuming that a key issue is the likelihood that a generalization will generalize to a particular, or more specifically, whether and to what extent predictive power changes across applications or settings, the clinician needs greater guidance than is usually available. Perhaps the typical response is to call for more research on generalization. For example, it might be proposed that a particular method be applied across settings to examine whether and how predictive formulas must change, or whether local knowledge makes much of a difference. This could be considered begging the question, because similar concerns are likely to remain about generalization of the findings to a new clinician's particular sample. Further, this type of grind-it-out empiricism, in which we set out to examine many possible comparisons, often, after much effort, produces a confusing set of findings (due partly to the very variation in settings and populations that we are addressing), is highly inefficient, and does not address the need for methods to assist such judgments.

Some sense of the type of work I believe is needed can be conveyed through two examples of possible approaches for improving the generalization of research to practice and enhancing our abilities to determine or predict generalization. Such research is mainly directed toward developing methods, rather than accumulating facts.

First, in many studies, there are serious reasons to doubt either the representativeness of samples relative to the population of clinical interest, or that clinical samples are properly matched with control groups. Further, there may be no direct means to obtain a representative sample of the clinical population. Finally, there may be no method for checking on how closely the sample represents the target population or the ultimate adequacy of the match between the clinical sample and the control group. Lacking such a method, even if one happens to obtain a representative sample or an excellent match, it does little good because one cannot evaluate whether the desired outcome has been achieved. What good does it do to have the right answer if there is no way to identify it as such or distinguish it from wrong answers?

For example, in research on the detection of malingering, some investigators try to determine the characteristics of fakers through detailed study of those that are caught (or presumably caught). The problem is that no one knows what percentage of malingerers escape detection, and, of course, we are most interested in those whom we do not know how to detect. To complicate matters more, those who are caught are likely to be systematically different from those who are not caught, because getting caught is probably associated with other features, such as lack of skill in malingering, that distinguishes this group from the undetected group. As a result, studies on those who are caught are generally of little applied use and may be systematically misleading. Or, if we are studying head injury, characteristics that make one more likely to experience such an event may overlap considerably with possible effects (e.g., impulsivity). As a result, it may be problematic to determine the appropriateness of matching or whether differences from control groups pre-date the injury. Obviously, it would be ethically reprehensible to solve the problem by random assignment and experimental manipulation of injury (and path analysis will not solve the problem either; see Faust, 1997).

To deal with these problems, I have (see Faust and Ackley, in press) proposed the Group Membership by Chance (GMC) method. Taking the example of malingering, some individuals are caught mainly by chance or bad luck (e.g., they happen to be seen at exactly the wrong time performing some activity they absolutely should not be able to do). In the case of head injury, some individuals "self-select" through their actions (e.g., drinking and driving) and others are just terribly unlucky (e.g., they are struck when walking on the sidewalk). In essence, ending up in these groups due almost entirely to bad luck is directly parallel to random selection. Although such cases may not come along very often, national data banks and other technological innovations greatly enhance the capacity to identify and pool cases. By compiling a sufficient number of cases, it should be possible to construct the equivalent of randomly selected, and hence representative, groups. (I realize that many questions can be raised about this method, some of which are touched on in Faust & Ackley, in press, and will be covered extensively in Faust, 1997.)

If the GMC method permits the researcher to obtain a representative group, she can also determine the extent to which the overall group of naturally selected individuals, or those not included by chance, match that group's characteristics. Additionally, by deriving discrepancy indices and examining their relation with representativeness, it might be possible to develop methods for predicting the extent to which matches really do achieve comparability, and to construct procedures that correct for degree and type of misrepresentation.

As a second example, most judgments about the potential generalization of research findings across populations, settings, and context depend on subjective data integration. Although the great bulk of journal articles in psychology contain a section describing the possible extent and limits of generalization, such discussions usually represent little more than educated guesswork or conjecture. These conjectures are usually based on rules of thumb with uncertain predictive value and which may conflict with one another. For example, we are likely to consider the range of situations in which a finding has been reproduced, effect sizes, whether independent replications have been conducted, and the similarity between the situations that have been investigated and new potential applications.

We thus have a classic problem domain for the judgment researcher: decisions must be made under conditions of uncertainty; higher order and well-corroborated theory is lacking; there are various potential predictors of uncertain value; and we need to determine the validity, strength, and redundancy of predictors in order to find ways of combining them properly. It is exactly in such situations that decision aids and actuarial procedures almost always equal or exceed subjective judgment. To the extent that generalization is predictable—and if it is not we should not be wasting our time guessing about it or criticizing those who do not accept application in their settings—it should be possible to identify the valid variables and work out formalisms that maximize the use of available information.

For example, as Faust and Meehl described (Faust, 1984; Faust & Meehl, 1992; Meehl, 1992, 1993), working from episodes within the history of science, one could derive and validate predictive formulas. It should be possible to examine how well the variables we usually use to appraise and predict generalization really work, how they ought to be combined, and whether there are other predictive variables we usually do not consider that have utility. Although these types of proposals might seem fantastic, there are emerging and large databases on scientific episodes that make such work feasible (Sulloway, 1996), and the basic methodology seems viable (see Faust & Meehl, 1992). To the reader who wonders why someone would not just test generalization, we would again note that there are serious constraints to this approach as an overall program, that methods that allow one to better anticipate outcomes are of great advantage, and that in the pragmatic context of prediction we often cannot await full or final tests. The clinician who must decide whether to follow his own clinical generalizations or a research finding often has an immediate situation to manage, one in which doing nothing has potentially serious consequences. In practice, we often must guess, and we would certainly welcome methods that produce better choices.

Ironically, any meta-scientific findings about the likelihood of generalization will itself take the form of a generalization. For example, we might be able to say that the likelihood of generalization is 9 in 10. At some point in time, it will remain for the clinician treating or assessing a patient to decide, when inconsistent conclusions result, whether the generalization about generalization to a particular is a better bet than his individualized judgments. I would end by stating the belief that the power of individualized judgment is often overestimated and that of generalization underestimated, resulting in many avoidable mistakes, and that the balance will continue to shift in favor of generalization as the science of psychology improves and as a true meta-science emerges. I hope and anticipate that psychologists will lead efforts on both fronts.

ACKNOWLEDGMENTS

I thank Leslie J. Youce and Paul E. Meehl for their many helpful suggestions, and especially Charles M. Boisvert for his extensive input and efforts.

REFERENCES

Butcher, J. N., Dahlstrom, W. G., Graham, J. R., Tellegen, A., & Kaemmer, B. (1989). *Minnesota Multiphasic Personality Inventory–2: Manual for administration and scoring.* Minneapolis: University of Minnesota Press.

Dawes, R. M. (1979). The robust beauty of improper linear models in decision making. *American Psychologist, 34,* 571–582.

Dawes, R. M., & Corrigan, B. (1974). Linear models in decision making. *Psychological Bulletin, 81,* 95–106.

Dawes, R. M., Faust, D., & Meehl, P. E. (1989). Clinical versus actuarial judgment. *Science, 243,* 1668–1674.

Faust, D. (1984). *The limits of scientific reasoning.* Minneapolis: University of Minnesota Press.

Faust, D. (1989). Data integration in legal evaluations. Can clinicians deliver on their premises? *Behavioral Sciences & the Law, 7,* 469–483.

Faust, D. (1991). What if we had listened? Present reflections on altered pasts. In D. Cicchetti & W. M. Grove (Eds.), *Thinking clearly about psychology. Vol 1: Matters of public interest* (pp. 185–216). Minneapolis, MN: University of Minnesota Press.

Faust, D. (1997). *GMC (Group Membership by Chance): A method for determining the representativeness of naturally occurring and potentially confounded samples in the social sciences.* Manuscript in preparation.

Faust, D., & Ackley, M. A. (in press). Did you think it was going to be easy? Some methodological suggestions for the investigation and development of malingering detection techniques. In C. R. Reynolds (Ed.), *Detection of malingering during head injury litigation.*

Faust, D., & Meehl, P. E. (1992). Using scientific methods to resolve questions in the history and philosophy of science: Some illustrations. *Behavior Therapy, 23,* 195–211.

Faust, D., & Nurcombe, B. (1989). Improving the accuracy of clinical judgment. *Psychiatry, 52,* 197–208.

Faust, D., & Willis, G. W. (in press). *Counterintuitive imperatives: A guide to improving clinical assessment and care by predicting more accurately.* Boston: Allyn & Bacon.

Goldberg, L. (1991). Human mind versus regression equation: Five contrasts. In D. Cicchetti & W. M. Grove (Eds.), *Thinking clearly about psychology. Vol. 1: Matters of public interest* (pp. 173–184). Minneapolis: University of Minnesota Press.

Grove, W. M., Boodoo, G. M., Cohler, B. J., Dahlstrom, W. G., Dawes, R. M., Faust, D., Frazer, D. W., Holtzman, W. H., Iacono, W. G., & Lezak, M. D. (1997). *"Assessment for the Twenty-First Century": Designing a Model Assessment Curriculum.* Report of American Psychological Association Division 12 (Clinical) Presidential Task Force in preparation.

Grove, W. M., & Meehl, P. E. (1996). Comparative efficiency of formal (mechanical, algorithmic) and informal (subjective, impressionistic) prediction procedures: The clinical-statistical controversy. *Psychology, Public Policy, and Law, 2,* 1–31.

Heaton, R. K., Grant, I., & Matthews, C. G. (1991). *Comprehensive norms for an expanded Halstead–Reitan Battery.* Odessa, FL: Psychological Assessment Resources.

Kennedy, M. L., Faust, D., & Willis, G. W. (1995). Social-emotional assessment practices in school psychology. *Journal of Psychoeducational Assessment, 12,* 228–240.

Kuhn, T. S. (1970). *The structure of scientific revolutions* (2nd ed.). Chicago: University of Chicago Press.

Lambert, M. J., & Bergin, A. E. (1994). The effectiveness of psychotherapy. In A. E. Bergin & S. L. Garfield (Eds.), *Handbook of psychotherapy and behavior change* (4th ed., pp. 143–189). New York: Wiley.

Meehl, P. E. (1978). Theoretical risks and tabular asterisks: Sir Karl, Sir Ronald, and the slow progress of soft psychology. *Journal of Consulting and Clinical Psychology, 46,* 806–834.

Meehl, P. E. (1990). Appraising and amending theories: The strategy of Lakatosian defense and two principles that warrant it. *Psychological Inquiry, 1,* 108–141.

Meehl, P. E. (1992). Cliometric metatheory: The actuarial approach to empirical, history-based philosophy of science. *Psychological Reports, 71,* 339–467.

Meehl, P. E. (1993). Philosophy of science: Help or hindrance? *Psychological Reports, 72,* 707–733.

Meehl, P. E. (1996). *Clinical versus statistical prediction.* Northvale, NJ: Aronson (Original work published 1954 by University of Minnesota Press)

Polanyi, M. (1966). *The tacit dimension.* New York: Doubleday.

Reitan, R. M., & Wolfson, D. (1993). *The Halstead–Reitan Neuropsychological Test Battery* (2nd ed.). South Tucson, AZ: Neuropsychology Press.

Russell, B. (1948). *Human knowledge, its scope and limits.* New York: Simon & Schuster.

Sawyer, J. (1966). Measurement and prediction, clinical and statistical. *Psychological Bulletin, 66,* 178–200.

Schmidt, F. (in press). Statistical significance testing and cumulative knowledge in psychology: Implications for training of researchers. *Psychological Methods.*

Smith, M. L., Glass, G. V., & Miller, T. I. (1980). *The benefits of psychotherapy.* Baltimore: The Johns Hopkins University Press.

Sulloway, F. J. (1996). *Born to rebel: Birth order, family dynamics, and revolutionary genius.* New York: Pantheon.

Wechsler, D. (1981). *WAIS–R Manual: The Wechsler Adult Intelligence Scale–Revised.* New York: Psychological Corporation.

Wilks, S. S. (1938). Weighting systems for linear functions of correlated variables when there is no dependent variable. *Psychometrika, 3,* 23–40.

PART III

Advances in Statistical Methods for Personality Assessment Research

Chapters in this part are devoted primarily to overviews of several statistical methods that are employed infrequently in personality assessment research, but have great potential in contributing to the understanding of the complex data sets often encountered in the measurement and study of personality. These articles should serve both as an introduction and a brief tutorial for personality researchers who are unfamiliar with them. Clinicians should find these articles to be valuable references that will serve as a basis for evaluating the appropriate use of these methods in published research in their areas of interest.

In the first of these chapters, John Schinka and his colleagues present the results of a frequency analysis of types of statistical methods employed in published articles. Their findings provide an empirical basis for understanding the need for the other chapters in this section. Leo Davis and Kenneth Offord then provide an overview of logistic regression, a technique that should be considered more frequently than the traditional reliance on chi-square analyses. They illustrate the use of logistic regression with an application to hypothetical Rorschach data that is very easy to follow. Their clearcut exposition of this technique, and its availability in most statistical packages for personal computers, should make its use straight-forward, particularly for researchers who are familiar with the methods of multiple linear regression and discriminant analysis.

In the third chapter, Susan Crowley and Xitao Fan provide an introduction to structural equation modeling and employ the most commonly used application of structural equation modeling, confirmatory factor analysis, to examine the under-lying structure of a data set of self-report anxiety and depression measures in children. Their presentation will be appreciated both for its comprehensive over-view of the modeling method and because of the substantive import of their findings for the measurement of anxiety and depression in children.

The authors of the remaining two chapters use the topic of item analysis/selection as a vehicle to illustrate the application of a particular statistical method. Richard Gorsuch, long recognized for his contributions to the development and use of exploratory factor analysis, provides an update on the application of this procedure. His presentation will be used by researchers, reviewers, and clinicians alike as a guideline for the well-reasoned and productive use of the method in personality assessment research. Additionally, his discussion of the structure of commonly used measures of anxiety and depression in adults will be valuable to clinicians. In the last chapter, Abigail Panter and her colleagues provide an introduction to item response theory, an application that has been rarely directed to instruments other than ability measures. They show how, and under what conditions, item response models can be considered to be special cases of general item-level, factor analysis models for dichotomous (e.g., true/false) data. Use of data from the MMPI-2 in their examples emphasizes the potential robust power of this methodology in personality assessment.

14

Statistical Methods in Personality Assessment Research

John A. Schinka

James A. Haley VA Medical Center
and
Department of Psychiatry
University of South Florida, College of Medicine

Leif LaLone

James A. Haley VA Medical Center
and
Department of Psychology
University of South Florida

Jo Ann Broeckel

Department of Psychology
University of South Florida

Emerging models of personality structure and advances in the measurement of personality and psychopathology suggest that research in personality and personality assessment has entered a stage of advanced development. In this article we examine whether researchers in these areas have taken advantage of new and evolving statistical procedures. We conducted a review of articles published in the *Journal of Personality Assessment* during the past 5 years. Of the 449 articles that included some form of data analysis, 12.7% used only descriptive statistics, most employed only univariate statistics, and fewer than 10% used multivariate methods of data analysis. We discuss the cost of using limited statistical methods, the possible reasons for the apparent reluctance to employ advanced statistical procedures, and potential solutions to this technical shortcoming.

Progress in any scientific endeavor is typically marked by stages. The early stages are usually characterized by initial discovery of the phenomena of interest, rough theory-building, and the invention of appropriate methodologies and procedures of analysis to explore the phenomena of interest. The later stages, which build on both the successes and failures of the first, are marked by increasing complexity of underlying models, theories, and research hypotheses. New experiments must take into account the findings and implications of previous research. Theories and models are altered, and alternative hypotheses forged. More complex research methodologies and data analysis procedures are designed to facilitate more rigorous tests of new theories. Reis and Stiller (1992) called this later epoch of increasing complexity *second-generation research,* and note that it reflects a growth in the maturity of the scientific endeavor. As we approach the end of the century, it is perhaps an appropriate time to ask whether research in the areas of personality and personality assessment have entered the stage of second-generation research. Specifically, is research in these areas characterized by (a) evolving and more sophisticated models, (b) improved methods of measurement, and (c) more refined and powerful methods of data analysis?

MEETING CRITERIA: MODELS, MEASURES, AND METHOD OF ANALYSIS

Models in Personality and Personality Assessment

One substantive demonstration of progress in research in personality and personality assessment is the development of the Five-Factor (Extraversion or Surgency, Emotional Stability or Neuroticism, Agreeableness, Conscientiousness, and Culture or Openness) model of normal personality. The past decade has seen a growing consensus on both the number and kinds of trait domains that are necessary to provide a parsimonious description of personality. In his review of personality theories, for example, Digman (1990) stated: "research on the five-factor model has given us a useful set of very broad dimensions that characterize individual differences. ... Taken together, they provide a good answer to the question of personality *structure*" (p. 436).

The status of the five-factor model (FFM) at this time is such that the emphasis has switched from constructive replications of the factor structure across samples, sources of ratings, and types of instruments to more precise definitions of the five major domains and the exploration of lower level descriptors that could be used to provide more detailed descriptions of personality (e.g., Goldberg, 1990). Relations between models of childhood temperament and the FFM are also being explored (e.g., Digman, 1994), with the goal of examining the linkage and developmental pathways that connect early childhood temperament factors with the five adult personality domains. Not all personality researchers endorse the FFM (e.g., Benet & Waller, 1995; Ben-Porath & Waller, 1992), however, and some have questioned the comprehensiveness of the model and noted the importance of exploring the limitations of the model (Paunonen, 1993). Nevertheless, the model represents a major step forward in the examination of normal personality functioning and, as exemplified in the numerous studies examining aspects of the model, serves an important heuristic function in the exploration of normal personality structure.

Although currently perhaps the most influential of models in terms of driving subsequent research hypotheses and studies, the FFM is certainly not the only indicator of increasing sophistication in personality models. Numerous major theories and mini-models have been proposed in the last decade. Examples include Millon's (1981, 1986a, 1986b) evolving theory of psychopathology and models of specific types of normal personality function (e.g., Wiggins, 1982).

Measures in Personality and Personality Assessment

Significant advances in the development and refinement of measures to examine personality and psychopathology have characterized the past decade. Among the more notable of these are the publication of the revised Minnesota Multiphasic Personality Inventory (MMPI–2; Butcher, Dahlstrom, Graham, Tellegen, & Kaemmer, 1989), the Personality Assessment Inventory (Morey, (1991), the revised NEO Personality Inventory (Costa & McCrae, 1992), the third revision of the Millon Clinical Multiaxial Inventory (Millon, 1994), the Multidimensional Personality Questionnaire (Tellegen & Waller, in press), and the series of revisions to the Comprehensive System for Rorschach interpretation (e.g., Exner, 1986). Development and revision of these broadband inventories involved not only updates of normative data, but substantive item selection and scale development work, guided primarily by rational-empirical models of test construction.

Numerous other measures have gone through several stages of refinement and are commonly used in research on personality, psychopathology, and diagnosis, such as the revised Personality Diagnostic Questionnaire (Hyler & Rieder, 1987). Over the same time we have also seen the development of highly focused narrow-band instruments designed to provide measures of very specific areas of personality functioning. Among these are measures such as the revised Interpersonal Adjective Scales (Wiggins, Trapnell, & Phillips, 1988), the State–Trait Anger Expression Inventory (Spielberger, 1988), and the Yale–Brown Obsessive–Compulsive Scale (Goodman, Price, Rasmussen, & Mazure, 1989).

Methods of Analysis in Personality and Personality Assessment

Few would doubt that the past two decades have shown important developments in statistics and measurement. Procedures and techniques for a broad range of multivariate statistics have been refined (e.g., see Stevens, 1992; Tabachnick & Fidell, 1989). These would appear to be especially important in research in personality assessment because of the complexity of relations among personality variables. Personality theory has clearly evolved to the point where complex interrelations among traits, environmental influences, and developmental factors can be hypothesized. Assessment instruments have also evolved such that specific dimensions of many behavioral variables can be quantified. Multivariate procedures provide the opportunity to examine the complexity of these interactions by providing methods of analysis for multiple independent (predictor) and multiple dependent (criterion) variables (Cohen & Cohen, 1983).

In addition, structural equation modeling (SEM; see Bentler, 1986; Jöreskog & Sörbom, 1979) and multivariate techniques for analyzing categorical variables, such as logit and probit analysis (e.g., Aldrich & Nelson, 1984), have been well explicated. Multidimensional scaling (e.g., Schiffman, Reynolds, & Young, 1981) and item response theory (e.g., Hambleton & Swaminathan, 1984; Lord, 1980) are recent developments that have been applied successfully in several areas of measurement. Several of these developments in statistics appear especially suited to the nature of research in personality assessment.

Have researchers in personality assessment taken advantage of these new and evolving statistical procedures? In contrast to advances in model development and the evolution of new and improved measures in personality assessment, here the evidence is not so obviously positive. To examine this issue, we conducted a review of articles published in the *Journal of Personality Assessment* (*JPA*). We selected *JPA* because it is the oldest of journals that focus on the evaluation and application of methods of personality assessment. We reviewed all articles published in the past 5 years (1990–1994) that included any form of data analysis. The results displayed in Table 1 illustrate the degree to which various statistical procedures have been used during this time period. Of the 449 articles that included some form of data analysis, 12.7% used only descriptive statistics. For the remaining articles (393), the average number of procedures used was 2.36 (*SD* = 1.46). Univariate and bivariate statistics (*t* test, chi-square, *r,* analysis of variance [ANOVA]) were the most frequently used procedures. With the exception of factor analysis (including principal components analysis), multivariate procedures were used infrequently (in less than 10% of studies). Fewer than 1% of the studies used some form of SEM.

COST OF USING LIMITED STATISTICAL METHODS

The results of our study of *JPA* articles suggest that researchers in personality assessment, or at least those who publish in *JPA*, rely heavily on more traditional descriptive and univariate methods of analysis at the expense of more recently refined procedures. Unfortunately, this preference is executed at some cost to research progress, primarily for two reasons.

TABLE 1
Use of Various Statistical Procedures in Studies Published in the
Journal of Personality Assessment from 1990 Through 1994

Procedure	Percentage of Studies Employing Procedure
Descriptive statistics only	12.7
Analysis of variance	29.2
Analysis of covariance	5.1
Chi-square	21.8
Cluster analysis	3.8
Discriminant analysis	6.8
Factor analysis	16.9
Multivariate analysis of variance	11.8
Multivariate analysis of covariance	2.4
Multiple linear regression	12.0
Simple correlation	50.1
Structural equation modeling	0.7
T test	24.5

Note. Total is greater than 100% because some studies employed more than one type of data analysis.

First, designs employing multiple independent and/or dependent variables generally provide the optimal test of a research hypothesis. In a recent article, for example, Patterson (1995) described an application of SEM to the description and development of antisocial personality characteristics and delinquency in children and adolescents. Briefly, the analyses described by Patterson involved behavioral and personality ratings, in self-, teacher, and parent formats, of a large group of boys. These boys were evaluated in Grades 4, 6, 8, and 10 as part of a larger longitudinal study of parenting practices and childhood development. Simple reliability analyses of ratings of antisocial behaviors and characteristics across time periods (e.g., Grades 4 and 8) were found to be highly stable, suggesting a stable trait pattern and a single path to delinquency. At the same time, data from the longitudinal study revealed that delinquency, defined by violations of the law, occurred at varying ages in developmental. In fact, earlier analyses had suggested that boys meeting the delinquency criterion fell into two subgroups, early and late onset delinquency.

Several alternative models, each testing a different pattern of relations among the independent and dependent variable, were examined. The SEM analysis revealed that early severity of antisocial characteristics was substantially influenced by ineffective parenting practices, and that early onset delinquency was largely a function of greater severity of antisocial characteristics. In contrast, boys with late onset delinquency were likely to show lesser severity of antisocial characteristics at younger and older ages. Wandering (presence on the street) and heavy commitment to a deviant peer group were the primary variables in explaining the presence and expression of late onset delinquency. In this study, therefore, SEM procedures allowed an analysis of the contribution of several independent variables (personality characteristics, parental influence, peer influence) on a dependent variable (delinquency) within a longitudinal (developmental) time frame—a simultaneous examination of these variables that would be virtually impossible to conduct and interpret within a traditional, univariate framework.

The second cost of reluctance to consider more advanced statistical procedures is that the full range of substantive variables that might be examined to address comprehensive issues cannot be evaluated. For example, the potential effects of patient demographic variables on the accuracy of MMPI interpretation have long been a source of concern for clinical researchers. This area of research has been characterized primarily by traditional experimental approaches; that is, studies that basically examine scale score differences between two participant groups that differ only on the variable of interest (e.g., ethnic identification) and attempt to control for all other variables (e.g., age, education). We (Schinka and LaLone) recently completed a study in which we took an alternative, multivariate approach. We used multiple linear regression analyses to examine simultaneously the relations of seven participant demographic variables to MMPI–2 scores in the MMPI–2 restandardization sample. These multivariate analyses provided little evidence that demographic variables, alone or in combination, explain meaningful amounts of variance in scale scores for the MMPI–2 validity, clinical, and content scales. Demographic variables did appear to be a potentially meaningful concern, however, for the MMPI–2 supplemental scales.

REASONS FOR THE LACK OF PROGRESS

Why have researchers in personality assessment been reluctant to examine more advanced statistical procedures? We believe that there are at least two reasons, the first of which was elucidated by Aiken, West, Sechrest, and Reno (1990) in their survey of graduate training in statistics. Their survey revealed that graduate training in design and statistics continues to focus on methods that support traditional laboratory research, as opposed to the "field" research that is generally the model in personality assessment. As a result, there is heavy emphasis on multifactor ANOVA, repeated measures ANOVA, cell contrasts and comparisons, and nonparametric statistics. From the standpoint of formal training, the primary emphasis has changed very little in the past 25 years, except that training in measurement (e.g., classical test theory, item-response theory) has declined substantially.

Second, and perhaps most important for most researchers, there are few venues for postdoctoral training in statistics. A substantial portion of researchers in the area of personality and personality assessment are located in clinical settings, with limited time and access to coursework and seminars provided in academic settings. Continuing education opportunities at professional meetings and via home study are almost nonexistent. Alternatively, it might be argued that current state-of-the-art statistical packages for desktop computers offer a vast array of sophisticated procedures—a substantial improvement in both computing and method resources over the days of mainframe, batch-processing computing. For many researchers, however, these programs present a bewildering array of options for the more advanced statistical procedures. As a result, many researchers ignore these procedures in favor of less sophisticated, but tried and true, methods.

RECOMMENDATIONS

Is there hope that these newer statistical procedures can be brought into the mainstream in personality assessment research? If the answer to this question is to be yes, then it is likely that solutions will need to come from within the community of personality researchers. Several suggestions might be considered:

1. Encouraging increased detail in descriptions of multivariate analyses in journal articles. Such descriptions should include the rationale for the statistical procedure, assessment of assumptions underlying use of the procedure, reasons for selecting particular forms of the procedure (e.g., standard versus hierarchical multiple regression), methods and caveats of interpretation, and references supporting the use of the analysis. Studies that might serve as a first step in meeting this standard include the cluster analysis experiment by Kinder and Curtiss (1990) and the confirmatory factor analysis study reported by Hau (1995). Tabachnick and Fidell (1989) provided excellent examples of the reporting of results from different statistical procedures.

2. Promoting the dissemination of large datasets among personality assessment researchers to facilitate exploration of statistical procedures. We have found that the availability of large datasets has greatly facilitated exploration of statistical procedures and research questions in our assessment training sites. An excellent dataset for exploration is the MMPI–2 standardization sample dataset, now available commercially at a very reasonable price.

3. Encouraging journal reviewers to expand their critique of articles submitted for review. Too often reviews simply cite the inadequacy or inappropriateness of statistical procedures reported in a submitted article. It would be far more helpful if reviewers would provide more specific critiques of unacceptable statistical analyses and recommend more specifically the appropriate alternatives. Suggesting references (e.g., Stevens, 1992) for alternative approaches would probably be

welcomed by many authors. In cases with complex research designs, it would even be appropriate to recommend that authors enlist the aid of a statistical consultant.

4. Recommending that authors have statistically knowledgeable colleagues review articles before submitting them for publication. Many successful authors routinely enlist the aid of colleagues, both locally and nationally, to review articles for potential problems with research design, statistical analysis, interpretation of results, and overall clarity. These relations often provide the opportunity for consultation prior to conducting analyses.

SUMMARY

In this article we have provided data and opinion indicating that advances in personality assessment research are likely being restricted by a failure to incorporate powerful multivariate statistics. Our comments should not be interpreted, however, as suggesting that these statistical procedures should be used simply because they are sophisticated and powerful. Sophistication in the absence of a well-focused research question, clarity of research design, and a good understanding of the nature of the underlying phenomena is simply obfuscation. As Weiner (1991) noted, the implication of research results always outweighs the elegance of the data analysis. We hope our comments spur researchers to increase the robustness of their analyses with the overriding goal of extracting more of nature's truth from personality assessment data.

ACKNOWLEDGMENTS

This research was supported in part by the Department of Veterans Affairs. We thank Glenn Curtiss and Rodney Vanderploeg for their comments on a previous draft of the chapter.

REFERENCES

Aiken, L. S., West, S. G., Sechrest, L., & Reno, R. R. (1990). Graduate training in statistics, methodology, and measurement in psychology: A survey of PhD programs in North America. *American Psychologist, 45,* 721–734.

Aldrich, J. H., & Nelson, F. D. (1984). *Linear probability, logit and probit models.* Beverly Hills, CA: Sage.

Benet, V., & Waller, N. G. (1995). The big seven factor model of personality description: Evidence for its cross-cultural generality in a Spanish sample. *Journal of Personality and Social Psychology, 69,* 701–718.

Ben-Porath, Y. S., & Waller, N. G. (1992). "Normal" personality inventories in clinical assessment: General requirements and the potential for using the NEO–PI. *Psychological Assessment, 4,* 14–19.

Bentler, P. M. (1986). Structural modeling and *Psychometrika:* An historical perspective on growth and achievements. *Psychometrika, 51,* 335–51.

Butcher, J. N., Dahlstrom, W. G., Graham, J. R., Tellegen, A., & Kaemmer, B. (1989). *Minnesota Multiphasic Personality Inventory–2: Manual for administration and scoring.* Minneapolis: University of Minnesota Press.

Cohen J., & Cohen, P. (1983). *Applied multiple regression/correlation analysis for the behavioral sciences.* Hillsdale, NJ: Lawrence Erlbaum Associates, Inc.

Costa, P. T., Jr., & McCrae, R. R. (1992). *Professional manual for the Revised NEO Personality Inventory.* Odessa, FL: Psychological Assessment Resources.

Digman, J. M. (1990). Personality structure: Emergence of the five-factor model. *Annual Review of Psychology, 41,* 417–440.

Digman, J. M. (1994). Child personality and temperament: Does the five-factor model embrace both domains? In C. F. Halverson, G. A. Kohnstamm, & R. P. Martin (Eds.), *The developing structure of temperament and personality from infancy to adulthood* (pp. 323–338). Hillsdale, NJ: Lawrence Erlbaum Associates, Inc.

Exner, J. E., Jr. (1986). *The Rorschach: A comprehensive system: Vol. 1. Basic foundations* (2nd ed.). New York: Wiley.

Goldberg, L. R. (1990). An alternative "Description of personality": The Big-Five factor structure. *Journal of Personality and Social Psychology, 59,* 1216–1229.

Goodman, W. K., Price, L. H., Rasmussen, S. A., & Mazure, C. (1989). The Yale–Brown Obsessive–Compulsive Scale. *Archives of General Psychiatry, 46,* 1012–1016.

Hambleton, R. K., & Swaminathan, H. (1984). *Item response theory: Principles and applications.* Boston, MA: Kluwer-Nijhoff.

Hau, K. (1995). Confirmatory factor analyses of seven locus of control measures. *Journal of Personality Assessment, 65,* 117–132.

Hyler, S. E., & Rieder. R. O. (1987). *Personality Diagnostic Questionnaire–Revised.* Unpublished manuscript.

Jöreskog, K. G., & Sörbom, D. (1979). *Advances in factor analysis and structural equation models.* Cambridge, MA: Abt Associates.

Kinder, B. N., & Curtiss, G. (1990). Alexithymia among empirically derived subgroups of chronic back pain patients. *Journal of Personality Assessment, 54,* 351–362.

Lord, F. M. (1980). *Applications of item response theory to practical test problems.* Hillsdale, NJ: Lawrence Erlbaum Associates, Inc.

Millon, T. (1981). *Disorders of personality.* New York: Wiley.

Millon, T. (1986a). Personality prototypes and their diagnostic criteria. In T. Millon & G. L. Klerman (Eds.), *Contemporary directions in psychopathology: Toward the DSM–IV* (pp. 671–712). New York: Guilford.

Millon, T. (1986b). A theoretical derivation of pathological personalities. In T. Millon & G. L. Klerman (Eds.), *Contemporary directions in psychopathology: Toward the DSM–IV* (pp. 639–669). New York: Guilford.

Millon, T. (1994). *Manual for the MCMI–III.* Minneapolis, MN: National Computer Systems.

Morey, L. C. (1991). *Personality Assessment Inventory.* Odessa, FL: Psychological Assessment Resources.

Patterson, G. R. (1995). Orderly change in a stable world: The antisocial trait as a chimera. In J. M. Gottman (Ed.), *The analysis of change* (pp. 83–102). Hillsdale, NJ: Lawrence Erlbaum Associates, Inc.

Paunonen, S. (1993, August). *Sense, nonsense, and the Big Five factors of personality.* Paper presented at the meeting of the American Psychological Association, Toronto, Canada.

Reis, H. T., & Stiller, J. (1992). Publication trends in *JPSP*: A three-decade review. *Personality and Social Psychology Bulletin, 18,* 465–472.

Schiffman, S. S., Reynolds, M. L., & Young, F. W. (1981). *Introduction to multidimensional scaling: Theory, methods and applications.* New York: Academic.

Spielberger, C. D. (1988). *State–Trait Anger Expression Inventory.* Odessa, FL: Psychological Assessment Resources.

Stevens, J. (1992). *Applied multivariate statistics for the social sciences* (2nd ed.). Hillsdale, NJ: Lawrence Erlbaum Associates, Inc.

Tabachnick, B. G., & Fidell, L. S. (1989). *Using multivariate statistics* (2nd ed.). New York: Harper Collins.

Tellegen, A., & Waller, N. G. (in press). Exploring personality through test construction: Development of the Multidimensional Personality Questionnaire. In S. R. Briggs & J. M. Cheek (Eds.), *Personality measures: Development and evaluation* (Vol. 1). London: Jessica Kingsley.

Weiner, I. B. (1991). Developments in research in personality assessment. *Journal of Personality Assessment, 56,* 370–372.

Wiggins, J. S. (1982). Circumplex models of interpersonal behavior in clinical psychology. In P. Kendall & J. S. Butcher (Eds.), *Handbook of research methods in clinical psychology* (pp. 183–221). New York: Wiley.

Wiggins, J. S., Trapnell, P., & Phillips, N. (1988) Psychometric and geometric characteristics of the Revised Interpersonal Adjective Scales (IAS–R). *Multivariate Behavioral Research, 23,* 119–134.

15

Logistic Regression

Leo J. Davis and Kenneth P. Offord

Mayo Clinic and Mayo Foundation

Logistic regression has probably been underutilized in clinical investigations of personality because of its relatively recent development (dictated by the need for computer programs to obtain maximum likelihood estimates), and the fact that use has been largely confined to the fields of biostatistics, epidemiology, and economics. Its use should be given serious consideration when the outcome of interest is dichotomous (or polychotomous) in nature and the predictors of interest may be categorical or continuous. The logit transformation is quite tractable mathematically, and it embodies the notion of threshold, which may have relevance for many of the variables that are of interest to investigators in the field of personality. Furthermore, investigators with experience in multiple linear regression or contingency table analysis should have little trouble in transitioning to logistic regression. Logistic regression programs are readily available in the major statistical packages, all of which provide fairly standard output.

Multiple linear regression and discriminant analysis are statistical tools that are much more familiar to investigators in clinical psychology and personality than logistic regression. The latter has wider use in such fields as biostatistics, epidemiology, and economics. When we began to assemble information on logistic regression for this article, we found scant reference to it in the psychology literature. References such as Cohen and Cohen (1983) and Pedhazur (1982) either do not mention it, or do not treat it as a formal analytic technique. A computer search of PsychInfo (1984 to 1995), by keyword, revealed 225 published studies using multiple regression (presumably linear) with personality variables, but only 28 published studies in the English literature that had made use of logistic regression and personality variables. The majority of these latter studies, however, were not in psychology journals. Yet, investigators who use, or plan to use, multiple regression or discriminant analysis should carefully consider the possible use of logistic regression.

Investigators should think about logistic regression if the dependent variable is categorical in nature. Use of multiple linear regression with such a dependent variable is likely to result in the violation of basic assumptions requisite to it. In personality and psychopathology research, many variables of interest have a categorical basis. Personality typologies and the presence or absence of disease (when treated as outcomes of interest) lend themselves nicely to analysis by means of logistic regression. In particular, a dichotomous dependent variable is a common occurrence in research relating to health where degrees of "caseness" are difficult to measure, and a disease is considered to be either present or absent.

The issue of appropriateness of assumptions is a key factor in the choice of techniques. For example, the distribution of error in the dependent variable in linear regression is assumed to follow a normal distribution. This, however, is not possible with a dichotomous dependent variable, which follows a binomial distribution. The result of using multiple linear regression with a dichotomous or polychotomous dependent variable is that the obtained significance tests and confidence intervals will not be valid. Similarly, in the case of discriminant analysis, the distribution of the predictors is assumed to be multivariate normal, an unlikely occurrence in practice. As Hosmer and Lemeshow (1989) noted, "application of the normal discriminant function when its assumptions do not hold may result in substantial bias, especially when some of the covariates are dichotomous variables" (p. 182). There are additional reasons for giving serious consideration to the use of logistic regression in those situations where multiple linear regression or multiple discriminant analysis might be used. First of all, the binary logistic function is bounded by 0 and 1 and, when the dependent variable is coded 0 for absence and 1 for presence of an outcome, yields a probability estimate of the occurrence of the outcome (dependent) variable, given the values of the predictors. For example, using logistic regression in a study of Minnesota Multiphasic Personality Inventory variables and the occurrence of bipolar disorder might yield the following statement: The probability of bipolar disorder, given a Scale *9 T* score of > 80, a Scale *3 T* score < 50, and a Scale *0 T* score of < 50, in a woman < 50 years of age is 0.6. Second, logistic regression makes use of the odds ratio, a concept of great use to epidemiologists. Thus, given certain values of the predictors, the odds favoring a certain outcome can be computed. The change in the odds ratio estimates when the values of one or more predictors are changed can be studied.

A third reason for considering logistic regression concerns the relation between the predictor (independent) variables and the outcome (dependent) variable. In multiple linear regression, this relation is a straight-line function, whereas in logistic regression, it is S-shaped. That is, the logistic transformation is S-shaped, which implies a threshold concept. Also, the increment in the probability estimate of the outcome per unit increase in the dependent variable is not constant across all levels of the independent variable. For logistic regression, the logarithm of the odds is linearly related to the independent predictor variables. In much research, the relation between the independent and dependent variables does not change for low values of the predictor. However, when predictor variable values reach a certain threshold, the predicted probability of the occurrence of an outcome increases and continues to do so until the predictor reaches high values, beyond which there is no visible change in the probability of occurrence of the outcome.

Fourth, when predictor variables are categorical, analysis of data using logistic regression is closely akin to contingency table analysis. In particular, it lends itself nicely to presentation with a four-fold table. Furthermore, the odds ratio can be computed easily from such a table. This latter feature has led some authors to approach logistic regression from a contingency-table perspective. At any rate, readers who are comfortable with chi-square and contingency table analysis will find the learning curve for logistic regression considerably shortened. Other writers, such as Hosmer and Lemeshow (1989), stressed the similarities of linear and logistic regression; thus, investigators who have considerable experience with multiple linear regression should find much that is familiar.

The use of a logarithmic function is not the only functional form that could be used, and in fact there are a number of other functions that have been proposed (see Aldrich & Nelson, 1984, p. 33, for other functional forms), including the probit model (based on normal probability theory). For practical purposes, however, only the logit and probit functions have generated much interest and may be the only ones available in standard computer packages. These last two models display a great deal of similarity and choosing between the two may hinge on rather minor considerations. The probit model is more computationally complex, but because computations will not be done by hand in either case, that is not an issue for the user. Probably the most telling argument for the user is the mathematical tractability of the logistic regression model.

METHOD OF ESTIMATION

The method of estimation used in linear regression is least squares. This method assures that the sum of the squared deviations of observations from the fitted regression line are at a minimum. Least squares estimation cannot be used with logistic regression because of the binary or polychotomous outcome and binomial distribution of errors. The method of choice with logistic regression is the method of maximum likelihood. Least squares and maximum likelihood are alternative methods of estimation that yield the same results with a normally distributed dependent variable. The maximum likelihood method has been known for many years, but has found favor only recently because of its computational complexity. The development of computer programs that quickly yield a solution has made the method feasible.

The distinction between maximum likelihood and least squares estimation procedures may have little meaning for clinical investigators, but the essence is this: Whereas the problem in least squares estimation lies in obtaining regression coefficient estimates that minimize the squared deviations around a regression line, the problem in maximum likelihood estimation is obtaining coefficients that maximize the likelihood of obtaining the observed set of data in the context of the model being proposed. Actually, the computing algorithm used to obtain maximum likelihood estimates in most computer packages is an "iterative reweighted least squares algorithm" (Hosmer & Lemeshow, 1989, p. 18). Another possible method is discriminant function analysis, but, under certain conditions, such as with the use of dichotomous independent variables, this technique will "overestimate the magnitude of the association" (Hosmer & Lemeshow, 1989, p. 20).

An additional consideration when using logistic regression and maximum likelihood estimators, is whether to use *conditional* or *unconditional* maximum likelihood methods. The conditional method should be used if the number of variables is large, relative to the number of participants. On the other hand, the unconditional method should be used if the number of variables is small, relative to the number of participants, or if participant matching is employed (Kleinbaum, 1994).

EVALUATION OF RESULTS

The evaluation of a study using logistic regression is similar to that for linear regression and contingency table analysis. T statistics are used to test hypotheses about the individual coefficients in both linear and logistic regression. In linear regression, the F ratio can be used to test the null hypothesis that all coefficients (with the exception of the intercept) are zero, while various logistic regression models can be compared using chi-square statistics. In particular, logistic regression models are compared by means of the likelihood ratio test. This ratio compares the log likelihood statistics for two different models (one model being "nested" in the other). It can be shown that the difference between these two statistics has a chi-square distribution, with degrees of freedom equal to the difference in the number of coefficients (beta weights) in the two models. The likelihood ratio test is written: $-2 \, ln_e L_1 - (-2 \, ln_e L_2)$, or, equivalently as: $-2 \, ln_e (L_1/L_2)$. This latter version indicates that the likelihood ratio test is a "ratio of likelihoods" (see later). The model labeled L_1 in this example is the likelihood for the reduced model, with the variable(s) of interest excluded. The model labeled L_2 includes the variable(s) of interest. If the variable(s) of interest makes a large contribution to prediction of the outcome (dependent variable), the L_1/L_2 ratio will be small, but multiplying the natural logarithm (ln_e) of a small fraction by -2 will yield a larger positive value, which is what one would expect for the chi-square value in this case. Computer packages typically show the log likelihood statistic for each model being considered. It is then a simple matter to compare log likelihoods for the models of interest. Confidence interval estimation for logistic regression parameters (i.e., regression coefficients/beta weights) is similar to that for multiple linear regression. Logistic regression does not have a good equivalent to the coefficient of determination, R^2, which is familiar to users of multiple linear regression as a measure of the percentage of total variance accounted for by the model (Aldrich & Nelson, 1984, pp. 56–59). Various pseudo-R^2 measures have been proposed but none has met with widespread acceptance, and all have certain disadvantages. Aldrich and Nelson suggested that investigators may want to construct a table of predicted-versus-observed tallies so that they have true-positive and false-positive rates to inspect. Such information is essential in the assessment of sensitivity and specificity of tests, and their positive and negative predictive power. Also, the indices of sensitivity, specificity, positive and negative predictive power, along with odds ratios, may provide a better overall measure of the goodness of fit of a particular model than chi-square-based measures of fit.

Odds ratios were mentioned earlier but deserve more extended discussion. Epidemiologists are quite familiar with the odds ratio, but investigators in other fields may not be as well acquainted with these intuitively appealing indices. The antilogs of the logistic regression coefficients yield odds ratio estimates that, for each variable, express the increase (or decrease) in odds of the outcome (e.g., thought disorder) being present in individuals who have the risk factor in question ($M-> 2$ on the Rorschach) versus those who do not have the risk factor ($M- \leq 2$). Odds ratios can also be obtained from contingency table analysis of results. This is demonstrated easily with a 2×2 table in which cells $a \times d$ are divided by cells $b \times c$ (see Figure 1). The odds of a patient with $M-> 2$ having a thought disorder is:

$$(a / a + b) / (1 - (a / a + b)) = a / b$$

While the odds for someone with $M- \leq 2$ having a thought disorder is:

$$(c / c + d) / (1 - (c / c + d)) = c / d$$

The ratio of these two odds is:

$$(a / b) / (c / d) = ad / bc$$

This last equation shows why the odds ratio is literally a "ratio of odds."

Odds ratios may change with varying levels of the independent variable in question. Using our example, the odds of thought disorder being present is 28/8 = 3.5, when the number of $M-$ responses on the Rorschach is > 2, but is 16/68 = .235 when $M- \leq 2$. This yields an odds ratio of 14.88. An odds ratio of 1.0 would

Rorschach Human Movement	Thought Disorder		
	Yes	No	
M- > 2	a 28	b 8	36
M- <= 2	c 16	d 68	84
	44	76	120

Odds Ratio=ad/bc=(28 x 68)/(8 x 16)= 14.88

Regression Coefficient= -2.6997 $(e^{2.6997})$ = 14.88

FIGURE 1   Relation between logistic regression and contingency table analysis for a 2 × 2 table.

suggest a null effect, or lack of association between $M-$ responses and the presence of thought disorder. Similarly, an odds ratio of <1 (say .5), would suggest an inverse relation between the presence of $M-$ responses and thought disorder. Although in reality this inverse relation is counterintuitive, it illustrates the interpretation of odds ratios <1.

EXAMPLES

To help the reader get started with logistic regression, the following examples, using fictitious data, are presented. One hypothetical study involves Rorschach variables derived from the Comprehensive System (Exner, 1986). Data were generated for 120 participants on the relation between $M-$ responses, Level 2 Special Scores, age, sex, and the presence or absence of thought disorder. In the first example, the independent variables are dichotomous (Table 1). The analysis was performed using Logit, an independent module using the same commands and syntax as Systat (Wilkinson, 1988) and sold as a supplemental program. Similar results could be expected from using any of the major microcomputer statistical packages. The results that are pertinent to this discussion are shown in Table 2. This full model (consisting of a constant, $M-$, Special Scores, age, and sex) yielded a log likelihood of -40.86, after six iterations, using the method of maximum likelihood. The chi-square value for this full model is 75.99 (with $df = 4$), which is highly significant ($p < .001$), indicating not all regression coefficients are simultaneously zero. Inspection of the Wald statistics (the t statistics) suggests that the logistic regression

TABLE 1
Distribution of Variables

Variable	Number of Patients
Dependent	
Thought disorder	
Yes	44
No	76
Independent	
Movement	
M– > 2	36
M– ≤ 2	76
Special score	
> 24	44
≤ 24	76
Sex	
Female	52
Male	68
Age (years)	
> 45	44
≤ 45	76
(M, SD)	(38.0, 14.3)

Note. N = 120.

TABLE 2
Logistic Regression Output for the Dependent Variable Thought Disorder

Parameter	Estimate	Standard Error	t Statistic
Constant	3.127	.914	3.4
Movement	–3.198	.694	–4.6
Special scores	–2.728	.642	–4.2
Sex	–0.657	.591	–1.1
Age	1.029	.592	1.7
		Log likelihood: –40.8593	

coefficients (i.e., β weights) for age and sex individually are not different from zero (have no independent multivariate effect on the dependent variable). Testing whether both of these potential predictors can be deleted can be evaluated by testing a reduced model. The first reduced model omits sex as a variable and yields a log likelihood of –41.485. When this value is subtracted from the log likelihood for the full model (–40.86), and the remainder is multiplied by 2, the resulting chi-square is 1.25 ($df = 1$), which has a p value > 0.20. Establishing 95% confidence intervals around the regression coefficient for sex would have yielded endpoints of the interval at –1.81 and .50, indicating that the confidence interval includes a regression coefficient of zero. If we continue with this example by omitting only the variable of age, we obtain a log likelihood of –42.383, which when subtracted from –40.86 leaves a remainder that, when multiplied by 2, yields a chi-square value of 3.05 ($df = 1$), which has a $p = 0.081$. Again, a 95% confidence interval around the regression coefficient for age yields endpoints of the interval of –0.14 to 2.18, and includes a regression coefficient of zero. On the other hand, an influential predictor in this example is poor quality human movement ($M-$). If we were to omit this variable from the full model, we would obtain a log likelihood of –55.623, yielding a chi-square value of 29.53 ($df = 1$), which has a $p < 0.001$. Confidence interval endpoints for $M-$ are 1.84 and 4.56, an interval that does not include zero. Incidentally, confidence intervals can be established around the odds ratios, but the usual procedure is to apply them to the regression coefficients. In this instance, the odds ratio confidence interval for Movement responses would be $e^{1.84} = 6.3$, and $e^{4.56} = 95.58$.

Evaluation of the $M-$ independent variable provides an opportunity to illustrate the relation between logistic regression coefficients (β weights), odds ratios, and contingency table analysis. Analysis of this variable yields the results shown in Figure 1. All of the major logistic regression packages provide an option for saving (and printing) predicted probabilities for each participant for each value of a dichotomous (or polychotomous) dependent variable. This allows the investigator to construct a table of actual-versus-predicted outcomes. In our example, the odds of a participant who is positive for $M-$ (i.e., more than two $M-$ responses) having a diagnosis of thought disorder is 14.88 times greater than a participant who is not positive for $M-$ (two or less $M-$ responses). This odds ratio is derived in two ways. One is obtained by taking the antilog of the regression coefficient (i.e., $e^{2.699682}$), which equals 14.88. The other way is by taking the 2 × 2 table and obtaining the product of cell a and cell d, and dividing this product by the product of cell b and cell c. In this case, that would be 28 × 68 (ad), divided by 8 × 16 (bc), or 1904/128, which equals 14.88! This illustrates the fact that in logistic regression with a dichotomous dependent variable, the regression coefficient has an interpretation that is directly related to the output from a four-fold table, and that both, in turn, have a direct relation to the odds ratio, a concept that has great intuitive appeal. This also illustrates the fact that the regression coefficient can be interpreted as the change in the log of the odds ratio per unit increase in the independent variable.

In regard to the relation between contingency table output and exponentiation of the regression coefficient, it is important to note that this relation holds when the independent variable of concern is dichotomous and is coded 0 or 1, or anytime the difference in coding equals 1. The user needs to ascertain how the particular computer package being used codes design variables.

To this point, the example has been limited to dichotomous independent variables. But logistic regression is not limited to point variables because continuous variables, such as age in years, can also be used. In this example, treating age as a continuous variable produces the results shown in Table 3. When we recalculate the model with the continuous variable of age omitted, we obtain a log likelihood of –42.383, which, when compared to the log likelihood for the full model, yields a chi-square value of 8.234 (df = 1), and a p value = 0.004. In contrast to the results obtained with age as a dichotomous variable, the 95% confidence interval for age treated as a continuous variable does not include zero (0.018, 0.113).

Interactions between variables is a concept familiar to users of analysis of variance. In logistic regression, interaction carries a similar meaning and should be included in the model if there is reason to believe that the relation between a predictor and an outcome variable is dependent on the level of another predictor variable. The term *effect modifier* is used to describe this situation and may be encountered in the literature, because this is the term often used by epidemiologists. One implication of the presence of interaction is that the odds ratio is not a single index but changes depending on the level of the effect modifier.

A word of caution about interactions! In models where there are a large number of variables, the number of interaction terms can be considerable, and inclusion of these terms in the model can use up degrees of freedom that are necessary for testing the goodness of fit of a particular model. It is suggested that only those interaction terms that are theoretically relevant be retained in the model. The inclusion of more variables makes the analyses more numerically unstable and the model is not likely to generalize to the wider population of interest. This is merely an example of the need for a parsimonious approach to model-building.

The mention of parsimony brings up another issue in logistic regression: namely, the use of stepwise variable selection procedures. This technique is

TABLE 3
Logistic Regression for Thought Disorder With a Continuous Variable (Age)

Parameter	Estimate	Standard Error	t Statistic
Constant	.809	1.236	.65
Movement	–3.289	.707	–4.7
Special scores	–2.818	.650	–4.3
Sex	–0.383	.614	–.6
Age	.065	.024	2.7
		Log likelihood: –38.26640	

widely used in multiple linear regression in the search for a "best" subset of predictors. The technique is equally applicable to logistic regression, as are the cautions associated with the use of stepwise procedures. Perhaps the best defense against letting the statistical algorithm select a predictor subset for us is the presence of good theory to guide us in the selection of variables thought to have real-world significance.

SUMMARY

Logistic regression has probably been underutilized in clinical investigations of personality because of its relatively recent development (dictated by the need for computer programs to obtain maximum likelihood estimates), and the fact that use has been largely confined to the fields of biostatistics, epidemiology, and economics. Its use should be given serious consideration when the outcome of interest is dichotomous (or polychotomous) in nature, while the predictors of interest may be categorical or continuous. The logit transformation is quite tractable mathematically, and it embodies the notion of threshold, which may have relevance for many of the variables that are of interest to investigators in the field of personality. Furthermore, investigators with experience in multiple linear regression or contingency table analysis should have little trouble in transitioning to logistic regression. Logistic regression programs are readily available in the major statistical packages, all of which provide fairly standard output.

ANNOTATED REFERENCES

Aldrich, J. H., & Nelson, F. D. (1984). *Linear probability, logit, and probit models*. Beverly Hills: Sage.
   This short book is #45 of the Sage series in Quantitative Applications in the Social Sciences. It serves as a good and inexpensive introduction to the topic and contains an excellent numerical example with raw data. Users can compare their results with those in the book. Also useful is the presentation of alternative models to logistic regression, and why logit and probit make good choices.
Hosmer, D. W., & Lemeshow, S. (1989). *Applied logistic regression*. New York: Wiley.
   This book is the standard reference for logistic regression. It is usable even by nonstatisticians, and is especially useful for those with a background in multiple linear regression. Although written from a linear regression perspective, the authors do a fine job of relating logistic regression, contingency table analysis, and the concept of the odds ratio, which is a familiar phrase to epidemiologists. The publication is recent enough to include references to the major microcomputer statistical packages. This text is highly recommended for anyone contemplating the use of logistic regression.

Kleinbaum, D. G. (1994). *Logistic regression: A self-learning text.* New York: Springer-Verlag.

As the title indicates, this is a self-learning text that should speed up the learning curve for those who are not familiar with logistic regression. The examples favor those with epidemiology backgrounds, but this is not a major obstacle. The text explains the difference between conditional and unconditional logistic regression programs and has a number of computer data sets for practice use. This is another book to consider seriously if one wishes to learn about logistic regression.

REFERENCES

Aldrich, J. H., & Nelson, F. F. (1984). *Linear probability, logit, and probit models.* Beverly Hills: Sage.

Cohen, J., & Cohen, P. (1983). *Applied multiple regression/correlation analysis for the behavioral sciences* (2nd ed.). Hillsdale, NJ: Lawrence Erlbaum Associates, Inc.

Exner, J. E., Jr. (1986). *The Rorschach: A comprehensive system: Vol. 1. Basic foundations* (2nd ed.). New York: Wiley.

Hosmer, D. W., & Lemeshow, S. (1989). *Applied logistic regression.* New York: Wiley.

Kleinbaum, D. G. (1994). *Logistic regression: A self-learning text.* New York: Springer-Verlag.

Pedhazur, E. J. (1982). *Multiple regression in behavioral research* (2nd ed.). Fort Worth, TX: Holt, Rinehart & Winston.

Wilkinson, L. (1988). *SYSTAT: The system for statistics.* Evanston, IL: SYSTAT.

16

Structural Equation Modeling: Basic Concepts and Applications in Personality Assessment Research

Susan L. Crowley and Xitao Fan
Department of Psychology
Utah State University

Structural equation modeling (SEM) has become an increasingly used methodological strategy in psychology. Nevertheless, many psychologists continue to be unclear about how to apply this analytic tool in their research. This article reviews SEM from a conceptual perspective, particularly focusing on confirmatory factor analysis. Additionally, the relation between SEM and other analytic techniques (e.g., exploratory factor analysis) are addressed. A confirmatory factor analytic example is presented and reviewed in detail. Finally, limitations of SEM and other considerations are discussed.

The appropriate application of multivariate statistical methods in research has been emphasized by many authors (e.g., Fish, 1986; Johnson & Wichern, 1988; Loehlin, 1992). Two major arguments are generally put forth supporting the use of multivariate statistics: (a) multiple univariate statistical tests inflate the experimentwise error rate and (b) the realities that behavioral science research faces are not univariate in nature, and this reality needs to be honored in our research by adopting appropriate multivariate strategies. As pointed out by Loehlin (1992),

> Scientists dealing with behavior ... rarely have the luxury of the simple bivariate experiment, in which a single independent variable is manipulated and the consequences are observed for a single dependent variable. Even those scientists who think they do are often mistaken. The variables they directly manipulate and observe typically are not the ones of real theoretical interest, but are merely some convenient variables acting as proxies. ... A full experimental analysis would again turn out to be multivariate, with a number of alternative experimental manipulations on the one side, and a number of alternative response measures on the other. (p. 1)

One multivariate method that is increasingly being utilized by psychologists in personality research and instrument development is structural equation modeling (SEM), also known by a variety of other names including covariance structure analysis, latent variable modeling, or causal modeling. The power and versatility of SEM and its increasing use in psychological research requires an elevated level of knowledge for psychologists working with substantive issues such as personality assessment. This article is intended to serve as a basic and practical introduction to SEM, focusing on the submodel of confirmatory factor analysis (CFA). It is hoped that, through concrete examples, the utility of SEM will be demonstrated, and it will become more accessible to those psychologists interested in adopting an SEM approach in personality research and instruments.

SEM

In recent years, SEM has become a useful method in social and behavioral sciences for specifying, estimating, and testing hypothesized interrelationships among a set of substantively meaningful variables. Much of its attractiveness is due to its generality and applicability in a wide variety of research situations, a versatility that has been amply demonstrated (Baldwin, 1989; Bollen & Long, 1993; Byrne, 1994; Jöreskog & Sörbom, 1989; Loehlin, 1992; Pedhazur & Schmelkin, 1991; SAS Institute, Inc., 1989). Because of such generality, SEM has been heralded as a unified model that joins methods from econometrics, psychometrics, sociometrics, and multivariate statistics (Bentler, 1994).

SEM expresses relations among several variables, and these variables can be either directly observed variables or unobserved hypothetical variables. Many widely used statistical techniques can be considered as special cases of SEM, including regression analysis, canonical correlation analysis, CFA, and path analysis (Bagozzi, Fornell & Larcker 1981; Bentler, 1992; Jöreskog & Sörbom, 1989).

However, several aspects of SEM qualitatively distinguish it from both univariate techniques (e.g., multiple regression analysis, analysis of variance) and other multivariate procedures (e.g., multivariate analysis of variance, exploratory factor analysis [EFA]). Univariate techniques are methodologically limited in examining the relations among multiple outcome variables because only one such variable can be examined at a time, leaving some relations and interactions largely unexplained. Compared with most other multivariate techniques, SEM takes a confirmatory rather than an exploratory approach to data analysis (Byrne, 1994), that is, the pattern of relations among variables are specified a priori based on theoretical expectations. This distinctive characteristic of SEM lends itself especially well to using empirical data for testing theoretical models. In contrast, most other multivariate techniques are descriptive and exploratory in nature, making them less appropriate for model testing.

ANATOMY OF SEM

A graphic representation is probably the easiest way to explain SEM. Figure 1 presents a hypothetical full SEM model. Conventionally, in SEM models, a circle or an oval represents a *latent variable,* that is, a hypothetical construct that is not directly measured. A square or a rectangle represents an *observed variable* on which measurement is taken. A latent variable can have one, or preferably more, observed variables as its indicators. A straight line with an arrow at one end represents a hypothesized "effect" one variable has on another, while a curved line with arrows on both ends represents a hypothesized correlation between two variables without implying any "causal" relation.

In SEM terminology, variables (latent or observed) that only exert an "effect" on other variables are called *exogenous variables,* while those that receive an effect from any others are called *endogenous variables.* In the model in Figure 1, all the measured variables (X_1 to X_5, Y_1 to Y_5), and two latent variables (F_3 and F_4) are endogenous variables. F_1 and F_2 are two exogenous latent variables because they exert effect on F_3 and F_4. As indicated in Figure 1, the SEM model can be viewed as consisting of three components: two measurement models and one structural model. The first measurement model describes the relations between exogenous latent variables (F_1 and F_2)and their indicators (X_1 to X_5). The second measurement model describes the relation between endogenous latent variables (F_3 and F_4) and their indicators (Y_1 to Y_5). The structural model, on the other hand, describes the relations among latent variables (Jöreskog & Sörbom, 1989). In other words, the measurement model deals with relations between measured variables and latent

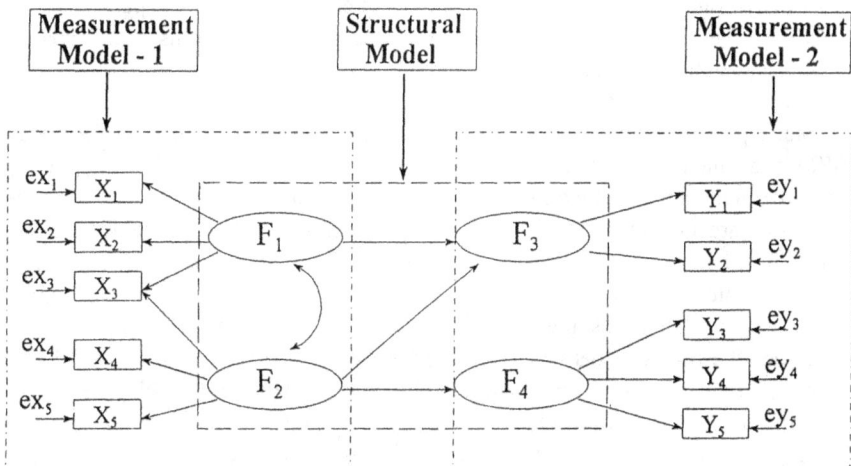

FIGURE 1   A hypothetical full structural equation model.

variables, and the structural model describes the relation among latent variables themselves. In the measurement models, the Xs and Ys represent the variance in the observed variables that are not accounted for by the latent constructs. In measurement terms, they are often treated as measurement errors. In SEM applications, it is not always necessary to implement the full model as depicted in Figure 1 because a submodel such as measurement model – 1 can be implemented by itself, as is the case of CFA in the later example.

Conceptually, the model in Figure 1 can be understood as follows: F_1 and F_2 are correlated latent constructs that have X_1 to X_3 and X_3 to X_5 as observed indicators, respectively. Similar relations exist for Y variables (Y_1 to Y_5) and latent constructs F_3 and F_4. The construct F_3 is causally affected by both exogenous latent constructs F_1 and F_2, and the latent construct F_4 is causally affected only by F_2.

Path Analysis, CFA, and SEM

Many researchers have used traditional path analysis to investigate causal relations among variables. Using a multi-step regression analysis, path analysis attempts to solve for hypothesized causal effects among a set of variables by decomposing correlations among variables into four components: direct effect, indirect effect, unanalyzed (due to correlated causes), and spurious (due to common causes). The major weaknesses of path analysis are (a) all variables are assumed to have been measured without error and (b) lack of statistical mechanisms to test the fit between the hypothesized path model and empirical data. The assumption that all variables are measured without error is not realistic because psychological measurement invariably contains considerable measurement error. Furthermore, path analysis only describes causal relations among measured variables and thus is not capable of dealing with situations in which several variables are hypothesized to be the indicators of the same latent construct.

Many psychologists know CFA, which is simply a measurement model under SEM (i.e., measurement model – 1 in Figure 1). In instrument development, multiple items are developed to form a subscale; and different, often correlated, subscales are developed to form a full measurement scale. Substantively, the different subscales often represent different constructs, or latent variables, which have multiple items as measured indicators. These subscales, or latent variables, are often correlated to some degree. Because the measurement model in SEM describes the relations between measured variables and latent constructs, it becomes particularly useful for construct validation in instrument development.

From the discussion presented earlier, it clear that CFA and path analysis can be subsumed under SEM. In practice, the difference among path analysis, CFA, and a full structural equation model can be briefly summarized as follows: path analysis examines the causal links among observed variables; CFA examines causal links between observed variables and latent constructs (factors); a full structural equation model examines the causal links both between observed variables and latent constructs, and among latent constructs themselves.

Because CFA is the primary use of SEM in personality assessment and is widely used for construct validation of psychological measurement instruments, our focus in later sections is primarily on this submodel of SEM. First, however, the differences between EFA and its confirmatory counterpart will be reviewed.

CFA Versus EFA

Conceptually, factor analysis can be considered to have two types: EFA and CFA. Historically, "factor analysis" has been used to mean EFA, and little confusion resulted from such use of the phrase. With the increasing popularity of CFA, the situation is changing and, it is important to make a theoretical distinction between EFA and CFA. The distinctions between CFA and EFA are numerous from both a theoretical and a mathematical perspective. For the purposes of this article, the following discussion focuses on a few of the theoretical differences between EFA and CFA.

Most important, CFA is mainly driven by substantive theories and expectations, while EFA, as the name implies, is primarily a data-driven technique for discovering what underlying structure the sample data may possess (Bollen, 1989; Jöreskog & Sörbom, 1989; Pedhazur & Schmelkin, 1991). In other words, EFA is applied because we want to explore the data to see what kind of characteristics, interesting features and relations may exist. In doing so, we usually do not impose any hypothesized model on the data and all variables "load" on all factors. EFA is useful for the purpose of generating structure, theoretical model, and empirically testable hypotheses (Gorsuch, 1983). Important insights about the data structure can often be gained through EFA in the early stages of experimentation or measurement instrument development.

CFA, on the other hand, starts with a theoretically plausible model that is assumed to describe, explain, or account for the empirical data. The construction of the model is based either on a priori information about the nature of the data structure, or on substantive theories in the field (Jöreskog & Sörbom, 1989; Long, 1983a; Pedhazur & Schmelkin, 1991). As such, variables are limited to only "load" on one, or a few, of the factors.

In the application of CFA to measurement problems, the model is often a given classificatory design for items or subtests according to the objective features of content and format, that is, which items should group together because of their common features, and which subscales should group together to form a higher order construct. The purpose of using CFA is to test the hypothesis that the proposed theoretical model fits the empirical data. As mentioned earlier, although EFA can be useful for generating hypothesis, it is highly desirable to subject such a hypothesis to the test of statistically more rigorous CFA.

Finally, EFA differs from its confirmatory counterpart in terms of the potential effect of sampling fluctuations on research results. Being data-driven in nature, EFA tends to be heavily influenced by the idiosyncracies of a particular sample. Unless there are adequate cross-validation or replication procedures, the structure derived from EFA should be viewed with caution, because sampling errors and sample idiosyncracies are being capitalized on in such a data-driven approach.

To a considerable degree, CFA avoids this problem by fitting a prespecified theoretical model to sample data. As a theory-driven technique, the construction of the model is not affected by particular sample data, and the likelihood of capitalizing on the sampling fluctuations and sample idiosyncracies is greatly reduced. Thus, CFA is generally considered to have some advantages over its exploratory counterpart in substantive theory building and theory testing (Duncan, 1975; Jöreskog & Sörbom, 1989; Long, 1983b; Pedhazur & Schmelkin, 1991). But due to the late development of the theory, and even later development of special software programs required for the analysis, CFA has been less popular among personality researchers than EFA.

Model Specification

Obviously, having a model for testing is a prerequisite for conducting CFA. The model specified should adequately represent theoretical expectations about the relationship structure of variables (e.g., as identified in previous research, or as predicted by a theory). Once the model is constructed, the population parameters of all the path coefficients in the model need to be estimated from sample data. There are three mutually exclusive ways to estimate these coefficients: free, fixed, or constrained. When the value of a coefficient needs to be estimated from the empirical data, it is free. When the value of a coefficient is specified to be zero (no "effect" or relation), it is fixed. When the value of a coefficient is specified either to be equal to a certain value (e.g., 1.0), or to be equal to another coefficient in the model that needs to be empirically estimated, it is constrained.

Once the model and all its path coefficients are specified, the sample data are used to test the fit of the model to the data. First the free parameters are estimated using mathematical algorithms (e.g., maximum likelihood estimation [MLE], generalized least squares [GLS], etc.). Then the parameter estimates, both those specified by the researcher (fixed and constrained), and those empirically estimated (free), are used to reconstruct the covariance or correlation matrix of the observed variables. The question of which matrix should be used for analysis is discussed in a later section under "Assumptions and Other Topics." The reconstructed covariance or correlation matrix is compared with the original sample covariance or correlation matrix to see how different the two matrices are. If the difference is small, it is said that the model fits the data well; if the difference is large, the model will likely be rejected as fitting the data poorly.

Degrees of Freedom and Model Identification

In SEM analysis, the concept of degrees of freedom deserves specific discussion. In SEM, degrees of freedom are not based on sample size as is usually the case in most other statistical analyses. The degrees of freedom in SEM are the difference between the number of unique elements in the convariance matrix and the number of parameters to be estimated (i.e., the number of freed coefficients, the values of which are to be estimated based from sample data). In general, if we have k variables, the number of unique elements in the covariance matrix is equal to $k(k + 1) / 2$. The number of estimated parameters can be obtained by simply counting the number of freed paths in your model (e.g., Figure 2). The difference between the number of unique elements and the number of estimated parameters is the degrees of freedom for the analysis. Thus, the more free parameters, the lower the number of degrees of freedom for the analysis.

The discussion about degrees of freedom in SEM naturally leads to the issue of model identification. Model identification in SEM is one difficult issue. Without going into more technical details, we will simply say that model identification is concerned about whether or not a unique set of parameter values can produce the observed covariance matrix, or the data. In other words, model identification asks this question: Are all the parameters uniquely defined? A nonidentified model may have more than one, or even infinite number of, sets of parameters that can produce the same covariance matrix. Thus, there is not a unique solution to the problem.

It is difficult, or even impossible, to specify the sufficient conditions for model identification (Jöreskog & Sörbom, 1989; Long, 1983a). But the degrees of freedom in SEM does give us one indication about model specification, although such indication only constitutes one necessary condition for model specification. Put simply, in any SEM model, the number of independent parameters to be estimated cannot exceed the number of unique, or nonredundant, elements in the data covariance matrix. For example, if we have two variables, and we want to test a model with four independent parameters, the model is not identified because we only have three nonredundant elements in data covariance matrix. In this case, no solution exists for the model. This does not mean that the model is hopeless, however. One way to solve this problem is to constrain or fix some parameters in the model, if this is theoretically reasonable, so that the number of independent parameters will not exceed the number of nonredundant elements in the covariance matrix. In counting the number of independent parameters, the fixed and constrained parameters must be taken into account. If one parameter is fixed, it does not need estimation, thus it does not "consume" any degree of freedom. If one parameter is constrained to be equal to another, then these two parameters only consume 1 degree of freedom, instead of 2.

There exist other necessary conditions for model identification, such as rank condition, order condition, the condition for the covariance matrix being positive definite, and so forth (Jöreskog & Sörbom, 1989; Long, 1983). Interested readers may consult other sources for this difficult issue, for example, Long (1983a), Bollen and Jöreskog (1985), and Jöreskog and Sörbom (1989).

Model Testing

Although the concept of model testing in SEM sounds straightforward, in practice this is where a considerable degree of uncertainty and subjective judgment often arises. There is no universally accepted criterion to judge how well the model fits the data, thus leaving much room for subjective opinions, and consequently, disagreements.

The statistical significance test for CFA is the χ^2 test. The null hypothesis in SEM is that the model fits the data. So contrary to most other hypothesis testing situations, in SEM we want to see that the null hypothesis is not rejected, because the specified model represents our theoretical expectations about the data structure. However, as is well known, χ^2 significance testing is heavily influenced by sample size, and SEM usually requires relatively large sample sizes for the results to be valid (Bentler, 1992; Boomsma, 1987; Jöreskog & Sörbom, 1989). Thus, researchers using an SEM methodology are in a dilemma. On the one hand, we do not want to see our null hypothesis rejected. On the other hand, SEM requires a large sample size and the large sample contributes to the power of the χ^2 test, making it easy to reject our null hypothesis. Because of the power of the χ^2 test with large samples, it is not surprising that the χ^2 test may declare a model as having poor fit with the data, even if the reconstructed covariance matrix differs minimally from the original sample covariance matrix, and the model makes strong substantive sense.

Largely due to the dissatisfaction with the χ^2 test, other indices for assessing model fit have mushroomed, with a lack of consensus among researchers with regards to which one(s) should be consulted for decision making. To get a sense of this current state of affairs, we only need to look at what types of fit indices are provided by the three most influential programs for SEM: LISREL (Jöreskog & Sörbom, 1989), EQS (Bentler, 1992), and PROC CALIS procedure of SAS (SAS Institute, Inc., 1990).

It is important to note that the number of fit indices proposed by researchers and the number of fit indices provided by software packages is increasing rapidly. Therefore, rather than an exhaustive discussion of numerous fit indices, we briefly discuss a few of the earlier indices. LISREL programs have historically provided three basic indices for assessing model fit: Goodness of Fit Index (GFI), Adjusted Goodness of Fit Index (AGFI), and Root Mean Square Residual (RMS; Jöreskog & Sörbom, 1989). EQS provides Bentler–Bonett's Nonnormed Index and Bentler–Bonett's Normed Index (Bentler, 1992), among others. The SAS program PROC CALIS, the newest of the three, goes further. Besides the regular χ^2 test and the indices provided in both LISREL and EQS programs, CALIS provides a dozen more fit indices, including some newer ones such as the Parsimonious Index and two of Bollen's indices (Mulaik et al., 1989; SAS Institute, Inc., 1990). To provide more fit indices seems to be the trend of SEM softwares. For example, the newest LISREL version, LISREL 8, outputs substantially more fit indices than previous LISREL versions.

For most researchers without sophisticated statistical training, it is difficult to have a good understanding of all the differences and nuances among the available fit indices. It is generally advised that information from three sources should be synthesized to make reasonable judgment about the model fit: (a) χ^2 test results, (b) fit indices (GFI, AGFI, RMR from LISREL, Nonnormed and Normed Bentler–Bonett's indices from EQS), and (c) fitted covariance matrix residuals (the difference between original sample covariance matrix and the reconstructed covariance matrix). As pointed out by many authors (Bentler, 1985; Bentler & Bonett, 1980; Costner & Schoenberg, 1973; Jöreskog & Sörbom, 1989; Pedhazur & Schmelkin, 1991), solely relying on one index, especially relying on the χ^2 test, may cloud our judgment.

Some researchers have argued that the major goodness-of-fit indices fail to take into account the fact that in many cases, the less we know about our model, the better fit indices we tend to obtain. If little is known about the model under study, there is no way to specify our parameter estimates and the sample data is used to drive the estimation process. The result is a less rigorous theoretical model that, ironically, tends to have better fit indices. We always tend to obtain better fit indices by letting more parameters be estimated (freeing the parameters) instead of being specified by the researcher (fixed or constrained). In this situation, when we do obtain good model fit, it is unclear whether the fit has been achieved through correct model specification, through capitalizing on sample idiosyncracies (i.e., by freeing more parameters), or both.

To penalize for freeing too many parameters, or for not having a theoretically rigorous model, indices based on model parsimony were introduced (Mulaik et al., 1989). If both high fit indices and high parsimonious indices are obtained, we have confidence that the good fit of the model is not at the expense of freeing more parameters. So it is more likely that our model specification is correct. If, on the other hand, the discrepancy between the fit indices and parsimonious indices is too large, we are informed that there is the possibility that our good fit might have been achieved by freeing too many parameters, not necessarily through correct model specification.

The concept of parsimony has strong appeal. A model with more constraints is a more rigorous theoretical model in the first place. Furthermore, the more constraints we have on the model, the more likely that our solutions will be unique. If we can achieve good fit under more stringent conditions, we have more confidence that our model may be a correct one. The parsimonious indices can be particularly useful when competing theoretical models are being compared. If two or more theoretical models have been proposed, empirical data can be used to see which model provides a better fit to the data. Parsimony indices can be used to evaluate whether a theoretical model is considered "better" merely because it is less rigorous than an alternative proposed model.

A PRACTICAL APPLICATION PROBLEM

To exemplify the concepts discussed in the article thus far, a research example using CFA is presented. This example was chosen for both methodological and substantive reasons. First, methodologically, CFA is probably the most common application of SEM in the area of personality assessment, and therefore the methodology readers and researchers are most likely to use. Second, substantively, the debate continues in the personality literature about whether depression and anxiety should be considered to be two independent constructs, or if they should be treated as a single construct such as negative affectivity (for reviews, see Finch, Lipovsky, & Casat, 1989; Stavrakaki & Ellis, 1989). This CFA example empirically sheds some light on this substantive issue.

CFA is commonly used in investigating the structure of an assessment tool in two ways: testing whether individual items fit on a subscale, and testing whether subscales within or between measurement instrument(s) actually assess claimed latent construct(s) (e.g., do the Beck Depression Inventory and Scale 2 of the Minnesota Multiphasic Personality Inventory–2 both assess the same latent construct of "depression"?). Because of the large measurement error contained in single test items, modeling the relation between individual items and instrument subscales tends to be a more difficult task (Floyd & Widaman, 1995). Thus, for greater heuristic value, our example has been chosen so that the relation among subscale or total scores from different measures is the focus. The example was obtained from a recent article by Crowley and Emerson (1996) that investigated the relation between anxiety and depression in children.

CFA is particularly well suited to analytic questions such as that posed in the anxiety and depression literature. Two theoretical positions have been discussed extensively in the adult and child literature. One position asserts that there is a sufficiently high correlation between anxiety and depression; it states that they are not two separate constructs but a single construct, often labeled *negative affectivity*.

Conversely, other researchers argue that although the constructs of anxiety and depression overlap in that both include painful, dysphoric affect, each construct also has distinctive, unique distinctive features. These researchers assert that anxiety and depression should be considered as separate, but related, constructs. Thus, two competing models regarding the relation between anxiety and depression have been put forth, that is, that depression and anxiety should be treated as two separate constructs, or that they should be treated a single construct, negative affectivity. Using CFA, the two competing a priori models can be empirically investigated to see how well each model fits the data.

In this research example, CFA is applied to self-report data from a nonclinical sample of children. Measures employed to assess anxiety and depression were as follows: Children's Depression Inventory subscales (CDI; Kovacs, 1992), Reynolds Child Depression Scale (RCDS; Reynolds, 1989), Revised Children's Manifest Anxiety Scale subscales (RCMAS; Reynolds & Richmond, 1985), and the trait scale of the State–Trait Anxiety Inventory for Children (STAIC; Spielberger, 1973).

Model Specification

To begin addressing the substantive problem under study, the two theoretical relations between anxiety and depression must be translated into measurement models, one model having a single latent variable, negative affectivity, and the second model have two latent variables, anxiety and depression. Ten observed variables from self-report anxiety and depression inventories were used to conducted both analyses: CDI–negative mood, CDI–interpersonal problems, CDI–ineffectiveness, CDI–anhedonia, CDI–negative self-esteem, RCDS, STAIC–trait, RCMAS–worry, RCMAS–physiological, and RCMAS–concentration. In this example, the observed variables are all endogenous variables, whereas the latent variables are exogenous variables. Note that only the measurement model under SEM, which describes the relation between the measured variables and the latent variables, is being considered here.

The next step in model specification is to decide what variables should be fixed, free, or constrained. As shown in Table 1, the pattern of fixed and free variables is different for the two models under study. The parameters for all 10 observed variables are free to be estimated in the one-factor model. Only the variance of the latent variable is constrained to be 1.0. This constraint imposes an arbitrary measurement scale on the latent variable, which does not have a measurement scale of its own.

With the two-factor model, the pattern of fixed and free elements becomes slightly more complex. The observed variables assessing depression load on the latent variable depression, and their path values are free to be estimated from the data. Similarly, the observed variables assessing anxiety load on the anxiety latent variable, and their path values are estimated from the data. However, the depression

TABLE 1
Variable Idenfication for One- and Two-Factor Models

Observed Variable[a]	One Latent Variable	Two Latent Variables	
	Negative Affectivity	*Depression*	*Anxiety*
	Fixed/Free	*Fixed/Free*	*Fixed/Free*
CDI Negative Mood	Free	Free	Fixed
CDI Interpersonal Problems	Free	Free	Fixed
CDI Ineffective	Free	Free	Fixed
CDI Anhedonia	Free	Free	Fixed
CDI Negative Self-esteem	Free	Free	Fixed
RCDS	Free	Free	Fixed
STAIC Trait	Free	Fixed	Free
RCMAS Worry	Free	Fixed	Free
RCMAS Physiological	Free	Fixed	Free
RCMAS Concentration	Free	Fixed	Free

Latent Variable[b]	*Variable Label*	*Fixed/Free/Constrained*
One factor	Negative Affectivity	Constrained, variance = 1
Two factors[c]	Depression	Constrained, variance = 1
	Anxiety	Constrained, variance = 1

Note. CDI = Children's Depression Inventory; RCDS = Reynolds Child Depression Scale; STAIC = State–Trait Anxiety Inventory for Children; RCMAS = Revised Children's Manifest Anxiety Scale. [a]All observed variables are endogenous variables in these two models. [b]All latent variables are exogenous in these models. [c]The relationship (correlation) between the latent variables is free to be estimated from sample data.

variables are not allowed to load on the latent variable anxiety, so the path values are fixed to be zero (and are consequently not drawn in the model). The converse is true for the anxiety variables. Again, the variances of the latent variables are constrained to be 1.0. The correlation between the two latent variables is free to be estimated.

As previously stated, the error terms in SEM are directly estimated. In both the one- and two-factor models, the error terms are estimated from the data. However, the error terms are not allowed to correlate, thereby fixing the relation between error terms to zero. The one- and two-factor solutions are depicted in Figures 2 and 3, respectively.

Model Testing

Models for this study were fitted to the data through LISREL 7, and the analysis was based on the variance–covariance matrix (Cudeck, 1989) presented in Table 2. The "fit" of the model to the data was evaluated according to information from the three sources previously discussed: the χ^2 statistic, fit indices, and the fitted residuals. Additionally, path values and the fit of individual parameters are reviewed. For the purposes of comparison, both the one-factor and two-factor models are discussed with regard to each aspect of model fit.

Chi-square statistic. For the one-factor model, the χ^2 value was 272.52 with $df = 35$ ($p < .001$). The χ^2 value for the two-factor model was 112.02 with $df = 34$ ($p < .001$). Recall that the χ^2 statistic measures the error in the model and is interpretatively counterintuitive in that a statistically significant result means that

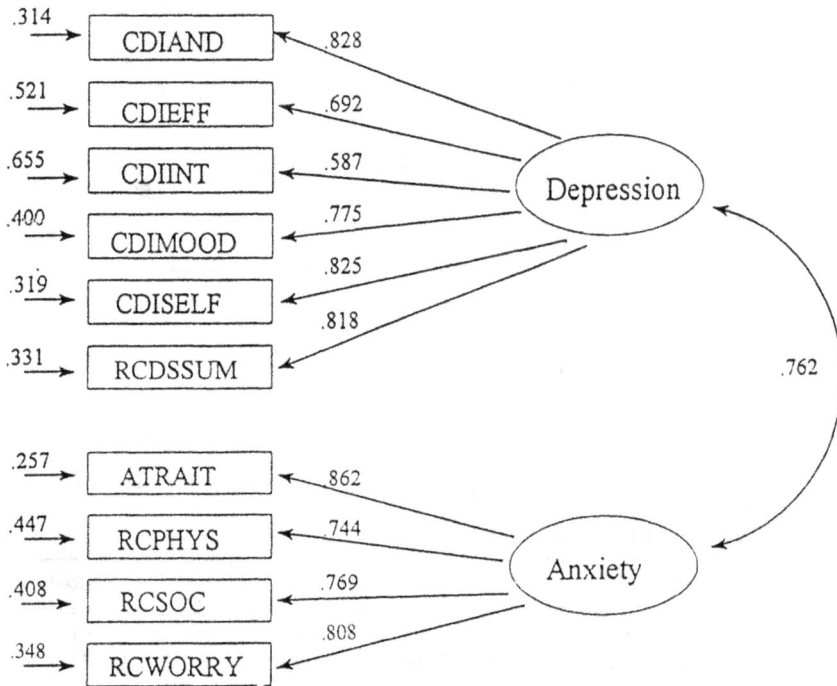

FIGURE 2   Two-factor model with parameter estimates.

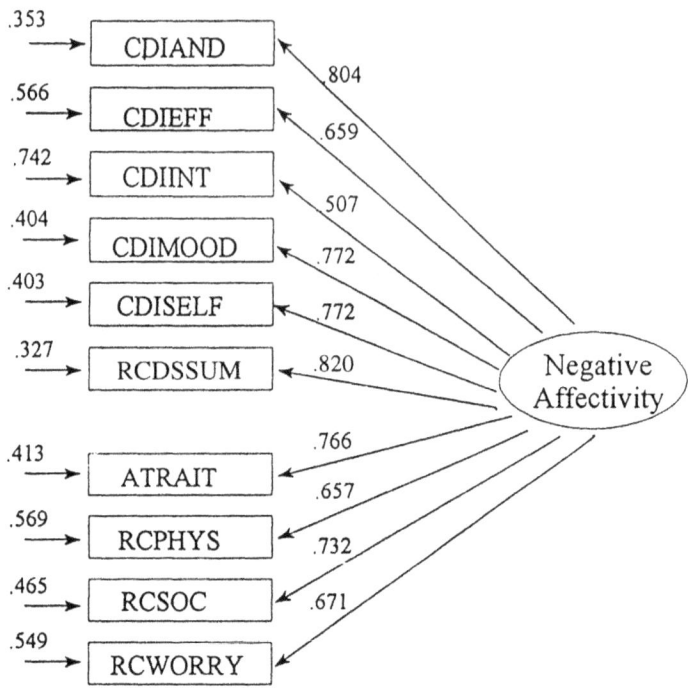

FIGURE 3   One-factor model with parameter estimates.

TABLE 2
Covariance Matrix of Self-Report Anxiety and Depression Scales

	1	2	3	4	5	6	7	8	9	10
1	5.886									
2	2.199	2.351								
3	1.421	.763	1.282							
4	2.820	1.436	.911	3.326						
5	2.767	1.602	1.129	1.949	2.910					
6	19.547	9.713	6.019	13.864	13.902	145.027				
7	10.669	5.215	2.100	8.741	6.824	60.956	64.297			
8	3.047	1.325	.573	1.987	1.780	14.366	12.578	5.919		
9	2.839	1.484	.480	2.034	1.745	15.069	10.602	2.777	4.340	
10	2.938	1.440	.550	2.446	1.837	16.522	15.304	4.054	3.582	7.26

Note. 1 = Children's Depression Inventory (CDI)–Anhedonia; 2 = CDI–Ineffectiveness; 3 = CDI–Interpersonal Problems; 4 = CDI–Negative Mood; 5 = CDI Negative Self-Esteem; 6 = Reynolds Child Depression Scale; 7 = State–Trait Anxiety Inventory for Children–Trait; 8 = Revised Children's Manifest Anxiety Scale (RCMAS)–Physiological; 9 = RCMAS–Concentration; 10 = RCMAS–Worry.

the model does not fit the data (e.g., that there is a statistically significant difference between the model and the data). In this example, both χ^2 values are statistically significant. The statistical significance may not be surprising to those using CFA in personality assessment, as most χ^2 results "achieve" statistical significance if the sample becomes large enough. Note that there is a difference in the degrees of freedom for the one- and two-factor analyses. As previously stated, the difference between the number of unique elements in the covariance matrix and the number of freed parameters is the degrees of freedom. For each analysis, there are 10 observed variables resulting in 55 unique elements (calculated by $10(10 + 1) / 2)$). The number of estimated parameters can be obtained by examining Figures 2 and 3. With the two-factor model, 21 parameters are estimated from sample data (i.e., 10 error terms, 10 path coefficients between observed and latent variables, and the path between the latent variables). Thus, there are 34 degrees of freedom (55 unique elements – 21 estimated coefficients) in the two-factor analysis. With the one-factor analyses, 20 parameters are estimated resulting in 35 degrees of freedom.

In judging whether one model is significantly better than another, Byrne (1989) noted that the change in χ^2 for nested models[1] can be considered. She states that "since the change in χ^2 is distributed as χ^2 with degrees of freedom equal to the difference in degrees of freedom between the two models, the significance of this value can be tested statistically" (pp. 58–59). The difference in χ^2 between the one- and two-factor models is 160.50 with 1 degree of freedom. This χ^2 difference is statistically significant at $p < .001$. Thus, the first piece of information used to assess model fit suggests that the two-factor model provides a better fit to the data.

Another approach often used to assess the results of the χ^2 tests is to compare the χ^2 value from the proposed model with the χ^2 results from a baseline model. Bentler (1992) suggested that the baseline χ^2 serves as a useful standard against which other models can be compared. Although baseline models can be specified in a variety of ways, for this study the baseline model proposed that each observed measure assessed a different latent construct. The χ^2 test result for the baseline model was 1654.53 ($df = 45, p < .001$). Both the one- and two-factor models provide a statistically significantly better fit to the data, with decreases in χ^2 value of 1382.01 and 1542.51, respectively. These results suggest that fewer latent variables improved model fit, but offers little in evaluating whether the one- or two-factor model would be "better."

---

[1]Two models are considered to be nested (or hierarchical) if one can be derived by imposing one or more constraint(s) on the other. In our example, the one-factor model is nested under the two-factor model. This is because in the two-factor model, the correlation between the two factors is free. But, if we constrain that correlation coefficient to be 1 ($r = 1.00$), statistically we get another model, that is, our one-factor model (see Loehlin, 1992, pp. 65–70 for more details on this topic).

Fit statistics. As previously noted, several authors have highlighted the limitations of the χ^2 statistic (e.g., Bentler, 1992; Byrne, 1989; Jöreskog, 1993), and a multitude of other fit indices have been developed to compensate for the influence of sample size on the χ^2 statistic. Interpretatively, fit indices generally range in value from 0 to 1.00, with higher values indicating a better fit. Although there is no absolute value with which one can state that the fit is acceptable, values larger than .90 are generally considered as suggesting a psychometrically acceptable model fit. In this study, the fit indices from LISREL (e.g., GFI and AGFI), as well as the Bentler–Bonnet fit index provided by the EQS program, and the parsimony index were all calculated.

Table 3 presents the fit statistics associated with the two models fitted to the data. Values for the fit indices for the one-factor model ranged from .636 for the parsimony index to .835 for the Bentler–Bonnet fit index. For the two-factor model, fit indices ranged from .618 for the parsimony index to .932 for the Bentler–Bonnet fit index. Not surprisingly, the parsimony index is the lowest for both models because relative to the number of observed variables, a large number of parameters were freed (i.e., estimated from the data in hand). Assessment of the fit indices also suggests that the two-factor model provides a better fit to the data in hand. The parsimony index for the two-factor model is lower, although similar in magnitude to the index for the one-factor model. For every other index, the two-factor model resulted in higher fit indices. Additionally, fit indices for the one-factor model are generally below the conventionally acceptable level. Based on fit indices, these results suggest that the two-factor model provides a better overall fit to the empirical data.

The overall fit of the model can be augmented by looking at the fit of individual parameter estimates. In the LISREL program, t values are provided for each parameter estimated in the model. EQS and CALIS both provide similar significance tests of individual model parameters. Parameters that do not achieve statistical significance are not significantly different from zero, and thus may suggest an area of model misspecification. In this example, assessment of the fit of individual

TABLE 3
Fit Statistics for One- and Two-Factor Models

	One-Factor Model	*Two-Factor Model*
Number of variables	10	10
Null χ^2	1654.53	1654.53
Model	272.52	112.02
Model *df*	35	34
Goodness-of-Fit Index	.778	.926
Adjusted Goodness-of-Fit Index	.651	.881
Parsimony Index	.636	.618
Bentler–Bonnet Index	.835	.932

parameter estimates provides limited information. Parameter estimates in both the one- and two-factor models all achieved statistical significance at the $p < .001$ level with t values ranging from 10.2 to 17.1 for the two-factor model, and ranging form 8.6 to 16.1 for the one-factor model.

Standardized residuals.   The standardized residuals identify the difference between the sample covariance matrix and the covariance matrix reconstructed based on the model fitted to the data. Residuals are standardized to circumvent the measurement scale differences for the variables involved, and are analogous to z scores. Byrne (1989) noted that standardized residuals greater than 2.00 or 3.00 are clues to identifying model misspecification. Essentially, a large standardized residual indicates a large discrepancy between the actual covariance between two observed variables and the reconstructed covariance based on the model.

For the one-factor model, the standardized residuals ranged from −5.104 to 7.523, with a median value of 0.00. In total, 20 residuals had absolute values greater than 3.0, with 8 large positive residuals and 12 large negative residuals. Standardized residuals for the two-factor model ranged from −4.762 to 4.255, again with a median of 0.00. Nine residuals were larger than 3.0 in absolute value, with 5 large negative residuals and 4 large positive residuals. Based on the standardized residuals, the two-factor model again fared better. There were fewer large residuals for the two-factor model as compared to the one-factor model, suggesting that the covariance matrix reconstructed from the two-factor model was closer to the sample covariance matrix. Of course, the greatest value in looking at the standardized residuals is to identify specific points of model misspecification. This information, although beyond the scope of this article, is particularly useful in suggesting problem areas in the theoretical model.

Path values.   The path values provided in the two figures are standardized coefficients ranging from 0.00 to 1.00, and can consequently be interpreted in a similar fashion as standardized regression coefficients, or beta weights. From the point of view of construct validity, the individual path coefficients are essentially reliability estimates of the observed variable, that is, how well each observed variable assesses the latent construct.

From the one-factor solution in Figure 2, all the measured variables assess the latent construct, negative affectivity, fairly well. The CDI Interpersonal Problems scale is the poorest indicator with a coefficient of .507, whereas the CDS summary score and the CDI Anhedonia scale are the best indicators with coefficients of .820 and .804, respectively.

Looking at the two-factor solution in Figure 3, we again see that the CDI Interpersonal Problems scale has the lowest path coefficient (.587) and, consequently, is a relatively poorer indicator of the latent construct "depression." Several path coefficients are greater than .80, including CDI Anhedonia, CDI Self-Efficacy,

RCDS Summary score, Trait Anxiety, and the RCMAS Worry Scale. These values suggest that these scales are reliable measures of the constructs in question, that is, anxiety and depression.

ASSUMPTIONS AND OTHER TOPICS

If applied appropriately, SEM, or its submodel CFA, can be a powerful analytic tool in personality research. Like other statistical techniques, appropriate application of SEM or CFA partially depends on whether or not some basic assumptions have been met. Three assumptions may warrant brief discussion here: multivariate normality, matrix to be analyzed, and sample size. Besides these three assumptions, some other relevant topics are discussed in this section.

Multivariate Normality

In application of SEM or CFA, the MLE method is the most widely used estimation procedure (e.g., it is the default for all major SEM softwares). ML assumes that the variables involved have a multivariate normal distribution. An extension of univariate normal distribution, discussion related to multivariate normal distribution can be found in books on multivariate analysis (e.g., Johnson & Wichern, 1988, pp. 120–162; Stevens, 1992, pp. 245–256). Procedures for assessing multivariate normality have been proposed, and some special computer programs for implementing these procedures have become available (e.g., Fan, 1996; Thompson, 1990).

The major reason for the normality assumption in the application of SEM or CFA is that ML is sensitive to departure from multivariate normality. When the assumption is not met, "the statistical basis of the method is lost and standard errors and chi square tests have little meaning" (Bentler, 1982, p. 421). When there is evidence that the data under study are multivariately nonnormal, two approaches can be taken (Byrne, 1994). First, estimation methods can be used which do not require multivariate normality (e.g., asymptotic distribution-free). Alternatively, the test statistic can be corrected to take the nonnormality into account (e.g., the Satorra–Bentler Scaled Statistic). When a corrected test statistic is used, standard errors that take the nonnormality into consideration are also computed.

Matrix to Be Analyzed

In the strict statistical sense, it is assumed that it is the covariance matrix that is being analyzed for the χ^2 test and the standard errors of the coefficients to be valid. This is primarily because the statistical theories for the estimation methods (e.g.,

MLE, GLS) were developed for covariance matrices, not correlation matrices. As pointed out by some researchers (Cudeck, 1989; Jöreskog & Sörbom, 1989; Loehlin, 1992), to analyze a correlation matrix may be problematic in several ways, such as unintentional alteration of the model being tested due to scale change caused by converting covariance matrix to correlation matrix, possible incorrect χ^2 test and other fit indices, and possible incorrect standard errors for parameter estimates. In practice, however, the correlation matrix is sometimes substituted for the covariance matrix to circumvent the interpretation problem caused by different measurement scales of the observed variables (Loehlin, 1992; Pedhazur & Schmelkin, 1991). This practice is deemed acceptable in some practical situations. Although the substitution of a correlation matrix for a covariance matrix may have certain interpretational advantages in some circumstances (Loehlin, 1992), this practice should be treated as the exception, rather than rule. Because the negative statistical consequences of analyzing a correlation matrix are not entirely clear in all situations, it would be well-advised that the covariance matrix should be analyzed whenever possible. Besides, the interpretational difficulty caused by different measurement scales when a covariance matrix is analyzed can partially be compensated for by producing a standardized solution. For more in-depth discussion about correlation or covariance matrices in SEM analysis, interested readers may consult Cudeck (1989), Lee (1985), and Jöreskog and Sörbom (1989).

In our experience, one practical situation where a researcher may attempt to use a correlation matrix is when initial values become necessary in specifying models. For the correlation matrix, reasonable initial values are much easier to specify due to the restricted range of possible values. A covariance matrix, on the other hand, may pose special problems because it tends to be much harder to provide reasonable initial values, due to unlimited range of variances and covariances.

To some extent, the interpretation problems posed by analyzing a covariance matrix are analogous to regression analysis where either unstandardized or standardized regression coefficients can be interpreted. More detailed discussion concerning the relative advantages and disadvantages of the two types of coefficients is readily available from some popular books (e.g., Loehlin, 1992, pp. 75–77; Pedhazur, 1982, chap. 17 & 18; Pedhazur & Schmelkin, 1991, p. 650).

Sample Size

Researchers using SEM or CFA in their analysis often face the dilemma related to sample size. As explained previously, in the application of SEM or CFA, the model fitted to the data represents a researcher's theoretical expectation about the data structure. So contrary to most research situations, it is desirable that the model is not rejected and statistical significance is not achieved. Like other statistical techniques, in fitting the model to data, the power to reject the null hypothesis (the model fits the data) increases as the sample size increases.

Statistical theory underlying SEM or CFA, on the other hand, is such that, for the χ^2 test to be valid, it is assumed that the sample size is sufficiently large. Although there is no agreed-upon criterion about what sample size is sufficient, 200 has been suggested as some kind of bottom-line number (Boomsma, 1987). Obviously, the sample size must also be considered in light of the complexity of the model and the number of parameters to be estimated, and 5 to 10 participants per estimated parameter has been suggested (Floyd & Widaman, 1995). However, generally, the larger the sample the more stable the parameter estimates. Nevertheless, the requirement for sufficiently large sample size in SEM or CFA creates a dilemma for researchers: Large sample size increases the power of the test, and consequently, minor discrepancies between sample data and the theoretical model will tend to be declared statistically significant.

Model Modification and Cross-Validation

In research practice, the model fitted to empirical data is often found to have poor fit. What should be done in this situation? Should the researcher's model be revised so as to obtain better fit? Indeed, it often becomes very tempting to modify the model for this purpose. Furthermore, computer programs routinely provide "modification indices" that pinpoint where changes should be made in the model so that the fit between the model and data can be improved. But before making any modifications for a theoretical model, it is important to understand the consequences of such post hoc model modification.

First, as discussed previously, a distinct advantage of SEM or CFA lies mainly in its confirmatory approach. Some authors have objected to such model modification practice, arguing that by so doing, the powerful confirmatory analysis of SEM is transformed into exploratory analysis; and we can always obtain better fit by continuously modifying our model, with or without the guidance of substantive theory (Cliff, 1983, 1987; Pedhazur & Schmelkin, 1991). In practice, however, it is often the case that there may be several competing substantive models. So it may be necessary to fit competing models in a study. In doing so, it is important to have model modification guided by substantive theory.

Second, any particular sample data set always contains some idiosyncracies. In fitting a theoretical model to empirical data, what we want to obtain is a model that will fit future similar data well, not just to obtain good fit for this particular sample. Put differently, researchers "want genuine improvement in measurement or theory, not just a procedure for decreasing chi-square in the *present* sample" (Loehlin, 1992, p. 187, italics added). If modifications are made that are based purely on sample data, rather than on theoretical considerations, it will be likely that the revised model may have capitalized on the idiosyncracies of the sample data; consequently, when tested against different sample data, the fit may decrease appreciably.

This discussion naturally leads to the topic of model validation. In research practice, if model modification based on sample data becomes necessary either due to statistical, or due to substantive considerations, it becomes imperative that after such modification, cross-validation procedures be carried out with independent sample data to make sure that sampling idiosyncracies are not driving the research results. Ideally, the cross-validation data should be collected from a new sample, but in practice, this is often not possible. However if the original sample is reasonably large, the model validation issue can be readily accommodated by randomly splitting the original sample into two independent data sets: one used for fitting the initial model and making necessary modifications, and the other used for testing the revised model.

Computer Programs for SEM

SEM, and its submodel CFA, can now be readily implemented using any of the major statistical packages available either in mainframe or PC versions. Although new programs are continually being developed, researchers new to SEM analyses will likely be best served by major commercial software that come with more extensive documentation and ancillary support materials, greater availability of third-party manuals, and support personnel to answer questions. Briefly, the three most widely used programs, LISREL, EQS, and PROC CALIS in SAS, will be reviewed.

LISREL (LInear Structure RELations), the pioneer program in the field, is available in both PC and mainframe version forms. In its PC version, LISREL can either be a stand-alone package, or it has historically been used as part of SPSS Window version. Relying on matrix algebra concepts, the LISREL program traditionally has a reputation of being somewhat esoteric. The newest version, LISREL 8, becomes much more user-friendly due to the addition of SIMPLIS, a much easier language for model specification. In some sense, due to its long history, its influence and popularity, LISREL almost becomes a synonym of SEM.

EQS, which was developed with the purpose of being more user-friendly than LISREL, is available through Multivariate Software as a PC Window version. The advantage of the EQS program is its easier model specification than LISREL, using a group of linear equations for the purpose. For those unfamiliar with matrix algebra, the EQS program may offer an easier start.

The PROC CALIS (Covariance Analysis of LInear Structures) procedure is part of regular SAS procedure that handles full SEM (SAS Institute, Inc., 1989). One advantage of PROC CALIS is its flexibility in specifying models. Four alternative methods can be used for the purpose, including one very similar to EQS.

SUMMARY

As originally stated, the purpose of this article was to offer a brief overview of SEM. For as many topics as have been reviewed, many others have not been discussed (e.g., recursive models, modeling latent variables, dealing with missing data). Although some limitations of SEM have already been reviewed (e.g., sample size), some final caveats regarding SEM are also warranted. First, SEM, like any other statistical technique, is merely a tool. It is up to the researcher to use the tool appropriately, and the results from an SEM analysis are not "truth," or definitive proof of the model in question. Secondly, it is important to remember that a great deal of researcher judgment is involved with specifying and testing a model, and those judgments should be made explicit. For the results to be judged accurately, authors need to include key pieces of information other than a causal diagram. Important elements include: the correlation or covariance matrix on which the analysis was based; the estimation procedure used; and explicit information on the pattern of fixed, free, and constrained elements (Biddle & Marlin, 1987). Finally, the trade-off for a powerful statistical tool like SEM is additional, often more restrictive, assumptions. Whether the data in hand can support any SEM analysis is a question each researcher must address.

REFERENCES

Bagozzi, R. P., Fornell, C., & Larcker, D. F. (1981). Canonical correlation analysis as a special case of structural relations model. *Multivariate Behavioral Research, 16,* 437–454.

Baldwin, B. (1989). A primer in the use and interpretation of structural equation models. *Measurement and Evaluation in Counseling and Development, 22,* 100–112.

Bentler. P. M. (1982). Confirmatory factor analysis via noniterative estimation: A fast, inexpensive method. *Journal of Marketing Research, 19,* 417–424.

Bentler, P. M. (1985). *Theory and implementation of EQS. A structural equations program.* Los Angeles: BMDP Statistical Software.

Bentler, P. M. (1992). EQS: Structural equations program manual. Los Angeles: BMDP Statistical Software.

Bentler, P. M. (1994). Forward. In B. M. Byrne, *Structural Equation Modeling with EQS and EQS/Windows* (pp. vii–ix). Thousand Oaks, CA: Sage.

Bentler, P. M., & Bonett, D.G. (1980). Significance tests and goodness of fit in the analysis of covariance structures. *Psychological Bulletin, 88,* 588–606.

Biddle, B. J., & Marlin, M. M. (1987). Causality, confirmation, credulity, and structural equation modeling. *Child Development, 58,* 4–17.

Bollen, K. A. (1989). *Structural equations with latent variables.* New York: Wiley.

Bollen, K. A., & Jöreskog, K. G. (1985). Uniqueness does not imply identification. *Sociological Methods & Research, 14,* 144–163.

Bollen, K. A., & Long, J. S. (1993). Introduction. In K. A. Bollen & J. S. Long (Eds.), *Testing structural equation models* (pp. 1–9). Newbury Park, CA: Sage.

Boomsma, A. (1987). The robustness of maximum likelihood estimation in structural equation models. In P. Cuttance & R. Ecob (Eds.), *Structural modeling by example: Applications in educational, sociological, and behavioral research* (pp. 160–188). New York: Cambridge University Press.

Byrne, B. (1989). *A primer of LISREL: Basic applications and programming for confirmatory factor analytic models.* New York: Springer-Verlag.

Byrne, B. M. (1994). *Structural equation modeling with EQS and EQS/Windows: Basic concepts, applications, and programming.* Newbury Park, CA: Sage.

Cliff, N. (1983). Some cautions concerning the application of causal modeling methods. *Multivariate Behavioral Research, 18,* 115–126.

Cliff, N. (1987). *Analyzing multivariate data.* San Diego, CA: Harcourt Brace Jovanovich.

Costner, H. L., & Schoenberg, R. (1973). Diagnosing indicator ills in multiple indicator models. In A. S. Goldberger & O. D. Duncan (Eds.), *Structural equation models in the social sciences* (pp. 167–199). New York: Academic.

Crowley, S. L., & Emerson, E. N. (1996). Discriminant validity of self-reported anxiety and depression in children: Negative affectivity or independent constructs? *Journal of Clinical Child Psychology, 25,* 139–146.

Cudeck, R. (1989). Analysis of correlation matrices using covariance structure models. *Psychological Bulletin, 105,* 317–327.

Duncan, O. D. (1975). *Introduction to structural equation models.* New York: Academic.

Fan, X. (1996). A SAS program for assessing multivariate normality. *Educational and Psychological Measurement, 56,* 668–674.

Finch, A. J., Jr., Lipovsky, J. A., & Casat, C. D. (1989). Anxiety and depression in children and adolescents: Negative affectivity or separate constructs? In P. C. Kendall & D. Watson (Eds.), *Anxiety and depression: Distinctive and overlapping features* (pp. 171–202). San Diego, CA: Academic.

Fish, L. J. (1986). Why multivariate methods are usually vital. *Measurement and Evaluation in Counseling and Development, 21,* 130–137.

Floyd, F. J., & Widaman, K. F. (1995). Factor analysis in the development and refinement of clinical assessment instrument. *Psychological Assessment, 7,* 286–299.

Gorsuch, R. L. (1983). *Factor analysis.* Hillsdale, NJ: Lawrence Erlbaum Associates, Inc.

Johnson, R. A., & Wichern, D. W. (1988). *Applied multivariate statistical analysis* (2nd ed.). Englewood Cliffs, NJ: Prentice Hall.

Jöreskog, K. G. (1993). Testing structural equation models. In K. A. Bollen & J. S. Long (Eds.), *Testing structural equation models* (pp. 294–316). Newbury Park, CA: Sage.

Jöreskog, K. G., & Sörbom, D. (1989). *LISREL 7: A guide to the program and application.* Chicago: SPSS.

Kovacs, M. (1992). *Children's Depression Inventory manual.* North Tonawanda, NY: Multi-Health Systems.

Lee, S.-Y. (1985). Analysis of covariance and correlation structures. *Computational Statistics and Data Analysis, 2,* 279–295.

Loehlin, J. C. (1992). *Latent variable models: An introduction to factor, path, and structural analysis.* Hillsdale, NJ: Lawrence Erlbaum Associates, Inc.

Long, J. S. (1983a). *Confirmatory factor analysis* [Sage university paper series on Quantitative Applications in the Social Sciences, 07–033]. Newbury Park, CA: Sage.

Long, J. S. (1983b). *Covariance structure models. An introduction to LISREL.* Newbury Park, CA: Sage.

Mulaik, S. A., James, L. R., Van Alstine, J., Bennett, N., Lind, S., & Stilwell, C. D. (1989). Evaluation of goodness-of-fit indices for structural equation models. *Psychological Bulletin, 105,* 430–445.

Pedhazur, E. J. (1982). *Multiple regression in behavioral research: Explanation and prediction* (2nd ed.). New York: Harcourt Brace.

Pedhazur, E. J., & Schmelkin, L. P. (1991). *Measurement, design, and analysis: An integrated approach.* Hillsdale, NJ: Lawrence Erlbaum Associates, Inc.

Reynolds, W. M. (1989). *Reynolds Child Depression Scale.* Odessa, FL: Psychological Assessment Resources.

Reynolds, C. R., & Richmond, B. O. (1985). *Revised Children's Manifest Anxiety Scale.* Los Angeles: Western Psychological Services.

SAS Institute, Inc. (1989). *SAS/STAT user's guide* (Version 6, 4th ed., Vol. 1). Cary, NC: Author.

SAS Institute, Inc. (1990). *SAS/STAT user's guide* (Version 6, 4th ed., Vol. 1). Cary, NC: Author.

Spielberger, C. D. (1973). *The State–Trait Anxiety Inventory for Children.* Palo Alto, CA: Consulting Psychologists Press.

Stavrakaki, C., & Ellis, J. (1989). The relationship of anxiety to depression in children and adolescents. *Psychiatric Clinics of North America, 12,* 777–789.

Stevens, J. (1992). *Applied multivariate statistics for the social sciences* (2nd ed.). Hillsdale, NJ: Lawrence Erlbaum Associates, Inc.

Thompson, B. (1990). MULTINOR: A fortran program that assists in evaluating multivariate normality. *Educational and Psychological Measurement, 50,* 845–848.

17

Exploratory Factor Analysis: Its Role in Item Analysis

Richard L. Gorsuch
Graduate School of Psychology
Fuller Theological Seminary

The special characteristics of items—low reliability, confounds by minor, unwanted covariance, and the likelihood of a general factor—and better understanding of factor analysis means that the default procedure of many statistical packages ("Little Jiffy") is no longer adequate for exploratory item factor analysis. It produces too many factors and precludes a general factor even when that means the factors extracted are nonreplicable. More appropriate procedures that reduce these problems are presented, along with how to select the sample, sample size required, and how to select items for scales. Proposed scales can be evaluated by their correlations with the factors; a new procedure for doing so eliminates the biased values produced by correlating them with either total or factor scores. The role of exploratory factor analysis relative to cluster analysis and confirmatory factor analysis is noted.

Exploratory factor analysis (EFA) has been widely used as a technique to develop scales and subscales. For example, using the terms "factor analysis" and "item" for a *Psychological Abstracts* search for 1990–1995 suggested that 400 to 500 studies used factor analysis with items; of these about 75% used EFA.

The several situations in which EFA may be helpful with items are explored in the first section of this article, where its relation to classical, simple scale development is outlined. A brief comparison of the role of EFA in relation to cluster and confirmatory factor analysis (CFA) is also made.

The second major section of this article, "Decision Making for Item Factor Analysis," addresses the practical details of the use of factor analysis with item data. It begins with a discussion of the special problems of factoring items and why the standard factor analytical procedure—principal components extraction with Varimax rotation (the standard default option in most computer packages and referred to as "Little Jiffy")—can produce misleading results with items. This section then speaks to several practical questions: What type of sample of items?

309

How large a sample size? Is component or common factor analysis best? How many factors? Which rotation? How, then, are items selected for scales? We shall find that the last 20 years have clarified some of these questions so that some answers given in, for example, Gorsuch (1974) and Nunnally (1967) are now out-of-date and can no longer be recommended. This section is designed to merge the worthwhile older conclusions with more recent knowledge. The last section of this article is a set of conclusions.

FACTOR AND ITEM ANALYSES

The goal of item analysis is to select those items that are most related to the construct. This goal is aided by evaluating how each item relates to its own construct, as well as how it relates to other associated or similar constructs. Each construct is understood to be unidimensional. The desired result is that all items measuring the same construct are scored together to give the best estimate of each person's score on that construct.

The purpose of factor analysis is to identify the fewest possible constructs needed to reproduce the original data. Mathematically, it seeks the set of equations that maximize the multiple correlations of the factors to the items. The equation for each item is:

$$i_1 = p_{1A} A + p_{1B} B + p_{1C} C + \ldots + u_1$$

(1)

where i is the response to Item 1; A, B, and C are the factor scores (the "...") indicating there may be more factors), the ps are the weights used to best reproduce the original standardized Item 1 responses, and u is the residual for Item 1 when the fit is not perfect. There are as many equations as there are items. Note the emphasis on reproducing the original item responses; all equations for factoring data are derived from the aforementioned equation (Gorsuch, 1983) and so are directly linked to the original data. This is an important theoretical difference from, for example, cluster analysis.

The relations of each variable to each of the factors tells whether the item is related to only one of the factors (constructs) or to more than one. Those items most clearly related to only one factor can then be recommended as a scale for the construct underlying that factor. Using the results of the factor analysis helps achieve the goals of item analysis in several ways. First, it provides information on the constructs. Is there only one? If so, then a single factor will, assuming no methodological problems, result. Is there more than one construct among the pool of items? If so, there will be one factor for each construct. The correlations of each item with each factor allow for selection of the best items.

Common methods for evaluating an item are special cases of factor analysis. Correlating each item with the total score from the set of items and then selecting those items with the highest item-total correlations is a special case of factor analysis. The total score is the general factor—technically a centroid factor with the items weighted as a function of their standard deviations—and the item-total correlations are the ps in Equation 1.

As an illustration of item analysis with one factor, analyses of the first six items of the Beck Depression Scale (BDI; Beck, Ward, Mendelson, Mock, & Erbaugh, 1961) were computed from Lee's (1995) data. The first six items were chosen so that the total score from all items could be considered the item domain. Item domain correlations are therefore available against which to compare the several procedures. These correlations are in the first column of Table 1.

The second and third columns of Table 1 give the usual item-total and item-remainder correlations. The former are, as expected, inflated because each item is correlated with its own error as well as the common variance among the items. The item-remainder are too low because only five items do not give a good, reliable estimate of the domain.

The last two columns of Table 1 give component and common factor correlations. Component analysis gives inflated loadings (see also Snook & Gorsuch, 1989), and so is not recommended. Common factor analysis gives the best estimate of the domain correlations.

Another special case in traditional item analysis occurs when a set of ability items, for example, are scored to measure two constructs, verbal and numerical abilities. To evaluate the items, each item is correlated with the sum of the verbal items and the sum of the numerical items. The items selected for a revised scale are those that correlate well with one of the scores but not the other (e.g., verbal items correlating with the verbal scale score but not the numerical scale score). This is

TABLE 1
Item Analysis Correlation by Traditional and Factor Analyses (One Dimension)

				Factor Analysis	
Item	Item-Domain	Item-Total	Item-Remainder	Component[a]	Common
1.	.55	.63	.45	.65	.55
2.	.49	.51	.36	.55	.44
3.	.56	.69	.46	.68	.58
4.	.64	.71	.49	.70	.61
5.	.45	.59	.41	.61	.49
6.	.44	.61	.35	.55	.43

[a]Also known as "Little Jiffy," and the default in most statistical packages.

technically a multiple group factor analysis with one centroid factor for each construct. Equation 1 could be solved by using multiple regression to estimate the item scores from the verbal and numerical factor scores.

Both of the aforementioned examples defined the factors by adding together a preidentified set of items (e.g., the verbal items or the numerical items). In traditional item analysis, the definition of the factor is only as good as the judgment of the investigator as to which items are to be added together. At this point, factor analysis offers an improvement. Instead of basing the factors on investigator judgment, it bases each factor on a set of highly correlated items. Hence, misjudgments about what items measure are less likely to distort the operationalization of the construct. Additionally, new constructs may emerge that the investigator did not realize were being measured. Such new constructs might be variations of the original constructs by which the item pool was built or contaminants that may otherwise have gone unnoticed. In either case, the investigator needs this information to properly evaluate the items.

For example, most scales are designed to measure just one construct, to be homogeneous. It is often incorrectly assumed that a measure of internal consistency (e.g., coefficient alpha) provides a means to address this question. However, it is easy to design a set of items that measure more than one independent construct and yet produce a coefficient alpha of .9 or better when scored as if they measured only one construct. Factor analysis provides a better means of examining scale homogeneity.

In traditional item analysis, potential scales are evaluated by trying out subsets of items. Thus the three items with the highest correlations are scored and correlated with the total item set, then the best four items, and so on. However, this common procedure has the same problem as item-total correlations. The fact of the item being in both the scale and the total produces an inflated correlation. Consider an extreme case where the item-domain correlations are all 0.0; a 3-item scale correlates .72 with the total from six items and a 4-item scale correlates .82. The latter is higher than the former solely because the fourth item is included in the total score, and all correlations appear important because of the built-in bias to which item-total and scale-total correlations are heir.

A new factor analytic procedure (Gorsuch, 1997) is now available for the problem just noted. It uses the same common factor approach that makes the item-common factor correlations better estimates of the item-domain correlations than either item-total or item-remainder correlations, but the correlations of proposed scales with the factor(s) are unaffected by any item being both in a proposed scale and in the factor analysis. Items too exploratory to be in the original total/remainder scores can be evaluated by this extension analysis without the bias favoring the items in the total score.

EFA can also be used with the confirmatory and cluster techniques discussed later. Roth and Roychoudhury (1991) did so and noted that many of the conclusions of factor analysis and clustering were the same, but they had more confidence that the results were independent of the methodology by including the factor analysis.

CONFIRMATORY FACTOR ANALYSIS

CFA requires clear predictions as to which factors exist, how they relate to the variables, and how they relate to each other. Without such predictions, exploratory analyses are needed. Of course, factor analysis can be used as a purely exploratory technique. This can occur when a set of items are developed to represent an area of interest with the sampling being broad and without specific subareas. The question addressed is whether one scale, one scale that can be subscaled, or a set of scales is needed in the area. Techniques recommended later (but not the "Little Jiffy" solution) can readily decide between such options.

EFA can also be used as an adjunct to CFA. Exploratory methods may be valuable in a preliminary study to focus hypotheses for the confirmatory analyses. It may also be useful as a follow-up in a confirmatory structural modeling analysis. Because of the stringent requirements for excellent hypotheses and data (see Gorsuch, 1996), many confirmatory structural model analyses fail to provide clear results—the chi-square of the residuals is still significant, an improper solution occurs, or the correlations between factors are too high. Often adjustments are subsequently made to the structural equations model to "cure" the problem, but such exploratory adjustments are dangerous for two reasons. First, the probabilities are no longer accurate but can be much smaller than they should be due to capitalization on chance. Second, MacCallum (1986) found that with Ns of 300 and only one or two adjustments needed, only half of the adjustments were toward the population values. The results were worse with Ns less than 300. (Rumor has it that most published CFAs have had adjustments made and so should have no significance levels reported; most of these adjustments do not seem to be reported.) In the situation when the CFA does not work, an EFA is an appropriate alternative to attempting to adjust the confirmatory model.

Note that confirmatory analysis comes in several types. An argument can be made that confirmatory multiple group factor analysis is one of the most useful approaches for items (Bernstein, Jaremko, & Hinkley, 1994, 1995; Bernstein & Keith, 1991; Gorsuch, 1974, 1983; Nunnally & Bernstein, 1994). It is much less prone to the problems noted earlier with confirmatory structural equations modeling.

EFA is also used for confirmatory purposes. First, it is conceptually a "multi-tailed" test as compared to CFA being conceptually a "one-tailed" test. If the same factors appear again in another exploratory analysis, they would surely—except for the limitations of structural modeling CFA—occur in a confirmatory analysis. Second, the test of whether a particular factor replicated is given only indirectly in most confirmatory structural modeling factor analyses. Generally there is no way of determining the degree of replication of any one factor. But the correlation of each exploratory factor as found in the first EFA with each factor in a second exploratory analysis is readily calculated, tested for significance, and interpreted (Gorsuch, 1996, in press).

CLUSTER ANALYSIS

Although cluster analysis is sometimes used instead of factor analysis, the limitations of cluster analysis in comparison to factor analysis are several. First, it has no direct link to the raw scores like factor analysis has (see Equation 1). Instead it is generally—there are many variants—a method of grouping objects that have high coefficients of similarity. The coefficients could be correlations or distance measures. This provides versatility, but also moves a step away from the data. Earlier, the basic equation of factor analysis was shown to be directly based on the item scores, just as is multiple regression, analysis of variance, and other common statistical procedures.

Second, cluster analysis has no built-in method for identifying the most parsimonious set of clusters. A four-cluster solution may be found when there are only three factors, making the data look more complex than would a factor analysis.

Third, the usual requirement that an object be either in or out of a cluster oversimplifies most results. Instead, a factor analysis provides the correlation of each item with each factor, and the complexity of the item (as determined by its pattern of loadings across factors) is useful in item rewriting or selection (see later). This information is lost in a cluster analysis.

DECISION MAKING IN ITEM FACTOR ANALYSIS

Special Problems of Item Analyses

Given that traditional item analyses are special cases of factor analysis, why not just use the same methods of factor analysis for items as are used for scales? This is certainly done, but the methods of factor analysis were developed for analysis of scales. Items have different properties that require special factor analytic techniques to avoid misleading results, as is shown in following examples (cf. Cattell, 1957, for an early discussion of the problems.)

Items differ from scales in four ways that influence a factor analysis. The differences and their impacts are:

1. Items have lower reliabilities than scales. This is a major reason why we develop scales. Adding together a set of items with low reliabilities averages out the error of the items while combining the shared variance. For example, consider

a 20-item scale with an internal consistency reliability of .8. Using the Spearman–Brown correction formula to "work backwards," the reliability of a 1-item scale is estimated to be .17! A population correlation of .9 for the latent measure perfectly measured would have a population correlation of .81 for the scale, but only .37 for the "average" item. If the N were 100, the observed correlation for the scale could be .7 and .9 in two samples, whereas the same observed correlation for the average item would, due to lower reliabilities, be .27 and .47. The variation of observed correlations across typical samples would be approximately 12% for the scale but approximately 27% for the item, for a N of 100. This means item correlations are lower and more difficult to work with than scale correlations. Because items correlate lower than scales, the factors are weaker with a higher percentage of the covariations being error.

2. Items often contain confounding variance in addition to the construct being measured. For example, one item of the BDI addresses the symptom of crying. This item thus contains possible gender specific information that may be unrelated to the question of whether the person is depressed. Almost every item of every scale has a word or phrase that may be interpreted by someone in an idiosyncratic manner. Scales avoid these minor confounds by adding across the confounds found in multiple items to average them out.

3. Item distributions often differ from each other, in part deliberately. These differences may be in either skew or kurtosis. To measure all variations of a construct well, it is necessary to have items with means that vary across values of the response range. The items with means at the extremes usually have skewed distributions. The skewed distributions impact the correlations because a correlation can only be high and positive if the two items being correlated have the same distributions. Different distributions among the items, therefore, reduce the correlations among the items. Scales sum across items, thus averaging the distributions. As a result, scales generally show higher intercorrelations than items do.

Factors produced by different distributions have been traditionally called *difficulty factors*. For example, in analyses of ability scales, it is commonly found that the least difficult items and the most difficult items form separate factors. The factors result from the fact that easy items are positively skewed (and difficult items negatively skewed) and so correlate more highly than they do with difficult items not sharing that skew.

4. Item scores are almost always a set of ordered categories rather than a continuous value. The categories may be "correct" or "incorrect," as in ability tests, or a range of responses as in a 5- or 7-category response scale ranging from *strongly disagree* to *strongly agree*. Because there are not a large number (e.g., 100) of points on the response scale, item scores can only reflect major differences among individuals on the underlying construct. Any 50 people with an item score of 5 will still have some differences on the underlying construct, and another item may distinguish between them. These two items then correlate lower than they would

be if both were measured as continuous variables. (Because total scale scores reflect the sums of the component item scores, scales have many more possible scores and so function more like continuous variables.)

The number of response options has an impact on item distributions. When only two responses are allowed—correct or incorrect, or yes/no—the skew can be great. This problem is not eliminated by the use of tetrachoric correlations, which introduce new problems. (See Comrey & Lee, 1992, and Nunnally & Bernstein, 1994, who recommend regular correlations over tetrachoric or biserial correlations.) With multiple-point response scales (e.g., 7 points ranging from *strongly disagree* to *strongly agree*), item means can vary with a greater likelihood of a less skewed distribution, all other things being equal, but skew problems often exist.

Bernstein and Teng (1989) discussed the problems of item distribution and item categorization and their implications for item factor analysis. They also discussed another potential problem. As more categories to the response option are added, a distribution difference that was previously obscured may be produced and reduce the correlation between items. For example, one item may have a 50/50 split by a normal distribution being cut in half. Another may have a 50/50 split by being cut at the median but be heavily skewed or have a nonnormal kurtosis. The two category versions of the items can correlate 1.0 but multiple category items (and continuous items) cannot correlate 1.0. Nevertheless, more categories of response do provide more information and can be generally expected to give higher correlations.

The impact of different distributions in item analysis can be easily demonstrated by factoring a perfect Guttman scale of 20 items using a Yes/No answer format. In such a scale, each item does exactly what it is supposed to do: it separates the respondents into two halves based on the underlying latent variable. Each item is perfectly reliable. The items also form a perfect Guttman scale in the sense that (a) each item has a different mean so that they, as a set, measure the entire range and (b) they are cumulative (i.e., if a person answers "Yes" to Item 3, then that person will have answered "Yes" to Items 1 and 2 also). The data set consists of five people at each of the possible scores, from 0 (no item answered "Yes") to 20 (all items answered "Yes"), for a total N of 105.

The results of the standard "Little Jiffy" analysis are presented in Table 2. The items are ordered from the highest percentage to the lowest percentage answering "Yes." Four uncorrelated factors were extracted despite the fact that each item measures exactly the same thing! The problem is that the conditions needed for "Little Jiffy" to be applicable were ignored. The "Little Jiffy" procedure is applicable to highly reliable variables with the same distributions with strong correlations from several uncorrelated domains. The different distributions of items in a perfect Guttman scale result in items of similar distributions correlating more highly together than they do with items of dissimilar distributions. These different patterns

TABLE 2
"Little Jiffy" of a Perfect Guttman Scale

Items	Factors			
	1	*2*	*3*	*4*
1.	.82	.06	.13	−.02
2.	.87	.26	.11	.03
3.	.78	.46	.09	.07
4.	.64	.63	.09	.10
5.	.49	.76	.12	.12
6.	.35	.83	.18	.12
7.	.24	.86	.27	.11
8.	.15	.84	.38	.09
9.	.10	.78	.49	.08
10.	.07	.69	.61	.08
11.	.06	.58	.71	.09
12.	.06	.47	.80	.12
13.	.08	.35	.85	.18
14.	.10	.24	.86	.27
15.	.11	.15	.83	.38
16.	.11	.09	.74	.52
17.	.09	.07	.61	.66
18.	.06	.07	.44	.80
19.	.02	.10	.23	.88
20.	−.03	.12	.04	.82

of correlations were interpreted by "Little Jiffy" to mean that different factors were being measured. Note that each item loads the same factor as other items with similar means and therefore similar distributions, producing technical rather than substantive factors.

Each of the following sections explain how to take item characteristics into account when conducting an item factor analysis. General presentations of factor analysis that are consistent with this exposition have been presented by Gorsuch (1983) and Nunnally and Bernstein (1994).

Sample of Items

From the aforementioned discussion, it is apparent that items that are more like scales are better for factoring. They should be highly reliable, measure only one construct, and have the same distributions as produced by a continuous response scale. But if we had perfect items, who would need scales? The point is that the items should be selected to be closer to the ideal rather than farther from it. The easiest component to manipulate in this regard is the scale for responses. With the possible exception of ability measures, or to meet needs for ease of administration or scoring, response options limited to two or three categories should be replaced with seven or more response categories. This is particularly important if the items are selected, as they should be, so that the means are systematically different.

It is always wise to pretest a set of possible items; if an item shows a strange distribution, it can then be rewritten to avoid the response category/distribution interaction noted by Bernstein and Teng (1989). The item selection has a major impact on what type of rotation is appropriate, as discussed later.

Not all the items need be in the factor analysis itself. Only those items that clearly help define the domain are in the factor analysis. If desired, the analysis may be extended to additional items not in the factor analysis. Extension analysis (Gorsuch, 1997) gives the correlations of the nonfactored items with the factors. For example, the factor analysis may be restricted to the classical set of items used in past literature to evaluate replicability of past factors. Then a new set of items are also evaluated to improve measurement by replacing some of the original items or by adding more items to increase the length of the scales. The new items would be in the extension analysis.

Sample of Respondents

The two issues to be confronted with regard to a sample of participants are the type of respondent and the size of the sample. The sample should consist of people similar to those with whom the scale will be ultimately used. For evaluating anxiety in everyday life, the sample should be of people in everyday life. For evaluating depression in patients being treated in an outpatient mental health clinic, the sample should consist of mental health clinic outpatients. Lee (1995), for example, sampled Korean students because the scales he evaluated are frequently used in student counseling centers.

Any analysis is enhanced if the sample has a wide variety of people. There should be many who would score low on the proposed scale(s) and many who would score high. The sample need not closely represent any clearly identified population so long as those who would score high and those from that population who would score low are well represented.

The sample size needed was in former times given as a function of the number of items (e.g., 10 cases for every item). This was a recommendation proposed largely out of ignorance rather than theory or research. We now have information for EFA from several sources suggesting that the "10-case-per-item" rule sets the sample size above the minimum needed. Cattell (personal communication, 1950) found the same factors in a small sample size as in a larger sample size even when the smaller sample size was less than twice the number of variables. Guadagnoli and Velicer (1988) used a simulation study to evaluate the stability of results across several conditions. They concluded that a N of 150 was sufficient for up to 40 or 50 variables (they did not investigate more variables), which is a ratio of 3 to 1 rather than the 10 to 1 formerly suggested. Reddon (1990) evaluated the sample size necessary to be able to extract any factors from a correlation matrix and reached a similar conclusion.

The general current conclusion is that the sample size needed is a function of the stability of a correlation coefficient without any correction needed for the number of variables, at least for situations of up to 40 or 50 variables. The stability of a correlation is a function of the square root of the sample size. To reduce by half the impact of error, the square root of the sample size would need to double. Thus if the N were 100, the error would be halved with a N of 400. To halve it again would require a N of 1600. A better sense of the needed precision can be gained from considering the expected size of the correlations among items. Note that if two items both are loaded by the same factor at .5, then their expected correlation is .25. Hence a sample size for which a .25 would be highly significant should be chosen; this is approximately 125. This is similar to the N of 150 that the aforementioned studies suggest is probably sufficient if there are clear sets of highly significant correlations.

The lower the expected correlations, the greater the sample size needed for the factors to stand out from the error variance. If loadings of .4 are of interest, then the expected correlation between two variables loaded by the same factor is .16 and a N of 300 is needed. For most item analyses of previously untested items, the traditional item analysis recommendation of 300 is also a good one for item factor analysis.

What of item analyses with more items than 50? The crucial issue here is not so much the number of items but rather the number of decisions that will be made and the level of selection at which they will be made. Picking the 10 items with the highest correlations with a factor has little capitalization on chance with a total item pool of only 11, but considerable capitalization on chance with an item pool of 100 from which to choose the 10. This requires an increase in the sample size; large sample sizes always help.

There is a check on whether the sample size is clearly too small for the factors extracted: Bartlett's significance test (Gorsuch, 1983). It is based on the eigenvalues of the correlation matrix and tests whether a residual matrix is significant after a given number of factors has been extracted. Any factor of interest should be highly significant by this test. Most item factor analyses with at least 200 to 300 cases can be assumed to be significant but the test should be computed on smaller sample sizes as a safeguard. Borderline sample sizes should not be rejected out-of-hand, for capitalization on chance is influenced by other factors than just the sample size. For example, if the item-factor correlations are high, a smaller sample size will give higher quality results than if the correlations are low. Both Type I and Type II error rates should be considered important. The final criterion for the needed sample sizes, however, is that of replicability. With borderline sample sizes, decent cross-validation of the factor structure needs to be demonstrated.

Component Analysis Versus Common Factor Analysis

Within the factor analysis paradigm one can distinguish between principal component and common factor analysis. Gorsuch (1983) proved that they vary only in that common factor analysis has the last element of Equation 1, an error term, and principal component analysis does not. Using the latter assumes that the variables are conceptualized as reproduced perfectly by the factors. Perfect reproduction generally means that the variables are almost perfectly reliable and correlate highly with at least one other variable. From our theoretical analysis of items, we concluded that items are unlikely to be highly reliable and may contain more than one factor. Error is also introduced by distribution and categorization problems. Hence, including the last element of Equation 1 is appropriate for item analysis, and so common factor analysis is preferred.

There is considerable support for using principal component analysis despite its theoretical inappropriateness (cf. the special issue of *Multivariate Behavioral Research,* Vol. 25, No. 1, 1990). The reasons appear to be four-fold. First, common factor analysis has a technical problem: There is no unique set of factor scores that can be calculated from a common factor analysis, but there is from a component analysis. This is less relevant to item factor analysis because the purpose is to select a subset of items to score each factor, and that does give a unique set of factor scores for common factor analysis.

A second reason principal components are occasionally recommended is that they are easier to compute. Of course with modern personal computers, this is rarely a problem. But such was not the case when "Little Jiffy" was introduced by Kaiser (personal communication, 1960). The computer he was using was Illiac I, which was considerably smaller and slower than the first of the desktop personal computers. But with the second generation of computers—only somewhat larger and faster than the original personal computers and considerably smaller and slower than any personal computer now manufactured—Kaiser recommended common factor analysis (Kaiser, 1970). The common factor analyses used as illustrations in this article took very little time—perhaps 1 min each—on a personal computer.

Third, some comparisons of principal component and common factor analysis use maximum likelihood common factors with highly iterated communalities, a type of common factor analysis that shows an occasional problem. But this is a type of common factor analysis I have never recommended (Gorsuch, 1974, 1983, 1990). These problems do not occur with principal axis common factor analysis with two or three iterations for communalities. Empirical analysis shows that such common factor analysis produces factor loadings not significantly different from population values whereas component analysis gives inflated loadings (Snook &

Gorsuch, 1989). Hence, this reason for preferring principal components appears to be outdated.

A fourth reason is that the results are about the same regardless of whether principal component or common factor analysis is used. This is true, but only when the variables correlate highly with each other or there is a large number of variables per factor. Item factor analysis always has a hard time meeting the first condition, but if 50 or so items are being factored with only five or so factors rotated, it may meet the second condition.

Note that Equation 1 is the general case, and principal component analysis is a special case in which the u is zero. Thus principal component analysis is a special case of common factor analysis. If a component analysis is appropriate, common factor analysis will produce it. But the reverse is not true; without the u in the equation, the principal component analysis procedures force a common factor situation as much as possible into a component model. Gorsuch (1983) provided examples where this forcing distorts loadings (also see Snook & Gorsuch, 1989). No such conditions exist for common factor analysis.

Consider the example in Table 3. All the items have some significant correlation except for the last item, which is a random variable and has no significant correlation with any of the four variables. In the common factor analysis, it is obvious that the item should not be used. In the principal component analysis it has a high loading of .60, leading to the conclusion that the item should be used. Because the loading is based on nonsignificant correlations, however, it will neither replicate nor help that scale.

An analogy to the choice between principal component and common factor analysis is item-total versus item-remainder correlations. The item-total correlation is inflated because the item's own error variance is part of the total score; item-remainder correlations are less misleading. Mistakes will seldom be made with item-remainder correlations, but will occasionally occur with item-total correla-

TABLE 3
Example of Component Analysis Making a Nonsignificant Item Appear Significant

Item	Component		Common Factor	
	1	*2*	*1*	*2*
1.	.08	.82	.14	.58
2.	.08	.82	.14	.58
3.	.70	.33	.57	.28
4.	.81	.00	.58	.06
Random variable	.60	.01	.32	.09

Note. $N = 90$. The shrunken squared multiple correlation for the random variable was .04. None of its correlations with the other items were significant.

tions. In like manner, principal component analysis will occasionally produce an erroneous judgment as in Table 3, but such errors seldom occur with common factor analysis.

Number of Factors

A major decision affected by the special conditions of item factor analysis is the number of factors. This is particularly relevant with "Little Jiffy" because it uses the "roots greater than 1" (abbreviated as R > 1) criterion. For this criterion all of the characteristic roots of the correlation matrix are extracted. The number of these roots greater than 1.0 is the number of factors to extract. The rationale for R > 1 is based on the roots of a population correlation matrix with no factors. In that case, all roots will be 1.0. If there is a factor in the population matrix, the root for the factor will be greater than 1.0; because the roots must total to the number of variables, the other roots with no factors will be less than 1.0. So the number of factors in the population is the number of roots greater than 1.0. This analysis is for the population matrix; with no factors, all correlations are 0.0 and all roots 1.0. But with a sample, there are chance correlations. In this case, the average number of R > 1 will be one half the number of variables (i.e., .5v where v is the number of variables). Hence the use of the R > 1 criterion produces many factors for a set of random variables.

In a well-designed factor analysis, the factors are clearly larger than random factors and so their roots are clearly larger than the other roots. Let's assume that we have 10 variables per factor, so the population matrix would have .1v roots meeting the R > 1 criterion. But as the correlations among the variables drop due to poor quality variables, the number of roots is a comprise between random data, which has .5v R > 1 factors, and the population number of factors, which is .1v R > 1 factors for this example. While the situation is more complex than can be described here, in general the observed R > 1 ranges from being accurate to being an overestimate of the number of factors. In simulations the R > 1 criterion has been found to give reasonable results with good data but to overestimate the number of factors with data having lower correlations. As noted earlier, item factor analyses have lower correlations than well-designed studies of scales. This is due to their lower reliabilities, among other problems. Hence, the R > 1 criterion will produce too many factors for items.

The problem of the R > 1 criterion was obvious in early research using item factor analyses. Gorsuch (1968) reduced the number of factors by running an initial analysis with the R > 1 criterion, rotating the factors to Varimax, and counting the number of factors that had at least three items salient on the factor. (*Salient* is defined as a loading that is greater than |.4| and is the highest loading for the variable.) This was used as an estimate of the number of factors. Also some random variables were included, and the factoring was stopped when a factor appeared with a high loading by a random variable. Gorsuch (1974, 1983) continued to recommend counting the number of factors with three or more salient loadings to establish the number of item factors.

The Gorsuch recommendation to restrict the number of factors to those having three salient variables was, it can now be seen, useful for two reasons. First it helped correct for the $R > 1$ tendency to indicate too many factors due to the low correlations among items. But it also served another goal as well. One of the problems with items noted earlier is that they have reliable variance that is unique to a couple of items but not to a general construct. For example, two items may be about one's family life, and so vary together in addition to the variation from the construct being measured. These items would therefore load a small factor together, but it would be a trivial factor. (*Trivial* is defined as lacking salient variables, both by few items loading the factor and also by most of its items having higher loadings with other factors.) Keeping only the larger factors eliminates these trivial factors that occur among items.

Other criteria may also be useful for item analysis. These include parallel analysis, the scree test, and, if the sample is large enough, separate factoring in two halves of the sample to evaluate the number of factors that replicate across random samples (each subsample would need to have at least 150 cases). No systematic evidence is available on the use of these procedures for estimating the number of item factors.

Additional evidence supports two general conclusions that appear applicable to item factor analysis. First, it is better to overfactor than underfactor (Fava & Velicer, 1992; Wood, Tataryn, & Gorsuch, 1996). Thus, keeping an additional factor or two is not likely to be a problem. Second, extracting too few factors can radically change one or more factors while extracting an additional factor when "in the right range" leaves the earlier ones unchanged.

In practice, it is recommended that several factor analyses be computed. The first one would be based on $R > 1$ and then, in the rotated solution, the number of trivial factors noted. Then the analysis is rerun with the trivial factors dropped. The two solutions would be compared. If any factor in the second analysis changed dramatically, then the analysis would be redone with an additional factor or two. With contemporary computers, this can be done in a half hour or so of the investigator's time.

Rotation

Simple structure rotation. The basic principle of factor rotation is *simple structure*. This seeks to minimize the number of variables that load on a factor—and so keep the factor simple—and to minimize the number of factors both loading the same variables—and so keep the solution simple. This means that the ideal variable loads on only one factor. And the rotation procedures are designed to rotate to a solution in which each factor has several loadings for variables not loading other factors. Hence programs rotating to simple structure are most appropriate when the items clearly load several different factors. The rotation procedures work well, perhaps too well. They almost always produce a solution in which the factors each have a set of items loading them high that do not load other factors. Even if a solution exists in which all items load the same factor, that solution will be avoided if at all possible so that all factors can also have high-loading variables that do not load another factor.

Many factor analyses of scales use a sample of scales for which simple structure rotation is appropriate. Each scale is expected to correlate high with some scales but low with the other scales in the analysis. This is appropriate for simple structure rotation.

Items, however, may not be sampled so that each item is expected to correlate with only a few other items. Instead, many item sets consist of items expected to correlate well with all the other items, not just some. Items on the BDI are all expected to measure depression, and so all items should correlate with every other item. Hence, the sampling of items is radically different than the sampling that fits simple structure rotation. When the sampling does not match simple structure, the programs do the best they can to produce a simple structure fit. Therefore the results look like simple structure even if every item primarily measures one factor—such as depression—but also measures some another trivial factor.

A good example of what simple structure does is shown with the perfect Guttman scale in Table 2. Instead of all loading the same factor—which they do in the underlying model—they load four factors that show simple structure. Our interpretation would go astray here unless we remember this is a function of the rotation technique, not of the items' substantive content.

Overcoming simple structure bias.   How, then, can we test if the items do all relate to one theoretical factor? There are two methods in theory but only one in practice. In theory the initial unrotated factor can be examined. It almost always produces a general factor. However, it is as biased toward a general factor as simple structure rotation is biased away from it. It also ignores the other factors loading these items which may give information about biases among the items. Instead of allowing these to shift to separate factors, the first unrotated factor has as much of all the variance, including the bias variance, in the general factor as is possible. As a result, this method is seldom used in practice.

In practice, the method to test for a general factor underlying the item set is to extract one or more higher order factors. This begins by avoiding any rotation that restricts the factor intercorrelations (note that Varimax rotation restricts them to being uncorrelated). The correlations among the rotated factors are used as the correlations for a second factor analysis. The original factors—called primary factors—thus become the "variables" for the second, or higher order, factor analysis. This procedure tests whether the primary factors are correlated and, if so, how those correlations are structured. Items can then be correlated with the higher order factors by extension analysis (Gorsuch, in press). If most items correlate well with the higher order factor, then it can be considered a general factor.

Consider, for example, the perfect unidimensional Guttman scale discussed earlier that produces four primary factors instead of one. The results of an item factor analysis leaving the correlations among the factors unrestricted is presented in Table 4. These factors correlate, and a higher order factor can be extracted. All of the four primary factors are loaded by the higher order factor and all items

TABLE 4
Item Factor Analysis of a Perfect Guttman Scale

	Factor				
	Primary				
	1	*2*	*3*	*4*	*Higher Order*
Primary factor					
1.	1.00	.52	.27	.18	.64
2.	.56	1.00	.57	.27	.81
3.	.27	.57	1.00	.58	.81
4.	.18	.27	.56	1.00	.68
Item					
1.	.65	.29	.17	.09	.40
2.	.87	.44	.24	.13	.56
3.	.90	.58	.29	.17	.66
4.	.85	.71	.33	.21	.71
5.	.77	.82	.39	.24	.74
6.	.67	.89	.45	.26	.77
7.	.58	.93	.53	.28	.78
8.	.50	.93	.61	.30	.79
9.	.44	.90	.70	.32	.79
10.	.39	.84	.78	.35	.79
11.	.35	.77	.85	.39	.79
12.	.32	.69	.90	.44	.79
13.	.30	.60	.93	.51	.79
14.	.28	.52	.93	.59	.78
15.	.26	.44	.89	.68	.77
16.	.24	.38	.81	.77	.74
17.	.21	.33	.71	.85	.71
18.	.17	.28	.58	.90	.65
19.	.13	.24	.43	.87	.56
20.	.09	.17	.29	.65	.40

Note. Items are ordered from the "easiest" to the "hardest."

correlate with it. Our interpretation is simple: All items relate to the single, higher order factor, which is the general factor we know underlies all the items. In addition, different distributions cause subsets of items to correlate together as seen in the primary factors. This then produces a complete understanding of how the items relate to each other.

The importance of a higher order factor analysis to evaluate whether there is a general factor is also shown with analyses of anxiety. Gorsuch (1966) rotated the previously found factors of the Test Anxiety Questionnaire without, as had been done in the previous analyses, restricting the factor correlations. He found the factors to be highly correlated and discovered a higher order factor that matched the author's intent of measuring test anxiety. The trait or state items from the State–Trait Anxiety Inventory (STAI; Spielberger, Gorsuch, Lushene, Vagg, & Jacobs, 1983) have often been factored. Despite a reliability of .9, two factors emerge from these items. When rotated to simple structure, half of the items are loaded by each factor. One of the primary factors has all the items that are scored in the positive direction (e.g., "Yes" to "Are you anxious?"), and the other has all the reversed-scored items (e.g., "No" to "Are you calm?"). If the factor analysis is stopped at this point, there appears to be no such thing as anxiety. If the analysis is continued without restricting the rotation, then a higher order, general factor is found that is the trait of anxiety. The scale includes items scored in both the positive and reverse-scored directions.

It follows that it is critical to note that simple structure bias against a general factor requires an unrestricted rotation to allow compensation for the bias. Restricting the rotation to uncorrelated factors, as Varimax does, precludes any general factor. Varimax is the worst method for item factor analysis because there is no way to overcome the simple structure bias, a bias that is present when the items come from the same domain (e.g., are all ability items, motivational items, or depression items). It should also be noted that nonrestricted solutions—such as Oblimin or Promax—will give uncorrelated factors when that provides a reasonable solution (they are only called *oblique* rotations because they may give correlated factors; Varimax is called *orthogonal* because it only gives uncorrelated factors).

Using unrestricted rotation, the two primary factors and the general factor structure of the STAI have been replicated. For example, Chan (1989) replicated these factors in Chinese, Lee (1995) in Korean, and Courelli (1991) in Greek monolingual respondents.

The BDI has often been factored with a variety of techniques, and comparing the results here with other studies helps to evaluate the impact of different procedures on a practical level. Table 5 presents the results of a BDI item factor analysis from Lee's (1995) work examining a Korean translation in a monolingual sample. The R > 1 criterion indicated six or seven factors, but only four meet the criterion of having four items with their highest loading on the factor in an initial rotated solution. Communality estimates were squared multiple correlations with two

TABLE 5
Item Factor Analysis of the Beck Depression Inventory

	Factor			
	Primary			
	1	2	3	Higher Order
Primary factor				
1.	1.00	.57	.70	.87
2.	.57	1.00	.45	.45
3.	.70	.45	1.00	.73
Item				
1.	.48	.28	.52	.49
2.	.45	.31	.45	.45
3.	.42	.26	.61	.49
4.	.61	.25	.58	.55
5.	.28	.28	.51	.41
6.	.28	.24	.44	.38
7.	.51	.24	.66	.54
8.	.47	.27	.56	.50
9.	.49	.40	.48	.50
10.	.50	.34	.41	.46
11.	.51	.33	.45	.48
12.	.55	.27	.33	.45
13.	.44	.26	.35	.41
14.	.50	.27	.45	.48
15.	.71	.40	.49	.58
16.	.25	.50	.20	.28
17.	.53	.35	.36	.46
18.	.32	.62	.23	.34
19.	.19	.50	.16	.24
20.	.38	.48	.25	.35
21.	.50	.38	.31	.44

iterations. The factors were rotated by Promax (using Varimax for the target matrix and setting k to 4). As can be seen in Table 5, the factors—when rotated without any restriction for uncorrelated or for correlated factors—were clearly correlated, and so a higher order factor was extracted and its correlations with the items computed. Table 5 shows that the primary factors all correlate highly with the higher order factor, as do almost all the items. Comparing Table 5 with Table 4 shows the BDI general factor to have more items with the highest correlation being with the general factor in the BDI than with the general factor of the perfect Guttman scales. There is clearly strong evidence for a single general depression score for the BDI. This evidence would not have been found if only Varimax had been used for the rotation. The primary factors may be technical factors, just as in the case of the Guttman scale of Table 4.

Technical factors need not replicate. They may be a function of idiosyncrasies of some trivial characteristic of the population sampled. We have found this to be so in factor analyses of the BDI in samples from different populations. Factoring the BDI items is factoring a set of items that were selected by Beck et al. (1961) to have a general factor, depression, and that would, we hope, function much the same across cultures. Chan (1989) collected data from Hong Kong Chinese, and compared the factors with the results of other analyses. She found several primary factors and a second-order factor with which all the items correlated. Thus there appeared to be some technical factors but items also measured a general factor, depression. The comparisons with other studies showed that the primary factors did not replicate any previously found; however, the general, higher order factor replicated quite well.

The check for replication is to use the past study's factors as hypotheses for multiple group factors (Gorsuch, 1983). Multiple group factor analysis is a type of CFA in which each factor is defined by a weighted subset of the variables. The correlations of these multiple group factors with the exploratory factors is the degree to which the prior study's factors replicate. (Note that coefficients of congruence can be misleading and are to be avoided.) The UniMult statistical package (Gorsuch, 1994) has multiple group factor analysis as an option and computes the correlations with other factors from the same data as well. If such a program is not available, an "almost as good" procedure is to sum the items salient for each factor of the

TABLE 6
Correlations of Korean Factors With Other Analyses

| | Korean Factor | | | |
| | Primary | | | |
Factor	1	2	3	Higher Order
Chinese (Chan, 1989)				
1.	.57	.75	.43	.55
2.	.68	.35	.79	.68
3.	.72	.32	.82	.71
Greek (Courelli, 1991)				
1.	.82	.38	.82	.77
2.	.80	.34	.61	.69
U.S. confirmatory factor analysis (Byrne, 1994)				
1.	.87	.34	.81	.79
2.	.85	.34	.80	.78
3.	.64	.88	.39	.60

prior factor analysis as one set of scales and sum items for the factors of the exploratory analysis as a second set of scales, and then compute the correlation between these two sets of scales.

We have related Lee's (1995) factors using UniMult to the factors resulting from other factor analyses. One set of factors was with another Asian sample, Chinese (Chan, 1989). Another was with Courelli's (1991) Greek elderly people. A third was with the three-factor structure Byrne (1994) used with CFAs. Table 6 shows the correlations of the factors of other studies with those of Lee.

The most striking aspects of Table 6 are twofold. First, none of the primary factors replicate. They all have odd mixtures of correlations but do not correlate highly with just one factor from the other study. This was also found in comparisons that Chan (1989) and Courelli (1991) made with other factor analyses in their samples. It may be that the primary factors are technical factors specific to a sample or are culturally specific factors. Either way, they do not replicate in these samples. Subscoring the BDI therefore appears to be of limited value, applicable only within one subculture, and of little use in evaluating the general applicability of the BDI. Second, there is a strong general factor that does replicate well. Even the factors restricted to being uncorrelated in an American sample (by using Varimax) were highly correlated when measured in a new sample such as Chan's, Courelli's, or Lee's. Additionally, all of the primary factors correlate well with the second-order factor of depression, as do the items. The results point clearly to the conclusion that the BDI measures one construct. While the item correlations will show different minor patterns that either vary by subculture or are nonreplicable, the strongest and most consistent replication is of the general depression factor.

Note how wrong we would have been if only "Little Jiffy" had been run. It would, by the uncorrected R > 1 criterion, have given too many factors and then, by the restrictions of Varimax rotation, have suggested that there were a set of uncorrelated factors with no general depression factor. And, the Varimax factors are unreplicable. The conclusion, based on poor methodology, would have been that the BDI had no replicable structure and so was meaningless. The correct conclusion is that the BDI has a strong general factor just as Beck et al. (1961) aimed it to have, and this general factor is highly replicable even across cultures.

Other examples of nonrestricted rotation in item factor analysis with higher order factors can be found. For example Dura, Bernstein, and Kiecolt-Glaser (1990) analyzed dementia items. Johnson and Johnson (1993) analyzed items regarding school life (although they probably should also have used confirmatory multiple group analysis to test the original author's subscales). Procter's (1993) brief presentation of factor analysis for attitude scales assumed higher order analysis. All found higher order factors meaningful.

In item factor analysis, "Little Jiffy" is not just a "personal choice"; it is a way of guaranteeing that any general, replicable factor is lost. In the case of BDI analyses by "Little Jiffy," the several samples would have strongly suggested that there are no replicable factors for the BDI when the opposite is true.

Interpretation of Factors

Before construing an item factor as substantive, the alternative interpretation that it is a technical factor must be ruled out. This happens by rejecting a set of alternative technical factor hypotheses:

1. The first alternative hypothesis is that the factor is nonreplicable. Using multiple group factor analysis to relate the factors to those found by others is helpful. However, this assumes that the previous analysis was an appropriate item factor analysis.

2. The second alternative hypothesis is that the factor is too small to be considered further. Assuming the number of factors has been examined as noted earlier, there are several salient items to measure it. Nevertheless, it could still be unmeasurable. This is found by scoring all factors as if they were scales (see selecting items later), computing the reliabilities, and correlating the scales. A usable scale has a reasonable reliability and has no correlation with another factor scale approaching either's reliability.

3. The third alternative hypothesis is that the factor is caused by items having different distributions. These are classically called difficulty factors because they were first found in ability items. The less difficult items had negative skew and correlated well with each other, and the more difficult items had positive skew and correlated well together. But the phenomena applies to any data set, just as in the aforementioned Guttman scale example. It may, for example, be the reason that Ross, Joshi, and Currie (1991) found a factor for common, everyday disassociative states and other factors for uncommon, rare disassociative experiences. To evaluate this interpretation, the distribution of each item should be examined. If it is the same among items of the same factor but differs from items not related to the factor, then it is probably a distribution factor.

4. The fourth alternative hypothesis is response style. Do all the items for the factor require the same response set? This could be as simple as the acquiescence response set possible for half of the STAI items, but it could also be more complex. Perhaps the items all require the same radical judgment be made. If that is a response style factor, then the items for other factors will not require a radical statement be made. Chan (1991) found order effects among the items of personal distress that may be a shift in response set while answering the items.

5. The fifth alternative hypothesis is that the items are not linear combinations of the factors. For example, an adjective list for rating one's roommate on dominance may include the terms "domineering," "reasonable person," and "a doormat

for others." But these items are curvilinearly related to the latent variable of dominance-submission. The "reasonable person" phrase would be checked only if neither of the other two items had been picked. Note how different this is from the Guttman scale, with each item linearly related to the factor. A person has a moderate score if and only if all items lower on the scale were also selected. For these three phrases to be linearly related to the same factor, the "reasonable person" could only be checked if "a doormat for others" were also checked. And "domineering" could only have been checked if both of the other items were checked. When items are nonlinearly related to factors, they can be analyzed conceptually and statistically as "unfolding" (see van Schuur & Kiers, 1994). Probably such factors correlate, leading to a single higher order factor, but that has not yet been shown. It has been shown that items curvilinearly related to factors produce an extra primary factor.

A useful procedure to aid in evaluating whether the possible technical factors may be substantive factors is to relate them to other variables. If the factors function as only technical factors and not substantively, then they should have the same beta weight as do the other substantive factors in a multiple regression to other relevant variables. This is tested by summing across the possible substantive factors and entering that sum first into a hierarchical multiple regression to the dependent variable. Then the technical factors are, as the second step in a hierarchical regression analysis, added to the multiple regression and tested as a set. If they are only technical factors, they function with the same weight; adding them together and then entering the total gives each the same weight. Entering them at the second step would not add significantly to the prediction. But if they function as separate substantive factors, then they would have different weights. In that case, the separate factors would be most predictive when weighted separately, and Step 2 would add significantly to Step 1. Gorsuch and McPherson (1989) found the positively and negatively worded items measuring intrinsic religious commitment to form two factors. The multiple regression, however, found no significant increase in predictive power by considering them two substantive factors rather than just one. Roberts, Lewinsohn, and Seeley (1993) also found positive and negative factors among loneliness items but, again, found the same pattern of relations to other variables.

If it is unlikely that the factor is a technical factor, then a substantive interpretation is warranted. These are generally based on the item content, but it is useful if other checks are made. Such checks are dependent on other data being available. If relevant data are available, they can be analyzed for increased understanding.

Indirect Item Factor Analysis

The problems of items—low reliabilities, varying distributions, noncontinuous response formats—have long been known. Cattell (1957) confronted these problems (and the problem of low computer capacity) and used "item parcels," or miniscales, to reduce them. He formed his items into groups that were all of one kind, and scored each set of items for one variable for the factor analysis. These miniscales were then factored and the items correlated back with the factors. Comrey and Lee (1992) advocated this procedure also.

The miniscale approach reduces all the problems inherent in factoring items:

1. The reliability of a miniscale is higher than that of an item.
2. The items for a parcel can be selected to have the range of means/distributions desired in the final scale. When summed together, each miniscale would have a more normal distribution.
3. The miniscales have a wider possible range. If each item is scored on a 3-point scale and there are five items, then the scale ranges from 5 to 15.
4. The idiosyncratic content that leads to two items loading a separate factor is averaged out across the miniscales, and so methods such as the R > 1 number of factors criterion are more applicable. There can still be ample basis for multiple factors; Cattell found 16 personality factors using this method.

Why, then, is this procedure not more widely used? Perhaps because it is not widely known, or perhaps because it requires the additional effort of building the parcels and then relating the items to the factors in addition to the factor analysis. Many scales have too few items for this type of analysis. Finally, investigators may be uncomfortable with determining which items are "alike" on an a priori basis and so should be in the same parcel.

The procedure recommended earlier of extracting higher order factors from primary factors is, in a sense, an empirically based miniscale assignment and factoring procedure. The primary factors group together those items that correlate highest, thus forming them into implicit miniscales. Factoring the primary factors for second-order factors is equivalent to factoring miniscales. The higher order factor approach has the advantage of less work and being more empirical than the parcel approach to building miniscales. Because it does minimize subjective judgments, it should also be more replicable. The drawback is that it does not reduce distribution problems as well as miniscales. Instead, the items with the same distributions will be placed together. Overall, this does not seem to be a serious handicap.

Selecting Items for Scales

Pattern or structure or weight matrix?   Whether the items are factored directly or indirectly, the result is a set of coefficients relating each item to each factor, including any higher order factors. There are several measures of relation between the items and the factors. First are the factor-item correlations; the matrix containing all these correlations is called the *factor structure*. Second are the standardized weights to be used to reproduce the item scores from the factor scores, called the *factor pattern*. Third are the standardized weights to be used to estimate factor scores from item scores, called the *factor weight matrix*.

Early tradition was to use the factor pattern (or the reference vector structure). The pattern is a matrix of the weights to be used to reproduce the variable standard scores from the factor standard scores (the reference vector structure contains the correlation of each item with each factor with the other factors partialled out). This was done primarily because of the limits of the computers which made calculating the actual correlations of the items with the factors difficult.

The correlations of each item with each factor—the factor structure—is an appropriate statistic to use to select items. It is either the equivalent of the item-total correlation if it is a component analysis, or the equivalent of the item-remainder or item-domain coefficient if it is a common factor analysis. The correlation reflects directly how the item will function as part of a scale, and the correlations of that item with other factors indicate how it will contribute to the relations of its scale to other scales based on these factors (the pattern only indirectly reflects the first and can be misleading about the second).

The other possible matrix to use to select items is the weight matrix for scoring the factors. The values in this matrix give the beta weights to be used with each item standard score to best estimate the factor standard score. It is the same as if one ran a multiple regression with each of the scale's items as predictors and the total scale as the dependent variable, and then picked items based on their beta weights. But beta weights are not used in item selection for two reasons. First, they are unstable and highly influenced by what other items are in the equation, including items not selected. Second, direct comparisons between beta weights are dangerous because each has a separate standard error; a beta weight of .3 may be significant for Item 1 while a beta weight of .4 may be insignificant for Item 2. How then can we decide which item should be on the scale? Third, multiple regression devalues redundancy and values differential contributions to the estimate. Hence two items that correlate highly together will not both be given high beta weights even if both correlate highly with the factor. Instead, both will be given moderately low weights or one will be weighted high and the other low. However redundancy is highly desirable in the items for a scale (and increases internal consistency reliability). Correlations have none of these problems.

In a comparison of using the correlations and using the weight matrix, ten Berge and Knol (1985) found that the full multiple regression weights lead to the highest correlation with the factors but that using the correlations lead to the highest internal consistency reliability. This is to be expected because the evaluations were in the original sample. Research in factor scoring (Gorsuch, 1983) has, however, found that the regression weights generalize poorly compared to just summing the items, as has been found in other areas. Summing the salient items is the most generalizable procedure. The ten Berg and Knol results would, in cross-validation, find the high internal consistency generalizing but not the highest correlation. Hence these results are in keeping with the recommendation to use the item-factor correlations.

How high a correlation? The same answer is given here as in any item selection based on correlations. First, the item should have a highly significant correlation. But note that the significance level should be smaller than might be normally used for two reasons: (a) factor-item correlations are suspected to have a higher standard error than regular correlations and (b) as in any item selection, many correlations are computed but only a few are chosen, thus leading to capitalization on chance.

Second, the item-factor correlation should be high enough that, given the items already chosen, it will add to the reliability and validity of the scale rather than reduce it. If the first 10 items correlate at least .6 and the next .3, adding that 11th item may do more harm than good. It appears that the best procedure is to try several sets of items and evaluate what happens to the correlation of the resulting scale with the factor by extension analysis (Gorsuch, in press).

How are the correlations with other factors used? The use of the other factors depends on whether they are technical factors or substantive factors. If technical factors exist, it is often impossible to find items that load only the substantive factor and no technical factors. So we counterbalance the technical factors so that the test score is not particularly associated with any of the technical factors. For the technical factors of different distributions of Guttman scale items, we counterbalance by including an equal number of items at each level of response frequency. For the STAI, we counterbalanced by including equal numbers of positive and negative items. (Note that the reliability of a counterbalanced scale is best defined by a parallel form coefficient, not the usual coefficient alpha. Using the latter is, in effect, assuming that no technical factors exist.)

The correlations of substantive item factors need to be monitored in light of the items already selected for each substantive factor and the correlations among the factors. The items selected should, as a group, have a set of loadings with other factors so that the focal factor scale will have the appropriate correlations with the other factor scales. For example, if the first three items correlate with another factor higher than their factor does with the other factor, the scale will correlate higher with the other factor than the factor analysis suggests it should. Hence the next item should have a much lower correlation with the other factor. This strategy also applies if the first items correlate much too low with the other factor.

Remember that, in selecting items as a function of the correlation with other substantive factors, items have attenuated correlations. Due to their low reliabilities they correlate lower with everything than do scales (see earlier example). Hence the individual items should correlate very low with the other substantive factors because the resulting scale will correlate higher than the items. Generally the lowest possible correlation of items with other factors is sought.

Testing proposed scales.   How well did the item selection work? Are the correlations with the factor the scale should measure high and the correlations with other factors low? Would another subset of items perform better?

There are two methods to provide correlations of proposed scales with the factors. The first—and no longer recommended—is to compute estimated factor scores and then correlate these with the scores for each proposed scale. The problem is that the factor scores contain nonfactor covariance among the items, leading to inflated values (just as item-total correlations are inflated).

The second method is Gorsuch's extension analysis (Gorsuch, 1997, which also shows prior extension procedures have the same problems as item-total correlations and estimated factor scores). In that procedure, the factors are located within the hyperspace defined by the items being factored. The factor analysis is then extended to the proposed scales by locating them in the item hyperspace also. The correlations of each proposed scale with the factors are computed. As shown in Gorsuch (1997), this procedure gives appropriate, noninflated correlations.

CONCLUSIONS

Items have lower reliabilities than scales. They can also be characterized by a greater degree of idiosyncratic content such as response bias (which is averaged out in a good scale). Hence, establishing the number of factors by the R > 1 criterion—whose rationale is based on an error-free matrix—gives too many factors. If component analysis is used—which has no error term in the model—the loadings will be inflated. Using multiple methods to determine the number of factors and extracting factors by a method allowing community estimates are recommended.

If the items are all from one conceptual domain or a set of conceptually related domains, restricting the rotation to uncorrelated factors (as in Varimax) obscures the general factor or broader constructs the test may measure. It also allows technical factors—factors occurring for methodological reasons—to obscure substantive factors. Using a nonrestricted rotation and extracting higher order factors, if any, allows for narrow to general factors to emerge and for constructing scales that minimize technical factors.

Proposed scales can be evaluated by a new extension analysis (Gorsuch, 1997), which gives better estimates of scale-domain correlations than either traditional item analysis or other factor analytic procedures.

"Little Jiffy," the default in many statistical packages, is designed for high reliability scales sampling several unrelated substantive domains. It is therefore seldom appropriate for item factor analysis; if it is used with items, it generally produces too many factors and prevents broad or general factors from being identified. An author's hypothesis that the items measure one construct will almost always be rejected solely because "Little Jiffy" was used even when the hypothesis is warranted; in such cases the "Little Jiffy" factors may be unreplicable. Using the procedures recommended earlier allows an unbiased test for a general or other broad factors and produces factors more likely to replicate.

REFERENCES

Beck, A. T., Ward, C. H., Mendelson, M., Mock, J., & Erbaugh, J. (1961). An inventory for measuring depression. *Archives of General Psychiatry, 4,* 561–571.

Bernstein, I. H., Jaremko, M. E., & Hinkley, B. S. (1994). On the utility of the SCL–90–R with low-back pain patients. *Spine, 19,* 42–48.

Bernstein, I. H., Jaremko, M. E., & Hinkley, B. S. (1995). On the utility of the West Haven–Yale Multidimensional Pain Inventory. *Spine, 20,* 956–963.

Bernstein, I. H., & Keith, J. B. (1991). Reexamination of Eisen, Zellman, and McAlister's Health Belief Model Questionnaire. *Health Education Quarterly, 18,* 207–220.

Bernstein, I. H., & Teng, G. (1989). Factoring items and factoring scales are different: Spurious evidence for multidimensionality due to item categorization. *Psychological Bulletin, 105,* 467–477.

Byrne, M. B. (1994). *Structural equation modeling with EQS/Windows: Basic concepts, applications, and programming.* Thousand Oaks, CA: Sage.

Cattell, R. B. (1957). *Personality and motivation structure and measurement.* Yonkers, NY: World Book.

Chan, M-Y. A. (1989). *Development and evaluation of a Chinese translation of the State–Trait Anxiety Inventory and the Beck Depression Inventory.* Unpublished doctoral dissertation, Graduate School of Psychology, Fuller Theological Seminary, Pasadena, CA.

Chan, J. C. (1991). Response-order effects in Likert-type scales. *Educational and Psychological Measurement, 51,* 531–540.

Comrey, A. L., & Lee, H. B. (1992). *A first course in factor analysis* (2nd ed.). Hillsdale, NJ: Lawrence Erlbaum Associates, Inc.

Courelli, P. S. (1991). *A screening battery of tests for the detection of dementia among Greek elderly.* Unpublished doctoral dissertation, Graduate School of Psychology, Fuller Theological Seminary, Pasadena CA.

Dura, J. R., Bernstein, R. A., & Kiecolt-Glaser, J. K. (1990). Refinements in the assessment of dementia-related behaviors: Factor structure of the memory and behavior problem checklist. *Psychological Assessment, 2,* 129–133.

Fava, J. L., & Velicer, W. F. (1992). The effects of overextraction on factor and component analysis. *Multivariate Behavioral Research, 27,* 387–415.

Gorsuch, R. L. (1966). The general factor in the Test Anxiety Questionnaire. *Psychological Reports, 19,* 308.

Gorsuch, R. L. (1968). The conceptualization of God as seen in adjective ratings. *Journal for the Scientific Study of Religion, 7*, 56–64.

Gorsuch, R. L. (1974). *Factor analysis.* Philadelphia: Saunders.

Gorsuch, R. L. (1983). *Factor analysis* (2nd ed.). Hillsdale, NJ: Lawrence Erlbaum Associates, Inc.

Gorsuch, R. L. (1990). Common factor analysis vs. component analysis: Some well and little known facts. *Multivariate Behavioral Research, 25*, 33–39.

Gorsuch, R. L. (1994). *UniMult guide.* Pasadena, CA: UniMult.

Gorsuch, R. L. (1996). *Relating factors across studies.* Manuscript submitted for publication.

Gorsuch, R. L. (in press). New procedure for extension analysis in exploratory factor analysis. *Educational and Psychological Measurement, 57.*

Gorsuch, R. L., & McPherson, S. (1989). Intrinsic/extrinsic measurement: I/E–Revised and single-item scales. *Journal for the Scientific Study of Religion, 28*, 348–354.

Guadagnoli, E., & Velicer, W. F. (1988). Relation of sample size to the stability of component patterns. *Psychological Bulletin, 103*, 265–275.

Johnson, W. L., & Johnson, A. M. (1993). Validity of the quality of school life scale: A primary and second-order factor analysis. *Educational and Psychological Measurement, 53*, 145–153.

Kaiser, H. F. (1970). A second generation Little Jiffy. *Psychometrika, 35*, 401–415.

Lee, C-K. E. (1995). *Evaluation of a Korean translation of the State–Trait Anxiety Inventory and the Beck Depression Inventory.* Unpublished doctoral dissertation, Graduate School of Psychology, Fuller Theological Seminary, Pasadena, CA.

MacCallum, R. (1986). Specification searches in covariance structure modeling. *Psychological Bulletin, 100*, 107–120.

Nunnally, J. (1967). *Psychometric theory.* New York: McGraw-Hill.

Nunnally, J., & Bernstein, I. (1994). *Psychometric theory.* New York: McGraw-Hill.

Procter, M. (1993). *Measuring attitudes.* In N. Gilbert (Ed.), *Researching social life.* London: Sage.

Reddon, J. R. (1990). The rejection of the hypothesis of complete independence prior to conducting a factor analysis. *Multivariate Experimental Clinical Research, 9*, 123–129.

Roberts, R. E., Lewinsohn, P. M., & Seeley, J. R (1993). A brief measure of loneliness suitable for use with adolescents. *Psychological Reports, 72*, 1379–1391.

Ross, C. A., Joshi, S., & Currie, R. (1991). Dissociative experiences in the general population: A factor analysis. *Hospital and Community Psychiatry, 42*, 297–301.

Roth, W. M., & Roychoudhury, A. (1991). Nonmetric multidimensional item analysis in the construction of an anxiety attitude survey. *Educational and Psychological Measurement, 51*, 931–942.

Snook, S. C., & Gorsuch, R. L. (1989). Common factor analysis vs. component analysis. *Psychological Bulletin, 106*, 148–154.

Spielberger, C. D., Gorsuch, R. L., Lushene, R., Vagg, P. R., & Jacobs, G. A. (1983). *Manual for the State–Trait Anxiety Inventory for adults.* Palo Alto, CA: Consulting Psychologists Press.

ten Berge, J. M. F., & Knol, D. L. (1985). Scale construction on the basis of components analysis: A comparison of three strategies. *Multivariate Behavioral Research, 20*, 45–55.

van Schuur, W. H., & Kiers, H. A. (1994). Why factor analysis often is the incorrect model for analyzing bipolar concepts, and what model to use instead. *Applied Psychological Measurement, 18*, 97–110.

Wood, J. M., Tataryn, D. J., & Gorsuch, R. L. (1996). Effects of under- and overextraction on principal axis factor analysis with varimax rotation. *Psychological Methods, 1*, 354–365.

18

Factor Analytic Approaches to Personality Item-Level Data

A. T. Panter, Kimberly A. Swygert, and
W. Grant Dahlstrom
University of North Carolina, Chapel Hill

J. S. Tanaka
University of Illinois, Champaign-Urbana

Factor analysis models have played a central role in formulating conceptual models in personality and personality assessment, as well as in empirical examinations of personality measurement instruments. Yet, the use of item-level data presents special problems for factor analysis applications. In this article, we review recent developments in factor analysis that are appropriate for the type of item-level data often collected in personality. Included in this review are discussions of how these developments have been addressed in the context of two different (but formally related) statistical models: item response theory (IRT; Hambleton, Swaminathan, & Rogers, 1991) and structural equation modeling (Bollen, 1989) for item-level data. We also discuss the relevance of item scaling in the context of these models. Using the restandardization data for the Minnesota Multiphasic Personality Inventory–2 Scale (cf. Butcher, Dahlstrom, Graham, Tellegen, & Kaemmer, 1989), we show brief examples of the utility of these approaches to address basic questions about responses to personality scale items regarding: (a) scale dimensionality and general item properties, (b) the "appropriateness" of the observed responses, and (c) differential item functioning across subsamples. Implications for analyses of personality item-level data in the IRT and factor analytic traditions are discussed.

Factor analytic approaches to personality assessment have been central to both scale construction and theory testing in issues such as personality structure and development (cf. Ozer & Reise, 1994). Yet, despite widespread use of factor analysis as a statistical method for analyzing data from major personality instruments, relatively little discussion has been forwarded regarding the specific assumptions that are necessary to draw appropriate inferences from item-level data. With few exceptions

339

(Bernstein & Teng, 1989), reviews of the factor analytic literature have focused on general aspects of the factor analysis models and, in fact, have advised against the use of item-level data (e.g., Comrey, 1978). However, applications of the factor analysis model in the personality literature frequently are conducted using dichotomous or Likert-type ordinal data obtained at the item level.

Our goal in this article is to extend earlier reviews of the factor analytic literature and to provide a nontechnical discussion of modeling frameworks designed to handle more easily the item-level data that are so often the heart of personality research employing factor analysis. In developing the discussion, we outline two statistical models that have emerged for the analysis of item-level data and summarize the few applications using these approaches that have appeared thus far in the personality literature. These statistical models have had independent histories of intellectual development in their respective literatures, yet we show that they are formally more similar than different (cf. Takane & de Leeuw, 1987; Muthén, 1984). The similarities between approaches will be developed to encourage thought about the research goals and decisions common to the two methods, and the different assumptions made in these models will also be noted.

To facilitate the presentation of this issue, we provide brief examples of how these approaches can be used in the personality research context. In these examples we use the normative sample data (for women, $N = 1462$; for men, $N = 1138$) from the restandardization of the Minnesota Multiphasic Personality Inventory (MMPI–2; cf. Butcher, Dahlstrom, Graham, Tellegen, & Kaemmer, 1989) to address basic questions about observed responses to personality scale items concerning: (a) Scale dimensionality and general item properties, (b) the "appropriateness" of the observed responses, and (c) differential item functioning across subsamples. Content scales from the MMPI–2 will serve as the basis for examples, including the Depression scale (e.g., especially one of its associated subscales, the 10-item Harris–Lingoes Brooding scale) and the Hypochondriasis scale. These empirical examples also allow us to demonstrate the different interpretational emphases of these models, along with the standard factor analysis model that is well-known to personality researchers. We hope to draw attention to different underlying measurement models and their implications for how a research might collect and analyze assessment data.

We begin by briefly reviewing the features associated with the standard factor analysis model and by outlining some weaknesses in this model when applied to item-level data. We next discuss the two models for item-level data: Item response models (Hambleton, Swaminathan, & Rogers, 1991) and structural equation models (Bollen, 1989) for item-level data. Because the models to be discussed are all intrinsically nonlinear, issues in item scaling can also be addressed, thereby linking these models to recent work in nonlinear multivariate analysis and optimal scaling discussed by the Dutch Gifi group (Gifi, 1990).

We follow this presentation with our empirical examples, highlighting some practical implications, differences, and similarities across the two methods, and conclude by discussing the implications of these methods for personality scale construction and research.

FACTOR ANALYSIS: A CONCEPTUAL REVIEW

We do not intend to provide a complete review of the exploratory and confirmatory factor analysis model here, as accessible introductions for the personality readership exist (exploratory: Comrey & Lee, 1992; Gorsuch, 1983; confirmatory: Hoyle, 1995; Tanaka, Panter, Winborne, & Huba, 1990). More technical presentations of both types of factor analysis can be found in Bollen (1989), Mulaik (1972), and Harman (1976).

The utility of the factor analytic approach within the personality literature is, in large part, attributable to the great emphasis that the field places on hypothetical constructs and testing interrelations among constructs. Within personality, these constructs (e.g., Extraversion, Agreeableness, Dominance, Nurturance, Depression, Ego-Resilience) and their interrelations are central components of both theory and assessment. For each of these constructs it is assumed that their observable manifestations as data capture only part of the information necessary to describe the underlying dimension. From this operating model, observable features, responses, signs, and symptoms are imperfect indicators of the underlying construct of interest.

The empirical application of exploratory factor analysis seeks to identify these meaningful, underlying constructs or dimensions by evaluating the observed covariation among observed features, responses, signs, and symptoms. The model, in general, says that observed behaviors can be described in terms of an underlying construct, with the assumption that only in very rare cases can there ever be an exact correspondence between a specific observed behavioral index or operationalization and the underlying construct to which it is related. In the confirmatory mode of factor analysis (a type of structural equation modeling [SEM]), these interrelations between indicators and unobserved constructs are specified in advance of testing the model, and assessments of fit are obtained to determine the extent to which the a priori theoretical conceptions match the observed covariation. Factor analysis thus is well-suited for and consistent with much of the thinking in personality, both when underlying structure is theoretically known or unknown in advance.

In previous reviews describing the application of the standard factor analysis to personality data, observed indicators thought to index unobserved (latent) constructs have been generally assumed to be continuously measured interval-level data, as is consistent with the basic statistical assumptions of the factor analysis model. It easily could be argued, however, that none of the data typically obtained by psychologists actually meets this assumption. At best, such continuous data are approximated by aggregating information from units (e.g., item responses, behaviors) into clusters, parcels, or scale scores. Comrey (1978, 1988) mentioned this in the context of developing item parcels or factor homogenous item dimensions to serve as the basic unit to be analyzed in factor analysis. We will return to this issue later.

Thus, a worst case scenario, one often encountered in research, would be to employ item-level data in factor analysis. In such an analysis, single item responses (such as those measured as a dichotomy or perhaps on a 5- or 7-point Likert-type scale ranging from *strongly disagree* to *strongly agree*) are analyzed. Clearly, such data fail to meet strict assumptions of continuous data. For convenience, we couch our discussions of item-level data in terms of dichotomous responses, without loss of generality, as parallel results exist for ordered categorical data (Muthén, 1984; Samejima, 1969).

To date, there are two key approaches that exist to analyze and model relations between indicators and underlying constructs or dimensions using dichotomous or ordered categorical item-level data.

APPROACH ONE: ITEM RESPONSE THEORY (IRT)

IRT has a prominent history of both research and implementation in educational measurement and test scoring (Hambleton et al., 1991). The methodology continues to be the dominant way that major testing programs evaluate the adequacy of items, score tests, and equate scores from one test administration to another on data from large groups of individuals. Item response models have also been applied more sporadically with depression and psychiatric epidemiological data in the sociological literature (e.g., Kessler & Mroczek, 1994; Reiser, 1989; Schaeffer, 1988), as well as in some areas of personality; namely, in instrument development (Childs, Dahlstrom, Kemp, & Panter, 1992; Reise & Waller, 1990, 1993; Reise, Widaman, & Pugh, 1993; Steinberg & Thissen, 1995; Swygert, Panter, Dahlstrom, & Reise, 1996; Tenopyr, 1994; Waller & Reise, 1989).

The IRT model explicitly addresses the case in which a single underlying dimension (e.g., Depression) is thought to generate a set of observed dichotomous item responses (cf. Hambleton, 1989). The model, which can be viewed as a multivariate logistic model with a single unobserved predictor (or factor), has a primary focus on item properties and a secondary focus on person estimates or scores along the underlying attribute dimension, called θ. The probability of endorsing the ith item in a set—for example, indicating that a particular MMPI–2 Depression item is true or self-descriptive—is given as a function of two components: (a) item characteristics or parameters (for the ith item) and (b) a single parameter (for the jth person), reflecting the location along the underlying attribute dimension (e.g., Depression) where that person falls. Each scale item (e.g., "I cry easily") can be represented graphically with an item trace line, and that line's form and location characterizes that item's specific properties. The trace line is a nonlinear function that takes the general form of the familiar S-shaped function, with the cumulative normal (normal ogive) or logistic functions being most typical. Because of development of this model has most commonly been in educational settings and in the context of problems such as scoring standardized tests, most often in discussions and applications of IRT in the educational literature responses in the "keyed" direction on a dichotomous item have been referred to as obtaining the "correct" as opposed to the "incorrect" answer. Similarly, in the educational context, the underlying latent dimension (θ) for a set of items typically has been labeled as an *ability,* such as verbal, quantitative, and the like. For personality contexts analogous general concepts from IRT apply to describe how individuals respond to inventory items, the characteristics of those items, and the estimates that each individual has on the underlying personality dimension.

One-, two-, or three-parameter IRT models appear most frequently in the literature, with the choice of IRT model being a function of research design considerations such as sample size, number of items being modeled, and interpretability of these parameters in the context of the data. Two very strong assumptions must hold prior to the implementation of these item response models in a set of data.

The first model assumption is that the item set should be unidimensional. With our example, this condition implies that the 57-item MMPI–2 Depression scale must be characterized by a single dominant dimension, as determined by a statistically appropriate factor analysis for dichotomous data. Though dimensionality can be approached theoretically (i.e., these items all involve content that have been traditionally associated with depressive symptomatology), it is only an empirical examination of the interrelations among items (using an exploratory factor analysis program designed for analysis of dichotomous data) that can reveal whether the unidimensionality assumption is indeed tenable. According to findings based on item response models reported in Childs et al. (1992), this is likely not to be the case for the MMPI–2 Depression scale in the restandardization sample. Additionally, the principle of local independence must hold, which means that the observed dependence of item responses must only be based on their common association with the underlying attribute rather than other effects, such those based on the order in which items are presented, carryover of content/context from other items, or dependence arising from items based on a common stem (i.e., a reading passage with a set of items that follow; e.g., Panter, Tanaka, & Wellens, 1992; Steinberg, 1994). When such assumptions hold, a number of desirable properties of model are present: (a) the aspects or characteristics of the administered items are independent of the specific population of respondents completing the items, (b) the underlying attribute estimates are independent of the specific items administered, and (c) precision of measurement can be determined for all attribute estimates along the underlying dimension.

In the three major types of IRT models, the one-parameter IRT or Rasch model (Rasch, 1960) is the most simple but, it has been argued, perhaps the least descriptive of actual item responding (cf. Hambleton, 1989). In this model, a single parameter, b, describes the probability of endorsing the ith item. This parameter, sometimes called the *item threshold* or *difficulty*, reflects the inflection point of the item trace line (curve) at which the probability of endorsing (or rejecting) the item is exactly .5. The parameter indicates the transition point between the probability of rejecting the item as not self-descriptive to endorsing the item as self-descriptive, with lower values denoting high endorsement, "non-difficult" items.

Figure 1 shows two Depression item trace lines that vary in their b values ($b = -.5; b = 1.0$). Thus, as seen in the figure, with lower values of b (an "easy to endorse" item) along the horizontal axis (reflecting values of the underlying dimension) the S-shaped item curve is shifted to the left along the horizontal axis. With higher values of b (a "difficult to endorse" item), on the other hand, the S-shaped item curve is shifted to the right.

The less restrictive, two-parameter model (Birnbaum, 1968) is as follows:

$$P_i(1|\theta_j) = [1 + e^{-ai(\theta j - bi)}]^{-1} \quad i = 1,2,3,4,\ldots p$$

This two-parameter model shows that the probability that the jth randomly selected respondent will endorse the item; that is, from 0.0 (*not at all probable*) to 1.0 (*absolutely certain*), given their level on the underlying dimension, is a function of the threshold parameter described earlier, and the parameter, a. This second parameter reflects *item discrimination,* a function of the item response curve's slope

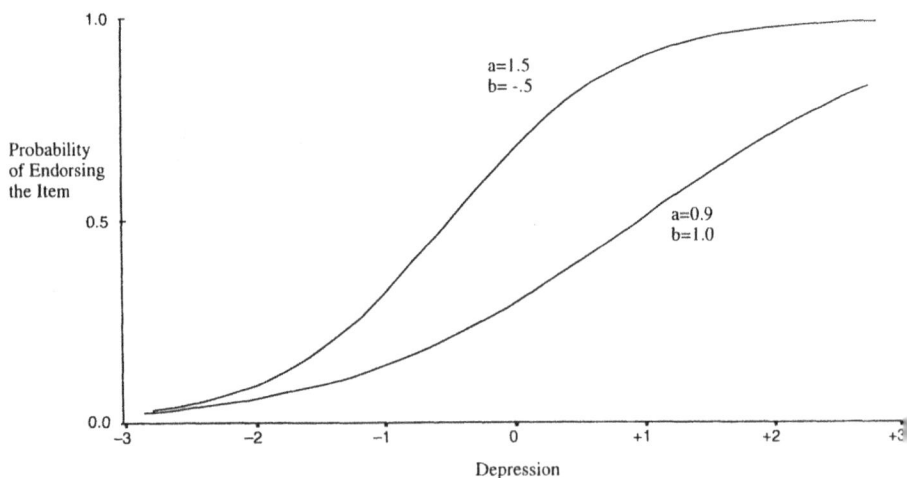

FIGURE 1   Example of two Depression item trace lines with varying parameters.

at the threshold point. As seen in Figure 1, two item trace curves can vary in their discrimination values ($a = 1.5$; $a = .9$). Item discrimination indexes how strongly related a particular item is to the underlying attribute, with steeper slopes (larger, positive as) implying greater differentiation at the corresponding point or points along the attribute dimension than less steep slopes. In our empirical analyses using the MMPI–2 data, we have focused solely on the two-parameter IRT model, due to the direct link with the item-level factor analytic models that we discuss later. Discrimination can be defined in terms of a point biserial correlation, and both parameters are directly related to the standard psychometric concept of difficulty.

A three-parameter IRT model has been thought to characterize accurately item responses in standardized testing settings. This model includes the item threshold parameter, the item discrimination parameter, and a third parameter called the *lower-asymptote parameter* (c). This third parameter denotes the nonzero probability that even respondents with low levels of the underlying construct (non-Depresssed individuals) might endorse an item as true or self-descriptive. In the educational literature, it is often referred to as the "pseudo-guessing" parameter, recognizing the possibility that even low-ability examinees have some nonzero probability of providing a correct response to an item through a guess. Within the personality domain each parameter the three-parameter model is conceptually interpretable; however, researchers outside of educational measurement generally have focused only on two-parameter IRT models.

In an IRT analysis data are modeled by specifying the probability of the observed response patterns over the set of p items (e.g., for MMPI–2 Depression, 57 true/false items). An immediate issue in the modeling is that when p gets large, the number of possible response patterns also becomes very large. Because the observed patterns are likely not to be sufficiently distributed across the total possible patterns over p items, sparse response patterns or cells typically will result in the observed item response data. For instance, the 57-item MMPI–2 Depression scale yields a total of 2^{57} possible response patterns over which the observed patterns must be distributed. For a construct where certain response patterns are more probable (such as in the Depression case for a nonclinical sample), certain patterns are likely to have high representation over the total possible patterns whereas other patterns will have very little representation.

A number of computer programs exist to model dichotomous and ordered categorical data using the IRT approach with very popular programs being BILOG (Mislevy & Bock, 1986) and MULTILOG (Thissen, 1991). An excellent review of the specific features, advantages, and disadvantages of each program is provided in Hambleton et al. (1991). For example, this review provides information about the types of models that can be estimated (one-, two-, and/or three-parameter models), data that can be used (dichotomous and/or ordered categorical data), different estimation procedures, computer requirements, user friendliness, cost, and additional features such as provision of standard errors, measures of fit, residual analyses, ways to handle missing data, and ability to handle more than one dimension to a data set. Decisions about which program to use in particular research contexts requires balancing these concerns.

APPROACH TWO: ITEM-LEVEL FACTOR ANALYSES

Having presented some basic properties of IRT models as they apply to personality, we next go on to describe item-level factor analysis models. An important feature of the item factor analysis models is that they specifically correct for the kinds of statistical and interpretational problems that can arise when dealing with dichotomous or ordered categorical data. Recall that in the "traditional" factor analysis model the basic data that are modeled are assumed to be continuous, equal interval data. The correlation or covariance matrix of these data is the main ingredient of the factor analysis. Thus, in contrast to standard factor analysis models, item-level models simply assume that item-level data mimic interval-level data. In addition, the item-level model, unlike the traditional IRT model, is a more general case that allows for more than a single dimension to be present in the data (Takane & de Leeuw, 1987).

To facilitate understanding of the item-level factor analysis approach, we first review some problems that dichotomous and ordered categorical data (or "less-than-interval-level data") pose for the factor analysis model and then go on to describe how the item-level factor analysis models are designed to address these concerns.

PROBLEMS WITH FACTOR ANALYZING
CORRELATIONS BASED ON DICHOTOMOUS ITEMS

If a researcher were to conduct a traditional factor analysis using dichotomous item-level data (e.g., a set of true or false responses to a scale), the fundamental statistics that would be employed by factor analysis would be Pearson correlations (r) among the dichotomous items or ϕ coefficients. While Pearson correlations should lie in a range between the values of -1.0 and 1.0, this is not true of ϕ coefficients in general. This point can be illustrated with a brief example.

Consider a 2×2 cross-classification table obtained from two dichotomous items on the 10-item Brooding MMPI scale with response options, "true" and "false." The top panel of Table 1 gives an example of the proportion of respondents who provide one of the four possible response patterns along with the marginal probabilities of a "true" ("false") response to either item. If one calculates a ϕ coefficient from these data in the top panel of the table, one would find that the value of the statistic (the size of the association) is rather small ($r_\phi = .11$).

TABLE 1
Phi Sensitivity Due to Marginal Distributions: An Example Using Two Items
From the Minnesota Multiphasic Personality Inventory–2 Brooding Scale

Observed Marginal Split

			95. I am happy most of the time[a]		
			0	1	
127.	Criticism/scolding	0	.39	.03	.42
	hurts me terribly	1	.50	.08	.58
			.89	.11	

$\phi = .11$

Constrained Marginals

			95. I am happy most of the time[a]		
			0	1	
127.	Criticism/scolding	0	.42	.00	.42
	hurts me terribly	1	.47	.11	.58
			.89	.11	

$\phi = .30$

Note. Data shown in the top panel are from the sample of $N = 1,462$. $\phi = (\pi_c - \pi_x \phi_y) / \sqrt{[\pi_x(1 - \phi_x)\pi_y(1 - \phi_y)]}$, where π_c is the joint probability of endorsing both items, π_x is the probability of endorsing item x, and π_y is the probability of endorsing item y.

[a]Denotes reverse-keyed items.

However, the size of this ϕ coefficient is constrained by the marginal totals of responses to the two items. In this case, if one assumes fixed marginals (i.e., the proportion of the sample answering in the keyed direction remains fixed for the two items), it turns out that the largest possible value that the ϕ coefficient can take on is .30. This result is demonstrated in the bottom panel of Table 1. Thus, if the actual value of the ϕ coefficient (from the top panel) is compared to its possible maximum value (as seen in the bottom panel), we see that we would not conclude that the obtained correlation was negligible in size.

This type of situation has led to two different conclusions regarding the use of the ϕ coefficient in factor analysis models. The first conclusion is based on an old observation by Ferguson (1941; see also McDonald, 1967; McDonald & Alawat, 1974) that analysis of ϕ coefficients leads to what are referred to as *difficulty factors*. For example, within an educational testing context, more difficult items (i.e., items that tend toward inequality or skew in the item marginals) would have ϕ coefficients that were further away from attaining their maximum value and may lead to spurious factors that are solely due to item marginal skew. Working in the other direction, a ϕ coefficient of ± 1 would be obtained only when item marginals were equal, with each item having a .5 probability of a keyed response.

An second conclusion made for use with ϕ coefficients was to implement a correction for the association coefficients by the maximum value they could take on, given the observed item marginals. To accomplish this, some authors proposed use of the statistic $r_\phi/\max(r_\phi)$ or what is referred to as "phi-max." Comrey and Lee (1992) described the relative virtues of analyzing r_{phi} versus phi-max in dichotomous data.

Item-level factor analysis models do not use ϕ coefficients at all because of the adverse way that the coefficients are dependent on item marginals. Instead, these models take the observed dichotomies to another level of abstraction and employ tetrachoric correlations, when dichotomous data are being analyzed, or polychoric correlations, when ordered categorical data are being analyzed. We provide an overview of the logic of tetrachoric correlations and their applicability within the domain of personality measurement.

ALTERNATIVE CORRELATIONAL STATISTICS FOR FACTOR ANALYZING DICHOTOMOUS (AND ORDERED CATEGORICAL) ITEMS

Tetrachoric correlations proceed from the assumption that the observed dichotomous item responses (e.g., a respondent's indicating "true" or "false" to an Depression item) arise from cutting an underlying normal distribution (y^*) at some threshold point, τ_i such that:

$$y_i = 1, \text{ if } y_i^* \geq \tau_i$$

It is assumed that the observed dichotomies (e.g., "true" or "false"; presence or absence of a clinical syndrome) are actually proxies for unobserved, normally distributed variables. Thus, underlying each observed response of "true" or "false" is another variable, a latent response variable (e.g., the Depression construct), which is normally distributed and describes the set of items from which the single item is taken.

When tetrachoric correlations are computed among the interval-scaled latent response variables, a factor analysis can proceed directly on these correlations because the latent response variables would at least meet the distributional assumptions of the standard factor analysis model:

$$y_i^* = \lambda_i \eta + \varepsilon_i$$

where y_i^* is the latent response variable, λ_i reflects the factor loadings for each items on the underlying dimension η, and ε_i denotes the residuals that are both uncorrelated among themselves and with η.

One can immediately identify a number of concerns and questions that might be raised. First, it is clear that this approach has introduced an additional level of abstraction to the data analysis. Rather than analyzing the observed dichotomous data directly, one is actually analyzing the relations among latent response variables presumed to underlie the observed data. Furthermore, the latent response variables are assumed to have a particular distributional form (i.e., they are continuous), which may (e.g., for the construct, Extraversion) or may not (e.g., for the construct of clinical Depression) be reasonable given the data (Haertel, 1990; Reise & Gomel, 1995). While some work with alternative distributional assumptions with the latent response variable is underway (i.e., continuous versus discrete), ease in computation involved with making this assumption has guided applications thus far in the literature. Furthermore, even if underlying continua for the latent response variables can be presumed, it may not be the case that such continua follow a normal distribution. Statistical tests of this assumption are also available (Muthén & Hofacker, 1988).

When tetrachoric correlations (i.e., in the dichotomous item case) are obtained from data, information is present about both the association between the two latent response variables and where they are cut in their respective latent response variables to generate the dichotomies (τ_i). The thresholds and the tetrachoric correlations provide the basic data for the item-level factor analysis methods compared to Pearson correlations with the standard factor analysis methods involving variables that are from the start measured more or less on an interval level scale (e.g., scale scores).

While our presentation of these methods has primarily considered the case of dichotomous items, many of these same generalizations can be extended to ordered categorical data. Muthén and Kaplan (1985, 1992) and Olsson (1979) considered through a series of computer simulations the effects of ordered categorical distributions with varying degrees of skew and kurtosis on the calculation of Pearson correlations. They reported many of the same kinds of attenuation effects on correlation size seen in dichotomous data. These findings have led to the parallel development in ordered categorical data of polychoric correlations.

In the case of polychoric correlations, associations are again obtained among latent response variables, but rather than obtaining a single threshold (τ_i) for each item that cuts an underlying normal distribution for a generated observed dichotomy, $(k-1)$ cutpoints are obtained for k-level ordered categorical variable. So, for example, a five-level ordered categorical variable would have associated with it four cutpoints or thresholds that divide the underlying normal continuum into five distinct and adjacent regions. Each of these regions would then be associated with the five observed response alternatives.

RESPONSE FORMAT CHOICE AND IMPLICATIONS
FOR THE UNDERLYING MODEL

It is not always clear that meaningful differentiations can be obtained among multiple response alternatives generated from an underlying continuum. In the ability/educational domain it is often the case that, while multiple response alternatives are presented, interest is only in whether or not a respondent chooses the "correct" response from the set of possible responses. In this framework, none of the "incorrect" responses are assumed to provide any additional information, because responses are not ordered in any particular manner. Thus, despite the presence of a multiple option response format, observed responses can be simplified into a dichotomous response format. Some work in that literature has begun to focus on better describing the characteristics of the "incorrect" or distractor options for items (e.g., Green, Crone, & Folk, 1989).

In the domain of personality assessment, two arguments that can be made represent two different theoretical and conceptual orientations. On the one hand, if an investigator believes that the particular phenomenon is continuously distributed, choice of response options may be relevant to attempt to map the ordinal scaling of an observed item onto an underlying continuum. For example, if Depression is conceptualized in terms of a construct that ranges continuously from mild or no depression to behaviorally debilitating levels of depression, then it may make sense to operationalize this conceptual model in terms of ordered categorical observed data.

But a competing conceptual model of such phenomena would only be interested in identifying the "caseness" of a particular observation as might be true in a matched case-control study. While the assessment model may be arranged in terms of ordinal data, the guiding conceptual model is based on a dichotomy. In this case, it might be reasonable to use the measurement model in a manner that is consistent with the conceptual model and simply adopt a strategy for employing a cutpoint based on some external criteria on the ordered categorical data.

This brief digression is intended to elucidate implications of conceptual models for personality assessment and their impact on how one approaches these data statistically. This approach represents a model-guided effort emphasizing the congruence between psychological models and statistical/analytic models. In the models described from the IRT tradition and from the item-level factor analysis tradition, a particular underlying distribution is assumed and modeled. Recent work of Reise and Gomel (1995) has begun to use latent trait and latent class methods to assess hypotheses about the discreteness of the underlying construct and the extent to which different analytic strategies affect the psychometric conclusions that are drawn for personality inventory data.

TWO ESTIMATION METHODS FOR
ITEM-LEVEL FACTOR ANALYSIS

Within the domain of item-level factor analysis there are two dominant approaches that rely on the assumption of an underlying latent response variable or distribution (y^*). However, these approaches differ in important ways that have practical implications for decisions regarding the number of items (p) and the number of factors that can be analyzed by these methods. These differences, in turn, have implications about the kinds of data that can be analyzed with each of these competing approaches. We first introduce item-level factor analyses based on a limited information generalized least squares (GLS) principle, followed by a full-information maximum likelihood (ML) approach. More technical discussions of the differences between these estimations methods and computer programs implement these estimation methods can be found in Mislevy (1986); Bock, Gibbons, and Muraki (1988); and Waller (1993).

ESTIMATION METHOD ONE: GLS

Christoffersson (1975, 1978) introduced a method for factor analyzing dichotomous data using tetrachoric correlations. Muthén (1978, 1984) subsequently extended this method to provide a less computationally heavy approach that is implemented in the computer program LISCOMP (Muthén, 1987). The method can be also employed for SEM for the broader case of a full covariance structure model with dichotomous, ordered categorical, censored, and/or truncated data (or mixtures of these types of data). Both the Christoffersson and Muthén approaches are based on a GLS estimation method.

More recently, other approaches have emerged for the analysis of data that are dichotomous, ordered categorical, interval-level, or mixtures of these measurement types in the general SEM framework (e.g., Jöreskog & Sörbom, 1988a, 1988b; Lee, Poon, & Bentler, 1992). Although the precise details are not available for the statistical development of the method implemented even in the latest versions of LISREL (version 8), the Lee et al. (1992) procedure has some desirable features in the early part of the algorithm and provides parameter estimates that compare equally well to, and in some cases better than, those from the Muthén method.

The conceptual foundation of the Christoffersson–Muthén and Lee, Poon, and Bentler (1992) approaches requires thinking about factor models for dichotomous data at the level of abstraction discussed earlier. In this framework the typical factor analysis model requires thinking about two different levels of variables, unobserved factors and observed indicators of those factors (items). The GLS approach to the factor analysis of dichotomous data, on the other hand, requires one additional, intermediate level between the observed item-level data and the latent variables.

This level corresponds to the latent response variables, one for each observed dichotomy, which are cut with threshold points corresponding with observed judgments (e.g., "true" or "false").

Recall that a tetrachoric correlation was hypothesized to be an estimate of the relation between two unobserved continuous variables that have been cut at threshold points, then the latent response variables represent these continuous variables. At this level of abstraction, the regular factor analysis can be applied directly, because one is now dealing with continuous indicators, albeit unobserved ones.

Conceptually, the problem of using tetrachoric (polychoric) correlations in item-level factor analysis can be thought of as a multistage process. Beginning with responses to dichotomous (ordered categorical) items, one first estimates thresholds and tetrachoric (polychoric) correlations. Note that, unlike the standard factor analysis model, these basic statistics that serve as the data for conducting a factor analysis are estimated quantities, rather than ones computed directly from the data. After this first stage of estimating thresholds and correlations, these computed statistics are expressed in terms of the familiar factor analysis model parameters. In other words, as in the usual factor analysis model, between-variable correlations are expressed in terms of the relations of these variables to a set of unobserved factors (i.e., factor loadings) that summarize variables interrelations.

Thus, two levels of abstraction are involved in the analysis. Observed dichotomous (ordered categorical) items are linked to unobserved latent response variables via the thresholds and tetrachoric (polychoric) correlations. These unobserved latent response variables then serve as the indicators for the factors. In this model, the factors summarize the relations among latent response variables rather than directly among observed variables.

GLS approaches to this factor analysis problem, such as those implemented in the computer programs LISCOMP, LISREL, and those described by other authors (e.g., Lee et al., 1989, 1992), involve a "limited information" estimator that considers only marginal (first-order) and joint (second-order) item response probabilities. This estimation method is a limited information estimator in that it ignores the additional data information available in considering high-order joint probabilities. Space precludes a detailed discussion of this estimation scheme, but the interested reader is referred to Muthén (1984). We note, in passing, too, the similarity between this estimation approach and the asymptotically distribution-free (ADF) approaches given in Browne (1984), particularly in the construction of the discrepancy function to be minimized to solve for the model parameters. Further, as with the Browne (1984) ADF approach, the computational feasibility of the GLS estimator is inversely related to the number of observed items: As the number of observed items (p) increases, the GLS estimator becomes more computationally infeasible due to the increasing size of the weight matrix used in calculation.

The GLS approach to estimation can be contrasted with a ML approach to item-level factor analysis. Unlike the GLS estimator, the ML estimator is a "full-information" estimator, employing all of the information available in observed response patterns.

ESTIMATION METHOD TWO: ML ITEM-FACTOR ANALYSIS

Bock and Lieberman (1970) introduced a conceptual model for the factor analysis of dichotomous data that was limited in its applicability to data due to a heavy computational burden. This model was reexamined in Bock and Aitken (1981) who were able to ease the computational burden by employing the EM algorithm for ML estimation that was developed by Dempster, Laird, and Rubin (1977). Without developing the details of the EM algorithm, it operates on a "missing data" principle that, in the factor analysis context, can be construed as an attempt to estimate factor scores (or, at least a distribution of factor scores) against which observed variables might be regressed. This ML approach has been implemented in the computer program, TESTFACT (Wilson, Wood, & Gibbons, 1991), which allows for a statistically appropriate method for conducting exploratory factor analysis of dichotomous data.

As in the GLS case, tetrachoric correlations among items serve as the basic data for the ML approach. However, rather than iteratively solving a weighted least squares minimization problem (as in GLS), the ML approach approximates a numerical integration of a (hypothesized) distribution of observations (typically assumed to be normal) using weighted sums. Because the numerical and computational complexity of ML factor analysis increases with the number of factors hypothesized to underlie a given set of dichotomous items, an immediate differentiation can be made between the ML the GLS estimators (Mislevy, 1986).

The computational difficulties with the ML estimator that arise as a function of the number of hypothesized factors make this estimator relatively impervious to the number of items (p) that are being analyzed. Conversely, the GLS estimator, as previously noted, is more sensitive to the number of items that are simultaneously analyzed (i.e., with the method breaking down when $p >$ about 20). Thus, a guide that might be adopted is that the ML estimator is appropriate for a large number of items and a small number of factors, while the GLS estimator can handle larger numbers of factors, but with fewer items (Mislevy, 1986). Of course, the issue of what to do in cases, such as the MMPI–2 Depression scale, when there are many items ($p = 57$) and possibly, many factors, has not yet been fully solved in the factor analytic literature.

SOME MMPI–2 EXAMPLES

In the following sections we provide brief empirical examples of the application of item-level factor analysis and IRT to personality assessment data. Specifically, using the restandardization sample of the MMPI–2 we demonstrate some applications for construction and validation of items, assessment of response patterns to examine response validity, and examination of the items for possible bias. These functions are important steps in the development of a personality inventory and in the assessment of the appropriateness of its use. Classical test theory and the traditional factor analytic model have provided most of the guidance for such developments in the past, and a combination of item-level factor analyses and IRT-based methods can be used to build on these traditional methods. Steinberg and Thissen (1995) noted that IRT models: (a) allow the researcher to assess the relation of an item response to the underlying construct, (b) examine the information given in the item response patterns, and (c) look for item bias due to context effects. The first issue regarding scale dimensionality and item properties has been addressed in the personality context by Carter and Wilkinson (1984), Childs et al. (1992), and Steinberg and Thissen (1995). The second issue regarding the appropriateness of response patterns has been examined through the use of appropriateness indices by Reise and Waller (1993) and Swygert et al. (1996). Finally, issues regarding differential item functioning in personality have been examined in several contexts by Reise et al. (1993) and Steinberg (1994).

DIMENSIONALITY AND ITEM PROPERTIES
OF PERSONALITY SCALES

An example presented by Steinberg and Thissen (1995), using data from Kuhl's (1985) Action scale, described the separate analyses of the two-parameter IRT model from the Action and Thought dimensions of state-action orientation. This model produced two sets of trace lines for the items, with each showing the probability of endorsing each item on the Action and Thought dimensions as a function of the underlying constructs. The discrimination (a) parameters for the Thought items showed that certain items of the scale were more related to the underlying construct than other items, and that the threshold parameters (b) for the Action items differed across items as well. Examining the trace lines for each item on these dimensions allowed the researchers to see which items were useful for the measurement of each dimension, and which items could be dropped without decreasing precision of measurement. However, these empirical solutions are not substitutes for a close look at item content, to be sure that the items being asked related to the underlying construct (Steinberg & Thissen, 1995).

Another example of the use of IRT in the context of personality items was presented by Carter and Wilkinson (1984), using data from the original MMPI. In this study, the one-parameter (Rasch, 1960) model was fit separately to each MMPI clinical scale. Items with threshold/difficulty parameters of less than .5 were considered to be a poor fit to the construct underlying each scale. Several scales had high numbers of poor items, including Depression, Hysteria, and Paranoia scales. The researchers assumed that these scales were not unidimensional and so were not fit well by an IRT model (in fact, no statistics were provided as to how well the data fit a unidimensional model). The conclusion about MMPI multidimensionality hypothesis is supported by more recent full-information ML factor analyses (Bock et al., 1988) conducted on the MMPI–2 scales for the restandardization sample, in which 8 of the 10 scales on the inventory were found to have more than one factor (Childs et al., 1992; Swygert et al., 1996).

Thus, an item-level factor analysis can be used to identify the dominant dimensions that underlie an item set such as the MMPI–2 Depression scale, and either item-level factor analysis or IRT can be then used as follow-up analyses to understand the item properties of that scale. Item-level exploratory factor analyses on the 10-item Harris–Lingoes Brooding scale from the MMPI–2 Depression scale showed that a single dimension was consistent with these data.

Table 2 presents item information for the Brooding scale from the MMPI–2 restandardization sample as analyzed using two methods: (a) a two-parameter IRT model (from the computer program BILOG) and (b) item-level factor analysis (the methods implemented in LISCOMP and LISREL). Data were modeled separately for women and for men. The first two columns of the table provide item parameter information for the IRT solution, whereas the third and fourth columns provide analogous information (factor loadings) for two types of item-level factor analysis solutions. The estimates from each method are generally similar and show uniformly high loadings for all of the items in each sample. Differential item functioning (in IRT) and/or multiple-group analyses (in item-level factor analysis) could be employed to assess more formally the invariance of the solution across samples (e.g., Muthén & Lehman, 1985).

Recall that in IRT analyses, the threshold parameter, b, can be viewed as an overall propensity to endorse the item, with higher parameters indicating lower endorsement rates (e.g., compare across gender the threshold values for Item 146, "I cry easily," from the Harris–Lingoes Brooding scale). The discrimination parameter, a, is analogous to a factor loading and refers to the strength with which the item relates to underlying dimensions. Because the standard IRT model assumes unidimensionality, the discrimination value is with respect to the first dominant dimension. Values large in absolute value reflect items that are strongly related to the dimension (e.g., compare across gender the discrimination values for the Item 215, "I brood a great deal," from the Brooding scale). Again, the applicability of the third IRT parameter to personality data has not been fully developed to date, perhaps because, unlike in educational settings, respondents on the low end of the trait dimension should not be especially motivated to obtain a "correct" answer or, in personality terms, to endorse an item. Indeed, motivation may be only part of the issue. For certain items, low-trait respondents may simply be interpreting items differently, or items may differentially apply to these respondents. In either case,

TABLE 2
Item Response Theory and Item Factor Analysis Parameters for 10
Brooding Minnesota Multiphasic Personality Inventory–2 Items in the
Sample of Women (N = 1,462) and Men (N = 1,138).

	IRT_a	IRT_b	$IF1_a$	$IF2_a$
Women				
38. Periods when I couldn't "get going."	1.19	1.03	.56	.56
56. I wish I could be as happy as others.	1.57	.61	.66	.68
75. I usually feel that life is worthwhile.[a]	1.05	3.29	.49	.47
92. I don't seem to care what happens to me.	1.11	3.56	.40	.45
95. I am happy most of the time.[a]	2.16	1.59	.66	.68
127. Criticism/scolding hurts me terribly.	.88	−.44	.41	.41
130. I certainly feel useless at times.	1.58	.44	.53	.55
146. I cry easily.	.72	.22	.74	.74
170. I am afraid of losing my mind.	1.21	2.30	.46	.47
215. I brood a great deal.	1.98	1.23	.79	.78
Men				
38. Periods when I couldn't "get going."	.99	1.32	.56	.56
56. I wish I could be as happy as others.	1.42	.74	.68	.68
75. I usually feel that life is worthwhile.[a]	1.06	3.18	.47	.47
92. I don't seem to care what happens to me.	1.20	2.86	.42	.42
95. I am happy most of the time.[a]	1.79	1.74	.67	.67
127. Criticism/scolding hurts me terribly.	.88	.70	.39	.39
130. I certainly feel useless at times.	1.69	.57	.53	.53
146. I cry easily.	.57	3.55	.79	.79
170. I am afraid of losing my mind.	1.04	2.88	.47	.47
215. I brood a great deal.	1.50	1.60	.84	.84

Note. Items are keyed in the high Brooding direction. IRT_a is the discrimination parameter obtained from estimating a two-parameter item response model using MULTILOG (Thissen, 1991), as reported in Childs, Dahlstrom, Kemp, and Panter (1992); IRT_b is the item threshold value from that model; $IF1_a$ is the factor loading from an exploratory factor analysis (first factor) using Muthén's (1984) LISCOMP model; $IF2_a$ is the factor loading from an exploratory factor analysis using Jöreskog and Sörbom's (1988a, 1988b) PRELIS and LISREL model.
[a]Denotes reverse-keyed items.

in a personality scale construction case, it would seem to be optimal to ensure that the parameter either did not exist or was explicitly modeled.

In conjunction with exploratory item-level factor analyses that address the underlying dimensionality of the item set, IRT and confirmatory item-level factor analyses (such as those shown in Table 2) are thus useful for the construction and validation of personality inventories. Both approaches provide item parameter information as well as trait estimates (or factor scores) for each respondent. The assumption of unidimensionality is restrictive and can be a problem, but as seen in the MMPI–2 Depression example, scales often can be broken down into smaller, unidimensional scales before the analysis or the items can be regrouped into "testlets" (Wainer & Kiely, 1987). Testlets are groups of items within which unidimensionality can be expected to hold, and the sampling of a certain area with a group of items can be more precise than with single items. Reise and Waller (1990) noted, however, that composing an adequate sample of items for an IRT analysis can be challenging and may not be straightforward. The construction of items that have high discrimination at the extremes of a personality dimension can difficult (e.g., discriminating among respondents who are not anxious).

EXAMINING ITEM RESPONSE PATTERNS

Another important function of item-level models is in the assessment of item response patterns. These patterns can yield a great deal of information relevant to scoring and are uniquely addressed by the IRT approach as compared to the item-level factor analysis approach. IRT-based "appropriateness" indices, initially developed in the educational testing literature, are designed to assess aberrant responding to scale items that may occur for a number of reasons such as the state of the respondent and the environment in which the items are taken. For example, responses to a test (in the educational testing literature) would be considered aberrant if a low-ability respondent correctly answered difficult questions (e.g., perhaps due to cheating) or if a high-ability respondent failed to answer correctly easy items (e.g., perhaps due to language problems, mismarking answers). These responses are not viewed as valid measures of the underlying ability, and thus should be identified (Drasgow, Levine, & Williams, 1985; Levine & Drasgow, 1982).

In the personality domain, various "checks" or validity scales (such as in the MMPI and the MMPI–2) have been incorporated into inventories to identify those protocols that may be characterized by aberrant responding for a set of items. All respondents can be considered to possess some level of a trait (θ) such as Depression. Thus, responses are aberrant or inappropriate if respondents with low levels of the trait endorse items indicating high trait levels, or similarly, if respondents with high levels of that trait fail to endorse low-trait items (Reise & Waller, 1993; Swygert et al., 1996).

Reise and Waller (1993) examined the Social Closeness scale of Tellegen's Multidimensional Personality Questionnaire with the l_z appropriateness index. The l_z index (Drasgow et al., 1985) can be employed to identify inappropriate scores on a personality inventory with dichotomous items, as long as the IRT assumptions are satisfied (Birenbaum, 1985). These authors found that the l_z correctly identified respondents whose item endorsements were not consistent with their trait estimates and concluded that for respondents with low l_z (which indicates extreme aberrant responding), the Social Closeness scale did not appear to measure the same construct that it did for respondents with normal or high l_z values. The appropriateness index in that context was useful in determining the relative scalability of individuals on the inventory.

Swygert et al. (1996) used this same approach in the context of the restandardization sample of the MMPI-2. In this context each item can be thought to represent a trait symptomatic of underlying psychopathology, and while there is no set of "right answers," a set of responses to the MMPI-2 can be mapped exactly onto a set of responses to any true/false test. A specific item thought to be seldom endorsed as true or self-descriptive can be called "difficult," whereas an item often endorsed as true or self-descriptive can be considered an "easy" item. Once an IRT model (one-parameter, two-parameter, or three-parameter) has been chosen, an appropriateness index can then be calculated for each respondent for each clinical scale. However, it is first necessary to provide evidence for the unidimensionality assumption for IRT models by demonstrating that the clinical scales are unidimensional. Once evidence of unidimensionality is shown, the IRT-based appropriateness index (l_z) and the MMPI-2-based validity indices can be evaluated and compared.

In the Swygert et al. (1996) analyses, all 2,600 respondents used in the analyses scored within the normal range on the F, K, L, and $?$ scales. Thus, according to these criteria, "inappropriate" responses from the traditional measures were already removed from the sample. Item-level factor analyses using TESTFACT were first conducted to identify the MMPI-2 clinical scales that were predominately unidimensional, and both the Hs and the Pt scales were sufficiently unidimensional to satisfy IRT assumptions.

Items from the Hs and Pt scales were analyzed using the IRT computer program BILOG (Mislevy & Bock, 1986) to obtain item parameters for each scale item. These parameters were then used to calculate the l_z index, using a program provided by Drasgow et al. (1985). Indices were calculated for each scale, which resulted in a Hs–l_z and a Pt–l_z. A regression model was then developed to determine whether l_z could be predicted from three of the existing "traditional" MMPI-2 validity scales (*FB, Variable Response Inconsistency Scale [VRIN]*, and *True Response Inconsistency Scale [TRIN]*). Findings revealed that both Hs–l_z and Pt–l_z could be predicted from the MMPI-2 validity scales. Interrelations among the three validity indices, the two appropriateness indices, and the 10 clinical scale scores were then examined and are presented in Table 3. The Hs–l_z and the Pt–l_z scores were positively related with each other, fairly highly negatively related with the FB scale, moderately negatively related with the $VRIN$ scale, and not at all related the $TRIN$ scale. The Hs and Pt scales showed high negative correlations with their corresponding l_z scores and had moderate positive correlations with the FB scale. The Schizophrenia (Sc) scale was notable because scores on this scale had high positive and negative relations with many other scales and indices, including the FB, Hs–l_z, and Pt–l_z indices.

TABLE 3
Correlations of the *FB, VRIN, TRIN, Hs–l$_z$*, and *Pt–l$_z$* With the 10
Minnesota Multiphasic Personality Inventory–2 Clinical Raw Scale Scores
in a Sample of Women (*N* = 1,421) and Men (*N* = 1,099)

	Hs	*D*	*Hy*	*Pd*	*Mf*	*Pa*	*Pt*	*Sc*	*Ma*	*Si*
Women										
FB	.48	.40	.08	.46	−.12	.35	.61	.72	.33	.38
VRIN	.30	.29	.01	.29	−.05	.13	.40	.49	.13	.36
TRIN	.10	−.02	−.16	.03	−.08	−.02	.20	.22	.24	.02
Hs–l$_z$	−.87	−.49	−.43	−.31	.00	−.24	−.54	−.57	−.27	−.29
Pt–l$_z$	−.53	−.49	−.26	−.47	.13	−.33	−.65	−.71	−.31	−.31
Men										
FB	.48	.34	.01	.48	.04	.31	.63	.70	.32	.37
VRIN	.38	.28	−.05	.26	.01	.10	.44	.44	.13	.34
TRIN	.01	−.07	−.30	.01	−.02	−.01	.22	.20	.20	.06
Hs–l$_z$	−.86	−.48	−.32	−.30	−.05	−.22	−.49	−.53	−.20	−.27
Pt–l$_z$	−.50	−.48	−.12	−.37	−.07	−.32	−.70	−.70	−.23	−.40

Thus, the *FB* scale and the *VRIN* scale (but not the *TRIN* scale) predicted, to some extent, the IRT-based indices (*Hs–l$_z$* and the *Pt–l$_z$*) and appeared to be assessing the same pattern of inconsistent responding. The correlations revealed that the *FB* and the *VRIN* are moderately related to the l$_z$ indices, as well as being related to the raw scale scores for the *Hs* and *PT* scales. The *Sc* scale was highly correlated with many of the validity measures (the *FB, Hs–l$_z$* and *Pt–l$_z$*, as well as with other measures of psychopathology such as the *Pt, Hs,* and *Psychopathic Deviance* scales). Interestingly, for women the *Pt–l$_z$* was significantly more related with the *Sc* raw score than with the *Pt* raw score. In other words, scores on the *Sc* scale appear to be more strongly associated with how inconsistently an individual has responded to items on the *Pt* scale than to it is with the *Pt* scale score itself. The raw *Sc* scale score may be general measure of psychopathology and of inconsistent responding. Given that the two l$_z$s (one from *Hs* and one from *Pt*) were so highly related, inconsistent responding on one scale was correlated with inconsistent responding on the other. High intercorrelations between the appropriateness indices and several of the clinical scale scores suggest that scale by scale IRT-index of appropriateness may not be any more useful than the inventory-wise validity indices that exist now.

In sum, findings from this study showed that, with the MMPI–2 validity scales, it was difficult to differentiate between a respondent with high psychopathology levels and a respondent who was responding to items in what might traditionally be described as an inconsistent manner. Inconsistency on one scale was found to be predictive of inconsistent responding on the other scale, and the *Sc* scale score was most highly predictive indicator of a respondent's l_z value. Here, appropriateness indices were helpful in examining the validity of item responses and in highlighting that invalid responding on one scale of a personality inventory was likely accompanied by invalid responding on other scales. This research revealed that an IRT-based approach to quantifying response inconsistency would need to begin to address the more general multidimensional case.

DIFFERENTIAL ITEM FUNCTIONING

In addition to understanding inappropriate responding to a personality inventory, IRT and item-level factor analysis are also useful for testing bias or item parameter invariance across groups at the item level (Reise et al., 1993; Thissen, Steinberg, & Gerrard, 1986). For both item response models an underlying structure is assumed–for IRT the structure is unidimensional with all items serving as indicators of the underlying factor, and for item-level factor analysis the structure can be any structure that can be specified in advance, as in the confirmatory SEM case (unidimensional or not). Both approaches allow for researchers to test formally the extent to which aspects of the underlying model (e.g., item properties such as thresholds or discriminations and model properties) are invariant across distinct subpopulations such as gender, intervention group, or clinical status. Reise et al. (1993) provided an excellent review of the common rationale across these two approaches. In this case we provide an example of how differential item functioning can be evaluated using the standardization MMPI–2 data.

Formally, a specific case of item-level bias is differential item functioning (*dif*), in which respondents from two groups have different probabilities of endorsing the item, even when the two groups are at the same point of the underlying attribute dimension (cf. Holland & Wainer, 1993). For example, men and women who both have a Depression trait estimate of 1.5 should each have the same probability of endorsing a particular item. If the probabilities differ across gender (meaning that the item has a different threshold or *b* for the two groups), then the item is said to display bias. Thissen et al. (1986) referred to such bias as a Group × Item interaction in the data, and this situation differs from the case in which two groups actually have different mean scores for a set of items. For their study, they obtained data with the Forced Choice Sex Guilt Inventory, and the results showed that not only did men and women have different mean scores on the measure, but that certain items had different thresholds across gender. Steinberg (1994) examined *dif* due to context effects in the Trait Anxiety Scale of the State–Trait Anxiety Inventory (Spielberger, Gorsuch, & Lushene, 1979) by experimentally manipulating item order and evaluating whether item slopes (discriminations) stayed constant across condition.

In the MMPI–2 restandardization sample, exploratory factor analyses were first performed using TESTFACT (Wilson et al., 1991). Having determined that *Hs* was a unidimensional scale, IRT methods were then used to examine possible *dif* across gender. When evaluating *dif,* the first step was to obtain a model that satisfactorily fit the data (the full model) and then to constrain further that model. The difference between the full and restricted model was to be evaluated inferentially using fit statistics between the two models (distributed as a χ^2). In these analyses the two-parameter IRT model was chosen as the full model for the data and was fit to the entire *Hs* scale for men and for women separately. An examination of the resulting item parameters in both samples showed that several of the items had thresholds that were out of theoretical and practical range (due to extremely low discrimination values) so these items were dropped for the purposes of these analyses.

The smaller item set consisted of 11 items, and the two-parameter IRT model was fit to both sets of data. The one-parameter model was first tested to determine whether all discrimination values could be constrained to be equal across gender, and the chi-square difference showed that the discrimination values were not equal across gender.

Thus, the two-parameter model was retained for the remaining *dif* analyses. The *Hs* item discrimination and threshold parameters were then constrained to be equal across gender. If only a mean difference could be observed across gender, the new constrained two-parameter model would fit adequately. However, the constrained IRT model did not fit, meaning the items assessed different constructs and/or were weighted differentially for men versus women respondents.

Table 4 provides the threshold and discrimination parameters for men and for women for the *Hs* scale. Inspection of the item parameters across gender shows a clear example of *dif* with the item, "I seldom or never have dizzy spells." This item has similar discrimination parameters across gender (men: .62; women: .46) but discrepant threshold parameters (men: 1.75; women: .59). In other words, women were much more likely to endorse this item than were men. The threshold difference across gender was tested formally by identifying "anchor" items from the scale (item for which discriminations and thresholds were similar across gender). A model with the anchor items constrained to be equal was then compared with a model with anchor and the "dizzy" item constrained to be equal. The difference between the two models was statistically significant, meaning that the threshold parameter for the item is not invariant for men and for women.

GENERAL CONCLUSIONS: RELATIONS BETWEEN ITEM-LEVEL FACTOR MODELS

The item-level factor analytic models considered here can be contrasted with other psychometric models for dichotomous data. Specifically, the IRT model (e.g., Lord, 1980), while not often applied outside the domain of educational assessment (but

TABLE 4
Item Response Theory and Differential Item Functioning for a Shortened Version
of the Hypochondriasis Minnesota Multiphasic Personality Inventory–2 Scale
in a Sample of Women (N = 1,462) and Men (N = 1,138)

	Women		Men	
Item	IRT_a	IRT_b	IRT_a	$IRTb$
1. I have never vomited or coughed up blood.	1.24	1.73	1.60	1.31
2. During the past few years I have been well most of the time.	1.12	.85	1.01	1.21
3. I am neither gaining nor losing weight.	1.25	2.09	.97	2.53
4. I do not tire quickly.	1.38	2.16	1.39	2.57
5. I seldom or never have dizzy spells.	.46	.59	.62	1.75
6. I have very few headaches.	.70	1.29	.62	.92
7. I have no difficulty in keeping my balance in walking.	.85	1.46	.89	2.27
8. I hardly ever notice my heart pounding, and I am seldom short of breath.	1.43	2.19	1.43	2.33
9. I have few or no pains.	1.74	.83	1.19	.91
10. My eyesight is as good as it has been for years.	.55	.40	.44	.85
11. I do not often notice my ears ringing or buzzing.	.64	2.77	.69	2.05

Note. Items are keyed in the high Hypochondriasis direction. IRT_a is the discrimination parameter obtained from estimating a two-parameter item response model using MULTILOG (Thissen, 1991); IRT_b is the item threshold value from that model. Item 5 shows *dif* for the threshold parameter. Items 6, 8, and 9 served as anchor items for the *dif* analyses.

see Reise & Waller, 1990, 1993; Swygert et al., 1996; Thissen, 1992; Waller & Reise, 1989), represents another model that attempts to link observed dichotomous variables to an underlying latent variable. Within the typical IRT context, it is assumed that there is a single underlying attribute of interest.

As discussed earlier, the two-parameter IRT model includes, for each observed item, an item difficulty parameter and an item discrimination parameter. The item difficulty parameter provides a measure of the amount of the underlying attribute necessary to answer an item in the keyed direction. The item discrimination parameter maps how well a particular item measures the underlying construct in question.

The interpretation of these parameters in a general factor analytic framework is clear. If more than one underlying attribute is hypothesized, then the factor loadings obtained for each item reflect how well the item in question measures each of the underlying factors. If a Thurstonian simple structure criterion is applied, then it might be hoped that, even if a multifactor solution is obtained, items tend to load only on one factor. The resulting factor loadings can be considered analogous to the item discriminations for each of the underlying attributes.

Similarly, the item difficulty parameter from IRT can be thought of as mapping information from the single, unobserved attribute to the observed data. In other words, at the estimated value of difficulty for a given item, information is provided about the likelihood of a particular observed response (i.e., is the response likely to be in the keyed direction or not?). The threshold parameter from an item factor analysis provides the same information linking the observed response to the unobserved factors.

Thus, by analogy, we can see that two-parameter IRT models can be considered special unidimensional cases of general item factor analysis models. This notion is not at all new (cf. McDonald, 1967; Muthén & Lehman, 1985; Takane & De Leeuw, 1987). We believe that conceptualizing the IRT in this way has a number of benefits. First, rather than viewing IRT models as a new methodological development, they can be viewed as a specific application of factor analytic logic to item-level data that is interested in the unidimensionality of a set of items. This general approach to the considerations of item-level factor models may also mean that investigators will be able to couch their discussions in IRT-related terms, thus bridging gaps that have historically existed between investigators interested in factor analysis and those interested in IRT.

Finally, although we do not emphasize it in this article, we note that, like factor analysis models for continuous data, item-level factor analysis can be conceived in terms of both unrestricted (exploratory) and restricted (confirmatory) modes, where these approaches differ in terms of the number of overidentifying restrictions placed on the model by hypothesis. Given the links between IRT models and the item-level factor analysis models considered here, the exploratory-confirmatory distinction immediately broadens the possibilities for restricted IRT models, which traditionally have been limited to internal criteria regarding the interrelations among items (however, see Childs, 1992; Muthén, 1988). As one example of the kinds of restricted models that might be considered for item-level data, one could use the classical test theory distinctions between parallel and tau-equivalent tests and construct them within the context of item factor analysis models following the developments of Jöreskog (1974). Moreover, issues regarding the detection of differential item functioning that are so critical to the scale construction process could be further pursed using multiple-group IRT modeling (Muthén & Lehman, 1985).

ACKNOWLEDGMENTS

Portions of this chapter were presented by A. T. Panter at the symposium, Item Response Theory Applications to Personality Assessment, at the meeting of the American Psychological Association, Toronto, Canada, August, 1993.

This chapter is dedicated to the memory of J. S. Tanaka.

REFERENCES

Bernstein, I. H., & Teng, G. (1989). Factoring items and factoring scales are different: Spurious evidence for multidimensionality due to item categorization. *Psychological Bulletin, 105,* 467–477.

Birenbaum, M. (1985). Comparing the effectiveness of several IRT based appropriateness measures in detecting unusual response patterns. *Educational and Psychological Measurement, 45,* 523–533.

Birnbaum, A. (1968). Some latent trait models and their use in inferring an examinee's ability. In F. M. Lord & M. R. Novick (Eds.), *Statistical theories of mental test scores* (pp. 392–479). Reading, MA: Addison-Wesley.

Bock, R. D., & Aitken, M. (1981). Marginal maximum likelihood estimation of item parameters: Application of an EM algorithm. *Psychometrika, 46,* 443–459.

Bock, R. D., Gibbons, R., & Muraki E. (1988). Full-information factor analysis. *Applied Psychological Measurement, 12,* 261–280.

Bock, R. D., & Lieberman, M. (1970). Fitting a response model for *n* dichotomously scored items. *Psychometrika, 35,* 179–197.

Bollen, K. A. (1989). *Structural equations with latent variables.* New York: Wiley.

Browne, M. W. (1984). Asymptotically distribution-free methods for the analysis of covariance structures. *British Journal of Mathematical and Statistical Psychology, 37,* 62–83.

Butcher, J. N., Dahlstrom, W. G., Graham, J. R., Tellegen, A., & Kaemmer, B. (1989). *Manual for administration and scoring the Minnesota Multiphasic Personality Inventory–2: MMPI–2.* Minneapolis: University of Minnesota Press.

Carter, J. E., & Wilkinson, L. (1984). A latent trait analysis of the MMPI. *Multivariate Behavioral Research Monographs, 19,* 385–407.

Childs, R. A. (1992). *Applying item response theory to the analysis of educational test items with an external criterion.* Unpublished doctoral dissertation, University of North Carolina at Chapel Hill.

Childs, R. A., Dahlstrom, W. G., Kemp, S., & Panter, A. T. (1992). *Item response theory in personality assessment: The MMPI–2 Depression Scale* [Report 92–1]. Chapel Hill: University of North Carolina, L. L. Thurstone Psychometric Laboratory.

Christoffersson, A. (1975). Factor analysis of dichotomized variables. *Psychometrika, 40,* 5–32.

Christoffersson, A. (1978). Two-step weighted least squares factor analysis of dichotomized variables. *Psychometrika, 42,* 433–438.

Comrey, A. L. (1978). Common methodological problems in factor analytic studies. *Journal of Consulting and Clinical Psychology, 46,* 648–659.

Comrey, A. L. (1988). Factor analytic methods of scale development in personality and clinical psychology. *Journal of Consulting and Clinical Psychology, 56,* 754–761.

Comrey, A. L., & Lee, H. B. (1992). *A first course in factor analysis* (2nd ed.). Hillsdale, NJ: Lawrence Erlbaum Associates, Inc.

Dempster, A. P., Laird, N. M., & Rubin, D. B. (1977). Maximum likelihood from incomplete data via the EM algorithm (with discussion). *Journal of the Royal Statistical Society, 39*(Series B), 1–38.

Drasgow, F., Levine, M. V., & Williams, E. A. (1985). Appropriateness measurement with polychotomous item response models and standardized indices. *British Journal of Mathematical and Statistical Psychology, 38,* 67–86.

Ferguson, G. A. (1941). The factorial interpretation of test difficulty. *Psychometrika, 6,* 323–329.

Gifi, A. (1990). *Nonlinear multivariate analysis.* New York: Wiley.

Gorsuch, R. L. (1983). *Factor analysis* (2nd. ed.). Hillsdale, NJ: Lawrence Erlbaum Associates, Inc.

Green, B. F., Crone, C. R., & Folk, V. G. (1989). A method for studying differential distractor functioning. *Journal of Educational Measurement, 26,* 147–160.

Haertel, E. H. (1990). Continuous and discrete latent structure models for item response data. *Psychometrika, 55,* 477–494.

Hambleton, R. K. (1989). Principles and selected applications of item response theory (pp. 147–200). In R. L. Linn (Ed.), *Educational measurement* (3rd. ed., pp. 147–200). New York: Macmillan.

Hambleton, R. K., Swaminathan, H., & Rogers, H. J. (1991). *Fundamentals of item response theory.* Newbury Park, CA: Sage.

Harman, H. H. (1976). *Modern factor analysis* (3rd. ed.). Chicago: University of Chicago Press.

Holland, P. W., & Wainer, H. (Eds.). (1993). *Differential item functioning.* Hillsdale, NJ: Lawrence Erlbaum Associates, Inc.

Hoyle, R. H. (Ed.). (1995). *Structural equation modeling: Issues and applications.* Newbury Park, CA: Sage.

Jöreskog, K. G. (1974). Analyzing psychological data by structural analysis of covariance matrices. In D. H. Krantz, R. C. Atkinson, R. D. Luce, & P. Suppes (Eds.)., *Contemporary developments in mathematical psychology* (Vol. 2, pp. 1–56). San Francisco: Freeman.

Jöreskog, K. G., & Sörbom, D. (1988a). *LISREL 7: A guide to the program and application.* Mooresville, IN: Scientific Software.

Jöreskog, K. G., & Sörbom, D. (1988b). *PRELIS: A preprocessor of LISREL.* Mooresville, IN: Scientific Software.

Kessler, R., & Mroczek, D. (1994). *Scoring the UM–CIDI short forms.* Ann Arbor: University of Michigan, Institute for Social Research.

Kuhl, J. (1985). Volitional mediators of cognition-behavioral consistency: Self-regulatory processes and action versus state orientation. In J. Kuhl & J. Beckman (Eds.), *Action control: From cognition to behavior* (pp. 101–128). Berlin: Springer-Verlag.

Lee, S.-Y., Poon, W.-Y., & Bentler, P. M. (1989). Simultaneous analysis of multivariate polytomous variates in several groups. *Psychometrika, 54,* 63–73.

Lee, S.-Y., Poon, W.-Y., & Bentler, P. M. (1992). Structural equation models with continuous and polytomous variables. *Psychometrika, 57,* 89–105.

Levine, M. V., & Drasgow, F. (1982). Appropriateness measurement: Review, critique, and validating studies. *British Journal of Mathematical and Statistical Psychology, 35,* 42–56.

Lord, F. M. (1980). *Applications of item response theory to practical testing problems.* Hillsdale, NJ: Lawrence Erlbaum Associates, Inc.

McDonald, R. P. (1967). Nonlinear factor analysis. *Psychometric Monograph, 15.*

McDonald, R. P., & Alawat, R. P. (1974). Difficulty factors in binary data. *British Journal of Mathematical and Statistical Psychology, 27,* 82–99.

Mislevy, R. J. (1986). Recent developments in the factor analysis of categorical variables. *Journal of Educational Statistics, 11,* 3–31.

Mislevy, R. J., & Bock, R. D. (1986). *BILOG I maximum likelihood item analysis and test scoring with binary logistic models* [Computer program]. Mooresville, IN: Scientific Software.

Mulaik, S. A. (1972). *The foundations of factor analysis.* New York: McGraw-Hill.

Muthén, B. (1978). Contributions to factor analysis of dichotomous variables. *Psychometrika, 43,* 551–560.

Muthén, B. (1984). A general structural equation model with dichotomous, ordered categorical, and continuous latent variable indicators. *Psychometrika, 49,* 115–132.

Muthén, B. (1987). *LISCOMP user's manual.* Mooresville, IN: Scientific Software.

Muthén, B. (1988). Some uses of structural equation modeling in validity studies: Extending IRT to external variables. In H. Wainer & H. I. Braun (Eds.), *Test validity* (pp. 213–238). Hillsdale, NJ: Lawrence Erlbaum Associates, Inc.

Muthén, B., & Hofacker, C. (1988). Testing the assumptions underlying tetrachoric correlations. *Psychometrika, 53,* 563–578.

Muthén, B., & Kaplan, D. (1985). A comparison of some methodologies for the factor analysis of non-normal Likert variables. *British Journal of Mathematical and Statistical Psychology, 38,* 171–189.

Muthén, B., & Kaplan, D. (1992). A comparison of some methodologies for the factor analysis of non-normal Likert variables: A note on the size of the model. *British Journal of Mathematical and Statistical Psychology, 45,* 19–30.

Muthén, B., & Lehman, J. (1985). Multiple group IRT modeling: Applications to item bias analysis. *Journal of Educational Statistics, 10,* 133–142.

Olsson, U. (1979). On the robustness of factor analysis against crude classification of the observations. *Multivariate Behavioral Research, 14,* 485–500.

Ozer, D. J., & Reise, S. P. (1994). Personality assessment. *Annual Review of Psychology, 45,* 357–388.

Panter, A. T., Tanaka, J. S., & Wellens, T. R. (1992). The psychometrics of order effects. In S. Sudman & N. Schwarz (Eds.), *Context effects in social and psychological research* (pp. 249–264). New York: Springer-Verlag.

Rasch, G. (1960). *Probabilistic models for some intelligence and attainment tests.* Copenhagen: Danish Institute for Educational Research.

Reise, S. P., & Gomel, J. N. (1995). Modeling qualitative variation within latent trait dimensions: Application of mixed-measurement to personality assessment. *Multivariate Behavioral Research, 30,* 341–358.

Reise, S. P., & Waller, N. G. (1990). Fitting the two-parameter model to personality data. *Applied Psychological Measurement, 14,* 45–58.

Reise, S. P., & Waller, N. G. (1993). Traitedness and the assessment of response pattern scalability. *Journal of Personality and Social Psychology, 65,* 143–151.

Reise, S. P., Widaman, K. F., & Pugh, R. H. (1993). Confirmatory factor analysis and item response theory: Two approaches for exploring measurement invariance. *Psychological Bulletin, 114,* 552–566.

Reiser, M. (1989). An application of the item response model to psychiatric epidemiology. In C. C. Clogg (Ed.), *Sociological methodology* (pp. 66–103). Washington, DC: American Sociological Association.

Samejima, F. (1969). Estimation of latent ability using a response pattern of graded scores. *Psychometrika Monograph, 34*(No. 17).

Schaeffer, N. C. (1988). An application of the item response theory to the measurement of depression (pp. 271–307). In C. C. Clogg (Ed.), *Sociological methodology.* Washington, DC: American Sociological Association.

Spielberger, C. D., Gorsuch, R. L., & Lushene, R. E. (1979). *Manual for the STAI.* Palo Alto, CA: Consulting Psychologists Press.

Steinberg, L. (1994). Context and serial-order effects in personality measurement: Limits on the generality of measuring changes the measure. *Journal of Personality and Social Psychology, 66,* 341–349.

Steinberg, L., & Thissen, D. (1995). Item response theory in personality research. In P. E. Shrout and S. Fiske (Eds.), *Personality research, methods, and theory: A festschrift honoring Donald W. Fiske* (pp. 161–181). Hillsdale, NJ: Lawrence Erlbaum Associates, Inc.

Swygert, K. S., Panter, A. T., Dahlstrom, W. G., & Reise, S. (1996). *The use of appropriateness indices in the MMPI-2.* Chapel Hill: University of North Carolina, L. L. Thurstone Psychometric Laboratory.

Takane, Y., & de Leeuw, J. (1987). On the relationship between item response theory and factor analysis of discretized variables. *Psychometrika, 52,* 393–408.

Tanaka, J. S., Panter, A. T., Winborne, W. C., & Huba, G. J. (1990). Theory testing in personality and social psychology with latent variable models. *Review of Personality and Social Psychology, 11,* 217–242.

Tenopyr, M. L. (1994). Big Five, structural modeling, and item response theory. In G. S. Stokes, M. D. Mumford, & W. A. Owens (Eds.), *Biodata handbook: Theory, research, and use of biographical information in selection and performance prediction* (pp. 519–533). Palo Alto, CA: CPP Books.

Thissen, D. (1991). *MULTILOG* [Computer program]. Mooresville, IN: Scientific Software.

Thissen, D. (1992, August). *Item response theory in psychological research.* Invited address at the meeting of the American Psychological Association, Washington, DC.

Thissen, D., Steinberg, L., & Gerrard, M. (1986). Beyond group-mean differences: The concept of item bias. *Psychological Bulletin, 99,* 118–128.

Wainer, H., & Kiely, G. L. (1987). Item clusters and computerized adaptive testing: A case for testlets. *Journal of Educational Measurement, 24,* 185–201.

Waller, N. G. (1993). Seven confirmatory factor analysis programs: EQS, EzPATH, LINCS, LISCOMP, LISREL 7, SIMPLIS, and CALIS. *Applied Psychological Measurement, 17,* 73–100.

Waller, N. G., & Reise, S. P. (1989). Computerized adaptive personality assessment: An illustration with the absorption scale. *Journal of Personality and Social Psychology, 57,* 1051–1058.

Wilson, D. T., Wood, R., & Gibbons, R. (1991). *TESTFACT computer manual.* Chicago: Scientific Software.

For Product Safety Concerns and Information please contact our EU
representative GPSR@taylorandfrancis.com
Taylor & Francis Verlag GmbH, Kaufingerstraße 24, 80331 München, Germany

www.ingramcontent.com/pod-product-compliance
Lightning Source LLC
Chambersburg PA
CBHW070544270326
41926CB00013B/2194

9 781138 968646